DEMOCRACY AND HUMAN RIGHTS IN MULTICULTURAL SOCIETIES

Democracy and Human Rights in Multicultural Societies

Edited by
MATTHIAS KOENIG AND PAUL DE GUCHTENEIRE

UNESCO

United Nations
Educational, Scientific and
Cultural Organization

ASHGATE

Published by

Ashgate Publishing Limited
Gower House
Croft Road
Aldershot
Hampshire GU11 3HR
England

Ashgate Publishing Company
Suite 420
101 Cherry Street
Burlington, VT 05401-4405
USA

Ashgate website: http://www.ashgate.com

Published jointly with the United Nations Educational, Scientific and Cultural Organization (UNESCO), 7, place de Fontenoy, 75007 Paris, France.

UNESCO website: http://www.unesco.org

British Library Cataloguing in Publication Data
Democracy and human rights in multicultural societies
    1. Minorities - Legal status, laws, etc. 2. Human rights
    3. Democracy 4. Language and languages - Political aspects
    5. Freedom of religion 6. Politics and culture
    I. Guchteneire, P. F. A. de (Paul F. A.) II. Koenig,
    Matthias III. Unesco
    346'.013

Library of Congress Cataloging-in-Publication Data
Democracy and human rights in multicultural societies / edited by Matthias Koenig and Paul
    de Guchteneire.
       p. cm.
    Includes index.
    ISBN-13: 978-0-7546-7029-2 (hardback : alk. paper)
    ISBN-13: 978-0-7546-7030-8 (pbk. : alk. paper)
      1. Human rights. 2. Ethnic relations--Political aspects. 3. Minorities--Civil rights.
    4. Multiculturalism. 5. Pluralism (Social sciences) I. Unesco.
    JC571.D384 2007
    323--dc22

                       2006031595

Ashgate   ISBN 978-0-7546-7029-2 (Hbk)
            ISBN 978-0-7546-7030-8 (Pbk)

UNESCO ISBN 978-92-3104050-4

Printed and bound in Great Britain by MPG Books Ltd, Bodmin, Cornwall.

Contents

Preface   *xi*
About the Contributors   *xiii*

INTRODUCTION

1 Political Governance of Cultural Diversity   **3**
Matthias Koenig & Paul de Guchteneire
   Nation-states and the Problem of Cultural Diversity   4
   Transforming the Nation-State – The Impact of Human Rights   6
   Ethnic, Linguistic and Religious Politics of Recognition   7
      Territorially Based Ethnic or National Movements   8
      Linguistic Diversity and Language Policy   10
      Secularism and Religious Diversity   12
   Conclusion   14
   References   14

PART I   ETHNO-NATIONAL MOVEMENTS

2 Nationalism, Ethnic Conflict and Democratic Governance   **21**
Juan Díez-Medrano
   Theoretical Approaches   21
      Primordialism   22
      Social Constructivism   22
      Rational Choice   24
      State Policy and Ethnonationalism: Theoretical Predictions   26
   Case Studies   26
      The Basque Country   27
      Northern Ireland   27
      Québec   28
      Chiapas   28
      The Kurdish Question in Turkey   29
   Case Studies and Theoretical Predictions   29
   References   32

3   **Constitutional and Governmental Policies towards
    Basque Nationalist Extremism**   35
    Enric Martínez-Herrera
    Strategies of the State facing Nationalist Insurgent Extremism:
    Repressive and Responsive Frames   36
        Repressive Policies and Insurgent Nationalist Extremism   36
        Responsive Policies and Insurgent Nationalist Extremism   37
    Dimensions of Insurgent Nationalist Extremism in the Basque
    Country   39
        Victims of Terrorism   40
        Herri Batasuna/Euskal Herritarrok Voting   40
        Basque Exclusivist Identification   41
    Dimensions and Indicators of State Policies in the Basque Case   42
        Repressive Policies   42
        Responsive Policies   42
    Empirical Analysis   44
        The Development of Violence   44
        Development of Basque Extremist Nationalist Voting   50
        Development of Rejection towards Spain   51
    Implications for Theory and Policy   56
    Notes   57
    References   59

4   **Conflict Management in Northern Ireland**   61
    Stefan Wolff
    Introduction   61
    About the Conflict and its Solutions   62
    Settling the Conflict? Constitutional Reform, Institutional Change,
    Security Policy, and Economic and Social Development in their
    Effectiveness over Time   64
        Failure of the Sunningdale Process   65
        The Anglo-Irish Agreement   68
    Assessing the Success and Failure of British Conflict Management
    and Resolution Policies in Northern Ireland   79
        Reducing the Level of Violent Conflict   79
        Republican Violence   80
        Loyalist Violence   80
        Violence and Community Relations   81
        Establishing the Conditions for an Inclusive Political Process? 83
        Balance of Political Power Between and Within the Communities 83
    Afterword: Northern Ireland since the Good Friday Agreement—
    Stability or Collapse of the Peace Process   85
    Notes   87
    Appendix   89

References   91
    Note on Terminology   95

5   **The Decline of the PKK and the Viability of a
    One-State Solution in Turkey**   **93**
    Matthew Adam Kocher
    Violence and Demographic Shift   95
    Identity   101
    Public Opinion   104
    Implications for Future Policy   109
    Notes   110
    References   111

PART II   LINGUISTIC DIVERSITY

6   **Linguistic Rights as an Integral Part of Human Rights –
    A Legal Perspective**   **115**
    Fernand de Varennes
    Private Use of Minority Language   116
    Use of Minority Language by Public Authorities   118
    Significance of Linking Language Rights as Part of Human Rights   121
    Linguistic Rights, Stability and Multicultural Democracies   122
    Conclusion   124
    Notes   125
    Bibliography   125

7   **Protecting Linguistic Minorities – The Role of the OSCE**   **127**
    Sally Holt & John Packer
    Language in the OSCE Framework   127
        OSCE and Conflict Prevention   127
        Integrating Diversity   129
        Some Remarks Regarding States' Practice   130
        The Oslo and Hague Recommendations   132
        Survey of State Practice   132
    Role of OSCE Institutions in Addressing Specific Language-related
    Issues   133
        OSCE Institutions   133
        Public/Private Divide   136
        Resources   137
        Public Administrative Authorities   138
        Public Office and the Electoral Process   140
        Employment in the Public and Private Spheres   143
        Citizenship   144
        Economic/Commercial Sphere   145

Provision of Public Services   146
Education   147
The Media   152
Conclusion   154
Notes   156
References   163

8   **Language Legislation in the Baltic States**   **167**
    Boriss Cilevičs
    Development of Linguistic Legislation after the Restoration of
    Independence   168
    Status of Languages and Recognition of Minority Languages   169
    Use of Languages in Legislatures and Elected Municipal Bodies   171
    Right to Use Minority Language(s) before Public Authorities   173
    Professional and Occupational Language Requirements   174
    Languages in Media   176
    Use of Languages in Education   177
    Conclusions: Main Features of the Language Policies in the Baltic States 179
    Notes   182
    References   184

9   **Language Rights in South Africa: an Adequate**
    Level of Minority Protection?   **185**
    Kristin Henrard
    Definition of the Minority Concept and its Application to the
    South African Population   187
    Relevant Historical Events and Developments   189
    Constitutional Negotiations and Analysis of the Relevant
    Provisions of the 1996 Constitution of South Africa   189
    Certification Judgements as related to the 1996 Constitution of
    the Constitutional Court   193
    Implementation of the Relevant Constitutional Provisions   195
        Section 6 of the 1996 Constitution: Status of Languages
        Spoken in South Africa   195
        Language in Education: Section 29(2) of the 1996 Constitution 199
        Minority Rights *Sensu Stricto* and Language, Including the
        "Minorities" Commission   201
    International Framework regarding Language Rights for Minorities   203
    Standards   203
    Supervision   207
    Evaluation of the South African Norms and their Application
    in Light of this Framework   209
    Notes   210
    References   214

10 **The Impact of Language Policy on Endangered Languages**   **217**
Suzanne Romaine
Evaluating Policies and the Fallacy of Autonomy   219
Weak Linkages   223
Timing: Too Little Too Late?   230
Factors Other than Legal Status   231
Conclusion: The Proof is in the Pudding   233
References   234

PART III   RELIGIOUS DIVERSITY

11 **The Resurgence of Religious Movements in the**
   Processes of Globalization – Beyond the End of History
   or the Clash of Civilizations   **239**
Shmuel N. Eisenstadt
Resurgence of Fundamentalist and Communal-Religious
Movements and the Transformation of the Classical Nation-
State   241
Modernity and the Resurgence of Fundamentalist and Communal-
Religious Movements   242
Reinterpretations of Modernity – the Larger Context   243
Specificities of the New Fundamentalist and Communal-Religious
Movements   244
Impact of Civilizational Traditions on the Formation of
Modernities   245
Conclusion: Multiple Modernities beyond the End of History and
the Clash of Civilizations – New Potentials for Conflict   246
Notes   249
References   249

12 **Modes of Religious Pluralism under Conditions**
   of Globalization   **251**
Ole Riis
Concept of Pluralism   252
A phenomenology of religious pluralism   253
Religious Pluralism from the Perspective of the Sociology
of Religion   255
Public Recognition of Denominations as a Mode of Religious
Pluralism   258
Pillarization as a Mode of Religious Pluralism   260
Dilemmas of Pluralism   262
Notes   264
References   265

13 **Prison Chaplaincy in England and Wales – from Anglican
   Brokerage to a Multi-faith Approach**   267
   James A. Beckford
   Pluralism or Diversity?   267
   Growth of Religious and Ethnic Diversity   269
   Brokerage by the Church of England   273
   Resistance to Brokerage   275
   Towards Multi-faith Chaplaincy   277
   Conclusion   279
   Notes   281
   References   281

14 **The Challenges of Religious Pluralism in Post-Soviet Russia**   283
   Kathy Rousselet
   Religious Diversity and Social Conflicts   284
   State Management of Religious Diversity – Towards which Model
   of Secularism?   288
   Religion, Community and Territory   294
   Conclusion   296
   Notes   299
   Bibliography   300

Index

Preface

One of the biggest challenges of today's world is the need to balance cultural diversity with social cohesion. As a result of multiple factors related to globalization, we live in an increasingly heterogeneous society, where people have different religions, different languages, different cultural values and lifestyles, different traditions and beliefs. Cultural diversity can certainly be an important contribution to quality of life, conflict resolution and human security, but cultural differences may also lead to social tension and conflict.

Respect for our cultural differences is deeply rooted in the idea of human rights, as articulated in the freedom of opinion and expression, freedom of thought, conscience and religion, and freedom to participate in the cultural life of one's choice. At the same time, when people coming from different traditions live together there is also a strong need to share common values, to promote social cohesion, and to ensure that minorities may fully participate in the social, political and cultural life of the larger society. Traditionally, the ideas of citizenship and democracy assumed at least some sense of a shared national identity, based on ethnicity, language or religion. Yet in contemporary multicultural societies, with different ethnic identities, languages and religions, the issue of social cohesion becomes a challenge to democracy that requires new institutional arrangement and public policies.

In 2001, UNESCO's Member States adopted unanimously the *Universal Declaration of Cultural Diversity*, by which a new ethical approach to respect for diversity has been formulated as a guiding principle for democratic societies. Its basic idea is that only when cultural diversity is in balance with social cohesion, can we find ways of democratic participation and peaceful co-existence. Although the *Declaration* has received strong support in member states throughout the world, its principles still need to be translated into actual policy-making under specific local and regional conditions. There is indeed a growing awareness, among politicians and academics alike, that the democratic management of multicultural societies needs rethinking and further development. Thus, UNDP's recently published Human Development Report *Cultural Liberty in Today's Diverse World* stressed the need to find public policies which recognize difference, champion diversity and promote cultural freedoms.

Indeed this book explores different public policy responses to cultural diversity which try to balance the recognition of difference and the need for social cohesion. The contributions presented in this volume are revised and up-dated versions of articles previously published in UNESCO's *International Journal on Multicultural Societies* (IJMS). The IJMS, which has established itself as a successful electronic journal with a broad audience worldwide, forms part of UNESCO's initiatives to stimulate policy-relevant social science research on multiculturalism. With its case studies on ethnic, linguistic and religious diversity in various countries, written by leading experts in sociology, political science and law, I hope that this book contributes to the diffusion of solid and up-to-date social scientific knowledge about the political governance of cultural diversity.

PIERRE SANÉ
Assistant Director-General for
Social and Human Sciences

About the Contributors

James A. Beckford, Fellow of the British Academy, is Professor of Sociology at the University of Warwick and was President of the International Society for the Sociology of Religion from 1999 to 2003. His research is concerned with religious diversity, chaplaincies and politics and religion. His main publications include *Religious Organization* (1973), *The Trumpet of Prophecy. A Sociological Analysis of Jehovah's Witnesses* (1975), *Cult Controversies. The Societal Response to New Religious Movements* (1985), *Religion and Advanced Industrial Society* (1989), *Religion in Prison. Equal Rites in a Multi-Faith Society?* (1998 with Sophie Gilliat), *Social Theory and Religion* (2003) and *Muslims in Prison* (2005, with D. Joly and F. Khosrokhavar).

Juan Díez-Medrano is Professor of Sociology at the Universidad de Barcelona. He is the author of *Framing Europe* (Princeton University Press 2003), *Divided Nations* (Cornell University Press 1995), and articles in journals such as *American Sociological Review, Social Forces, Theory and Society*, and *Ethnic and Racial Studies*. His areas of interest are collective identities, social movements and European integration.

Shmuel N. Eisenstadt is Professor Emeritus of Sociology at the Hebrew University of Jerusalem and Research Fellow at the Van Leer Jerusalem Institute. He holds honorary doctoral degrees from the Universities of Harvard, Helsinki, Duke, Warsaw, Hebrew Union College and Tel Aviv and has received many academic awards and prizes – the latest one being the Holberg International Memorial Prize. His research is mainly concerned with the analysis of political change and the comparative sociology of civilizations. His main publications include *The Political Systems of Empires* (Free Press 1963), *Tradition, Change and Modernity* (John Wiley & Sons 1976), *Power, Trust and Meaning: Essays in Sociological Theory and Analysis* (Chicago University Press 1995), *Paradoxes of Democracy. Fragility, Continuity and Change* (Woodrow Wilson Press 1999), *Fundamentalism, Sectarianism and Revolutions. The Jacobin Dimension of Modernity* (Cambridge University Press 1999), and *Comparative Civilizations & Multiple Modernities* (Brill 2003).

Paul de Guchteneire is Head of the Programme on International Migration and Multicultural Policies at UNESCO and Director of the *International Journal on Multicultural Societies*. Before coming to UNESCO he worked as epidemiologist at the Netherlands Cancer Research Foundation, and as Director of the Steinmetz Institute of the Royal Netherlands Academy of Sciences. He is a former President of the International Federation of Data Organizations (IFDO) and published several works on data collection and data analysis in the social sciences, and a book on *Best Practices of Indigenous Knowledge*. His current research programme focuses on the human rights dimension of international migration, and the development of policies for migration management at the international level. Forthcoming publications include a book on *Migration without Borders*.

Kristin Henrard is Lecturer in Constitutional Law, Human Rights, Refugee Law and Humanitarian Law at the University of Groningen. She graduated at the Catholic University of Leuven, Belgium, in 1994 and obtained an LLM degree at Harvard Law School in 1995 during which she further specialized in human rights and humanitarian law. She received her doctorate at the Catholic University of Leuven in 1999. She also worked at the Constitutional Court of South Africa and monitored the South African constitutional negotiations in 1996 for the Flemish Government. Her main publications pertain to the areas of human rights, minority protection, Belgian constitutional law and international law.

Sally Holt is Research Fellow at the Centre for International Cooperation and Security(CICS), Dept. of Peace Studies, University of Bradford, UK. Prior to joining CICS in September 2004 she spent four years as Legal Officer at the Office of the High Commissioner on National Minorities (HCNM) of the Organization for Security and Co-operation in Europe (OSCE). She holds a masters degree in human rights from the University of London, Institute of Commonwealth Studies (conferred with distinction in 1998). Her research interests – and related publications – lie primarily in the field of human rights, minority rights and conflict prevention.

Matthew Adam Kocher is currently Professor/Researcher at the Center for Research and Teaching in Economics (CIDE) in Mexico City. He received his PhD in 2004 from the Department of Political Science, University of Chicago. He has previously taught at the University of Chicago, University of Notre Dame (Indiana) and Yale University. His doctoral dissertation, entitled *Human Ecology and Civil War*, focuses on linked processes of demographics, state formation and violence. His doctoral thesis, *Human Ecology and Civil War*, won the American Political Science Association's 2006 Gabriel A. Almond award for best dissertation in Comparative Politics.

Matthias Koenig is Professor of Sociology at the University of Göttingen, Germany. He obtained a master's and a doctoral degree in sociology at the University of Marburg. He was a Marie Curie fellow at the Institut de la Recherche des Sociétés Contemporaines (IRESCO), Paris, and visiting researcher at the London School of Economics and Political Science as well as the European University Institute, Florence. His main research interests are related to the sociology of religion, multiculturalism, and human rights.

He is author of several books and numerous articles in major journals such as *International Social Science Journal, Journal of International Migration and Integration,* and *Social Compass.* Since 1998, he has served as editor-in-chief of UNESCO's *International Journal on Multicultural Societies* (IJMS).

Enric Martínez-Herrera. M. García-Pelayo Fellow at the Centro de Estudios Políticos y Constitucionales (CEPC, Madrid). PhD in political and social sciences from the European University Institute (Florence). MA in data analysis from the University of Essex. He was awarded the national prize for the best doctoral thesis in constitutional law and political science in Spain. He has been a J. William Fulbright Fellow at the University of Maryland (CIDCM), an assistant lecturer at University Pompeu Fabra (Barcelona) and a visiting researcher at the universities of Edinburgh, Essex and Leuven. His research, which is concerned with political behaviour, institutions and governmental policies in comparative perspective, has been published in various international academic journals and edited books.

John Packer is an independent consultant currently advising a number of governments and inter-governmental and non-governmental organizations on matters of peace and security, conflict prevention and resolution, diversity management, prevention of genocide and the protection of minorities and human rights. He is also Principal Investigator and Project Coordinator of the global "Initiative on Conflict Prevention through Quiet Diplomacy" located at Human Rights Internet in Ottawa, Canada. He taught International Law at the Fletcher School of Law and Diplomacy at Tufts University and was a Fellow at the Carr Center for Human Rights Policy at the John F. Kennedy School of Government at Harvard University. Until February 2004, he was Director in the Office of the High Commissioner on National Minorities (HCNM) of the Organization for Security and Co-operation in Europe (OSCE), located in The Hague, where from 1995–2000 he was Senior Legal Advisor to the HCNM. He was previously a United Nations Staff Member and consultant to several specialized agencies. He is Associate Editor of the Human Rights Law Journal and a member of the editorial boards of the *International Journal of Minority and Group Rights,* the *European Yearbook of Minority Issues,* and the *European Diversity and Autonomy Papers,* and of the editorial advisory boards of the *Journal on Ethnopolitics and Minority Issues in Europe* and *The Global Review of Ethnopolitics.*

Ole Riis is Professor of Sociology of Religion at the Institute of Religion, Philosophy and History at Agder University College in Norway and involved in establishing a doctoral programme there. Ole Riis came from Denmark, where he was Associate Professor and councillor for the Danish Minister of Ecclesiastical Affairs on the public recognition of denominations. Ole Riis has participated in several international projects such as the European Values Survey and the project on 'Religious and Moral Pluralism in Europe'. He is presently working on a sociology of religious emotions in collaboration with professor Linda Woodhead, Lancaster.

Suzanne Romaine has been Merton Professor of English Language at the University of Oxford since 1984. Her research interests lie primarily in historical linguistics and sociolinguistics, especially in problems of societal multilingualism, linguistic diversity, language change, language acquisition and language contact in the broadest sense. She has conducted extensive fieldwork in Europe as well as in Papua New Guinea and Hawaii. She is the author of numerous articles and books, the most recent of which is *Vanishing Voices. The Extinction of the World's Languages* (jointly with Daniel Nettle, Oxford University Press 2000).

Kathy Rousselet is a research director at the Centre d'Etudes et de Recherches Internationales (CERI) at the Fondation Nationale des Sciences Politiques, Paris. She is a former student of the Ecole Normale Supérieure and a habilitated doctor in political science. Following her thesis on non-institutionalized religion in the Soviet Union, she has taken a particular interest in the new religious processes in post-Soviet Russia. She is the author of numerous publications on this subject. She also co-edited the book *La globalisation du religieux* (L'Harmattan 2001) and co-published *La société russe en quête d'ordre. Avec Vladimir Poutine?* (CERI-Autrement, 2004). Kathy Rousselet is editor-in-chief of *Revue d'Etudes Comparatives Est-Ouest*.

Boris Tsilevich is a member of the Latvian Parliament elected on the platform of the defence of minority rights, and a member of the Parliamentary Assembly of the Council of Europe. A journalist, scholar and political commentator, he has written extensively on minority rights, nation-building in multi-ethnic states, and conflict prevention in post-communist Europe. He is also the founder and moderator of MINELRES, a website providing information on minorities and ethnopolitics in Eastern Europe, and co-founder of the Consortium on Minority Resources (COMIR).

Fernand de Varennes is a Doctor of Law and former Director of the Asia-Pacific Centre for Human Rights and the Prevention of Ethnic Conflict at Murdoch University, Australia. He has written and published in eleven languages on the issues of human rights, minority rights and ethnic conflicts. His seminal work on *Language, Minorities and Human Rights* places him as one of the world's leading experts on linguistic rights, and he has worked on these issues with numerous international organizations such as the United Nations Working Group on the Rights of Minorities, UNESCO, the United Nations Mission in Kosovo and the OSCE High Commissioner on National Minorities. He is on the advisory board of numerous research centres and journals around the world and has been a research fellow at the European Academy in Bolzano, Italy, and Seikei University, Tokyo. He recently held the prestigious Tip O'Neill Peace Fellowship at INCORE (Initiative on Conflict Resolution and Ethnicity) in Derry, Northern Ireland and was awarded the LINGUAPAX prize from the Centre UNESCO de Catalunya. His most recent publications include a two-volume series on human rights documents on Asia. He is currently collating a three-volume series on peace agreements involving ethnic and internal conflicts worldwide.

Stefan Wolff is Professor of Political Science at the University of Nottingham in England, United Kingdom and Senior Nonresident Research Associate at the European Centre for Minority Issues in Flensburg, Germany. He holds an MPhil. in political theory from Magdalene College, Cambridge, and a PhD in political science from the London School of Economics. He has extensively written on ethnicity, ethnic conflict and conflict resolution. Wolff has authored and edited 11 books to date, including *Disputed Territories: The Transnational Dynamics of Ethnic Conflict Settlement* (Berghahn 2002), *Peace at Last? The Impact of the Good Friday Agreement on Northern Ireland* (Berghahn 2002, with Jörg Neuheiser), *Minority Languages in Europe* (Palgrave 2003, with Gabrielle Hogan-Brun), *Managing and Settling Ethnic Conflicts* (Hurst 2004, with Ulrich Schneckener), *The Ethnopolitical Encyclopaedia of Europe* (Palgrave 2004, with Karl Cordell), and *Ethnic Conflict: A Global Perspective* (Oxford University Press 2006). He is editor of the journal *Ethnopolitics* (Routledge) and co-chair of the Specialist Group on Ethnopolitics of the Political Studies Association of the UK.

INTRODUCTION

1 Political Governance of Cultural Diversity

MATTHIAS KOENIG &
PAUL DE GUCHTENEIRE

This book is about the political governance of cultural diversity. It analyses how public policy-making has dealt with the claims for cultural recognition that have increasingly been expressed by ethno-national movements, language groups, religious minorities, indigenous peoples and migrant communities in the past decades. Its major aim is to understand, explain and assess public policy responses to ethnic, linguistic and religious diversity. Adopting the perspective of comparative and interdisciplinary social sciences, it addresses the conditions, forms and consequences of democratic and human-rights-based governance of multi-ethnic, multi-lingual and multi-faith societies.

That cultural diversity has become a political challenge throughout the world stems from a complex set of factors. One of the major factors of cultural diversification in various societies is globalization. The intensified flow of capital, post-Fordist modes of production and the global spread of Western consumer culture have prompted a variety of social movements that emphasize their own ethnic, linguistic or religious distinctiveness. The emergence of transnational migrant networks, facilitated by growing inequalities in the capitalist world-system as well as by new technologies of transport and electronic communication, is another prominent aspect of such cultural diversification. What all these new social movements have in common, whether based on ethnicity, language or religion, is that they demand full and equal inclusion in society, while claiming the recognition of their particularistic identities in the public sphere. They criticize the assumption of congruence between political unity and cultural homogeneity which was characteristic of the classic model of the nation-state, and thereby contribute to its far-reaching institutional transformation.

In this book, we address the political governance of cultural diversity by focusing on this transformation of the nation-state and of political modernity in general. The contributions to this volume deal with specific aspects of governing ethnic, linguistic and religious diversity from different disciplinary perspectives. In our introduction, we situate them within a larger conceptual framework. Thus, in the first section, we argue that a major problem implicit in contemporary debates about cultural diversity is the ongoing transformation of the classical nation-state. In a second section, we highlight that a crucial aspect of this transformation is the emergence and development of international human rights regimes, which alter the external legitimacy structures of nation-states by providing new social arenas and new cultural repertoires of contention and claims-making. And thirdly, we analyse the particular challenges posed to the classical model of the nation-state by politics of ethnic or national, linguistic and religious recognition, respectively.

NATION-STATES AND THE PROBLEM OF CULTURAL DIVERSITY

Conceptualizing the political governance of cultural diversity poses a challenge to the social sciences, to the extent that these were for a long time impregnated by what some authors have called a "methodological nationalism" (Glick-Schiller and Wimmer 2003; see also Wallerstein et al. 1996; Wimmer 2002). By taking territorially bounded, socially closed and culturally integrated societies as their basic units of analysis, the social sciences have tended to ignore, to naturalize or simply to take for granted the nation-state as an institutional form of political modernity. However, seen in long-term historical perspective, this institutional form is highly contingent and problematic and therefore needs closer analysis.

The core feature of the modern nation-state is a structural coupling of political organization and collective identity which has deeply shaped our political vocabulary including such notions as constitutionalism, democracy and human rights. Thus, since the French Revolution popular sovereignty was conceived in terms of state independence and national self-determination, with the consequence that human rights were identified with citizen rights and attached to national identity. Perhaps the best illustration of this structural coupling of statehood and national identity is the institution of citizenship (Brubaker 1992; Hanagan/Tilly 1999). Understood as a set of institutionalized relations between the state and the individual, citizenship can be considered as being composed of two major elements: firstly, the rules of formal membership and individual rights through which individuals are incorporated organizationally into the state, and secondly, the forms of national identification through which individuals are incorporated symbolically. Of course, the close correspondence of political and cultural collectivity, assumed in the classical model of the nation-state, was rarely given in historical reality, as most states used to contain culturally heterogeneous populations. Yet, under the impact of that model, state-formation and nation-building were often accompanied by policies of cultural homogenization. Claims for recognition put forward by ethnic, linguistic or religious minorities were thus routinely seen as a threat to state stability and to national cohesion.

Today, conflicts about cultural diversity seem to contest the homogenizing assumptions of the classical nation-state model. Policies of assimilation or of differential exclusion are increasingly considered as illegitimate, both at domestic and international levels, while pluralistic policy responses, as exemplified by anti-discrimination legislation, affirmative action programmes or special minority protection, have gained momentum. Policies of "multiculturalism", as adopted by the governments of Australia, Canada, Sweden and some other countries in response to the poly-ethnic situation induced by international migration, are particularly noteworthy in this respect, as they aim simultaneously to achieve individual inclusion and respect for cultural differences (Castles 1995; Inglis 1996; Alexander 2001). That "consociational" democracies, such as in Belgium, the Netherlands or Switzerland (Lijphart 1977; Gagnon and Tully 2001), have recently become models for other multi-national democracies, is another indicator for changing assumptions about the nation-state. What we seem to witness is thus a certain decoupling of statehood and national identity. The question emerging from these developments is whether, and if so how, notions of constitutionalism, democracy and human rights may and need to be reformulated in such "post-national constellations" (Habermas 1998).

In political theory, the question of political governance in culturally diverse societies has, over the past decade, been extensively discussed in controversies surrounding the "politics of cultural recognition" (Gutmann 1994; Tully 1995) and "multicultural citizenship" (Kymlicka 1995; Kymlicka and Norman 2000; Mouffe 1992). Two major dilemmas are addressed in these debates. First, how can the recognition of cultural differences be reconciled with the social reproduction of trust and solidarity that is necessary for the maintenance of a democratic polity? Here, the question is which constitutional arrangements guarantee the functioning of a common sphere, while leaving room for the maintenance of diverse cultural practices and identities. The second dilemma is how to reconcile the recognition of minorities as groups with the concept of human rights, which focuses on the rights of the individual person. Put differently, how can constitutional arrangements mediate between different groups' collective rights of self-rule and the individual's rights to inclusion in the larger polity?

While a variety of policy experiences is reflected in the literature addressing these questions, the debates are often far more concerned with philosophical rather than empirical problems. Thus, a core issue of debate is the normative justification of policies in the light of classical traditions of political theory, such as liberalism, republicanism and social democracy. To be sure, such normative reflections on the triangle of democracy, human rights and cultural diversity have considerably helped to reconstruct the arguments put forward by political actors to legitimate (or contest) pluralistic policies. Yet, as Michel Wieviorka (2001) has recently argued, these philosophical approaches have sometimes tended to ignore the empirical dynamics of the cultural construction, social formation and political mobilization of collective identities. Lacking conceptual tools to analyse the institutional prerequisites, favourable factors, and social consequences of public policy-making, they cannot explain varying policy output and varying policy outcomes in different social situations. Here precisely lies, in our view, the genuine contribution of social science research to the debate on the political governance of culturally diverse societies. Which factors, globalization among them, give rise to politics of cultural recognition in the first place? Which public policies do governments adopt in reaction to cultural diversity, and how are these determined by existing institutional arrangements? And, finally, what is the concrete impact of pluralistic policies on the inclusion/ exclusion of minorities in different social contexts? In the following, we elaborate these questions in some greater detail.

TRANSFORMING THE NATION-STATE – THE IMPACT OF HUMAN RIGHTS

One of the major factors explaining the rise of politics of cultural recognition as well as more pluralistic policy responses to cultural diversity is the multi-faceted process of globalization. As a particularly important dimension of this process, we would like to highlight the institutionalization of human rights in cultural and social frameworks at a transnational or global level (Soysal 1994; Jacobson 1996). In fact, the evolution of international human rights regimes has contributed to far-reaching changes in the legitimacy structure of political modernity since the post-war period. Two transformations which directly affect the institution of national citizenship may be distinguished in this respect. Firstly, the transnational diffusion of ideas of human rights and their institutionalization in international organizations, both governmental and non-governmental, has established a status of "universal personhood" to which rights are, at least in principle, attached independently from formal state membership or nationality. And secondly, within the transnational human rights discourse there has been a proliferation of new rights which clearly go beyond the classical modern political tradition. Thus, rights of equality and non-discrimination have been specified in articles on individual rights to cultural identity and minority rights which oblige state governments to adopt a proactive approach to the promotion of the identity of ethnic or national, linguistic and religious minorities on their territory.

Within the United Nations (UN), where strong references to questions of minority protection had initially been avoided, the principles of non-discrimination and equality have been supplemented by the idea that states should not only protect, but also promote the identities of minorities (see Phillips and Rosas 1995; Symonides 1998). This trend is documented in the changing interpretation of Article 27 of the International Covenant of Civil and Political Rights (ICCPR), adopted by the United Nations in 1966. The article states:

> In those states in which ethnic, religious or linguistic minorities exist, persons belonging to such minorities shall not be denied the right, in community with other members of their group, to enjoy their own culture, to profess and practice their own religion, or to use their own language. (Article 27, ICCPR)

Whereas this article used to be interpreted in a rather restricted way (see Capotorti 1979), its content and coverage have recently been expanded so as to oblige the state to create favourable conditions for the maintenance of *group* identities and to include "new minorities". Thus, the Human Rights Committee, in its general comment on Article 27 ICCPR, has stated:

> Although the rights protected under article 27 are individual rights, they depend in turn on the ability of the *minority group* to maintain its culture, language or religion. Accordingly, *positive measures* by States may also be necessary *to protect the identity* of a minority and the rights of its members to enjoy and develop their culture and language and to practice their religion, in community with the other members of the group. (UN doc CCPR General Comment 23: The rights of minorities [8 April 1994], para. 6.2., emphasis added).

In its current understanding, Article 27 ICCPR thus constitutes the basis for broad conceptions of a "pluralism in togetherness" according to which minority identities are to be promoted by the state, while ensuring social integration in a common public sphere (see Eide 1994).

The same trend is manifested, for example, by the *Declaration on the Rights of Persons Belonging to National or Ethnic, Religious and Linguistic Minorities* adopted by UN General Assembly Resolution 47/135 in 1992 which calls upon states to "protect the existence and the national or ethnic, cultural, religious and linguistic identity of minorities within their respective territories and [...] encourage conditions for the promotion of that identity" (Article 1(1); see also Thornberry 1995). The *Universal Declaration on Cultural Diversity* adopted by the General Conference of UNESCO at its 31st session in 2001 points in the same direction. At the level of regional human rights regimes, similar developments can be observed, especially after the dissolution of the former Soviet Union, under the auspices of the Council of Europe and the Organization for Security and Co-operation in Europe (OSCE). The *European Charter for Regional or Minority Languages* (1992) and the *Framework Convention for the Protection of National Minorities* (1994) are the most notable documents in that respect.

All these developments in transnational human rights law contribute to a de-legitimization of the classical model of the nation-state with its assumptions of cultural homogeneity of its citizens. They strengthen the position of ethnic, linguistic and religious minorities and thus necessitate new public policies of governing diversity.

ETHNIC, LINGUISTIC AND RELIGIOUS POLITICS OF RECOGNITION

The social science literature dealing with policy reactions to cultural diversity seems to be highly fragmented along different disciplinary as well as thematic lines. Most notably, there is on the one side, a burgeoning literature that deals with policies of immigration and integration in industrial societies (Aleinikoff and Klusmeyer 2001; Bauböck et al. 1996; Bauböck and Rundell 1998; Castles and Davidson 2000; Joppke 1998) in which policy shifts from assimilation to "multiculturalism" – and back to assimilation (Brubaker 2001; Joppke 2004; Joppke and Morawska 2003) – are well documented and analysed. On the other side, social scientists have also been concerned with institutional contours of so-called "plural societies", characterized by long-standing ethnic and national cleavage structures (Stavenhagen 1996; Young 1998; Young 1999). While it is true that international migration has resulted in other types of cultural conflict than processes of nation-building in plural societies, both "old" and "new" types of identity politics equally challenge classical models of the nation-state. However, these commonalities are not further scrutinized due to this fragmentation of research agendas (for exceptions see for example Díez-Medrano 1995, Rex and Singh 2004).

In this book, we therefore adopt a slightly different approach. We focus on three dimensions of cultural diversity that challenge distinctive aspects of the classical nation-state model: *ethnicity, language* and *religion*. All these dimensions were, in multifaceted ways, closely related to processes of state-formation and nation-building. As a consequence, democratic states are in at least one of these dimensions less culturally neutral than is often assumed in political theory. To understand the complexities of governing cultural diversity, it is therefore imperative to capture the distinctive logics of ethnic, linguistic and religious politics of recognition.

Territorially Based Ethnic or National Movements

The most acute challenge to the coupling of political organization and collective identity within the classical nation-state is posed by territorially based ethnic or nationalist movements. Their claims for recognition not only call for equal respect in the common public sphere, but may turn into fully fledged strategies for secession. Cross-national comparative studies in the social sciences have shown that accelerated processes of globalization and the end of the Cold War have indeed brought about a resurgence and intensification of ethnic or nationalist movements (for example Gurr 1993). Furthermore, the growing robustness of the international human rights regime, in which the individual and collective rights of minorities are increasingly recognized, has strengthened the legitimacy of ethnic minorities' claims for self-determination (Tsutsui 2004).

Yet, while the initial formation and mobilization of ethnic or national movements has been widely explored, the impact of various government policies and constitutional arrangements on the support for secession and on the degree of violence involved in ethno-national conflicts is studied less. In fact, state governments have responded to claims for self-determination in a variety of ways, ranging from utmost repression to pluralistic policies such as communal representation, federalism or cultural autonomy (Ghai 2002). How the outcome of such policies can be evaluated is, however, far from clear.

In his contribution to this volume, *Juan Díez-Medrano* analyses the impact of government policies, by starting from available theoretical explanations of support for secessionist movements. Reviewing primordialism, social constructivism and rational choice theory, he highlights several structural and processual factors that contribute to popular support for secessionism and violence. From there, he develops a set of hypotheses on the extent to which these factors may be manipulated through state policy. Thus, while patterns of geographical and economic segregation may be difficult to reverse, state policy may shape a non-antagonistic public discourse about interethnic relations, respond favourably to non-violent demands of ethnic movements and adopt well-targeted public order policies. Comparative evidence suggests that non-indiscriminate public order policies, which only target radicals and not the ethnic group as a whole, combined with responsive policies might contribute to declining levels of violence and decreasing support for secessionism.

Thus, *Enric Martínez-Herrera* argues that the combination of efficacious but flexible public order policies, together with very substantial doses of responsiveness, contributes to the mitigation of Basque nationalist terrorism and extremism in Spain. His time-series multivariate analyses, aimed at evaluating policy outcomes in terms of support for violence and for secessionism, also show that certain specific policy choices have been either inefficacious or counterproductive, whereas terrorist violence itself tends, paradoxically, to decrease the attitudinal social bases of insurgent nationalist extremism.

Similar conclusions may be drawn from *Stefan Wolff*'s case study on the Northern Irish conflict in the United Kingdom. He analyses the different policies employed by the British government to manage the conflict in Northern Ireland between the late 1960s and the conclusion of the Good Friday Agreement in 1998. Drawing attention to the consequences of conflicting perceptions for the conflict management strategies, he evaluates success and failure of individual British strategies to manage the conflict in terms of policy objectives and, in particular, by the responses of paramilitary organizations and of the electorate. Here, as in the Basque case, the attempted or achieved solutions have involved political and institutional recognition of the ethnonational rights of the parties involved.

Yet it would be premature to argue that only pluralistic policies could settle conflicts with ethnonational movements, as is clearly shown by *Matthew Kocher*'s analysis of the Kurdish case. Prior to the 1990s, most regional experts insisted that only a negotiated settlement could provide a solution to "the Kurdish problem" in Turkey. It was widely assumed that the uncompromising stance of the government would result in a radicalization of the Kurdish population, which would further fuel violence. However, this has not happened. In the late 1990s, the Turkish state defeated the insurgent organization PKK militarily, without making any important concessions to Kurdish nationalism. That further polarization of Kurdish politics has still not ensued is due to intra-ethnic and cross-cutting political cleavage structures undermining support for nationalist extremism.

The results of these three in-depth case studies, if interpreted within the analytical framework of structural and process factors for support of ethnic or national violence and secessionism as laid out by Juan Díez-Medrano, suggest that non-indiscriminate public-order policies as well as responsive policies have a clear effect on reducing levels of violence, to the extent that they also secure the individual and collective rights of ethnic minorities in plural societies.

Linguistic Diversity and Language Policy

While not necessarily leading to secessionist movements, linguistic diversity also poses a considerable challenge to democratic polities. As language is the most fundamental tool of communication, states cannot be linguistically neutral. In fact, state-building was often accompanied by strong policies of linguistic homogenization, as evinced most notably in France (Weber 1979). In addition to its instrumental, communicative function, language also carries symbolic functions and has thereby contributed to the construction of collective identities. Corpus planning, that is, the standardization of scripts, semantics and grammar, and the canonization of literatures were among the most prominent policy tools in processes of nation-building worldwide (Anderson 1983; Wright 2004). Classical democratic theory in its assumption of a common sphere of public discourse was implicitly built on these linguistic characteristics of the nation-state.

However, the classical model of the nation-state is challenged by de facto linguistic diversity resulting from international migration and social networks based on new electronic media of communication, and by de jure linguistic pluralism imposed on nation-states by international human rights regimes. As a consequence, new policies need to be designed to ensure the respect for language rights while at the same time strengthening the reproduction of a common sphere of public discourse (see Koenig 1999; Kymlicka and Patten 2003).

In that context it is important to notice that, as *Fernand de Varennes* forcefully argues, language rights are generally conceived as specifications of basic human rights such as freedom of expression and non-discrimination, both under the global and various regional human rights regimes. His review of various international legal documents suggests that they are only inadequately captured by notions of (unenforceable) collective or minority rights. Rather, claims to the private and public use of minority languages are justified as individual human rights. But even as minorities are not in themselves bearers of collective rights, the transnational legal discourse of human rights does de-legitimize strong policies of language homogenization and clearly obliges states to respect and promote linguistic diversity (see also de Varennes 1996).

There are many organizational mechanisms by which transnational legal discourse affects national policy-making. International organizations, both governmental and non-governmental, certainly play a crucial role in this respect. *Sally Holt* and *John Packer* provide detailed information on one of the most prominent actors in the field of linguistic rights, the Organization for Security and Co-operation in Europe (OSCE). As an organization which is concerned primarily with peace and security, the OSCE approach to linguistic diversity and notably to the linguistic rights of national minorities has been one of conflict-prevention. Post-Soviet state-building and the resurgence of nationalist movements and inter-ethnic conflict in that region have achieved particular attention in this respect. Evidently, institutions such as the OSCE have mounted normative pressure on states to implement international legal standards aimed at protecting and promoting the linguistic rights of persons belonging to national minorities.

However, to what extent this changing transnational legitimacy structure of nation-states affects domestic policy output is open to scrutiny. Many case studies show that, in spite of such normative pressure, public policies continue to be influenced by historical trajectories of state-formation and nation-building along with other more contextual factors. Thus, as *Boriss Cilevičs* shows in his review of language legislation in Estonia, Latvia and Lithuania after the restoration of their independence, there are a number of inconsistencies with the provision of the international legal instruments on the linguistic rights of national minorities. The regulations determining the status of the state language and the languages of national minorities, and governing the use of languages in elected bodies, before public authorities, in media, in education, and in employment, bear the imprint of post-communist nation-building aimed at reversing the hitherto dominant status of the Russian language.

The Baltic case also shows that there may, in practical terms, be tensions between human rights standards and the process of democratization. In that respect, post-apartheid South Africa provides another interesting example. The country contains numerous linguistic population groups, all of which can be considered linguistic minorities, with the possible exception of the English-speaking group. Between 1910 and 1994 South Africa had two official languages, English and Dutch (later Afrikaans). Simultaneously, the indigenous and Indian languages were given a grossly inferior status. As *Kristin Henrard* demonstrates, during the negotiations for a constitution in post-apartheid South Africa, the status of the languages spoken in South Africa proved to be particularly sensitive. Although she finds the constitutional framework concerning the accommodation of South Africa's linguistic diversity rather promising, practice reveals a de facto denial of several constitutional principles concerning the status of languages and multi-lingualism, which goes hand in hand with the emergence of English as lingua franca.

If public policies continue to be affected by historical trajectories, their actual *outcomes* are supposedly even more determined by contextual social dynamics. To what extent language policies, including both status and corpus planning, alter the power-differentials between dominant and minority languages has been extensively discussed in socio-linguistic research. Of particular interest in this context are the intended and unintended consequences of interventions in favour of endangered languages. *Suzanne Romaine* argues that evaluating the potential and actual impact of language policies is complicated by lack of straightforward causal connections between types of policy and language maintenance and shift. Language policy, so her argument goes, is not an autonomous factor, and what appears to be ostensibly the same policy may lead to different outcomes depending on the situation in which it operates. Conventions and treaties adopted by international organizations and agencies recommending the use of minority languages in education usually lack power to be reinforced. Furthermore, policies have negligible impact on home use, which is essential for continued natural transmission of endangered languages. Although survival thus cannot depend on legislation as its main support, legal provisions may allow speakers of endangered languages to claim some public space for their languages and cultures.

Secularism and Religious Diversity

Religious diversity is perhaps the oldest dimension of social and political cleavages in many parts of the world (Rokkan 1970; Martin 1978). In fact, confessional identities provided the backbone for processes of state-formation and nation-building in early modern Europe. With confessional fragmentation, various institutional modes of governing religion developed, ranging from secularist exclusion of religion from the public sphere to corporative forms of religious inclusion. Yet, these constitutional arrangements have recently been challenged by a resurgence of religion and new patterns of religious pluralization triggered by globalization, international migration and the emergence of transnational religious networks.

However, political and academic debates on the so-called "resurgence of religion" often suffer from simplistic assumptions about modernity and the process of globalization. Some argue that globalization strengthens the differences between Western modernity and other, non-Western civilizations; in this perspective, most prominently formulated by Samuel Huntington (1996), religious diversity is interpreted, both on a global and a national level, as mirroring inter-civilizational conflict. Others, such as Francis Fukuyama (1992), promote an opposing view arguing that globalization processes imply a homogenization of civilizations in accordance with Western modernity; hence, compared to the impact of a globally diffused consumer culture, religious diversity would be judged as a marginal phenomenon without serious political implications. What both perspectives share is the assumption that (Western) modernity is characterized by "secularization", that is, by a decline of religion, the functional differentiation of politics and religion, and the privatization of religious beliefs. However, the rising politics of religious recognition in Western and non-Western countries attests to the public dimension of religion in modernity (Bader 2003; Casanova 1994; Koenig 2005).

In his contribution to this volume, *Shmuel N. Eisenstadt*, adopting a broad historical perspective on the rise and transformation of modernity, takes an explicit stance against both Huntington's and Fukuyama's theses. He situates fundamentalist and communal religious movements within the larger context of a structural transformation of the modern nation-state and increased global interconnectedness which allows for multiple interpretations of major principles of political modernity. These movements simultaneously draw on the religious dimension of the so-called "Axial civilizations" and on the totalitarian or Jacobin dimensions of modernity. In his view, new potential for conflict therefore arises from the multiplication of different, yet presumably universalistic, interpretations of modernity rather than from the confrontation of different particularistic cultures.

Thus, whereas religious pluralism may, on the one hand, lead to peaceful co-existence and even to ideological convergence among different religions, it may, on the other hand, also lead to social dissolution, as it intensifies the awareness of fundamental differences between religious world-views, thus potentially provoking social conflicts along religious lines. Hence, the major question is how political governance of religious diversity may respect the individual's right to religious liberty, while at the same time recognizing religious identities in the public sphere.

Ole Riis takes up this question in his contribution by discussing conceptual, theoretical and empirical problems of analysing public policy responses to religious diversity. Reviewing various theoretical approaches in sociology of religion, he distinguishes different ideal-typical "modes of religious pluralism", understood as an institutional framework of governing religious diversity. These modes of religious pluralism, which result from specific historical trajectories of state-formation and nation-building, may stress religious toleration, corporative rights of religious denominations or individual religious freedom. In so far as either of these aspects may be given priority, public policies responding to contemporary religious pluralization vary. The outcome of such policies, in turn, depends on a number of sociological aspects, including the distribution of political, economic and cultural resources.

The political challenge posed by religious pluralization is illustrated in *James Beckford*'s case-study on the governance of religious diversity in prisons in England and Wales. As is well known, the variety of faith traditions represented in the country has grown due to international migration, as have the numbers of, for example, Buddhists, Hindus, Jews, Muslims and Sikhs. More importantly, these faith communities have established themselves to the point where they can confidently demand "equal respect" and "equality of opportunity" to practise their religion in private and public. As a consequence, the importance of policies governing religious and ethno-religious diversity in England and Wales has increased in recent decades. Whereas the Anglican Church used to function as broker between the State and religious communities, there has recently been a shift to various forms of multi-faith chaplaincy. Contrary to those who fear that such even-handed pluralistic policies may increase segmentation along lines of ethno-religious difference, Beckford argues that they contribute to both the equal respect of religious human rights and social integration.

By comparison, politics of religious recognition have taken rather different forms in post-communist countries. Here, religion has regained political and public importance in several respects. Firstly, the reconstruction of national identities which has accompanied both the break-down of communist regimes and the process of democratization has often drawn on religious traditions which had been involved in nation-building and state-formation prior to the communist era. Secondly, a remarkable religious pluralization has led to public debates over the respect for the individual's rights to religious freedom and, hence, the recognition of religious diversity (Anderson 2003). These somewhat contradictory trends are well exemplified by the governance of religious diversity in the Russian Federation, as analysed by *Kathy Rousselet* in her contribution to this volume. On the one hand, the Russian Orthodox Church has actively participated in the reconstruction of Russian national identity while, on the other hand, de facto religious diversity has led to concerns, both domestic and international, about the full legal recognition of diverse religious identities, notably in those republics with a strong Islamic presence. Rousselet's analysis suggests that the governance of religious diversity may be considered as an indicator of the degree of democratisation.

From different angles, then, the contributions show that contrary to conventional theories of secularization there is an enduring place for religion within the public spheres of modern democratic polities. They suggest that secularism may not always be the most suitable policy to religious diversity, but that context-sensitive solutions have to be found which respond to claims of religious recognition, while at the same time furthering democratic participation in a common public sphere.

CONCLUSION

The governance of cultural diversity is a key issue in contemporary politics, both domestically and internationally. Accommodating increased cultural diversity by balancing the recognition of differences with the promotion of equal participation in the common public sphere is a task that will, for the foreseeable future, be with us to stay.

The contributions to this volume show that this task requires finding suitable public policy responses to ethnic, linguistic and religious claims for recognition that go beyond the classical institutional contours of the modern nation-state. They also show that while human rights do provide some normative yardsticks for policy-making in this respect, no single and simple solutions exist. The dynamics of ethnic, linguistic and religious diversity follow different logics, respectively, and they moreover vary as a function of different historical trajectories of state-formation and nation-building. Accommodating cultural diversity therefore requires finding highly context-sensitive pluralistic policy designs.

It is in this respect – by providing knowledge about the socio-historical contexts of, and preconditions for, successful pluralistic policies – that interdisciplinary and comparative social science research can make an important contribution to the debate about the political governance of cultural diversity in post-national constellations.

REFERENCES

Aleinikoff, Thomas A. and Klusmeyer, Douglas B. (eds) (2001), *Citizenship Today: Global Perspectives and Practices* (Washington, DC: Carnegie Endowment for International Peace)

Alexander, Jeffrey C. (2001), "Theorizing Modes of Incorporation: Assimilation, Hyphenation, and Multiculturalism as Varieties of Civil Participation", *Sociological Theory* 19, 238–249.

Anderson, Benedict (1983), *Imagined Communities. Reflections on the Origin and Spread of Nationalism* (London: Verso)

Anderson, John (2003). *Religious Liberty in Transitional Societies. The Politics of Religion* (Cambridge: Cambridge University Press)

Bader, Veit (2003). "Religious Diversity and Democratic Institutional Pluralism", *Political Theory* 31, 265–294.

Bauböck, Rainer, Heller, Agnes and Zolberg, Aristide R. (eds) (1996), *The Challenge of Diversity: Integration and Pluralism in Societies of Immigration* (Aldershot: Avebury)

Bauböck, Rainer and Rundell, John F. (eds) (1998), *Blurred Boundaries: Migration, Ethnicity, Citizenship* (Aldershot: Ashgate)

Brubaker, Rogers (1992), *Citizenship and Nationhood in France and Germany* (Cambridge, Mass.: Harvard University Press)

Brubaker, Rogers (2001), "The return of assimilation? Changing perspectives on immigration and its sequels in France, Germany, and the United States", *Ethnic and Racial Studies* 24, 531–548

Casanova, José (1994), *Public Religions in the Modern World* (Chicago: Chicago University Press)

Castles, Stephen (1995), "How Nation States Respond to Immigration and Ethnic Diversity", *New Community* 21, 293–308

Castles, Stephen and Davidson, Alastair (2000), *Citizenship and Migration. Globalization and the Politics of Belonging* (London: Macmillan)

Capotorti, F. (1979), *Study on the Rights of Persons Belonging to Ethnic, Religious and Linguistic Minorities* (New York: UN Publications)

de Varennes, Fernand (1996), *Language, Minorities and Human Rights* (The Hague: Martinus Nijhoff)

Díez-Medrano, Juan (1995), *Divided Nations* (Ithaca, NY: Cornell University Press)

Eide, Asbjørn (1994), *Peaceful and Constructive Resolution of Situations Involving Minorities* (Oslo: Norwegian Institute of Human Rights)

Fukuyama, Francis. (1992), *The End of History and the Last Man* (New York: Free Press)

Gagnon, Alain and Tully, James (2001), *Multinational Democracies* (Cambridge: Cambridge University Press)

Ghai, Yash Pal. (2002), "Constitutional Asymmetries: Communal Representation, Federalism, and Cultural Autonomy", in Andrew Reynolds (ed.), *The Architecture of Democracy. Constitutional Design, Conflict Management, and Democracy*, 141–70 (New York: Oxford University Press)

Glick-Schiller, Nina and Wimmer, Andreas (2003), "Methodological nationalism, the social sciences, and the study of migration. An essay in historical epistemology", *International Migration Review* 37, 576–610

Gurr, Ted R. (1993), *Minorities at Risk. A Global View of Ethnopolitical Conflicts* (Washington DC: United States Institute for Peace Press)

Gutmann, Amy (ed.) (1994), *Multiculturalism: Examining the Politics of Recognition* (Princeton, NJ: Princeton University Press)

Habermas, Jürgen (1998), *Die postnationale Konstellation. Politische Essays* (Frankfurt a.M.: Suhrkamp)

Hanagan, Michael and Tilly, Charles (eds) (1999), *Extending Citizenship, Reconfiguring States* (Lanham: Rowman & Littlefield Publishers)

Huntington, Samuel P. (1996), *The Clash of Civilizations and the Remaking of World Order* (London: Simon & Schuster)

Inglis, Christine (1996), *Multiculturalism: New Policy Responses to Diversity* (MOST Policy Papers, No. 4) (Paris: UNESCO)

Jacobson, David (1996), *Rights Accross Border. Immigration and the Decline of Citizenship* (Baltimore: Johns Hopkins University Press)

Joppke, Christian (ed.) (1998), *Challenge to the Nation-State: Immigration in Western Europe and the United States* (Oxford: Oxford University Press)

Joppke, Christian (2004), "The Retreat of Multiculturalism in the Liberal State: Theory and Policy", *British Journal of Sociology* 55, 237–257

Joppke, Christian and Morawska, Ewa (2003), *Toward Assimilation and Citizenship. Immigrants in liberal nation-states* (Houndsmill: Palgrave Macmillan)

Koenig, Matthias (1999), "Cultural diversity and language policy", *International Social Science Journal* 161, 401–408

Koenig, Matthias (2005), "Politics and religion in European nation-states - institutional varieties and contemporary transformations", in Bernhard Giesen and Daniel Suber (eds), *Religion and politics. Cultural perspectives*, 291–315 (Leiden: Brill)

Kymlicka, Will (1995), *Multicultural Citizenship. A Liberal Theory of Minority Rights* (Oxford: Clarendon Press)

Kymlicka, Will and Patten, Alan (eds) (2003), *Language Rights and Political Theory* (Oxford: Oxford University Press)

Kymlicka, Will and Norman, Wayne (eds) (2000), *Citizenship in Diverse Societies* (Oxford: Oxford University Press)

Lijphart, Arend (1977), *Democracy in Plural Societies: A Comparative Exploration* (New Haven/London: Yale University Press)

Martin, David (1978), *A General Theory of Secularization* (Oxford: Basil Blackwell)

Mouffe, Chantal (ed.) (1992), *Dimensions of Radical Democracy: Pluralism, Citizenship and Community* (London: Routledge)

Phillips, Alan and Rosas, Allan (eds) (1995), *Universal Minority Rights* (Turku/Åbo: Åbo Akademi University Institute for Human Rights)

Rex, John and Gurharpal Singh (2004), *Governance of Multicultural Societies* (Aldershot: Ashgate)

Rokkan, Stein (1970), *Citizens, Elections, Parties* (New York: McKay)

Soysal, Yasemin Nuhoglu (1994), *Limits of Citizenship. Migrants and Postnational Membership in Europe* (Chicago: Chicago University Press)

Stavenhagen, Rodolfo (1996), *Ethnic Conflicts and the Nation-State* (London: UNRISD/ Macmillan)

Symonides, Janusz (ed.) (1998), *Human Rights: New Dimensions and Challenges* (Aldershot: Ashgate/UNESCO)

Thornberry, Patrick (1995), "The Rights of Minorities", in David Harris and Sarah Jones (eds), *The International Covenant on Civil and Political Rights and United Kingdom Law*, 597–627 (Oxford: Clarendon Press)

Tsutsui, Kiyoteru (2004), "Global civil society and ethnic social movements in the contemporary world", *Sociological Forum* 19, 63–87

Tully, James (1995), *Strange Multiplicity. Constitutionalism in an Age of Diversity* (Cambridge: Cambridge University Press)

Wallerstein, Immanuel et al. (1996), *Open the Social Sciences. Report of the Gulbenkian Commission for the Restructuring of the Social Sciences* (Stanford: Stanford University Press)

Weber, Eugen (1979), *Peasants into Frenchman* (London: Chatto and Windus)

Wieviorka, Michel (2001), *La différence* (Paris: Éditions Balland)

Wimmer, Andreas (2002), *Nationalist Exclusion and Ethnic Conflicts. Shadows of Modernity* (Cambridge: Cambridge University Press)

Wright, Sue (2004), *Language Policy and Language Planning. From Nationalism to Globalization* (London/New York: Palgrave)

Young, Crawford (ed.) (1998), *Ethnic Diversity and Public Policy. A Comparative Inquiry* (London: Macmillan/UNRISD)
Young, Crawford (ed.) (1999), *The Accommodation of Cultural Diversity. Case Studies* (London: Macmillan/UNRISD)

PART I
ETHNO-NATIONAL
MOVEMENTS

2 Nationalism, Ethnic Conflict and Democratic Governance

JUAN DÍEZ-MEDRANO*

Research on nationalism and ethnic conflict has shown a tendency to focus excessively on aspects that do not directly relate to the problems that triggered the research on these topics in the first place: violence and movements towards secession in plurinational and multi-ethnic states (Díez Medrano 1995). Rather than addressing these specific topics, scholars have given priority to general problems such as the historical emergence of nationalism, the presence/absence of nationalist/ethnic mobilization, and the intensity of such mobilization. Whether these lines of inquiry respond to a deliberate effort by social scientists to distance themselves from the mundane and the specific, or to a misled conflation of similar but distinct problems, is an open question. Policy-makers and the general public are concerned, however, with the mundane and specific questions that scholars appear to ignore. The purpose of this chapter is to redirect attention to the problems of ethnic/nationalist violence and movements towards secession. More particularly, through the examination of several case studies, it seeks answers to the following questions: What is the effect of state policies on ethnic violence and/or support for secession? Can the state successively mitigate ethnonational violence and conduct policies that contribute to a decline in support for secession while simultaneously securing the individual and collective rights of ethnic and national minorities, as Paul de Guchtenaire and Matthias Koenig (in this volume) put it?

THEORETICAL APPROACHES

One useful approach to addressing the questions above is to examine current explanations for the problems of ethnic/nationalist violence and secessionism and, based on the variables invoked by these explanations, analyse the role that the state can play in changing the values of these variables so as to induce changes in the levels of violence and of support for secessionist solutions. Fearon and Laitin (2000) and Brubaker and Laitin (1998) in their

21

reviews of the literature on these topics, highlight two major approaches to the explanation of ethnic/nationalist conflict in general, which they label "primordialist" and "social constructivist". Furthermore, conscious of the fact that conflict rarely translates into violence, they discuss rational choice, international relations and game theory approaches directly related to the topic of violence. From these reviews of the literature, one can discern three major propositions about secessionist movements, corresponding to the primordialist, social constructivist and what they summarize as "rational choice approaches".

Primordialism

The first proposition is that ethnic/nationalist violence and movements towards secession are inevitable in pluri-ethnic or plurinational states. This proposition follows from an ideal-typical primordialist conception of ethnic and national identities, which posits that people are naturally emotionally attached to the ethnic and national groups to which they belong and that this attachment necessarily implies feelings of antagonism towards other groups that sooner or later express themselves through violence and/or, in plurinational states, in movements towards independence, regardless of state policy. Of course, this conception is, as Fearon and Laitin point out, a simplistic perspective found in the public sphere but rarely taken seriously by scholars. Regardless of the descriptive merits it may have, the primordialist approach is clearly insufficient to explain violence and secessionism, for the number of pluri-ethnic or plurinational states with high levels of ethnic/ national violence and/or strong support for the creation of independent states is very small relative to the number of such states.

Social Constructivism

The second proposition is that ethnic/nationalist violence and movements towards secession vary depending on how much antagonism towards other ethnic/national groups characterizes an ethnic/national group's identity. This is the proposition that follows from the ideal-typical social constructivist approach that prevails in the social sciences (for example Brass 1997; Deng 1995; Kapferer 1988; Prunier 1995; Woodward 1995). Social constructionists contradict the primordialist thesis that ethnic/national identities necessarily prescribe antagonism towards other groups; instead, they allow for variation across ethnic and national groups and thus potentially account for observed contrasts in levels of ethnic/nationalist violence and support for independence across these groups. However, social constructivists fail to discuss the causal mechanisms linking antagonism towards other groups with violence or support for independence; nor can they account for the low frequency with which antagonism translates into actual violence and/or support for secession. Moreover, the dynamic character of ethnic/national identities leads to the expectation that violence/efforts towards secession will move hand in hand with ethnic/national discourses that emphasize antagonism, such that it becomes impossible to demonstrate a causal link between the content of these identities and violence and/or support for secession. Despite these caveats, the factors that social constructivists invoke when explaining the different degree of ethnic/national antagonism that characterizes different ethnic/national identities direct our attention towards areas where state action could be effective.

Social constructionists emphasize three sets of factors when explaining the level of antagonism towards other ethnic/national groups contained in ethnic/national identities:

1. *Structural variables such as the levels of ethnic segregation and intra-group competition and the stability and non-controversial nature of ethnic/ national boundaries.* Ethnic segregation models predict that levels of ethnic antagonism increase with levels of ethnic segregation (Hechter 1975; Hechter 1978). In contrast, ethnic competition models predict a sharpening of antagonistic feelings when ethnic segregation breaks down (Hannan 1979). Explanations focused on the role of intra-group competition emphasize that the greater it is, the greater the propensity of competing factions to demonize other ethnic groups (Horowitz 1985; Gagnon 1994–96; Kaufman 1996). Finally, explanations focused on the role of the stability and non-controversial nature of ethnic/ national boundaries posit that unstable and controversial boundaries provide a favourable context for the construction of ethnic identities that stress antagonism towards other ethnic groups (Deng 1995).

2. *Discursive resources available to and deployed by ethnic/national groups against other ethnic/national groups.* Ethnic identities emphasize the antagonistic element in ethnic relations when the groups constructing these identities have more resources at their disposal than have their more moderate competitors in their own or other ethnic group. Many factors can determine the level of discursive resources available to different groups and thus create information asymmetries that eventually determine the dominant self-understandings among the population (De Figueiredo and Weingast 1999; Fearon and Laitin 1996). Language differentiation between ethnic groups is one of them. If two ethnic groups speak different languages and cannot understand each other's language, those speaking the same language as the population to which their discourse is addressed will have a greater capacity to make their definitions of ethnic identity prevail than will those who do not master this language. The level of ethnic segregation, whether spatial or socio-economic, also determines the discursive resources available to different groups. Discourse producers have less access to the population of another ethnic or national group when there is a higher degree of ethnic segregation. The level of concentration of the population can also affect the relative discursive resources of different ethnic or national groups. Constructions formulated by members of an ethnic or national group to define another ethnic or national group have a better chance of penetrating the group that they define

when this group's population is clustered in large cities than when it is scattered in small villages, in which personal acquaintance and micro-power dynamics play a more important role in the spreading of ideas than large-scale mechanisms of indoctrination such as control of the media. Finally, one may expect more economically advanced ethnic or national groups to have more discursive resources than their less economically advanced counterparts.

3. *State responses to ethnonational violence.* The main hypothesis advanced by scholars who focus on the dynamics of ethnic relations is that indiscriminate repression against an ethnic/national group generates more antagonism and violence among the members of the groups that are subjected to this violence than does a judicious and targeted used of public-order measures (Díez Medrano 1995). The former creates the impression that the whole ethnic or national group is targeted, whereas the latter makes clear that it is not the ethnic or national group that is targeted but, rather, particular individuals.

Rational Choice

Neither the primordialist nor the social constructivist approaches address the problem of the translation of ethnic/national antagonism into violence and/or movements for secession. Since this translation occurs very rarely, explaining it becomes crucial for an adequate understanding of the causes of ethnic/national violence or secessionism. Scholars in the rational choice tradition stand almost alone in having accepted this challenge (for explanations combining structural and rational choice variables, see Horowitz 1985). Their approach has consisted in subsuming the problems of ethnic/national violence and secessionism into the more general themes of violence and exit. Perceived costs and benefits of various courses of action are the causal mechanism that, according to scholars in this tradition, determines the political strategies followed by different ethnic/national groups (Fearon 1995; Hechter 1995). According to these authors, when the problem under examination is violence, the utility that individuals try to minimize is their personal security. When the problem under examination is secessionism, the utility on which authors in this tradition have focused is economic well-being. In other words, the main propositions advanced by the rational choice tradition are that members of an ethnic/national group will opt for violence only if it is perceived to bring more security than not relying on violence and that members of an ethnic/national group will opt for secession only if it is perceived to yield a better economic situation than remaining part of the state in which they find themselves.

Relative wealth with respect to other ethnic/national groups in a given state and trade interdependence are some of the variables that are viewed as having an impact on the cost–benefit calculations regarding secession (see Meadwell 1989; Hechter 1992). Confidence in the ability to maintain or even improve the ethnic/national group's economic situation is probably greater among ethnic/national groups that are better off than the rest of the population and/or do not depend on trade with the rest of the state to which they belong than it is among groups that are poorer than the rest of the population – unless this is caused by demonstrated ethnic discrimination – and/or that depend greatly on trade with the rest of the state to which they belong. The main variables entering the security equation are people's expectations about the penalties that members of the different ethnic/national groups will attempt to impose on them if they side or do not side with violent behaviour and about the relative capacities of these members to make these penalties effective. Citizens of the Basque Country, for example, will act in one way or another guided by more or less conscious estimations about the penalties that the Spanish Government, Basque institutions and other segments of Basque society will try to impose on them for participating in and/or supporting violent behaviour. As part of this more or less conscious calculus, they will also guess how likely it is that the Spanish Government, Basque institutions and other segments of Basque society will be able to impose these penalties. Finally, they will be guided by guesses about the penalties associated with not participating and/or not supporting violence and about the likelihood that these penalties will be made effective.

For the security argument to have policy implications, if it is indeed a valid one, one must link people's cost–benefit calculations to variables affecting this calculus. If we follow the social movement literature, we must take into account the relative resources available to the leading groups involved in ethnic or national conflict. These resources play a role in determining people's perceptions about each of the contending group's ability to penalize people who in some form or another support or do not support violence. If the state is one of the contenders, one would expect that under normal conditions, that is, to the extent that the state retains its monopoly over the means of violence, ethnic or national violence will be kept in check. The state's resource superiority will allow it to convince the population about its ability to inflict penalties on those who incur or support violence and about its ability to guarantee the security of those who do not follow the path of violence against retaliation by those advocating violence. Within this general expectation, there may be variation from case to case. Variables that may diminish the state's persuasive power are the mildness of its penalties compared with those of the groups advocating violence, a weak state (Posen 1993), and ethnic/national concentration in particular regions in which violent representatives of the ethnic/national groups in question enjoy what one could call "home advantage". The population's concentration in a particular region makes it easier for an ethnic/national group to counteract the superior resources of the state. If, at the same time, the population in this region is scattered in small villages rather than concentrated in large towns or cities, then the advantages for the local violent ethnic/national group are even greater because in small villages the cost of social control is cheaper and thus the marginal utility of the state's greater economic, repressive and technological resources diminishes (see Laqueur 1998; Laitin 1993).

State Policy and Ethnonationalism: Theoretical Predictions

The discussion above provides an analytical framework and various theoretical propositions about the structural and processual factors underlying support for ethnic/national violence and secessionism. Some of the hypotheses developed above invoke factors that are difficult to manipulate in the short term through state policies. Patterns of geographic and/or economic segregation, for example, are difficult to reverse; the same applies to the levels of economic development of a particular ethnic or national group. Other hypotheses invoke factors that are not subject to the state's manipulation, such as the level of its resources or its monopoly over the means of coercion. Other factors, however, are easier to manipulate. For example, here is a list of policies that, based on the above discussion, can contribute to diminish support for ethnic/national violence:

- increased and more efficient administration of the communication resources invested in shaping a non-antagonistic discourse about the nature of relations between ethnic/national groups;
- increased and more efficient enforcement of the resources devoted to fighting violent behaviour;
- increased state penalties attached to participating or supporting violence;
- avoidance of indiscriminate repression;
- efforts to diminish competition between moderates and extremists within ethnic/national groups by strengthening the moderates;
- responsive behaviour towards the non-violent demands of mobilized ethnic/national groups.

CASE STUDIES

We can start addressing the issues discussed above by comparing levels and trends in support for secession and/or violence in different peripheral regions of five different countries and the state policies that have been implemented to address these problems since the 1970s. These cases were intentionally selected for a special issue of the *International Journal on Multicultural Societies* (IJMS, 2002) so as to cover a broad geographic scope, varying levels of violence, and different degrees of state success in eradicating this violence. The cases are the Basque conflict in Spain, the Northern Irish conflict in the United Kingdom, the Kurdish conflict in Turkey, the Zapatista conflict in Mexico and the Québécois conflict in Canada. The selected cases represent different levels and trends in violence and support for secession. They vary from the very low level of support for secession among the Chiapas population in Mexico to the very high level among Québécois, from the very low level of nationalist violence observed in Québec to the very high level observed in Chiapas, from the stable levels of violence observed in Northern Ireland and the Basque Country to the increasing levels observed in Chiapas and the decreasing levels observed in the Turkish regions mainly inhabited by Kurds. Comparisons between these five cases are made easier because of the similar methodology that the investigators for the IJMS special issue cited above used in analysing their respective cases.

The Basque Country

The Basque Country is a highly divided community, with intense competition between Basque nationalist groups and state-wide parties, which is made even more complex by the high degree of intra-nationalist competition between moderates and extremists. The political context within which the Basque conflict has taken place has been one of democracy and a very high degree of political autonomy for the Basque Country, with Basque moderate nationalists ruling the regional government, alone or in coalition, since the first regional elections in 1981. Since the first democratic elections in 1977, support for political parties that advocate independence has remained stable, while exclusive Basque identification has declined somewhat, and levels of violence have declined significantly from close to 100 deaths per year around 1980 to averages between 10 and 20 deaths per year in the late 1990s. Taking advantage of the unusual wealth of quantitative data accumulated since the 1970s, Martínez has conducted what is probably the most systematic attempt to date to quantitatively assess the relative effects of public order and responsive state policies (see Martínez-Herrera 2002 and this volume). His findings suggest that both types of policy have played a role in affecting levels of violence and of exclusive identification as Basque, while they have had almost no effect on levels of support for separatist political parties.

Northern Ireland

The Northern Irish case is unique in that the state (the British for the most part and also the Irish) has largely played the role of arbiter in the intra-regional conflict between two communities – Unionists, favourable to remaining part of the United Kingdom, and Irish Nationalists, favourable to integration in the Republic of Ireland. As is well known, in Northern Ireland this political cleavage largely overlaps with the Protestant–Catholic divide. As Wolff shows, the political context in Northern Ireland since the 1970s has been less stable than it has in the Basque Country, with direct rule from Westminster alternating with periods in which somewhat autonomous regional assemblies have participated in the government of Northern Ireland (Wolff 2002 and this volume). Another contrast with the Basque Country has been the state's much greater reliance on harsh public-order policies to confront the problem. Finally, Wolff has shown that levels of violence in Northern Ireland have been significantly higher than in the Basque Country, with a peak around 500 deaths per year early in the 1970s followed by a decline to an average between 50 and 100 deaths per year until the mid-1990s and a recent decline to around 25 deaths per year in the late 1990s, that coincided with the reaching of the Good Friday Agreement. Wolff's findings suggest again that public-order policies have managed to maintain levels of violence under control and that political negotiation can also bear fruits in terms of a reduction of violence. As in the Basque Country, however, there does not seem to be a connection between state policies and levels of support for radical nationalist groups, for these have remained relatively stable throughout the period or changed for reasons that are independent of state policies.

Québec

In his analysis of conflict in the Canadian province of Québec Rocher has provided a useful counterpoint to other instances of peripheral nationalism examined here because Québecois nationalism has expressed itself mostly through peaceful channels (Rocher 2002). The Québec conflict opposes the francophone community to the dominant anglophone community and has played out in a very stable political context, with federal arrangements ensuring a great deal of political autonomy for the province of Québec. The only instances of francophone nationalist violence took place in the second half of the 1960s, causing nine victims. Violent groups were heavily repressed by the Canadian Government and rapidly disappeared. The absence of physical violence in Canadian nationalist politics is not indicative of lack of conflict. In fact, Québec nationalism displays the highest levels of support for independence of any of the cases examined here, as well as very high and increasing levels of exclusive ethnic identification. In this sense, the Québec example illustrates the very different factors at play in explaining various dimensions of peripheral nationalism and the need to develop theories tailored to the specific dimension or dimensions being studied.

Chiapas

Particularly violent instances of ethnic/nationalist violence are the Chiapas conflict in Mexico and the Kurdish conflict in Turkey. Whereas ethnic/ nationalist conflict in the cases discussed above has usually involved fewer than 100 victims a year, in the Chiapas and Kurdish conflicts the numbers of victims have been well above that number and total many thousands. Guillermo Trejo's work on Chiapas has given us privileged access to a contemporary instance of constructed ethnic identity (Trejo 2002). Largely a peasant movement for land and democratic reform, the Chiapas conflict turned ethnic under the leadership of the Zapatista movement in the 1990s. The Chiapas conflict also presents us with an exceptional case in which political identities (opposition to the Institutional Revolutionary Party (PRI)/ support for the PRI), religious identities (Protestant/Catholic), and ethnic identities (indigenous/non-indigenous) greatly overlap. Trejo has traced the history of the peasant movement for land reform and its transformation into an ethnic movement that has surprisingly shied away from demanding independence. The Chiapas movement, in contrast to those described above, has taken place in a rural society with relatively low levels of economic development and in a political context characterized by federal government and low levels of democracy. The author shows that violence by both the state and the rebels has predominated in this conflict and that levels of violence increased with the emergence of the Zapatista movement. In contrast to the other cases examined here, the insurgents have managed to partially attain their goals by force rather than negotiation and the conflict has been characterized by a spiral of violence in which state repression and violent protest have fed on each other.

The Kurdish Question in Turkey

The comparison between the Chiapas and the Kurdish cases provides useful insights about the role of state policies in determining levels of ethnic/nationalist violence. Matthew Kocher, in a highly provocative piece, suggests that public-order policies alone can successfully suppress ethnic/national violence even when, unlike the Canadian, Basque and Northern Irish cases, the initial level of violence is extremely high (see Kocher, this volume). The main cleavage in the Turkish case is the one between the Turkish state and the Kurdish minority. Kocher points out that, in contrast to Chiapas, this cleavage does not overlap with other important cleavages in Turkish society. In fact, it cross-cuts religious divisions in Turkish society. The context for the Kurdish conflict has been that of a rural society with relatively low levels of economic development but, unlike Chiapas, experiencing a rapid process of urbanization. From a political perspective, the Kurdish conflict presents similarities to the Chiapas conflict in that they have both taken place in societies with a heavy democratic deficit. In contrast to Mexico, however, Turkey is not organized as a federal state. Matthew Kocher eloquently describes how the Turkish state successfully eradicated Kurdish violence without making a single political concession (only after curbing Kurdish violence, and under a complex set of external pressures, has the Turkish state recently begun to grant cultural and political rights to the Kurdish minority). Kocher explains the Turkish government's success with reference to its policies of repression and, most significantly, forced rural evacuation. According to Kocher, the expulsion of the Kurdish population from rural areas and its relocation in urban areas made it much easier for the Turkish security forces to control while at the same time drastically reducing the control capacity of Kurdish extremists.

CASE STUDIES AND THEORETICAL PREDICTIONS

It is difficult to draw definite conclusions about the role of state policies in addressing violence and radical ethnonationalist demands with a small and unsystematic sample of cases such as the one examined here. None the less, a careful comparison of these cases in the light of the hypotheses developed above allows for some tentative conclusions. The authors cited above show that in all cases violence has been addressed by strong and non-indiscriminate public-order measures and, consistent with theoretical expectations about the role of state penalties in reducing support for violent behaviour, demonstrate that these policies are indeed effective irrespective of initial levels of violence. Whenever drastic public-order measures have been applied to fight violence, the levels of ethnonational violence have declined. The only exception to this conclusion seems to be the Chiapas conflict where the spiral of violence has remained largely unabated despite very strong state public-order measures. A comparison between the Chiapas and the Kurdish conflicts, similar in that they take place in societies with relatively low levels of economic development, with a strong democratic deficit and high initial levels of violence, invites the conclusion that beyond the resources invested in repressing violence, tactics and the context in which they are deployed – rural/urban – also count. One could say that the Turkish Government, in implementing a systematic policy of rural evacuation to urban areas that has short-circuited the ethnonational rebels' power to mobilize the population against the state, has displayed a level of tactical sophistication not present among Mexican security forces. This hypothesis deserves further research. One obstacle that the Spanish state has faced in fighting Basque violent groups, for example, has been its difficulty in breaking through the tight networks of social control developed by these organizations in the Basque urban landscape, formed by many small urban centres. Whether the contrast between a rapidly urbanizing Kurdish region and a largely rural Chiapas region explains the different rates of success of the Turkish and Mexican governments in eradicating violence remains an open question, however, for there are variables that one cannot control in this comparison. For example, the facts that economic grievances seem to play a more significant role in the Chiapas conflict than in the Kurdish conflict, and that in Chiapas economic, political, religious and ethnic identities overlap whereas they do not in the Kurdish case, could have favoured the development of more antagonistic anti-state identities in Chiapas than among the Kurdish population.

Whereas the role of public-order measures in reducing levels of ethnonational violence seems undisputed, the role of what Martínez-Herrera calls responsive policies is less evident and certainly more modest. The Kurdish case, in which ethnonationalist violence has been eradicated only through public-order policies, clearly shows that responsive policies play at most the role of sufficient but not necessary causes in curbing violence. None the less, ideally one would like to contribute to policy-making by highlighting state policies that affect both the decline in ethnonational violence and the securing of the individual and collective rights of ethnic minorities in plurinational states. In this sense, the Turkish case, while useful to illustrate the effect of public-order policies, would not seem to be the best example to follow. When we move to the other case studies – with the exception of the Québec case, where there has been hardly any violence – the empirical evidence suggests that when the state succeeds in meeting some of the demands of mobilized ethnonational groups, violence subsides somewhat, even though less than through the implementation of public-order policies. This is the case in the Basque Country after the approval of the Spanish Constitution in 1978 and the Statute of Autonomy in 1981, and in Northern Ireland after the Good Friday agreement in 1995. The Québec case illustrates the same point in a cross-national and thus less conclusive way. It might be argued that the federal structure of the Canadian state grants so much self-government to Québec that many of the francophone population's demands have been to a large extent satisfied. The Chiapas case appears again as an exception, for the Mexican state has made significant efforts over the years to redistribute land and, more recently, to democratize public life. If we follow Trejo's analysis, however, these efforts have taken the form of concessions from above rather than that of negotiated agreements. As Wolff suggests with respect to Northern Ireland, responsive government policies to address ethnonational demands have translated into less violence only when they have been legitimated from below rather than just imposed from above. Trejo's analysis provides another potential explanation for why reforms have failed in Chiapas, which is that the implementation of these concessions seems to have fallen short of the promises made by successive Mexican governments and run parallel to what appears to be a highly indiscriminate use of violence against insurgents.

The cases discussed in this chapter lend support to most of the hypotheses developed above about the role of state policies in diminishing levels of ethnonational violence through their effects on the antagonistic content of ethnic identities and the population's security calculations. There is also evidence that state policies may have an impact on levels of exclusive ethnonational identity and/or levels of support for political parties representing separatist ethnonational aspirations. The analysis of trends in exclusive ethnic identity in the Basque Country shows some impact of responsive policies such as the approval of the 1978 Spanish Constitution and the reinsertion of former Basque terrorists. Meanwhile, levels of exclusive ethnic identity in Québec have increased over time, partly because of federal attempts to homogenize Québec's constitutional status with that of the rest of the Canadian provinces, which have not taken the Québécois population's interests into account.

The effect of state policies on support for extreme ethnonationalist political formations is less easy to evaluate than those on ethnonational violence and exclusive ethnic identification. Support for ethnonational parties in general in the Basque Country, in Northern Ireland, in Québec and even in Turkey has remained stable through the period analysed by the present authors, despite contrasting policies. In the Basque Country and Northern Ireland, in particular, levels of support for extremist ethnonational parties have in fact shown minor fluctuations that seem to vary independently of state policies. A more optimistic reading of the Basque and Northern Irish cases, however, is that the stability in patterns of support one observes results from the adaptation of extremist ethnonational parties to changing circumstances created by the state's responsive policies. The articles show that in both the Basque Country and Northern Ireland, support for extremist ethnonational parties has rebounded after short periods of decline when they have showed signs of condemning or abandoning support for violence in the context of a delegitimation of this violence resulting from negotiated agreements between the state and moderate nationalists. By moderating their messages, they seem to have cancelled out the effects that the reaching of these agreements would otherwise have had on the support these political parties were able to attract.

In sum, the case studies discussed in this chapter demonstrate that one can address theoretically relevant questions pertaining to the social sciences while at the same time tailoring them to the practical concerns of the policy-making community. The conclusions reached upon examination of these case studies are good news for those interested in the impact that state policies can have on levels of violence, ethnic exclusiveness and separatism in plurinational states. Both non-indiscriminate public-order policies and responsive policies are effective in highly diverse cases, while at the same time granting and even strengthening the rights of ethnonational groups in plurinational states. It is certainly encouraging to see that, despite the intensity of conflict in the cases examined here, in all but the Kurdish case attempted or achieved solutions have involved political and institutional recognition of the ethnonational rights of the parties involved. More research is needed, however, to allow for more systematic conclusions than those obtained from the examination of the small sample of cases discussed above.

NOTE

*   I would like to acknowledge the assistance received from Carolina Greer de Miguel Moyer in the early stages of the preparation of this article.

REFERENCES

Brass, P. (1997), *Theft of an Idol*. Princeton (NJ: Princeton University Press)

Brubaker, R. and Laitin, D. (1998), "Ethnic and Nationalist Violence", *Annual Review of Sociology* 24, 423–452

De Figueiredo, R. and Weingast, B. (1999), "The Rationality of Fear", in Barbara F. Walter and Jack Snyder (eds), *Civil Wars, Insecurity, and Intervention* (New York: Columbia University Press), 261–302

Deng, F. M. (1995), *War of Visions: Conflict of Identities in the Sudan* (Washington DC: Brookings Institution)

Díez Medrano, J. (1995), *Divided Nations* (Ithaca, NY: Cornell University Press)

Fearon, J. (1995), "Rationalist Explanations for War", *International Organization* 49, 379–414.

Fearon, J. and Laitin, D. (1996), "Explaining Interethnic Cooperation", *American Political Science Review* 90:4, 715–35.

_____ (2000), "Violence and the Social Construction of Ethnic Identity", *International Organization* 54:4, 845–77

Gagnon, V. (1994–96), "Ethnic Nationalism and International Conflict: The Case of Serbia", *International Security* 19:3, 130–66

Hannan, M. (1979), "The Dynamics of Ethnic Boundaries in Modern States", in Michael T. Hannan and John Meyer (eds), *National Development and the World System: Educational, Economic, and Political Change, 1950–1970* (Chicago: University of Chicago Press), 253–75

Hechter, M. (1975), *Internal Colonialism: The Celtic Fringe in British National Development, 1536–1966* (Berkeley, Calif.: University of California Press)
_____ (1978), "Group Formation and the Cultural Division of Labor", *American Journal of Sociology* 84:2, 293–317
_____ (1992), "The Dynamics of Secession", *Acta Sociologica* 35:4, 267–283
_____ (1995), "Explaining Ethnic Violence", *Nations and Nationalism* 1:1, 53–68
Horowitz, D. (1985), *Ethnic Groups in Conflict*, (Berkeley, Calif.: University of California Press)
Kapferer, B. (1988), *Legends of People/Myths of State: Violence, Intolerance, and Political Culture in Sri Lanka and Australia* (Washington DC: Smithsonian University Press)
Kaufman, S. (1996), "Spiraling to Ethnic War: Elites, Masses, and Moscow in Moldova's Civil War", *International Security* 21:2, 108–38
Laitin, D. (1993), "National Revivals and Violence", *Archives Européennes de Sociologie* 36, 3–43
Laqueur, W. (1998), *Guerrilla Warfare: A Historical and Critical Study* (New Brunswick, NJ: Transaction Publishers)
Martinez-Herrera, E. (2002), "Nationalist Extremism and Outcomes of State Policies in the Basque Country, 1979–2001", *International Journal on Multicultural Societies* 4:1, 17–41
Meadwell, H. (1989), "Ethnic Nationalism and Collective Choice Theory", *Comparative Political Studies* 22, 139–54
Posen, B. (1993), "The Security Dilemma and Ethnic Conflict", *Survival* 35:1, 27–47
Prunier, G. (1995), *The Rwanda Crisis: History of a Genocide* (New York: Columbia University Press)
Rocher, F. (2002), "The Evolving Parameters of Québec Nationalism", *International Journal On Multicultural Societies* 4:1, 74–96
Trejo, G. (2002), "Redefining the Territorial Bases of Power: Peasants, Indians, and Guerrilla Warfare in Chiapas, Mexico", *International Journal on Multicultural Societies* 4:1, 99–129
Wolff, S. (2002), "Conflict Management in Northern Ireland", *International Journal on Multicultural Societies* 4:1, 41–63
Woodward, S. L. (1995), *Balkan Tragedy: Chaos and Dissolution After the Cold War* (Washington DC: Brookings Institution)

3 Constitutional and Governmental Policies towards Basque Nationalist Extremism

ENRIC MARTÍNEZ-HERRERA*

In order to reduce nationalist extremist behaviour, governments may develop a wide variety of public policies, which can be generally classified as "repressive" and "responsive" policies. In this chapter I evaluate the efficacy of different policies inspired from one or another approach in coping with Basque nationalist extremism in Spain, one of the most salient cases of nationalist violence in post-industrial societies. For this I make use of the unusual abundance of data that this case has generated.

Since the 1960s, different Spanish governments, first within the context of an autocratic political regime and then within a liberal-democratic one, have implemented different strategies that can be labelled as repressive policies and responsive policies. The itinerary of the former goes from a rather indiscriminate repression towards Basque nationalism to the selective incrimination of violent activists. Similarly, as for responsiveness, a long-standing rejection of the Basque cultural, social and political differences has changed into a constitutional recognition of the Basque nationality, which has provided the Basques with an unprecedented level of political autonomy.

This variation in policy sectors, of policy styles, and even political regimes, as well as the duration of the Basque conflict, optimizes the empirical foundations for exploring the short- and medium-term effects of repressive and responsive policies on different dimensions of nationalist extremism. Given the many variables and their interrelations, a multivariate methodology reduces the risk of spurious causal imputations. It is on this basis that I pursue, with a deliberately chosen empirical orientation, a thorough evaluation, though within its own limits, of the consistency of a number of theoretical hypotheses in the literature. It will be suggested that the mitigation of Basque nationalist extremism is best explained through a combination of efficacious but flexible repressive policies inspired in the respect of human rights, together with substantial doses of responsiveness.

STRATEGIES OF THE STATE FACING NATIONALIST INSURGENT EXTREMISM: REPRESSIVE AND RESPONSIVE FRAMES

The study of governmental response to insurgent nationalist extremism tends to confine itself to two areas of study hardly communicating with each other. Though with interesting exceptions, mainstream analyses and prescriptions focus either on repressive policies or on responsiveness policies vis-à-vis minorities.[1] Nevertheless, here they will be considered as two different but compatible dimensions. The view that authority and force are intrinsic to the nature of the state predominates in the former. By contrast, the latter corresponds to pluralistic views of public power where the authority of the state is viewed as sensitive to social needs and demands, and where communication, attention to the material and cultural bases of conflicts, as well as the search for mutual compromises, are regarded as equally useful or even more useful instruments than force.

Although a comparison of these two frames could be attempted, inquiring into which is the more effective in reducing insurgent nationalist extremism, one might suspect that the correct depiction of the problem is not so much of a disjunction than of a more complex dialectic nature. It is plausible that a strategy combining sanctions and rewards, with a reinforcing effect, tends to be the most efficacious. On the other hand, responsiveness does not need to entail a zero-sum game where improvement for some implies harm for others, but it can supply all the involved actors with a general improvement greater than the eventual costs of renouncing maximalist ambitions.

In order to limit the question, it must be specified that only "insurgent nationalist extremism" is under consideration here. The term "extremism" denotes the attitude of involved actors who perceive the conflict as a war, advocating, or at least accepting, the use of violent means. The analysis will only consider "insurgent" nationalist extremism, which seeks to increase the self-government of its social group of reference until secession.[2] Therefore, "surveying" nationalist extremism, though it has been also present in Spain, will not be examined here – this kind of nationalist extremism is typical of actors in favour of the status quo, as well as supporters of regression when faced with decentralizing or self-determining processes (cf. Reinares 1998).

Repressive Policies and Insurgent Nationalist Extremism

Viewed from an historical and international comparative perspective, more usual policies towards any extremism have been those of repression (Gurr 1993). These interventions develop an intrinsic attribute of the modern state (democratic or otherwise), namely that its authority is supported by violence (legitimate or not, legal or not, monopolized or not, normative considerations aside). By having the use, or threat, of force as its main resource of power, a hierarchic and coactive logic of imposition of values on the social environment tends to predominate in the state's policies. Authority and force materialize in coercion and eradication of different types of anti-system extremism, all the more so in its actual violent expression. Furthermore, another ideal-typical attribute of the framework of repression is the reception of conflict in terms of its symptoms. Either reactive or preventive, the objective of those policies is to combat violent or simply threatening *effects* of conflict rather than to face its deep causes (see Table 3.1).[3]

Table 3.1   Some ideal-typical differences between repressive policies and responsive policies towards political extremism

Repressive policies	Responsive policies
Attention to violence as a symptom	Attention to social causes of violence
Predominance of the principle of authority, hierarchic	Predominance of the principle of inclusion, egalitarian
Predominance of force	Predominance of compromise

Source: Author's elaboration

Apart from that, these policies can show a broad heterogeneity. Their character can be reactive (penalizing violent behaviour retrospectively) or preventive (with an emphasis on information and protection, dissuasion, or even prior deactivation). Moreover, the use of force can or cannot be limited by the state and international parameters of legality (for example with reference to fundamental rights). Also it can or cannot be liable to judicial and/or democratic control, and its social legitimacy can vary in scope. The segment on which force is applied can differ widely, ranging from the more selective and careful persecution of those acting violently to the more general application of force to the whole political environment of theirs, or even their whole social group. The policies can also vary in the judicial and penitential treatment of activists, implementation agencies (in their military or police character, and in their degree of specialization) and the degree of international collaboration (Reinares 1998; Hoffman and Morrison-Taw 1999). Several hypotheses invoking these factors will be regarded in the third section.[4]

Responsive Policies and Insurgent Nationalist Extremism

The term "responsive policies" alludes here to those polices oriented at reducing the social and political causes that lie in the background of political grievances that bring subsequent political conflict, contention and extremism, as well as reducing their effects or symptoms. Unlike repressive policies, which have a more enclosed classification, responsive policies imply much more diverse domains and means – hence my choice of an atypical qualifier. The approach that predominates in them tends to inclusiveness, typical for the pluralist democratic approach and, more generally, for regimes that are sensitive – though this could be in paternalistic, tutelary manners – to the needs and demands of every social group.

Within this approach, rulers seeks to know which are the demands the dissatisfied groups, they may even seek to anticipate their concerns, and they may be ready to engage in a dialogue with those groups. Rulers may also be ready to negotiate and cooperate with the groups in pursuit of mutual benefit. Thus, their instruments, rather than force, are: (a) the recognition – not necessarily formal – of either material or perceived conflicts; (b) reciprocal communication and compromise; and (c) a disposition to share, to some extent, material resources, prestige positions, and even power. Authority tends to be conceived in a pluralist, sensitive, responsive, even consensual manner, regarding the various social needs and concerns. In the face of the emergence or risk of extremist behaviour, the authorities pay attention to its social bases, both structural and cultural (see Table 3.1).

It should be stressed that responsiveness does not necessarily entail weakness or unilateral concessions; therefore, it does not necessarily satisfy any claim. Nor does this approach have to be the result of certain ultimate principles or values either, since it can also, for simply instrumental reasons, be developed in a tactical fashion.

As for the sectors, levels, and manners of action, these policies can be extremely heterogeneous. According to the roots of the conflict, responsive policies can involve many different policy fields (for example culture, religion, education and so on) as well as the very distribution of public power. As for their juridical rank and degree of institutionalization, they can be enforced in the form of constitutional engineering policies, as common legislation, or even as simple administrative decisions (cf. Gurr 1993; Hoffman and Morrison-Taw 1999).

From explanatory political science, the most outstanding example of a responsive approach is the "consociational" model of Arend Lijphart (1984 and 1999). He analyses institutions that induce the protection, possibility of expression, and possibility of decision of organized minorities in plural societies. These institutions are directed towards enabling the elites of those groups to participate in power and thus towards increasing the integration of political systems that otherwise tend to break up and/or to have a low performance. One of these institutions is federalism, which tends to reduce the levels of ethnic violence (Horowitz 1985; Saideman et al. 2002). However, I use the concept of responsiveness instead of Lijphart's "accommodation" because political integration is not always based on an institutionalization of minorities' rights and power. Other opportunities rest on pluralist policies (Dahl 1971) and on attempts at co-optation seeking the assimilation of minorities into the majority in exchange for economic and prestige advantages – less theorized but often put into practice (see Bloom 1990; Gurr 1993; Hoffman and Morrison-Taw 1999).[5]

DIMENSIONS OF INSURGENT NATIONALIST EXTREMISM IN THE BASQUE COUNTRY

The inclination to use violence for influencing public power I have called "political extremism". The most prominent materialization of the Basque nationalist extremism is terrorism, in which Euskadi ta Askatasuna (Euskadi and Freedom – ETA) stands out, almost incomparably. ETA is one of the most long-lived terrorist organizations in the Western world, with more than forty years of existence, more than thirty years of personal attacks and more than eight hundred homicides. I employ the term "terrorism" here in a simple descriptive and precise sense of the use of violence for intimidating a social group beyond the subgroup of direct victims, without any evaluative connotation (Reinares 1998).

Still, manifestations and consequences of extremism do not limit themselves to terrorism, however implacable and persistent it can be. Extremism must be observed from a broader perspective: to begin with, because the extremist repertoire of actions able to destabilize the political system is broader than terrorism; and then because, if one seeks to give an account, specifically, of armed struggle, one should try to understand the conditions in which it is formed and sustained.

The destabilizing effects of extremism upon the official political system are not confined to terrorism. First of all, not all political violence is "terrorist" in the sense that it intimidates a social group beyond its direct victims. Secondly, there exist varieties of equally destabilizing non-conventional, but also non-violent types of political behaviour – for example general strike, petty sabotage and civil disobedience. Thirdly, extremism can obstruct institutional performance and destabilize the system from within the system itself, by means of conduct that is formally legal but is actually contrary to the principles of the political regime. Finally and more generally, the presence of impenetrable political subcultures, strongly structured internally and antagonistic, makes cooperation and coordination in favour of the whole society exceedingly difficult – this is especially true where there is an inclination to justify, promote or practice violence.

On the other hand, ETA's origin and persistence could not be understood without its exchanges with the broader environment. Like other organizations, its own internal dynamics explain, to a large extent, its persistence and autonomy (organizational culture, opportunity costs for its members, internal incentives and sanctions and so on). Nevertheless, its interaction with the broader social context becomes crucial. Its obvious aspect is the success or failure of the police in arresting ETA activists and in the protection of ETA targets. However, the inputs that favour ETA are no less important. ETA's reproduction for decades has required, above all, a regular inter-generational replacement of its commandos. In the same way, the role of the environment in the provision of information, ammunition, infrastructure and moral support cannot be neglected (Reinares 1998).

In this sense, in the Basque case at least, it is possible to consider a system of concentric circles. In the centre, there are the terrorist organizations. In a broader circle, there is a network of interconnected support organizations, including political parties, trade unions, associations (among them, associations of prisoners' relatives), mass media, even firms, which altogether are often called the Basque National Liberation Movement (MLNV). Next, there are the voters for those parties. The external circle corresponds to those who share ideas of rejection towards Spain, independence for the Basque country, and come to terms with violence as a means. In the case of ETA and the MLNV, this portrait is consistent with a hierarchical relation empirically documented (Mata 1993). I shall now consider three indicators of Basque nationalist extremism that approximately correspond to these circles or layers.

Victims of Terrorism

Violence must be regarded as a dimension of extremism. All the more so when, by acquiring the form of terrorism, the perpetration of homicides results from the desire for public impact, and when terrorist organizations exert an outstanding ascendancy over the whole extremist movement. An annual number of fatalities (deceased victims) denotes, to a degree, the operability of the Basque nationalist terrorist organizations and their capability of psychologically influencing great numbers of people. I refer basically to ETA, but also to its several factional splinter groups, such as the ETA-m ("military"), the ETA-pm ("political-military"), and the Anti-capitalist Autonomous Commandos. As a measurement, this turns out somewhat unsatisfactory, since from a propaganda angle, the impact of every victim – a First Minister or an ordinary member of the public – is not identical, and from an operative angle, a massive attack with a car bomb, which is relatively safe, produces many more victims than one directed at a protected public personality, which is much more risky. However, these are the best available data both for their validity and time scale.[6]

Herri Batasuna/Euskal Herritarrok Voting

Extremism can also obstruct institutional performance and destabilize the political system while formally respecting legality. Here the evolution of the voting for the coalition Herri Batasuna (HB), related to the "military ETA", the only remaining branch of the terrorist organization, will be considered – for judiciary reasons HB changed its name to Euskal Herritarrok in 1998, and to Batasuna *tout court* in 2001.

The voting for HB provides us with three types of information. For one thing, by being a coalition that advocates secession of the Basque Country, accepting the use of violence and including many convicted ETA members on its electoral roll, the votes for HB publicly have expressed a disagreement with the fundamental rules of the political system, thus delegitimatizing it.

In the second place, these ballots are closely related to attitudes towards terrorism. In 1979 a team lead by Juan J. Linz (1986) surveyed the Basques about their perception of ETA members. They observed the rate of voters that considered ETA members as "patriots" (instead of "manipulated" or, even worse, "criminals", or lack of expressed opinion): at least, six out of ten HB voters, a third of Euskadiko Ezkerra (EE) voters (related to ETA's "political-military" branch, self-dissolved in 1982), and one out of ten Basque Nationalist Party (PNV) voters. Applying these percentages to actual voters for every organization, it came out that about 140 000 people (14 per cent of the active voters and 9 per cent of Basque enfranchised citizens) judged ETA militants favourably. Although from 1979 to 1989 the perception of ETA members as patriots decreased from 17 to 5 per cent (Linz 1986; Llera 1994), this was the fertile ground for ETA.

Finally, these votes have given to some convicted terrorists and, more generally, to extremist politicians, access into the Basque, Spanish and European parliaments, into Basque city councils and even some mayorships. These representatives and authorities often utilized their positions to challenge constitutional legality, obstruct the political process and/or allocate public resources, both in the symbolic and the material domains.

Basque Exclusivist Identification

At the basis of the extremist behaviour under consideration here lies a system of beliefs that constitutes a clear example of a political subculture. It is a consistent, structured and stable system of rejectionist attitudes towards Spanish identity, while adhering to a Basque national identification, preferences for secession and an inclination to violence.

A quite reliable expression of the Basque nationalist extremist subculture lies in the exclusive identification with the Basque Country, as expressed on a bipolar scale of identification preferences. The question asks interviewees about whether they identify themselves as either Basque only, more Basque than Spanish, equally Basque and Spanish, more Spanish than Basque, or Spanish only. I focus on the number of Basques that reject any degree of self-identification with Spain – namely, those individuals declaring to identify *only* with the Basque Country, thus not at all with Spain. These citizens not only strongly tend to express secessionist attitudes but, as Linz and his collaborators (1986) have shown, exclusively Basque identifications are also closely associated with a favourable perception about ETA members.

Specifically, the perception of ETA militants as patriots or idealists is much more likely to occur among citizens holding a primarily Basque identification than among the rest. As a matter of fact, the proportion of acquiescent attitudes towards ETA kept quite stable among the former during the 1980s (Llera 1994). Therefore, although certainly a part of these identifiers do not sympathize with terrorism, I shall consider the percentage of people feeling themselves to be Basque only as a reliable proxy indicator to extremist attitudes.[7]

DIMENSIONS AND INDICATORS OF STATE POLICIES IN THE BASQUE CASE

As stated above, the repertoire of state policies is extremely wide. Nevertheless, within this mixture, repressive frameworks and responsive frameworks stand as two relevant dimensions. Let us now look at what the main hypotheses and indicators are.

Repressive Policies

The repressive approach includes the development of policing, military, judiciary and foreign policies. All of these have varied greatly in relation to Basque nationalist extremism. The better quantified ones are: (a) the number of arrests of alleged ETA members; (b) the number of imprisonments; (c) a ratio denoting "policing social efficiency" in terms of the scope of repression; (d) the number of arrests in France, a consequence of foreign policy and international judicial and police collaboration; and (e) the number of reintegrated terrorists, product of a judicial policy.[8] Even the type of political regime (autocratic or pluralist) can be included in this dimension inasmuch as the former usually have less constrictions administrating force (Reinares 1998). Moreover, I shall consider what effects state terrorism against ETA and its environment has had.

Two general hypotheses can be postulated about the links between these policies and extremist behaviour and attitudes. In the first place, there is the position that the more efficacious – for example, in the number of imprisonments – the repression of violent conduct is, the more likely extremism will be reduced. Throughout history, this hypothesis has often been taken, in practice, as an assumption, from which a prohibition of any expression and organization – even peaceful – of extremist views has followed. Supposedly, this policy would produce a loss of influence of the core group of extremists over their social environment, and consequently the reduction of extremism among the population.

This proposition, however, can be substantially amended if one considers that the efficaciousness of the whole policy will be greater insofar as the violence of the state is considered legitimate in the relevant contexts, such as in the social milieu where force is applied and an international environment where human rights and political freedoms are highly valued. This involves aspects related to the public image of the whole policy, such as accuracy in the application of force and the respect of fundamental rights.

Responsive Policies

Responsive policies appear in a plurality of domains. In relation to Basque extremism and its social background, an historical dynamic of political centralization and decentralization synthesizs and articulates most of these sectoral policies. After the Spanish Civil War (1936–39), the winning side dismantled most Basque self-government institutions, minimizing the responsive framework. Contrary to this, however, the Spanish Constitution of 1978 and the Basque Autonomy Law (with the rank of constitutional law) of 1979 enacted an extraordinary, unprecedented political autonomy.

This juridical frame establishes a Basque parliament and a Basque executive chosen by universal suffrage. The matters over which they have jurisdiction include education, health, culture and social services, as well as the collection of the most important taxes, a share of which is then passed on to the central state, after mutual agreement. Moreover, the Basque Autonomous Community has also a regional police force that has largely taken over from state-wide policing corps. As a consequence, its administration has a considerable volume of staff, physical assets and financial resources. Moreover, importantly enough, these jurisdictions are guaranteed by a Constitutional Court and by exacting qualified majorities and referendums for eventual constitutional reforms affecting them (Aja 1999).

Responsiveness, however, also stands up in other domains. Accompanying its organizational dispositions, the current Constitution also bears an important symbolic intention, since it recognizes the existence of "nationalities" within the "nation" (Spain) and establishes, as a doctrinal fundamental principle of the constitutional state, the protection and fostering of minority languages and cultures.

Another factor is the type of political regime. One of the motives that originated nationalist extremism was the dictatorial context, which in the collective *imaginaire* associated the idea of "Spain" with the idea of oligarchic domination (cf. Pérez Díaz 1993). It could thereby be possible that the dissolution of such conditions has contributed to the mitigation of the rejection towards the Spanish political community. Even so, the type of regime entails a certain paradox, since in each one of the considered dimensions it would influence in an opposed direction: whereas autocracy has more "operability" in the administration of repression, it tends to provoke a greater rejection. The opposite, in both dimensions, seems to happen in a democracy.

In addition, the established electoral system particularly facilitates the representation of minorities that are territorially concentrated. Hence, during several legislatures, the parties ruling at the Spanish level (be they social-democrats, centre-right or conservative parties) but lacking the absolute majority in Parliament have reached agreements on investiture, even on legislature, with the Basque Nationalist Party (PNV). There have also been many coalition governments in the Basque Autonomous Community between this party and the social-democrats. In turn, both types of inter-partisan agreements have eased multilevel government collaboration (Aja 1999).

Prospects about an association between responsiveness and extremism can be synthetically expressed as a negative hypothetical causal relation. It is possible to expect that every governmental action satisfying a need – be this articulated or not as a demand – or making up for a motive of reactivity in different domains (culture, self-government, economy) of the social bases of

Basque extremism, will contribute to the reduction of both rejection towards Spain and support for insurgent nationalist violence.

Furthermore, the search of some Basque nationalist governments of an agreement with the organized extremist movement which could integrate the latter into the political system and thereby reducing its inclination to violence is also noteworthy. There have been dialogue round tables, meetings and certain agreements, including one concerning the investiture of the autonomic president.

Finally, in a general manner, it could be possible to reflect on the way in which responsiveness occurs: whether it tends to be impelled from a unilateral cooperative willingness or, on the contrary, it is part of a bilateral exchange (coordination) process that eventually leads to a dynamic of reciprocal cooperation. Whereas the first interaction scenario could allow for incrementalism and constant claiming from the insurgent movement and related parties, the latter could supply greater stability.

EMPIRICAL ANALYSIS

In order to reject spurious causal relations and to unveil hidden relations, after observing graphically the evolution of the main variables, multivariate regression analyses have been produced. In order to reach a relatively broad public, technicalities have been reduced to the minimum in the presentation of results.[9]

The Development of Violence

In this part of the analysis, I aim to explain changes in time-series of the number of physical victims of ETA attacks, including fatalities (deaths and casualties) between 1969 and 2003.[10] The maximum activity took place between 1978 and 1980, coinciding with the delicate period of transition to democracy, and the trend since then has been decreasing (see Fig. 3.1). The task is to explain this development through attending to the possible impact of the different state policies. In the first place, hypothetical relations between variations in fatalities and several repressive interventions will be examined, subsequently turning to those involving responsiveness. Table 3.2 summarizes the main variables in the analysis and their hypothetical relations to the number of ETA's victims. It is important to note that the multivariate analysis only accounts for changes since 1979, due to the lack of prior information about several factors.

The first general hypothesis is that repressive policies should reduce violence both directly, by removing active actors, and indirectly, by increasing the actual and perceived cost of those actions. Most prominent aspects of a punitive policy are arrests and imprisonments. Both variables are statistically associated to the number of fatalities. However, given a close correlation between imprisonments and arrests, but more information about the latter, after several trials I have chosen the arrests for statistical analysis.[11]

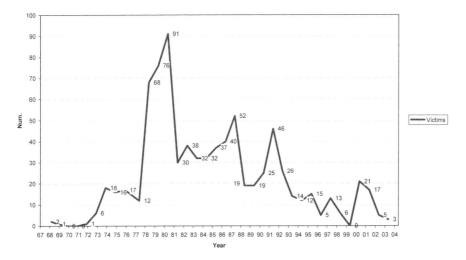

Figure 3.1   Homicides by ETA, 1968–2003

Source: Author's elaboration of police data

Understandably, police activity increases when a terrorist attack occurs. However, it would be more interesting to know the reverse impact of arrests on attacks. The foreseen association should be negative and its effect should have, at least, a delay of one year, since the substitution of commands needs some time. This relation does not show up at the first glance (see Table 3.2).[12]

However, an effect of the measurement method could influence the results. In an organization with a hierarchical structure, the arrest of a leader should have a greater impact than, say, the arrest of a militant in charge of logistics. Because of this, a (dummy) variable representing the detention of major ETA leaders in Bidart (French Basque Country) at the beginning of 1992 has also been computed.[13] These arrests were the result of international cooperation, as French judicial police carried them out after an investigation by the Spanish Guardia Civil. Its outcome was a drastic decrease in fatalities, apparently definite, possibly due to the organizational problems this implied for ETA in the short and long run, as well as the information obtained by security agencies. Once its impact was controlled, ordinary detentions in Spain show a negative effect with a delay of two years, though more than thirty arrests would have been required to save one victim (see Table 3.3, especially Model 2).[14] A comparison of the size of standardized betas points out these interventions among the most effective.

Therefore, another relevant factor is international coordination and collaboration. For many years ETA benefited from a de facto sanctuary in France. For this reason Spanish governments have set as a priority in their foreign policy to persuade the neighbouring country to prosecute the activities of the organization and to extradite its activists. Even more, as Reinares (1998) and Hoffman and Morrison-Taw (1999) plausibly argue, this

Table 3.2   **Variables utilized in the modelling of the number of victims**

Dependent variable	Observed period	Expected relationship
No. of victims of ETA	1968–2001	
Repression variables		
No. of arrested in Spain	1977–2001	Negative
No. of reinserted	1982–1990	Negative
Algiers negotiations (1989)	Dummy	Negative
No. of victims of GAL and BVE	1978–1987	?
Bidart intervention (1992)	Dummy	Negative
Responsiveness variables		
Constitution	Dummy	Negative
Exogenous variables		
Coup d'état (1981)	Dummy	Negative
ETA truce in 1992	Dummy	Negative

could become a key element of an efficacious antiterrorist policy. In 1983/84 a shift in French attitudes occurred that led to increasing antiterrorist collaboration, in both the police and judicial domains (Domínguez 1999; Jaime and Reinares 1999).

Another instrument employed early by democratic rulers was the social reintegration of fighters. By the mid 1980s, Spanish governments thus supplied an outlet for almost 150 activists, most of them from the "political-military" ETA splinter group, which had unilaterally renounced its armed struggle in 1982. Eighty-six amnesties were added between 1982 and 1990 (Domínguez 1999; Jaime and Reinares 1999).[15] In this manner sanctions derived from past actions were removed, hence important opportunity costs that could cause those ETA members to persist were avoided. This policy could produce, moreover, another three delayed effects: (a) an interruption of active recruitment by this faction; (b) a modification, among "military" ETA members, of the perception of their opportunities structure; and (c) a lower probability of new recruits, owing to an effect of reduction of the critical mass of armed collective action. The regression analysis gives consistency to this hypothesis. For each three reintegrated combatants, we

Table 3.3   Regression of the number of victims of ETA

Variable	Model 1 Coef.	t	Model 2 Coef.	t	St. Beta
Constant	88,11***	19,88	87,82***	20,59	
Arrested Spain (-2)	-0,03***	-3,34	-0,03***	-3,56	-0,421
Bidart	-40,52***	-6,11	-39,53***	-6,56	-0,901
Constitution (-2)	-31,44***	-4,48	-32,35***	-4,99	-0,407
Reinserted(-6)	-0,78***	-3,41	-0,72***	-4,06	-0,316
GAL-BVE (-2)	0,89 .11	1,70	0,91*	1,79	0,125
Ceasefire	-20,51**	-2,60	-20,31**	-2,64	-0,144
Coup d'Etat	-14,51**	-2,21	-14,10**	-2,22	-0,128
Algiers Negotiations	3,19	0,41			
Sample (adjusted)	79-03		79-03		
N	25		25		
R^2	0,95		0,95		
Adj. R^2	0,93		0,94		

Sign.: *** .01; ** .05; * .10; other in figures

find two victims less six years later (Model 2), and its standardized effect is comparable to that of ordinary arrests. However, the killing by ETA of a reinserted prominent former leader ("Yoyes") in 1986 seems to be the main motive to terminate this policy (Domínguez 1999).

Nevertheless, during the democratic period murders of ETA members or their sympathizers were carried out or organized from the structures of the state, too. The so-called "dirty war" almost always took place in the French Basque Country and was aimed at eliminating ETA's refuge there. Two periods can be distinguished. From 1978 to 1980, the centre-right cabinets of the Unión del Centro Democrático tolerated or were unable to control members of the security forces that, giving themselves the names of Batallón Vasco Español (BVE) and Triple A, committed ten murders of alleged ETA sympathizers. From 1983 to 1987, under social-democratic rule, the newly arrived Grupos Antiterroristas de Liberación (GAL) committed 28 homicides more. In this case, several policemen and politicians, including one former Minister of the Interior, would be imprisoned some years later as organizers of the criminal structure (Domínguez 1999).

On this issue two competing hypotheses exist: on the one hand, the responsible policemen and politicians could have thought that the illegal violent campaign would restrain ETA, forcing it to be much more cautious in its French refuge. On the other hand, it has been argued that this actually provided new arguments to ETA when its social legitimacy was in crisis (Unzueta 1994; Reinares 1998). The statistical analysis seems to agree with the latter, since every BVE, Triple A or GAL murder seems to produce, two years later, almost one ETA murder more than could have been expected without the intervention of this factor.

Other factors, though more difficult to operationalize, deserve equal consideration. One hypothetical factor consists of attempts of communication with ETA to negotiate reintegration of its members, a reduction of their sentences, or the attenuation of other consequences (particularly, transferring convicts to prisons near their social milieu), in exchange for an end to violence. The most important meeting between government and ETA representatives occurred in Algiers in 1989. Although a ceasefire was not reached even during the negotiations, the number of victims that year was relatively low. However, this decrease seems to reflect a period of insurgent weakness, since there was an equal number of victims in 1988 and the statistical effect of those talks is not significant (Model 1).[16]

Furthermore, at about the end of 1998 and until the middle of 1999, ETA proclaimed a unilateral ceasefire, represented as being inspired by the Ulster agreement and driven by a will to negotiate.[17] Although the trend could suggest another period of operative weakness, its coefficient predicts far fewer victims than could be expected without the truce (Model 2).

As seen above, various repressive interventions account for a good deal of variation in the number of victims (especially, the arrests in Bidart, the ordinary arrests, and social reintegration). Even so, it is also possible to concede plausibility to other factors located in the responsive frame. In this sense, an impact of Basque autonomy and democratization should occur. Their clearer effect is the above-mentioned self-dissolution of the "political-military" ETA. Along with the judicial facilities for reintegration of their activists, the political integration of these activists and the social segment that supported them can be explained by the realization of a substantial part of their political goals – namely, a democratic regime and an important degree of recognition and self-government for the Basque – and the possibility to pursue further objectives by seizing the new opportunities of political contest supplied by liberal democracy. Their subsequent devotion to the party Euskadiko Ezkerra speaks for this account.

For this reason, a dummy variable considering that the Constitution and the Autonomy Law of 1979 (vis-à-vis the dictatorial and centralized state), which should produce a substantial change in violence levels, has also been included in the displayed regression models. This factor seems to account for a change in level of thirty-two yearly murders from two years later up to the present day, with one of the strongest effects (see standardized betas).[18] This lends support to the hypothesis that responsiveness reduces the levels of ethnic violence.

On the other hand, the ceasefire of ETA "military" is the single factor able to account for the decrease in 1999. Police pressure and massive mobilization in favour of peace occurring by the end of 1998 must be regarded against the background of that decision, but also some factors of a political nature.[19] Immediately after the ceasefire announcement, important agreements of institutional collaboration between EH, PNV and EA (Eusko Alkartasuna, a splinter party from PNV) were reached, including the investiture of the President of the Basque government (Pact of Lizarra). The persistence of the truce for almost a year seems, to a large extent, to be due to that rapprochement. Even if, for this investiture agreement in 2000, other reasons could have played an important part, the result of an advance in integration would not have differed greatly.

The most recent development in the struggle against ETA has been a series of measures against the above-mentioned conglomerate of groups that provide it with different resources. For one thing, a few hundred members of Batasuna – one of the different names for the political branch of ETA – were sentenced in court for their proven implication as collaborators of the terrorist organization. Subsequently, in August 2002 the judge investigating Batasuna links with ETA – Baltasar Garzón – preventively suspended the party. Contemporarily, in September 2002 the parliament passed a new law on political parties, allowing the government, upon request from the parliament, to demand judicial procedures intended to outlaw political groups maintaining links with terrorist organizations. Thus, immediately afterwards the executive asked the Supreme Court to outlaw Batasuna, which was finally made illegal in March 2003.

These initiatives prompted a debate among both politicians and public opinion, especially in the Basque Country, and its outcomes on nationalist terrorism are an open question. Though the number of lethal terrorist actions has decreased throughout 2002–3, the unknown concerns what will occur in the middle and long run. On the one hand, as it could be hypothesized, ETA might regain popular support upon the discourse that radical nationalism is oppressed, as it did already in the past. On the other, the dismantling of those satellite structures supporting ETA, together with the increase of formal sanctions towards violent activism, could also further accelerate the decline of the terrorist organization, which would find even more difficulty in sustaining its recruitment and financing social networks and bases. However, it is too early to assess the impact of these new policies.

Finally, during the process of identification of this model I observed a pronounced temporary reduction in 1981. My ex post interpretation is that this could be due to the failed coup d'état attempt of that year. On the one hand, the leadership of "military" ETA precisely sought polarization, and according to some observers, even the returning of the dictatorship (Unzueta 1994). In this sense, the coup could be perceived as the most unequivocal expression of its apparent success at that time. Of course, the terrorist organization could have also seized the coup as an opportunity for having a rest after the exhausting terrorist campaign of 1978–80. On the other hand, many activists, especially those of the "political-military"

ETA faction, could take stock of the situation and ask themselves whether a return to dictatorship was what they actually wanted. Whichever the mechanisms involved, this factor accounts for a decrease of fourteen homicides that year.

It is worth ending this section by summarizing its main findings. The number of ETA victims has decreased dramatically since the beginning of the 1980s, putting forward an unequivocal decreasing tendency. According to the statistical multivariate model supplied, this development is the result of a combination of certain responsive and repressive approaches: police efficacy (ordinary arrests, and above all, the intervention in Bidart), the reintegration of combatants (a flexible but persevering repressive policy), and the twofold political change in establishing democracy and the Basque Autonomous Community (responsive policies). Another factor is ETA's ceasefire, which can either be considered as a consequence of political factors or – in a tautological but plausible manner – as a consequence of those very policing actions. In turn, state terrorism seems to have produced more ETA homicides. The failed coup d'état in 1981 – as a theoretically exogenous variable – adds to these factors.

Development of Basque Extremist Nationalist Voting

From the statistical point of view, the vote for HB/EH/Batasuna is distributed along time in a discrete and irregular manner, and only supplies twelve observations, taking regional and general elections together. This deprives us of a regression analysis like the preceding one. Despite that, observing its development in a descriptive manner is still revealing.

Observing the number of ballots in favour of this coalition out of the total enfranchised citizens, a remarkable stability can be noticed along the 1980–1990s, although with a slow downward slope from the mid 1980s (see Figure 3.2). When compared with the number of victims of ETA, no statistical association is apparent with regard to most of the theoretical factors considered above. However, there is an exception of the ETA ceasefire (1998 and 1999) that, along with the agreements between the Basque nationalist parties, which included a campaign in favour of "national self-determination", certainly improved the results for this organization in the 1998 elections. Yet the finishing of those pacts relatively accelerated the smooth decreasing trend in HB electoral support.

This core of nationalist extremist sympathizers remained quite unaffected in the face of the several factors considered, supporting the thesis of the existence of a strongly autonomous socio-political subculture and substructure autonomous within the social system. However, the frustration of a part of that movement's twofold expectations of peace *and* self-determination seems to explain that the greatest electoral success ever of HB/EH/Batasuna (1998) was followed by its worst result ever (2001) and the creation of the splinter new party Aralar, made of former Batasuna members that had criticized violent methods (Pallarés 2002).

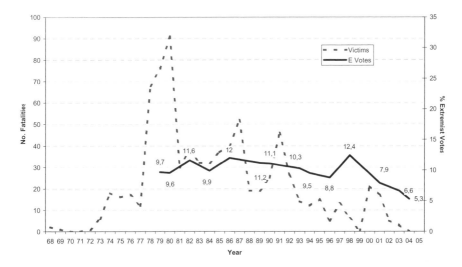

Figure 3.2   Extremist votes and victims of terrorism

Note: For 2003 and 2004 figures, see the text. Author's elaboration of voting data of Díez-Medrano (1995) and the Basque Parliament; for terrorist murders, police data.

Since 2003 the electoral situation of this political movement has changed dramatically. As said above, in August 2002 its electoral platforms were suspended by a judge of the counter-terrorist court upon evidence indicating strong structural links between Batasuna and ETA. Then, in March 2003 those platforms were outlawed by the Supreme Court on the basis of the new law of political parties. In response, regional members of parliament representing the outlawed Batasuna called for null votes in the 2003 local and 2004 general elections. This allows us to observe a further electoral decline, which can be partly accounted for by a transference of votes to its splinter Aralar.[20]

Development of Rejection towards Spain

The several policies in the face of extremism, adopted from the angle of both repression and responsiveness, could have an effect on the systems of belief from which behaviour then flows. As a proxy indicator to extremism, I consider the above-mentioned rejection towards Spain within the personal feelings of belonging, which correlates very strongly with preferences for secession and also strongly favourable attitudes towards ETA, and has been measured through surveys for more than twenty years.[21] Its trajectory can be observed in Figure 3.3. Between 1969 and 1982 approximately 40 per cent of Basques expressed this attitude in a number of surveys. However, since 1984 the average of "Basque only" identifiers is around 25 per cent.

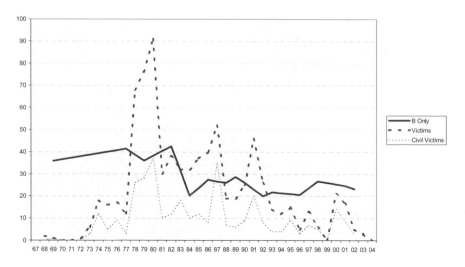

Figure 3.3   Basque-only identifiers, 1968–2002

Source: Author's elaboration of survey and police data.

As summarized in Table 3.4, it was initially previewed that policing social efficiency, social reintegration of fighters and the establishing of Basque autonomy and democracy could mitigate the refusal towards Spain, whereas the GAL-BVE homicides would prove to be counterproductive. On the other hand, the effect of ETA's violence has also been considered, leaving it as an open question. Moreover, the proportions of immigrants and autochthons' children are also included, a necessary control due to the fact that the family geographical origin is the most discriminating variable at the individual level (Martínez-Herrera 2002).[22] Nevertheless, the analysis will only account for variations since 1979, due to the lack of prior information about most factors.

Regarding the results in Table 3.5, the twofold institutional change ("Constitution") of democratization and political decentralization leads to a decrease in the average of ten percentage points with a delay of five years, the strongest effect from a political factor (notice the standardized beta).[23] Likewise, social reinsertion policies implemented between 1982 and 1990 confirm the predicted impact with a year's delay with a strong association, thus supporting the hypothesis that they also contributed to the re-legitimization of the Spanish state and its political community.

With regard to detentions it has been argued that their indiscriminate character causes unnecessary grievance and hostility among the population towards authorities (Hoffman and Morrison-Taw 1999; Reinares 1998). For this reason, at the very least, it would be desirable to carry out arrests in a more selective manner, and sticking both to legality, respect of human rights, and what common people consider legitimate in their own social milieu. In turn, insurgent movements can, precisely because of this, try to increase support for their cause by spurring on the

Table 3.4   Variables utilised in Basque exclusivism modelling

Dependent variable	Observed period	Expected relationship
% of Basque-only identifiers	1975–2001	
Repression variables		
Policing social efficiency	1982–2000	Negative
No. of reinserted combatants	1982–1990	Negative
No. of victims of GAL and BVE	1978–1987	Negative
Erzaintza	Dummy	Negative
No. of victims of ETA	1968–2001	?
Responsiveness variables		
Constitution	Dummy	Negative
Exogenous variables		
% of immigrants	1979–2000	Negative
% of second-generation Basques	1979–2000	Positive
Coup d'état 1981	Dummy	Positive

state to apply its violence indiscriminately on the whole population. In the case of ETA, its doctrine of "action-reaction-action" is well known. As a matter of fact, during the dictatorship and till the mid 1980s security agencies acted as aimed by ETA. Part of the explanation for this rests on the bad organization of the intelligence police services at that time, so that interrogations were their main information source (Domínguez 1999; Jaime and Reinares 1999).

Here an annual ratio between the number of detentions and the numbers of those finally processed has been calculated. This indicates not so much police efficacy as its "social efficiency", in the sense of avoiding unintended de-legitimizing effects. Figure 3.4 shows the remarkable improvement of security agencies' precision. From this the prospect of an improvement in the legitimacy of the Spanish political system would follow.[24] However, the statistical modelling does not provide a clear validation of its expected effect on Basque exclusivism.[25]

Table 3.5   Regression of the percentage of Basque-only identifiers

Variable	Coef.	t	St. Bela
Constant	-2,81	-0,25	
% of immigrants	1,34***	3,88	0,449
% of autochthon offspring	0,07	0,29	0,026
Constitution (-5)	-13,07***	-8,77	-0,847
Reinserted (-1)	-0,34***	-5,93	-0,522
GAL-BVE (-1)	0,72***	3,63	0,347
Victims of ETA (-1)	-0,11***	-3,37	-0,403
Sample (adjusted):	79-02		
N	24		
R^2	0,94		
Adj. R^2	0,92		

Sign.: *** .01; ** .05; * .10; other between brackets

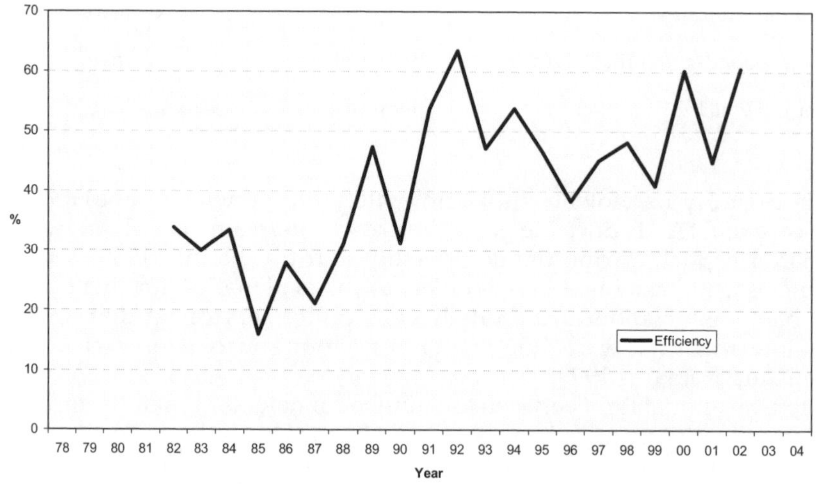

Figure 3.4   Policing social efficiency, 1982–2002

Note: Policing social efficiency is operationalized as the rate of judicially processed suspects out of those arrested. Author's elaboration of data in Domínguez Iribarren (1999).

As far as the "dirty war" is concerned, it has been argued (Unzueta 1994; Reinares 1998) that the killing of ETA members by security agents calling themselves BVE, Triple A or GAL supplied the extremist nationalist discourse with new legitimizing arguments, which would re-legitimize ETA among public opinion. As expected, the statistical analysis suggests that these murders increased the rejection towards Spain.

Finally, the impact of the number of victims of violence has also been examined. Paradoxically, this seems to strongly reduce exclusivism (with an annual lag, notice the standardized effect), eroding the bases of the secessionist movement against ETA's political strategy itself. In this sense, it is noteworthy that since the mid 1990s, when ETA has targeted many elected politicians for its attacks, a growing part of its social bases have questioned the practice of assassination (cf. Tejerina 2001). Thus, a hypothetical shift to non-violent methods in future might improve Basque national pride and the morale of this societal segment, thereby renewing their trust in secessionism, whereas as long as ETA persists in using terrorism, the results will foreseeably be the opposite.[26]

A more recent question is on what will the effects be, if any, of the above-mentioned banning of the electoral platforms of support to ETA, which occurred in March 2003, and more generally, of the judicial suspension of the activities developed by the conglomerate of groups that provide it with different resources, which occurred in August 2002. On the one hand, it can be hypothesized that support to extremist nationalism may grow upon a renewed claim that secessionism is oppressed, as it has done already in the past. On the other, the suspension of the activities of the satellite structures supporting ETA and fostering extremist nationalist socialization could also further accelerate the decline of these attitudes. Moreover, the former argument could not work as long as other openly secessionist parties are not outlawed, specifically, Eusko Alkartasuna (EA) and Aralar (recently splinted from Batasuna). Future survey data on exclusive Basque identification will help in testing these alternative predictions.

To summarize this section, the rejection towards Spanish self-identification has been significantly reduced from the first half of the 1980s to the benefit of some sort of shared identification with Spain. In the light of the data managed here, the explanation seems to rest, above all, on responsive policies, namely, on the twofold process of democratization of the Spanish political system and its political decentralization that provides the Basques with an unprecedented political autonomy. Furthermore, from the domain of repressive policies, the social reintegration of fighters renouncing armed struggle stands out for its effects on the Basques' national identification, while state terrorism became counterproductive. It is also worth underlining that the social efficiency of arrests since 1982 seems to be irrelevant in relation to the process of subjective integration of the Basques in Spain. In turn, the number of ETA victims seems to reduce the population's attachment to the idea of rejecting Spain.

IMPLICATIONS FOR THEORY AND POLICY

The addressing of Basque nationalist extremism has been based on policies placed in two dimensions: repression and responsiveness. By relying on available data with a multivariate statistical approach, much of the analysis has focused on the evolution of terrorist violence, and particularly on the efficacy of the struggle against it. The evidence is consistent with a combination of the perspectives of repression and responsiveness. A perseverant law-ruled but flexible repressive policy, materialized in the detention and the reintegration of fighters, and responsiveness, materialized in the twofold establishment of democracy and a Basque Autonomous Community, appear as the main means. On the other hand, it is more difficult to attribute the effect of ETA ceasefire in 1998/99 to one or the other policy approach, since it is possible to attribute it to both previous police efficacy – interpreting the truce as a tactical retreat due to ETA deterioration – and the agreements between nationalist parties and ETA during that period. Contrarily, state terrorism seems to have caused even more ETA violence. Therefore, this chapter backs a responsive policy that does not neglect repression in the sense of police efficacy, but allies it with the respect of law and human rights, with incentives to the abandonment of clandestine structures, and with the aim of being legitimated in the social milieu in which it is administered.

The study of voting has been limited by the nature of the data. However, the conclusion is that Basque nationalist extremist voting demonstrates great autonomy with respect to the factors under consideration. The social section closer to the extremist movement appears entrenched, firmly persistent within a hermetic socio-political subculture and substructure. However, a double disappointment after failures in both pacification and in the widening of the nationalist front that happened around the end of 1999 seems to explain the certain fall-off of this vote in 2001 and some subsequent excisions produced in the Batasuna coalition.

Finally, the refusal of self-identifying with Spain has significantly decreased over the last twenty years. Analysing the matter within the theoretical frame of this chapter, the findings suggest that, above all, responsive policies of democratization of the polity and the instauration of the Basque Autonomous Community as well as the flexible repressive policy of social re-integration of combatants have reduced that rejection. On the contrary, the so-called "dirty war" developed by the state intensified it for a time. In turn ETA violence seems to reduce it as well, against the very objectives of the movement supporting violence. Thus, the combination of a relatively flexible repressive policy with the satisfaction of demands of the extremist movement's social milieu seems to explain the increase in subjective integration of the Basques in Spain. Moreover, illegal exception state measures increased the rejection of any degree of Spanish identification, whereas insurgent violence has deeply and paradoxically eroded its own basis of social support.

In short, the results in this chapter support the hypothesis that a combination of repressive and responsive policies, rather than an exclusive choice of only one of them, accounts for the mitigation of Basque nationalist extremism in both its attitudinal and its behavioural forms.

NOTES

* I am grateful to Florencio Domínguez for the updating of essential data, to Osiris Parcero and Helmut Luetkepohl for their views on statistical modelling, to Aleksandra Djajic-Horvath and Ron Peek for the language editing, and to Juan Díez-Medrano, for his advice on both presentation and substantive aspects. Yet the responsibility for eventual mistakes remains entirely my own.

1   For an exception, see Gurr 1993.
2   In scenarios of irredentism, insurgent nationalism could have as its horizon incorporation into another already existing political system, which also implies a breaking up of the current polity.
3   Although much less expeditious, other customary means such as political acculturation and indoctrination of a reluctant population by means of the education system, military service, and propagandistic use of mass media (cf. Lipset and Rokkan 1967; Rokkan 1975; Hobsbawm 1990) also correspond to a framework of authority, but not directly to the "repressive" frame.
4   A good critical review of the literature focusing on the logic of what I call "repression" can be found in Fernando Reinares' book *Terrorismo y antiterrorismo* (1998). Another asset of the book lies in its numerous references to nationalist violence and anti-terrorist policies in the Basque Country and the whole of Spain.
5   My term "responsiveness" is similar to Gurr's (1993) "accommodation", but the latter should not be confused with Lijphart's one.
6   Apart from that, any attempt at weighting attacks would turn out quite controversial. The data on victims come from police sources.
7   I have compiled and treated these data from the Centro de Investigaciones Sociológicas, collecting frequencies in an almost exhaustive way and, often, resorting directly to the original data matrices. In addition, while trying to avoid mixing data from different sources, I have checked in some cases surveys with too reduced samples, and completed the series during deficit periods with other sources. In order to clarify the trends, where there is more than one survey per year, I have calculated a monthly and quarterly estimated average for that year. I have also interpolated for some gap periods of up to two years long (Martínez-Herrera 2002).
8   The data on detentions, imprisonments and social reintegration draw from Domínguez (1999 and personal communication for updating), except for those since 2001, which are drawn from the daily newspapers *El Mundo* and *El País* as well as the UDAT (Unidad de Documentación y Análisis sobre Terrorismo de la Universidad Rey Juan Carlos).
9   A more detailed report on the statistical procedures followed, including additional tests, and replications can be obtained from the author upon request. Replications consist of multivariate ARIMA and ML event-count modelling, both techniques yielding widely robust findings that are consistent with those presented here.
10 According to former social-democrat Spanish minister Professor Ernest Lluch, the first homicide occurred in 1961, when a baby died in an explosion of a device placed at a train stop. ETA, who disclosed the death of an alleged policeman torturer in 1969, has not confirmed that information.

11 They are 27 observations against 21. The correlation coefficient between arrests and imprisonments in Spain between 1982 and 2002 yields 0.93 (p=.000). Taking their first differences, 0.85 (p=.000).

12 None of the attempted specifications with delays at the bivariant level has yielded a significant negative coefficient. However, non-apparent relations that require a proper control to emerge often exist. Moreover, as long as first differences of both variables are considered (isolating variations between successive periods in the long-term tendencies of both series) instead of "levels", the result is more consistent with the hypothesis.

13 The dummy Bidart scores 0 till 1990 and 1 since 1991, hence modelling an effect of an "abrupt-permanent" type (McClearly and Hay 1980).

14 The proper length of delays has been identified by means of the method of McClearly and Hay (1980). The main step has been to select the strongest cross-correlation between the number of victims and the number of arrests once the series were differentiated, since both of them were non-stationary.

15 The handled data series on social reintegration includes 86 reinsertions, plus 10 amnesties conceded in 1990. The distribution of the remaining reinsertions and amnesties is not publicly available.

16 The dummy variable scores 1 in 1989.

17 The ceasefire in 1998 and 1999 has been operationalized with scores 0.25 and 0.75, respectively.

18 The length of this delay has been identified by the method of McClearly and Hay (1980); see note 15 above.

19 Peaceful mobilization against terrorism tends to be useful in several ways. In some contexts, however, these actions can be useless, or even counterproductive. In a society divided into hermetic blocks, mobilization of an opposed group can plausibly encourage insistence on and entrenchment of their own positions to counterbalance that mobilization. Despite this, I agree that collective action increases the costs for those attracted to extremism, while helping to organize the collective action, both coordinative and cooperative, of those harmed by violence and its many other consequences.

20 In the 2003 and 2004 elections there were attempts to circumvent the banning of the party under a new name, but courts noticed a clear continuity of candidates from previous contests. Then the movement called for null votes expressing a claim for "self-determination". The percentage of null votes was 7.06 and 5.77, respectively. From these I have subtracted 0.47 per cent, which is the average of null votes in the 1996, 1998, 2000 and 2001 elections, in which EH/Batasuna ran with their own rolls. Aralar received the support of 0.94 per cent of the electoral census in 2003, and 2.14 in 2004.

21 It is noteworthy that the risk of "ecological fallacy" is very small. In the first place, a study by the present author demonstrates that the trends are practically equal for all generational cohorts. Secondly, immigrants' entries almost ceased by the mid-1970s (Martínez Herrera 2002). Thirdly, here the proportions of immigrants and autochthons among interviewees are controlled.

22 These variables do not project co-linearity, because they are complemented with the ratio of autochthonous children of immigrants and mixed couples. Although this is not the right place to discuss this, the surprising finding that the more immigrants, and fewer autochthons' children there are, the more frequent exclusivism is, seems to be consistent with theories of ethnic competence (see Díez Medrano 1994).

23 The length of this delay has been identified by the method of McClearly and Hay (1980); see note 15 above.

24 Arrests are now included in police efficiency.

25 The coefficient is statistically significant at a .05 significance level if analysing the levels of the series, but not if analysing the differentiated series. This lack of consistency of the results between two different methods prevents me from showing potentially misleading results.

26 I also tried to observe the effect of the ceasefire in 1998/99. However, in 1999/2000 the CIS did not ask for details of national identity, hence the data for that period are an interpolation, which prevents me from observing a hypothetical immediate effect.

REFERENCES

Aja, E. (1999), *El Estado autonómico: federalismo y hechos diferenciales* (Madrid: Alianza)

Bloom, W. (1990), *Personal Identity, National Identity and International Relations* (Cambridge: Cambridge University Press)

Dahl, R. A. (1971), *Polyarchy. Participation and Opposition* (New Haven: Yale University)

Díez Medrano, J. (1994), "The Effects of Ethnic Segregation and Ethnic Competition On Political Mobilization in the Basque Country, 1988", *American Sociological Review* 59, 873–89.

_____ (1995), *Divided Nations. Class, Politics and Nationalism in the Basque Country and Catalonia* (Ithaca, NY: Cornell University Press)

Domínguez Iribarren, F. (1999), *¿El final de ETA? De la negociación a la tregua* (Madrid: Taurus)

Gurr, T. R. (1993), *Minorities at Risk. A Global View of Ethnopolitical Conflicts* (Washington DC: US Institute of Peace)

Hobsbawm, E. J. (1990), *Nations and Nationalism since 1780. Programme, Myth, Reality* (Cambridge: Cambridge University)

Hoffman, B. and Morrison-Taw, J. (1999), "A Strategic Framework for Countering Terrorism", in F. Reinares (ed.), *European Democracies against Terrorism* (Aldershot: Ashgate)

Horowitz, D. D. (1985), *Ethnic Groups in Conflict* (Berkeley: University of California Press)

Jaime, O. and Reinares, F. (1999), "Countering Terrorism in a New Democracy: The Case of Spain", in F. Reinares (ed.), *European Democracies against Terrorism* (Aldershot: Ashgate)

Lijphart, A. (1984), *Democracies. Patterns of Majoritarian and Consensus Government in Twenty-one Countries* (New Haven: Yale University Press)

_____ (1999), *Patterns of democracy. Government forms and performance in thirty-six countries* (New Haven: Yale University)

Linz, J. J. (1986), *Conflicto en Euskadi* (Madrid: Espasa Calpe)

Lipset, S. M. and Rokkan, S. (1967), "Cleavages, Party Systems and Electoral Alignments", in S. M. Lipset and S. Rokkan (eds), *Party Systems and Voter Alignments* (New York: Free Press)

Llera, F. J. (1994), *Los vascos y la política* (Bilbao: Universidad del País Vasco)

Martínez-Herrera, E. (2002), "From Nation-Building to Building Identification with Political Communities. Consequences of Political Decentralisation in Spain, the Basque Country, Catalonia and Galicia, 1978–2001", *European Journal of Political Research* 41, 421–53.

Mata, J. M. (1993), *El nacionalismo vasco radical. Discurso, organización y expresiones* (Bilbao: Universidad del País Vasco)

McClearly, R. and Hay, R. A. (1980), *Applied Time Series Analysis for the Social Sciences* (Beverly Hills: Sage)

Pallarés, F. (2002), "Las elecciones vascas de 2001", in E. Aja (ed.), *Informe Comunidades Autónomas* 2001 (Barcelona: Instituto de Derecho Público)

Pérez Díaz, V. (1993), *La primacía de la sociedad civil* (Madrid: Alianza)

Reinares, F. (1998), *Terrorismo y antiterrorismo* (Barcelona: Paidós)

Rokkan, S. (1975), "Dimensions of State Formation and Nation-building: A Possible Paradigm for Research on Variations within Europe", in C. Tilly (ed.), *The formation of National States in Western Europe* (Princeton University Press)

Saideman, S. M., Lanoue, D. J., Campenni, M. and Stanton, S. (2002), "Democratization, Political Institutions, and Ethnic Conflict. A Pooled Time-series Analysis, 1985-1998", *Comparative Political Studies* 35, 103-129

Tejerina, B. (2001), "Protest Cycle, Political Violence and Social Movements in the Basque Country", *Nations and Nationalism* 7, 39-57

Unzueta, P. (1994), "Las tres provocaciones de ETA", in J. Aranzadi, J. Juaristi and P. Unzueta (eds), *Auto de terminación* (Madrid: El País-Aguilar)

4 Conflict Management in Northern Ireland

STEFAN WOLFF

INTRODUCTION

As a result of the partition of a formerly British colonial territory in 1920, Northern Ireland is constitutionally a part of the United Kingdom, yet geographically it is located on the island of Ireland. Consisting of six counties, its population is just over 1.5 million. Since partition, a conflict has existed between one section of Northern Ireland's population, which has sought the restoration of a united Ireland, and another section aiming to secure the status of Northern Ireland as part of the United Kingdom. This conflict about fundamentally different political aspirations has been exacerbated by inequalities between the two communities, by the wounds inflicted through violence, but also by increasing intra-communal diversity.

"Nationalist" and "Unionist" are terms that refer very broadly to the political divide in Northern Ireland. This political divide, to some extent, coincides with the religious divide into Catholic and Protestant congregations. Considering the conflict in Northern Ireland to be about conflicting notions of national belonging, I will generally refer to political rather than religious communities throughout the following.

Defining the Northern Ireland conflict thus as an ethnonational one has important implications for its analysis and for the assessment of various attempts to resolve it. Thus, causes for failure and success of such attempts need to be sought at more than one level. While the situation in Northern Ireland itself is of great significance, it must not be seen in isolation from the political processes in the United Kingdom and the Republic of Ireland. Increasingly over the past two decades, factors in the international context have become more and more important as well – international connections of paramilitary groups, the influence of diasporas, and the consequences of European integration. The complex interplay between these four factors can explain the dynamics of conflict development and the successes and failures of attempts at resolving it.

This chapter analyses the different policies employed by the British government to manage the conflict in Northern Ireland over a thirty-year period. Following an introduction to the nature of the conflict and its conflicting interpretations (and their consequences for conflict-management strategies), the most significant British policies are analysed in their objectives and assessed in their efficiency: conflict-management approaches aimed at containment (deployment of the army, internment, Diplock courts, intelligence and security policy, criminalization of politically motivated terrorism, punctual measures aimed at economic and social development) and at resolving the conflict (Sunningdale, the constitutional convention, "rolling" devolution, the Anglo-Irish Agreement, and finally the peace process leading up to the 1998 Good Friday Agreement). Success and failure will be judged by the objectives sought with each policy, and by the response of paramilitary organizations (increase and decrease in conflict-related death tolls) and of the electorate (increase and decrease in votes for moderate and extremist political parties). In addition, the analysis will take account of other contextual factors having an impact on the development of the conflict so that a comprehensive picture emerges as to the success or failure of each strategy examined as well as to the reasons for such success or failure.

ABOUT THE CONFLICT AND ITS SOLUTIONS[1]

The conflict in Northern Ireland is primarily caused by incompatible conceptions of national belonging and the means to realize them. These two different conceptions are the goal of a united Ireland, pursued by Nationalists and Republicans, and the goal of continued strong constitutional links between the province and the United Kingdom, desired by Unionists and Loyalists. Historically, these two traditions have been associated with two different religions – Catholicism and Protestantism. These labels have played a significant role in the conflict as they have made possible the systematic pursuit of discrimination and segregation. Yet, this has not made the conflict an ethno-religious one. The same holds true for the issue of language. Although less significant, the equality and preservation of Gaelic and Ulster Scots has mobilized some sections of the population in Northern Ireland, yet overall, the conflict is not ethno-linguistic in its nature either. Similar cases could be made for other dimensions of this conflict, such as class or culture. What they all have in common is that they have polarized Northern Irish society for decades, leaving little room for cross-cutting cleavages, and eventually aligning all these various dimensions of the conflict behind two fundamentally different conceptions of national belonging.

Consequently, explanations of the Northern Ireland conflict vary widely between and within the two principal communities in Northern Ireland. Generally, a line can be drawn between external and internal accounts. The two external explanations are the Nationalist, and especially Republican, contention that the involvement of the British state into what is essentially described as internal Irish affairs is the major cause of the conflict; the alternative Unionist and Loyalist version is that the Republic of Ireland, in upholding its constitutional claim to the whole of Ireland in Articles 2 and 3 of its 1937 constitution, unnecessarily fuelled the existing tensions and encouraged the Nationalist/Republican tradition to strive for Irish reunification.[2]

Internal explanations, in contrast, see the roots of the conflict in a variety of factors within Northern Ireland itself by focusing on the implications of economic, religious and/or cultural conditions in the province. Economically, deprivation and systematic discrimination of Catholics in Northern Ireland is the most common argument to account for the conflict alongside suggestions of economic opportunism of those who actually profit from the ongoing conflict. As an explanatory concept, religion is either seen as a phenomenon that deepens and aligns already existing social divides, making positive intercommunal relationships virtually impossible, or the religious fanaticism of certain sections within each community is interpreted as the driving force behind the conflict policies of each community. Cultural accounts, finally, treat the conflict as either inherited, that is, simply as the tradition of being in conflict with the other community and/or the authorities, or as an ethno-centrist clash of two fundamentally different cultures.

As a consequence of this conflict about the conflict, proposed solutions have differed as well. They range from full integration of Northern Ireland into the United Kingdom, to devolution, independence, repartition and eventually to Irish unification, with a variety of different models for each of the major proposals.

Integration into the United Kingdom, defined as direct government by Westminster, is an idea mostly supported by various streams within the Unionist community and based on an understanding of the conflict as caused by the "Irish dimension". Full integration, in one version, aims at making Northern Ireland part of the United Kingdom such that it would neither be treated any differently from any other part of the country, nor would it have separate, or independent, or different institutions. Supporters of electoral integration propose a slightly different model. According to this model, the main British political parties should expand into Northern Ireland to create a party-political "normality" above sectarian divisions and thus eliminate or at least gradually realign Northern Irish political parties on other issues. Both of these models of integration suggested a modification of the system of direct rule introduced in 1972. However, there is a third group of integrationists who argue that, instead of attempting to change this system, it should simply have been made permanent.

In contrast to the various types of integration, the idea of devolving powers held by the Westminster government, has been favoured, in its various forms, and each of them with different degrees of support, by sections of both communities. While a return to simple majority rule, as it existed between 1921 and 1972, was, and still is, favoured among significant sections of the Unionist community, notably the Democratic Unionist Party (DUP) and some parts of the Ulster Unionist Party (UUP), this proposal enjoys no support from within the Nationalist camp. Majority rule with safeguards such as a bill of rights and an election system based on proportional representation is a more moderate approach which tries to take account of the historic concerns of the minority community. However, any significant support for such a solution has always been confined to Unionism. Another proposal for a devolutionist arrangement, supported by the explicitly cross-communal Alliance Party of Northern Ireland (APNI), and to some extent by sections of the UUP, was power sharing, giving political representatives from both communities the opportunity to be involved in the executive and legislative branches of a new system of government in Northern Ireland. While the moderate Nationalist community, primarily the Social Democrat and Labour Party (SDLP), supported the idea of power sharing, they wanted it to be qualified by some sort of executive and legislative involvement of the Republic of Ireland, which was unacceptable to Unionists before the 1990s.

Somewhere between suggestions for integration into the United Kingdom and Irish reunification stand proposals for repartition along the major demographic divides in the west and southwest of the province, the independence of Northern Ireland from both the United Kingdom and the Republic of Ireland, and joint authority of both states over Northern Ireland. With the exception of joint authority, which found significant support among Nationalists, none of these proposals was attractive to a majority within either of the two major traditions in Northern Ireland.

In contrast, the idea of a united Ireland has always been very popular as a long-term goal in the Nationalist community. While moderate Nationalists favour its achievement by consent and peaceful, constitutional and democratic means, Republican paramilitary groups, most notably the Irish Republican Army (IRA), have tried since 1921 to force the issue through violence. While this approach is rejected by large sections of the Nationalist community, a majority of the same community is nevertheless united over the desirability of the goal of Irish unification, which, in turn, is strongly opposed by Unionists and Loyalists.

Overall, this means that the demands made by both Unionists/Loyalists and Nationalists/Republicans stretch across the whole spectrum of output, regime and community-oriented demands, which implies that government responses need to be similarly "comprehensive" and address these demands at all the levels at which they occur in order to achieve a sustainable settlement. As the following analysis will demonstrate, this is a lesson that has been learned the hard way by successive British governments, which at different times have emphasized different types of responses while sidelining or neglecting others.

SETTLING THE CONFLICT? CONSTITUTIONAL REFORM, INSTITUTIONAL CHANGE, SECURITY POLICY, AND ECONOMIC AND SOCIAL DEVELOPMENT IN THEIR EFFECTIVENESS OVER TIME

Despite a number of relatively far-reaching reforms to combat inefficiency and discrimination introduced under the short-lived premiership of Terence O'Neill in Northern Ireland in the 1960s, community relations deteriorated quite rapidly. Despite these reforms, Unionist control of the entire state apparatus in Northern Ireland continued and meant that the evolving conflict was at the same time one between two communities and between one community and the institutions of the state. The often barely disguised goal congruence between Unionist community and what was essentially a Unionist state, that is, to assure the continued membership of Northern Ireland in the United Kingdom with all means available, clearly limited the possibilities of any successful conflict management within Northern Ireland. The violent escalation of the conflict in the late 1960s was ample evidence of that failure, and it prompted the British government to take a more active interest in the province. As it became clear that local security forces and policy were unable to deal with the increasing violence, in 1969 the British government deployed troops in Northern Ireland. Despite this extraordinary move, violence continued and, in fact, increased. This led to the introduction of internment in August 1971, that is, the mass detention without trial of all terrorist suspects, who happened to be almost exclusively Nationalists. The subsequent alienation of the entire Nationalist community in Northern Ireland provoked a further upsurge in violence and an increasingly heavy-handed police and army response, which culminated in thirteen civilians being shot dead by the army on "Bloody Sunday" in January 1972. When, after this unnecessary escalation, the Stormont government refused to hand over control of security matters to the British government in London, the then Conservative Prime Minister Edward Heath suspended the Northern Ireland legislature on 24 March 1972 temporarily for one year. This marked the beginning of the British government's formally taking charge of conflict management and resolution policies in Northern Ireland.

Failure of the Sunningdale Process

As direct rule had only been intended as a temporary measure, the government needed to develop an alternative system of government acceptable to both communities. In 1972 and 1973, it published *The Future of Northern Ireland: A Paper for Discussion* and subsequently constitutional proposals for the province. As a consequence, elections to a power-sharing assembly were held on 28 June 1973. Based on an electoral system according to which between five and seven candidates were elected by proportional representation in each of the parliamentary constituencies and on a turnout of 72.5 per cent, the elections returned 78 representatives of eight parties to the new assembly. The official Unionists won 29.3 per cent of the vote and sent 24 members to the assembly, followed by the SDLP with 22.1 per cent and 19 successful candidates. Together with the APNI, which won 9.2 per cent of the vote and eight seats, they formed a coalition government (Northern Ireland executive), initially supported by 52 of the 78 members of the assembly. The parties in the executive were generally in favour of both the idea of power-sharing in Northern Ireland and of a Council of Ireland to be established subsequently to address a long-standing demand by Nationalists for the recognition of the "Irish" dimension of the conflict.

Between 6 and 9 December 1973, representatives of the British and Irish governments and of the parties involved in the designated executive met at Sunningdale and discussed and agreed the setting up of the Council of Ireland. The provisions foresaw a Council of Ministers with executive, harmonizing and consultative functions, consisting of an equal number of delegates from the Northern Ireland executive and the Irish government, and a Consultative Assembly of thirty members from each of the parliaments, chosen by proportional representation on the basis of the single transferable vote system within each parliament. The Council was to have executive functions, by means of unanimous vote in the Council of Ministers, in the fields of environment, agriculture, cooperation in trade and industry, electricity, tourism, transport, public health, sport, culture and the arts. The conference also agreed on closer cooperation in security-related matters, on inviting the Council of Ireland to draft a human-rights bill, and on the possibility of a future devolution of powers from the parliament in Westminster to the Northern Ireland assembly and the institutions of the Council of Ireland.

This relative quick success on the constitutional front, however, had not prevented the British government from recognizing that it still had a very serious security situation on its hands. Already in November 1972, provisions had been made in the Detention of Terrorists (Northern Ireland) Order to replace and formalize earlier arrangements on internment that had had their basis in the 1922 Special Powers Act. This was followed in 1973 by the Northern Ireland (Emergency Provisions) Act and the 1974 Prevention of Terrorism (Temporary Provisions) Act (PTA). The 1973 act introduced trial without jury for so-called scheduled offences (that is, terrorist activities), allowed confessions made under psychological pressure as admissible evidence, and banned the IRA, Sinn Féin (SF), and the Ulster Volunteer Force (UVF) as legal organizations in Northern Ireland. Less than a year later, the then Secretary of State for Northern Ireland Merlyn Rees announced that he would de-proscribe the UVF and SF (and phase out internment). The further tightening of anti-terrorist legislation in the 1974 PTA was a direct response to the Birmingham pub bombings, which had brought the conflict in Northern Ireland to Britain's doorstep. Under this 1974 act, the IRA was banned in the rest of the United Kingdom, it became possible to ban Northern Ireland residents from travelling to other parts of the United Kingdom, and police powers of search, detention and arrest were extended. Together, both acts provided the foundation of the government's criminalization policy, that is, the attempt to treat politically motivated violence in Northern Ireland by means of the criminal justice system. In part, this was a recognition of the failure to address the violence-related aspects of the conflict through a wider framework of constitutional reform and institutional change only.

Ironically, the government's approach to security issues was subsequently vindicated, when the initially favourable situation for the implementation of the Sunningdale Agreement began to change dramatically early in 1974. The Westminster elections on 28 February had been turned into a referendum on power sharing and the Council of Ireland. Opponents of any change in the status quo united in a coalition called the United Ulster Unionist Council and won 51 per cent of the vote and 11 of the 12 seats in Northern Ireland, with the remaining seat going to the SDLP. Shortly afterwards, the newly established Ulster Workers' Council (UWC) called for new elections to the Northern Ireland assembly. When a motion against power sharing and the

Table 4.1   Conditions accounting for the failure of the Sunningdale process

- In Northern Ireland:
  - Vulnerability of the pro-Agreement parties to out-flanking by radicals in both communities
  - Traditional mistrust of large sections of the Unionist community towards all issues involving cross-border cooperation
  - Recent high level of violent interethnic conflict
  - Ability of the UWC to mobilize key sections of the Unionist community in a general strike against the agreement
  - Lack of popular and institutional support in defence of the agreement

- In the United Kingdom:
  - Failure to take decisive measures in support of the pro-agreement parties in Northern Ireland and to defeat the general strike in its early stages
  - Public comments by leading government officials that fuelled anger and fear within the Unionist and Loyalist communities
  - Lack of effective responses to the Irish Constitutional Court's ruling on the compatibility of the Sunningdale Agreement with Articles 2 and 3 of the Irish constitution

- In the Republic of Ireland:
  - Irish Constitutional Court's ruling on the compatibility of the Sunningdale Agreement with Articles 2 and 3 of the Irish Constitution
  - Lack of sufficient assurances by the Irish government to respect the constitutional status of Northern Ireland

- International context:
  - Lack of any pressure on, or incentives for, the conflict parties to resolve their differences through compromise

Council of Ireland was defeated in the assembly by 44 to 28 votes on 14 May 1974, the UWC called for a general strike. The following two weeks of the strike brought Northern Ireland to an almost complete standstill. The failure to break up the strike and the unwillingness to negotiate a settlement with the UWC, eventually, led to the resignation of the Northern Ireland executive on 28 May 1974. The assembly was prorogued two days later.

An analysis of the failure of this first attempt to settle the Northern Ireland conflict by means of constitutional and institutional change shows that the essential conditions for the success of power-sharing and a formal institutional involvement of the Republic of Ireland in the affairs of Northern Ireland had not been there, and even where they had appeared to be present, they were not stable enough to endure the pressures exercised on them (see Table 4.1). Even though the initial elections to the Northern Ireland assembly seemed to be a clear vote in favour of the new constitutional status, the reality of the situation in the province betrayed this superficial impression. The cooperating élites had a rather secure two-thirds majority *in* the assembly, but their influence and control over their (former) electorate on the *outside* was far less permanent and stable, in particular as far as Unionists in favour of the new arrangements and the APNI were concerned.[3] Apart from this lack of popular support for the settlement, there was also an essential lack of institutional support and failure of politicians to implement counter-measures. While British government policy was not to negotiate with the UWC, there were no decisive steps taken to prevent the breakdown of public life in Northern Ireland, nor was enough done to counter the pressure from UWC activists on members of the Unionist community who were opposed to the strike or undecided about their role in it. Sunningdale was not a treaty between two states, but an agreement reached between two states and a selected number of political parties. In order to work, it would have required substantial support for those partners in the agreement who were most vulnerable to pressures from within their own communities. The pro-agreement parties in both blocs were vulnerable to outflanking by hard-core radicals. That this support for pro-agreement politicians was not forthcoming was one of the major reasons for the failure of this early attempt to resolve the Northern Ireland conflict.

The Anglo-Irish Agreement

After the failure of Sunningdale, the British government on the one hand continued its security policy alongside a number of programmes aimed at economic development and an improvement of community relations in Northern Ireland, such as the creation of a Standing Advisory Commission on Human Rights (SACHR) and the Fair Employment Agency (FEA) in 1975. On the other hand, it also initiated several initiatives aimed at a new constitutional status for Northern Ireland. In the wake of Sunningdale, these initiatives were either strictly limited to Northern Ireland itself, such as the 1974/75 constitutional convention, or, when they had cross-border implications, they did not involve any Northern Irish political parties, as with the Anglo-Irish Inter-Governmental Council set up in 1981. Yet, none of these initiatives were succesful.

Between 1982 and 1984, another attempt was made to resolve the conflict by reintroducing devolution. A scheme of "rolling devolution" involving an assembly and a committee-style executive was proposed. The devolution of powers to elected representatives in Northern Ireland was supposed to be gradual and subject to 70 per cent agreement in the assembly to be elected. As, from their point of view, there was no adequate recognition of the Nationalist tradition in Northern Ireland, both Sinn Féin and the SDLP participated in the 1982 elections on an abstentionist platform and subsequently boycotted the assembly, which meant the failure of "rolling devolution".

In 1983 the Fianna Fail, Fine Gael and Labour parties of the Republic of Ireland met with the Northern Irish SDLP in Dublin at the so-called New Ireland Forum to discuss the future of Northern Ireland from their viewpoint.[4] Until February 1984, 11 public meetings were held. In September 1983 delegates from the Forum visited Northern Ireland and in January 1984 the United Kingdom. In conclusion, the Forum produced a report, in which the members gave their analysis of the problem, examined the situation in Northern Ireland, and presented three potential solutions to the conflict – a unitary Irish state, a federal or confederate Irish state, and joint British–Irish authority over Northern Ireland. While this report represented a determinedly Nationalist interpretation of the conflict and its solutions, it nevertheless signalled to the British government that there was a certain basis for negotiation and compromise.

Given this and a British desire to involve the Republic of Ireland in the responsibility of running the province amid the continuously serious security situation, alongside a growing Irish interest to stabilize the situation in the north and to prevent a spill-over of violence and/or Republican influence, a new and joint approach to the conflict seemed possible. Furthermore, the British government realized that it had failed in its campaign to criminalize Republicanism, and both governments faced a growing appeal of Republican ideology within the Nationalist community, in particular after some highly publicized hunger strikes by Republican paramilitary prisoners in the early 1980s. Based on these considerations, both governments decided to enter into negotiations, which resulted in the Anglo-Irish Agreement of 1985.

The agreement dealt with a variety of issues, including an intergovernmental conference, a human-rights bill for Northern Ireland, security and judicial policies, and cross-border cooperation on economic, social and cultural matters. The British attempt to address concerns of the Nationalist community was apparent, but as the implementation of the agreement did not effect any dramatic or even particularly noticeable change, the reward for the United Kingdom alienating the Unionist community was not forthcoming as expected. Although the influence of Sinn Féin within the Nationalist camp decreased towards the end of the 1980s, activities of the IRA did not decline. On the contrary, hard-line Republican opposition to the United Kingdom and IRA activity[5] increased. The declining electoral appeal of Sinn Féin in the mid-to-end 1980s set in motion a rethinking process among the leadership of the party. Eventually, the party moved away from its unqualified support for, or at least tolerance of, Republican violence to become one of the participants in the peace process(es) of the 1990s that finally brought about the Good Friday Agreement in 1998.

The more severe repercussions, however, originated from within the Unionist community. In a survey of January 1988, 55.1 per cent of those who declared themselves as Protestants voiced their opposition to the Anglo-Irish Agreement, compared with 7.9 per cent of those describing themselves as Catholics. Only 8.7 per cent of Protestants opted more or less in favour of the agreement, as compared with 31.8 per cent of Catholics who did so. Asked in the same survey for the biggest problem in Northern Ireland, only 8.6 per cent of Catholics, but 29.5 per cent of Protestants pointed to the Anglo-Irish Agreement (Hamilton 1990). Strong Unionist opposition failed to secure one of the central objectives of the British government, namely to strengthen moderate Unionism in the form of the UUP and marginalize the radicals of Ian Paisley's DUP. Similarly unsatisfactory were the working of the Inter-Governmental conference, the envisaged cross-border cooperation and the hoped-for improvement in the security situation.[6] The latter especially prompted a further tightening of security policy on part of the British government. The 1989 revisions to the PTA introduced a variety of measures to enable security forces to combat money laundering by terrorist organizations. Already in 1988, a broadcast ban had been pronounced against Sinn Féin, and the Criminal Evidence (Northern Ireland) Act of the same year had allowed judges trying terrorist offences without juries to draw, in certain circumstances, inferences from defendants' refusal to answer questions in court. This and the so-called supergrass trials of the early and mid 1980s were meant to make the judicial battle against terrorism in Northern Ireland more effective at a time when the government came under increasing criticism over an alleged "shoot-to-kill" policy by security forces in Northern Ireland.[7]

Although the Anglo-Irish Agreement had by no means failed as badly as Sunningdale, it did also not produce a significant breakthrough in the political stalemate in Northern Ireland (see Table 4.2). In some respects, such as the increasing alienation of parts of the Unionist community, it even worsened the situation and prevented major progress for years to come. However, although the stalemate continued, it did so on a different level. The agreement had shown that solutions were possible to which the two governments and a significant part of the Nationalist community could agree. This had a positive long-term effect on the opportunities to reduce the level of violent conflict and to increase the chances of achieving an inclusive agreement for the future of Northern Ireland, because it made uncompromising, hard-line Unionism less credible as a strategy to preserve Northern Ireland's link with the United Kingdom and, similarly, indicated that there was overwhelming support for constitutional, non-violent politics within the Nationalist community, the latter finding its expression in the poor electoral performance of Sinn Féin in the late 1980s and early 1990s. The limited success that the Anglo-Irish Agreement had in the short term was mostly a consequence of it being reached and implemented at intergovernmental level.[8] This being a recognition of the situation in the mid 1980s, in which cross-communal agreement was virtually impossible, the British and Irish governments also had to accept that no stable and durable solution would be possible without the involvement and consent of the parties representing the two traditions in Northern Ireland. However, despite continued economic and social-development programmes administered in the province, there is little evidence that the British government made any significant progress throughout the 1980s to facilitate such involvement and consent. On the other hand, the more decisive move towards a bilateral approach in the

Table 4.2   Conditions accounting for the limited success of the Anglo-Irish Agreement

- In the United Kingdom:
  - Deliberate attempt to address concerns of the Nationalist community, even at the price of alienating sections within the Unionist community
  - Failure to deliver on key aspects of the agreement, such as the Inter-governmental Conference, cross-border cooperation, and an improved security situation

- In the Republic of Ireland:
  - Upholding of the constitutional claim to Northern Ireland and its perception by Unionists as a threat to a non-negotiable aspect of their identity
  - Failure to deliver on key aspects of the agreement, such as the Inter-governmental Conference, cross-border cooperation, and an improved security situation

- In Northern Ireland:
  - Exclusion of the political parties in Northern Ireland from the formal negotiation process
  - No opportunity for the people of Northern Ireland to approve of, or reject, the agreement
  - Disappointment among Nationalists and Republicans about the lack of visible improvements in their situation
  - Increased hard-line Republican resistance against British policy
  - Radicalization of the Unionist community in opposition to the "Irish" dimension of the agreement
  - Continued high levels of violent interethnic conflict

- International context:
  - Lack of any pressure on the conflict parties to resolve their differences through compromise
  - Support of the IRA through Libyan arms shipments

Source: From the Joint Declaration to the Good Friday Agreement

1980s did provide part of the foundation upon which the peace process in the 1990s could be built.

The end of the 1980s and the beginning of the 1990s signalled new opportunities to move towards an inclusive settlement of the Northern

Ireland conflict. In 1988, the UUP, the DUP, the APNI and the SDLP had met in Germany without achieving any breakthrough. Talks had also been held between the SDLP and Sinn Féin in the first half of 1988. More significant than these talks, however, was an announcement by Sinn Féin president Gerry Adams in March 1989 that he sought to establish Sinn Féin as a democratic political movement in pursuit of self-determination. This and the public acknowledgement by the then Northern Ireland secretary Peter Brooke that the IRA could not be defeated militarily, that he would not rule out talks between the government and Sinn Féin should IRA violence cease, and that the British government had no selfish strategic or economic interests in Northern Ireland paved the way for the Brooke/ Mayhew talks, involving the UUP, the DUP, the APNI and the SDLP. These talks were held between March 1991 and November 1992 during a break in the operation of the Anglo-Irish intergovernmental conference to ensure the participation of the Unionist parties. The arrangements for the talks provided for three different strands – relationships in Northern Ireland, between the province and the Republic, and between the two governments. While talks about the relationships in Northern Ireland came to a standstill in June 1992 because there was little sign of compromise and the gap between the different positions seemed, at the time, impossible to bridge, the parties nevertheless agreed to move on to talks about Strand 2. With no major progress made, and decreasing willingness to cooperate on the part of the DUP, the process eventually collapsed when the resumption of the Maryfield secretariat[9] prompted the Unionists to withdraw from the talks.

In April of the following year it was revealed that Gerry Adams of Sinn Féin and John Hume of the SDLP had held a series of talks for two years discussing the contributions their parties could make to bringing about peace. After their talks had become public, they issued a first joint statement in April and a second one in September, which became known as the Hume/Adams Initiative, and outlined the Nationalist and Republican views of a road to peace. Unionist opposition to the Hume/ Adams Initiative coincided with a new series of violent attacks by and against both communities, of which an IRA bomb on the Shankill Road in Belfast was the most costly in human casualties.[10] It was also revealed that there had been secret talks between the British government and Sinn Féin. At the end of the year, following a series of meetings Irish Prime Minister Albert Reynolds and British Prime Minister John Major issued the Joint Declaration.

The significance of the declaration, and the single most important difference to the Sunningdale and Anglo-Irish Agreements, was the fact that the British government acknowledged that it was

> for the people of the island of Ireland alone, by agreement between the two parts respectively, to exercise their right of self-determination on the basis of consent, freely and concurrently given, North and South, to bring about a united Ireland, if that is their wish.

The explicit reference to the notion of self-determination had a highly symbolic value, positively connoted for the Nationalist community, with more negative implications for the Unionist tradition.

The Joint Declaration and its emphasis on inclusiveness was, to some extent, not an entirely new policy. However, it had been reinvigorated at the beginning of the 1990s with the creation of the Community Relations Council and the inauguration of "Education for Mutual Understanding" and revised curricular guidelines emphasizing the cultural heritage of both communities. Also falling in this period was the launch of another initiative – Targeting Social Need – which required all departments of the Northern Ireland Office to monitor policy impacts and distribute their funds in a way that, wherever possible, those areas and communities most in need of social and economic development would benefit most. Further confidence-building measures followed early in 1994 when the broadcast ban on Sinn Féin was lifted in the Republic of Ireland, when Gerry Adams was given a visa to enter the USA, and when the Northern Ireland Office issued a statement in which it addressed questions by Sinn Féin concerning the Joint Declaration. Although Sinn Féin remained critical of the Declaration, a secret meeting was held between the Secretary of State for Northern Ireland Sir Patrick Mayhew and a Sinn Féin delegation in August, which was followed by an IRA announcement about a "complete cessation of all military activities" on 30 August.

While relations between the Nationalist community and its representatives, on one side, and the Irish government, on the other, grew closer, the increasing degree of alienation between the DUP, which represented the more radical sections of Unionism and Loyalism, and the British government became apparent when John Major cut short a meeting with DUP leader Ian Paisley on 6 September 1994. Ten days later, the British government lifted the broadcast ban on Sinn Féin. On 13 October 1994, the Combined Loyalist Military Command announced its own ceasefire. At the end of the year, the British government, represented by officials of the Northern Ireland Office, began a series of talks with those political parties of Northern Ireland that had affiliations with paramilitary organizations, namely Sinn Féin (9 December 1994), the Progressive Unionist Party (PUP) and the Ulster Democratic Party (UDP) (both on 15 December 1994).

Thus, within a year of the Joint Declaration, ceasefires had been announced by the major paramilitary organizations which did not cover a specified period of time (as they had in the past), but seemed, if not permanent, at least longer-term. In addition, the British government had entered into official and formal talks with representatives of the paramilitary organizations of both communities, and Sinn Féin was heading back into the political process, being recognized as a necessary partner by both governments. Although Unionist opposition to the Anglo-Irish Agreement and the Joint Declaration remained, the conditions to move forward towards a lasting settlement seemed rather good.

Realizing that, despite these favourable conditions, the causes of conflict in Northern Ireland had not been removed, the British and Irish governments developed *A New Framework for Agreement*, which proposed structures for

North–South (or, Northern Ireland – Republic of Ireland) and East–West (British–Irish) institutions and sought to integrate the earlier suspended three-strand talks with a new effort of peacemaking (O'Leary 1995, 867). Both governments recognized that a settlement would not be possible without significant and substantial compromise from all parties to the conflict and reaffirmed the basic positions of the Joint Declaration – the principles of self-determination and consent, peaceful and democratic means as the only acceptable political strategies and tactics, and the recognition of the fundamental "rights and identities of both traditions". In addition, the British government proposed its own ideas for a possible solution of the conflict within Northern Ireland in a document called *A Framework for Accountable Government in Northern Ireland*.

Throughout 1995, contacts and official talks continued between the British government and Sinn Féin, and although no major progress was achieved an eventual settlement seemed to have come closer.[11] However, the end of the IRA ceasefire in February 1996 and the resumption of (Republican) violence throughout the region, primarily targeting the security forces, and in England, proved to be a major setback. Despite this, the British and Irish governments announced the beginning of all-party talks, following elections to them in May, for June 1996. Although Sinn Féin polled a record 15.5 per cent of the vote in these elections, the party was not allowed to take its seats at the negotiation table,[12] because IRA violence continued and the party did not sign up to the Mitchell principles of non-violence.[13] The multi-party talks commenced as planned but did not bring about any significant results in their first year.

The election of a Labour government in the general elections in May 1997, the emphasis Labour put on reaching a settlement in Northern Ireland, and the perception, especially among the Nationalist community, that there was a new approach in Northern Ireland policies opened new possibilities. In July 1997, the IRA renewed its ceasefire. After Sinn Féin had signed up to the Mitchell Principles, the party was allowed into the multi-party talks at Stormont, which, however, resulted in the DUP and the United Kingdom Unionist Party walking out. After more than six months of intensive negotiations with several setbacks, eight political parties in Northern Ireland and the British and Irish governments agreed to what has become known as the Good Friday Agreement.

This agreement established a 108-member legislative assembly elected by popular vote in Northern Ireland according to the Single Transferable Vote system. From within this assembly, an executive is elected according to the d'Hondt principle. A First Minister and a Deputy First Minister, who are also elected by the assembly, lead this executive. The assembly has legislative powers in a wide variety of areas, ranging from economic policy and health care to education and tourism. The Northern Ireland Secretary retains a certain measure of power, most crucially in the area of security and justice policy. Within the assembly, qualified majority voting procedures can be invoked on critical issues. The assembly can also veto any proposal by the North–South Ministerial Council that was set up by the Good Friday Agreement to coordinate cross-border cooperation between Northern

Table 4.3   Agreements on and in Northern Ireland, 1973–98

	Sunningdale Agreement	*Anglo-Irish Agreement*	*Good Friday Agreement*
Signatories	United Kingdom, Republic of Ireland, UP, SDLP, APNI	United Kingdom, Republic of Ireland	United Kingdom, Republic of Ireland, UUP, UDP, PUP, NIWC, L, APNI, Sinn Féin, SDLP
Consent principle	X	X	X
Self-determination	O	O	X
Reform of the policing system	X	X	X
Early release of prisoners	X	(X)	X
Bill of Rights	X	X	X
Abandonment of violence required	X	X	X
Security cooperation	X	X	X
Cross-border cooperation	X	X	X
Recognition of both identities	O	X	X
Intergovernmental cooperation	X	X	X
Institutional role for the Republic of Ireland	X	X	X
Cooperation between Unionists and Nationalists required	(X)	X	X
Inter-island cooperation	O	(X)	X
Devolution of powers	X	X	X

Key: X – issue addressed; (X) – issue implicitly addressed; O – issue not addressed.

Ireland and the Republic of Ireland. A new British-Irish Council operates on a similar premise and includes delegates from the two national governments and the three regions within the United Kingdom that have devolved powers (Northern Ireland, Scotland and Wales). The British-Irish Intergovernmental Conference, subsuming both the Anglo-Irish Intergovernmental Council and the Intergovernmental Conference established under the 1985 Agreement, was given the task to promote broad and substantial bilateral cooperation between the United Kingdom and the Republic of Ireland.[14]

Despite the apparent comprehensiveness of the Good Friday Agreement and its endorsement by what, at the time, looked like overwhelming majorities in Northern Ireland and the Republic of Ireland, the question remains whether it provides an effective framework for a permanent resolution of the conflict. In order to answer this question, it is useful to compare the Good Friday Agreement to previous settlement attempts both in terms of their content and the context of their implementation.

Starting with the first of these issues, a comparison between the Sunningdale Agreement, the Anglo-Irish Agreement and the Good Friday Agreement reveals that there is a core of issues dealt with by all or some of these agreements in a similar manner (see Table 4.3).

However, there are also a number of differences between the agreements. These relate, in the first place, to the signatories of each of the agreements. While the United Kingdom and the Republic of Ireland have signed all of them, the prior negotiation process did only on two occasions (Sunningdale and Good Friday Agreements) involve political representatives from the communities in Northern Ireland. Clearly, the participation has been far broader in the 1997/98 talks process and, even more significantly, included representatives of paramilitary organizations alongside the mainstream constitutional parties.

A second difference concerns the comprehensiveness and detail of the arrangements. Here the Good Friday Agreement, as it is based on an inclusive negotiation process, addresses the greatest number of issues and lays down, for most of these issues, in great detail the operational procedures for their implementation.

A third difference is the character of the implementation process. Only the Good Friday Agreement was proposed to the people in the Republic of Ireland and in Northern Ireland in a referendum, while all the others were more or less implemented by government decree, thus giving the people a sense of imposition. The majority with which the Good Friday Agreement was endorsed by the population north and south of the border and across the communities in Northern Ireland is so far unprecedented in the history of the conflict. However, it remains to be seen how long this majority will persist under the strains to which the agreement has been, and continues to be, subjected. In summer 2001 these pressures seem to have become overwhelming, and the future of the institutions established by the Good Friday Agreement is in serious doubt.

Fourth, since the beginning of the final round of the negotiation process in the autumn of 1997, the major paramilitary organizations on both sides have upheld their ceasefires.

Fifth, there is the question of what alternative arrangements would be put in place in case the Good Friday Agreement fails. A comparison with the situation that existed after Sunningdale reveals that the incentives for both communities to find a modus vivendi within the agreement structure are more compelling than they were before. The failure of Sunningdale meant the reintroduction of direct rule, an outcome that many in the Unionist community preferred to power sharing. A failure of the Good Friday Agreement, however, will most likely mean that the United Kingdom and the Republic of Ireland will move towards a form of shared sovereignty over Northern Ireland. Clearly, this is not an outcome that Unionists would prefer. Nationalists, however, would also lose out, as the influence of both communities on the decision-making in Northern Ireland would decrease to a level well below to what they have at present achieved. In particular, Sinn Féin, unless the party substantially increases its representation in the Irish parliament would lose an unprecedented power base.

Finally, the international context, especially the involvement of the United States, has been a critical factor in the success of the Good Friday Agreement to date. In particular, the international mediation of the talks process and the simultaneous and subsequent American pressure on, and incentives for, all parties in the process to come to an agreement and to implement it has played a significant role in the maintenance of the peace process. The vital role of former US Senator George Mitchell in brokering the Belfast Agreement in 1998 and in overcoming the decommissioning impasse in 1999, as well as the support from the European Union must not be underestimated in their importance. The early endorsement of the post-agreement peace process in the form of the award of the Nobel Peace Price to John Hume and David Trimble was similarly significant. It assisted in encouraging the pursuit of a long-term and stable peace in Northern Ireland and in putting the spotlight on the developments in the province in which the major protagonists can less and less afford to fail in their efforts to seek accommodation. The involvement of the European Union since the mid 1990s has made a positive contribution to economic development and, through various development projects, to an improvement of inter-communal relations.

The conflict in Northern Ireland in all its different aspects and dimensions and in its dependence on factors that can be influenced only to a limited degree by the political actors in Belfast, London and Dublin is not certain, but also not unlikely, to be resolved within and by the institutional framework set out in the Good Friday Agreement (see Table 4.4). The reason for this uncertainty is that the Good Friday Agreement, as any other agreement reached before, is dependent upon the cooperation and compromise of two communities with fundamentally different political aspirations and identities. These, of course, may change over time provided opportunities and incentives for such change exist, at present, however, there is little indication that such change has in fact taken place.

Table 4.4   Conditions accounting for the possibility of the Good Friday Agreement

- In Northern Ireland:
  - Inclusion of all parties in the negotiation process based on a prior election
  - Opportunity for the people of Northern Ireland to approve the agreement
  - Protection mechanisms built into the agreement to address concerns of both communities
  - Ceasefires of all major paramilitary organizations considerably reducing the level of violent interethnic conflict

- In the United Kingdom:
  - Change in government, fresh and more determined approach to achieve an inclusive settlement
  - Pressure on all sections of the communities in Northern Ireland to compromise
  - Greater degree of flexibility on key issues, such as Sinn Féin participation in the negotiation process, decommissioning, early release of prisoners and so on.
  - Negotiation of a new Anglo-Irish Agreement
  - Reiteration that any change in the constitutional future of Northern Ireland was subject to the approval of the people of Northern Ireland
  - Close cooperation with the government of the Republic of Ireland and the international chairmanship of the talks

- In the Republic of Ireland:
  - Preparedness to withdraw the constitutional claim to Northern Ireland
  - Pressure, particularly on Sinn Féin and the IRA, to appreciate the opportunity presented by the multi-party negotiations in 1997/98
  - Active steps to address concerns of the Unionist community in Northern Ireland
  - Close cooperation with the government of the United Kingdom and the international chairmanship of the talks
  - Opportunity for the citizens of the Republic of Ireland to approve the agreement

- International Context:
  - International, particularly American, involvement in the talks process, including official and unofficial pressure on both communities to come to a settlement and on the IRA to maintain its ceasefire

ASSESSING THE SUCCESS AND FAILURE OF BRITISH CONFLICT MANAGEMENT AND RESOLUTION POLICIES IN NORTHERN IRELAND

The overwhelming evidence from the previous discussion suggests that conflict management, that is, the containment of the conflict at a low intensity level, has been successful, while in spring 2002 an actual resolution of the conflict seemed as far away as ever before. In other words, punctual policy measures in the areas of economic, social and education policies in combination with an increasingly sophisticated and successful, albeit not uncontroversial, security policy has managed to keep levels of violence and civil unrest low. At the same time constitutional reforms and institutional changes have not been able to foster a common vision of Northern Ireland's future acceptable to both communities so that, measured in terms of support for political parties, unification with the Republic of Ireland remains the goal of a majority of people within the Nationalist community. Taken together, punctual policy measures and the failure of constitutional and institutional changes have hardened and deepened the existing divisions in Northern Ireland.

Reducing the Level of Violent Conflict

By global standards of death tolls in violent inter-ethnic conflicts, the one in Northern Ireland has not been very intense. Between 1969 and 1994, when the first IRA and Loyalist ceasefires were announced in the current peace process, about 3200 people had been killed.[15] Yet, these statistics tell only half the story. Apart from killings, paramilitaries have committed many more acts of violence, ranging from beatings, to kneecappings, to intimidation and directed both at the alleged "enemy" and at members of their own communities. These many forms of violence have had a significant impact on community relations in Northern Ireland, whose examination can provide a good understanding of the degree to which the conflict as a whole has affected society, and thus in turn has created the very conditions under which governments had to formulate and implement policies aimed at conflict resolution.

As Figures 4A.1 and 4A.2 in the Appendix indicate, British government policy has largely succeeded in reducing the level of violence, especially of fatalities, in Northern Ireland. Despite some setbacks, this has been the predominant trend since the mid 1970s. Yet, the impact of violence on the conflict cannot only be measured in these terms. Used by the paramilitary groups of both communities to realize their goals as well as by the British state and its institutions to preserve the status quo and prevent further escalation, violence has not only been a symptom of the incompatibility of communal identities in Northern Ireland, but has also intensified existing tensions and kept them at a high level for the past thirty-something years. Violence in Northern Ireland is not only a matter of paramilitary groups, the army and the police. It also occurs in the form of spontaneous and organized rioting and clashes between infuriated mobs and between them and the security forces. While these are better understood in terms of occasionally deteriorating relationships between sections of the two communities, the campaigns of Loyalist and Republican paramilitary organizations are a valuable source for analysing the reasoning of the radical factions in each community.[16] This will provide a deeper understanding of how the conflict as such is perceived and how the actions of the respective "other" side are interpreted. Such an analysis can then be used as a further element in an informed assessment of the situation in Northern Ireland and the reasons for success and failure of various government policies to find a solution.

Republican Violence

Violence by Republican paramilitaries has accounted for the greatest number of deaths by far in Northern Ireland as a whole. This overall picture, however, needs to be clarified in a number of important ways. Between 1969 and 1994, the time when the first ceasefires were announced in the recent peace process, Republican paramilitaries were responsible for more than half of all lives lost in the Northern Ireland conflict (58.8 per cent), and killed more than twice as many people as their Loyalist counterparts, and about six times as many as the security forces. Almost exactly one-half of their victims (50.7 per cent) were members of the security forces, about half from within and half from without Northern Ireland, but more than one-third (37.1 per cent) were civilians, including not only innocent bystanders but, for example, also contract workers for the "Crown forces". Loyalist paramilitaries, apart from the security forces, the other direct adversaries of Republican paramilitaries, accounted for only 1.5 per cent of their victims, while infighting among Republican paramilitary organizations and splinter groups caused significantly more casualties (10.7 per cent).[17]

As regards the religion of Republican paramilitaries' civilian victims, the greatest number of their victims were Protestants (37.4 per cent), which amounts to almost three-quarters of all Protestant deaths in the conflict. At the same time, they were responsible for most of the deaths among people whose religion could not be established (89.4 per cent) or among people from outside Northern Ireland (94.6 per cent). A quarter of all Catholics killed between 1969 and 1994 died as a direct consequence of Republican paramilitary action.

Even though the status of victims – civilian, Loyalist or Republican paramilitary, security forces – suggests a non-sectarian campaign against selected target groups with a high number of civilian bystanders killed, a look at the religion of these victims reveals that, in its results, Republican paramilitary warfare had a sectarian outcome.

Loyalist Violence

Loyalist paramilitaries have also contributed significantly to the overall death toll in Northern Ireland since 1969. Of all victims killed in the conflict,

Loyalist paramilitary violence has accounted for 29 per cent of them, of which 87.5 per cent were civilians. The next highest percentage of victims were from within the Loyalist paramilitary community itself (6.5 per cent), followed by Republican paramilitaries (4.3 per cent), and members of the security forces (1.2 per cent), most of them (91 per cent) from Northern Ireland.

As regards the religion of their victims, Loyalist paramilitaries killed almost half of all Catholic victims in the conflict (49.6 per cent), which equals more than three quarters (75.5 per cent) of all victims of Loyalist paramilitary violence.

These figures qualify the Loyalist campaign "in defence of their ancient rights" as one that has been strongly sectarian and very indiscriminate in the selection of targets and demonstrates the very wide concept of who and what is perceived as threatening.

The three major Loyalist paramilitary organizations are the Ulster Volunteer Force (UVF), the Ulster Defence Association (UDA), which has also operated under the cover name Ulster Freedom Fighters (UFF), and the Loyalist Volunteer Force (LVF). The UDA and UVF have operated under the Combined Loyalist Military Command (CLMC) and generally coordinated their strategy. However, during the final months of the talks process in 1997/98 the joint Loyalist command structure collapsed.[18]

Violence and Community Relations

Violence, and its increasing acceptance as a means to achieve political objectives among some sections of both communities, has had an impact on community relations and vice versa at three levels – segregation, polarization and alienation.[19] Violence may not be the primary cause for, or result of, any of these three dimensions of community relations, yet there is a strong interrelation between them.

Segregation, although it has been a long-term trend, has increased as a result of inter-communal violence. This was the case especially in the late 1960s and early 1970s, but on a lower level it has continued in subsequent decades. While intimidation from the "other" community and fear of violence have contributed to increasing residential segregation, peer pressure from within one's own community has also played a role in establishing the largely segregated structure of residence in Northern Ireland today. Segregation has important consequences in societies affected by interethnic conflict because it makes it easier to develop and maintain stereotypes about the other community and its intentions towards one's own community. Because of this, there will be even less understanding for the position of the other community, which, in its rejection, increases homogeneity and solidarity within one's own community. On this basis, violence against this other community becomes more easily acceptable and justifications for its use are more readily available.[20]

This is also the basis upon which polarization grows. The degree to which both communities differ in their perceptions of the nature of the Northern Ireland conflict and its potential solutions is influenced by more or less informed judgements about the other community and its political agenda. Violence and the interpretation of violent acts is likely to reinforce polarization. At the same time, the stark polarization between the two communities over what could be an acceptable and desirable future for Northern Ireland, and the inability to reach an agreement by peaceful means increased the preparedness of some sections within each community to engage in violence to either achieve their goals or, at least, prevent the other community from achieving theirs.

The lack of political progress over almost thirty years of violent conflict and the inability of the security forces to provide protection from acts of terrorist violence has also contributed, though unequally, to an increasing alienation of both communities from the British state and its institutions. While this has always been a feature of the relationship between the Nationalist community and Stormont and later the British political systems, alienation has also affected the Unionist community, especially after the Anglo-Irish Agreement and after the recent Good Friday Agreement. The sense of being left alone with unresolved problems has triggered processes in both communities in which paramilitary organizations have partly replaced organs of the state. This is more obvious and widespread within sections of the Nationalist community, where paramilitaries not only "protect" their community from sectarian attacks, but also police it and provide a number of community "services". Unionist alienation from the United Kingdom has its origins in the early days of partition in the 1920s when national political parties withdrew from campaigning in Northern Ireland, thus encouraging the build-up of an almost exclusively sectarian party system for decades to come. Likewise, the creation of a parliament in Northern Ireland was not the preferred option of Unionists because it marked Northern Ireland as different from the rest of the United Kingdom;[21] yet having a parliament elected by popular vote was at the same time perceived as a safeguard against a British sell-out, and thus still an option with a fairly positive connotation.

Community relations that are based on the historic experience of inequality, deprivation and discrimination are more likely to form the background against which intercommunal violence can develop and escalate. In general, the acceptability of violence has not only affected inter- but also intracommunity relations. Feuds between rival paramilitary groups in each community, such as the Loyalist turf wars of summer 2000, and punishment beatings, expulsions of individuals and entire families, intimidation and so on, have contributed to a deterioration of social relations, decline in trust in the effectiveness of state institutions to perform essential functions, and widespread disillusionment with the political process in Northern Ireland for several decades. With regard to civil society, Northern Ireland shows levels of social and political participation, cooperation and trust within each community that are quite high compared to those across the communities, that is, civil society is similarly polarized and organized along the fundamental ethnonationalist fault line as the rest of society. In fact, one can speak of two separate civil societies in Northern Ireland. This, too, is part of the complicated sociopolitical background against which conflict resolution policies in Northern Ireland must be judged.

The declaration of ceasefires by the major paramilitary organizations on both sides in 1994 and 1997 and their continuation despite opposition to the Good Friday Agreement from sections within both communities indicates that there is a growing understanding that it will not be possible to achieve any stable settlement of the conflict through violence. This, however, does not mean that the structure of community relations in Northern Ireland could not facilitate a renewed violent escalation of the conflict despite the settlement achieved in the Good Friday Agreement. Even though this may not lead to the same degree of guerrilla and sectarian warfare as before 1994, community relations could continue to deteriorate further as a result of, and cause for, violent eruptions. As the Good Friday Agreement is built largely on the assumption of the possibility and desirability of intercommunal cooperation, and as its implementation crucially depends upon the cooperation of both communities, violence has the potential to destroy the agreement, mostly because of the structure of communal interests and the design of the institutional process envisaged by the agreement.

Establishing the Conditions for an Inclusive Political Process?

Any durable solution, except for partition and/or resettlement (inasmuch as these can be considered durable), for a conflict such as the one in Northern Ireland requires a minimal but broad consensus among political leaders and the population at large about the desirability of a common future.

The balance sheet of British government policy in this respect is very mixed, and at the bottom line has not achieved its main goal. Despite managing to achieve fairer representation of both communities at all levels of the political process, government policy over the past thirty-something years failed to create the foundation upon which such a broadly supported political consensus could emerge. On the contrary, an analysis of the electoral process provides evidence, especially from recent elections, which suggests that the two communities as a whole support more hardline political parties and are politically moving even further apart (see Figures 4A.3 and 4A.4 in the Appendix).

Balance of Political Power between and within the Communities[22]

The two most important trends in relation to the balance of political power in Northern Ireland over the past 30 years are that the political influence[23] of Nationalist parties has grown at the expense of the Unionist community and that, at the same time, the diversity of political parties within all the three party blocs – Nationalist, Unionist and cross-communal – has increased.

The Unionist bloc consists of the UUP, the DUP and a number of smaller, and over time different, Unionist parties. The two main contenders for the Nationalist vote have been, since 1982, the SDLP and Sinn Féin. Between

1973 and 1982, the SDLP competed with a number of smaller Nationalist parties. Before 1973, the Nationalist Party, the Republican Labour Party and occasional independent candidates ran in elections. The most persistent element of the cross-communal bloc has been the APNI. Until 1977, its main competitor was the Northern Ireland Labour Party, after 1981, it was the Worker's Party, and more recently the Northern Ireland Women's Coalition. Other parties whose position cannot be determined on the confessional/non-confessional scale, such as the Natural Law Party, have also contested elections. The general trend of vote distribution among the three major blocs is exemplified in Figure A4.3 in the Appendix.

The increasing diversification within each of the blocs has had different effects. In the Unionist bloc, it has meant that the UUP, although it has just managed to retain its leading position (except in European elections, where the DUP has always been the strongest party), has lost votes and seats, mostly to its main contender, the DUP. This split of Unionist votes had the effect that the SDLP, for a brief but significant moment in Northern Ireland's recent history, became the party with highest percentage share of votes in the 1998 assembly elections.

In the Nationalist camp, the SDLP was unquestionably the stronger performer in elections until 2001, and has always, with some exceptions in the 1980s, won more than 20 per cent of the vote. Sinn Féin after a good performance in the early 1980s, lost significant electoral support after the Anglo-Irish Agreement, but could regain most of it and win new voters from the early 1990s onwards when the party managed to establish itself more credibly as a democratic, non-violent political force.[24] In both the 2001 Westminster and local-government elections, Sinn Féin has out-polled the SDLP and has become the strongest political force in the Nationalist community.

The APNI has always been the dominant party in the cross-communal sector, yet its electoral performance has only been satisfactory at local and provincial level and after the introduction of the Single Transferable Vote system (STV). The Worker's Party never had a share of more than 3 per cent of the valid vote. The Northern Ireland Women's Coalition, however, has managed to win seats both in the 1996 Forum and in the 1998 assembly elections.

In general, the balance of power has been altered at local and provincial levels towards fairer representation of the Nationalist and cross-communal vote with the introduction of STV. In parliamentary elections, the plurality system is still in operation for the 18 Northern Ireland constituencies, but the overall increase in Nationalist votes has brought about a more balanced representation of the electorate in Westminster as well. On the other hand, the success of Sinn Féin and the DUP at the expense of the more moderate and consensus-oriented SDLP and UUP suggests that attitudes towards the most recent settlement attempt – the Good Friday Agreement – are hardening in both communities. Against this background it is unlikely that the Good Friday Agreement will become the long-term acceptable framework in which the Northern Ireland conflict will finally be resolved for good.

AFTERWORD: NORTHERN IRELAND SINCE THE GOOD FRIDAY
AGREEMENT—STABILITY OR COLLAPSE OF THE PEACE PROCESS

Faced with the imminent collapse of the political institutions created
by the Good Friday Agreement, and under considerable national and
international pressure following the terrorist attacks on the USA and
the arrest of three alleged IRA members in Colombia, Sinn Féin publicly
called on the IRA in October 2001 to begin decommissioning its weapons,
which was followed by a subsequent announcement of the Independent
International Commission on Decommissioning that a first set of arms and
other equipment had been put beyond use. At the time it seemed that the
importance of this development could hardly be overestimated for the
future of the peace process in Northern Ireland. Devolved government was
duly restored within a matter of weeks. Yet, only a year later the next crisis
hit the peace process. Following allegations of an IRA spy ring gathering
intelligence at the Northern Ireland Assembly, the UUP withdrew from
government, prompting yet another suspension of the institutions. Intensive
negotiations over the following months bore no fruit and elections, initially
scheduled for May 2003, were first postponed and then cancelled. When a
carefully choreographed sequence of events that was supposed to lead to
the restoration of devolved government collapsed because the UUP was
not satisfied with the degree of transparency of a crucial round of IRA
decommissioning and refused to rejoin the Northern Ireland Executive, the
British government called the elections for November 2003. The result was
a sea change in the composition of the Northern Ireland assembly, with the
DUP and Sinn Féin emerging as the strongest parties.

Over the following nine months, it proved impossible to put the institutions
in Northern Ireland back on track. Intensive negotiations over the summer
of 2004 involving the DUP and Sinn Féin (mediated by the British and Irish
governments, since the DUP continued to refuse to engage in direct talks with
Sinn Féin) led to top-level negotiations at Leeds Castle, Kent, in September.
The key problems facing the negotiators were to achieve a complete
decommissioning of paramilitary weapons and an end to all paramilitary
activity, on the one side, and reforms of the institutions established under the
Agreement that would protect the basic bargain achieved in 1998 and at the
same time enable the DUP to sit in government with Sinn Féin, on the other.
When it emerged that the IRA was prepared to accept decommissioning
and an end to its activities, the focus of the negotiations shifted to the
DUP's preparedness to play an active and constructive role in the devolved
government.

Though no agreement was reached at Leeds Castle, it appears that
significant progress was made and that a formula now exists which might
allow the parties to overcome the hurdles still existing before a restoration
of the power-sharing institutions in Northern Ireland is possible. While it
remains to be seen whether the peace process can be reinvigorated, there is at
least sufficient evidence to suggest that a return to violence is highly unlikely.
It is also significant that the British government proposed an amendment
to the current decommissioning legislation, extending the amnesty period

from the end of February 2002 initially until 2003, with possible further extensions until 2007. Despite Unionist and Conservative concerns that this would take the pressure off the paramilitary groups, the Northern Ireland Decommissioning (Amendment) Bill was passed in the House of Commons on 9 January 2002 and sent to the House of Lords where it also passed before receiving Royal Assent.

The overall trend of decreasing violence has been reversed since 2001 with acts of spontaneous and organized mob and paramilitary violence once again becoming a feature of Northern Irish politics. The months-long stand-off and clashes between Catholics and Protestants around the Holy Cross Girls' Primary School in the Ardoyne area of North Belfast, the murder of a Catholic postal worker and the, subsequently withdrawn, UDA threat against Catholic schoolteachers and postal workers, as well as the threat by the Republican paramilitary group INLA against the Protestant staff at a Marks & Spencer distribution centre testify to the persistence of sectarian divisions and mindsets in Northern Ireland. However, what is equally, if not more significant, is that the murder of the Catholic postal worker was not only widely condemned by representatives from all major political parties in Northern Ireland, but also led to thousands of people from both communities participating in rallies against hatred and sectarianism. By the same token, it is interesting to observe that the clashes around the Holy Cross Girls' Primary School did not spread across Northern Ireland or even lead to wider rioting in Belfast itself, as similar events did over the past years. What this indicates is a decreasing acceptance of violence as a useful means to achieve political aims and, as such, points to a change in the overall political climate in Northern Ireland over the past several years that must not be underestimated in its significance for conflict resolution.

In terms of party politics, one of the smaller Unionist parties, the UDP, which functioned as the political arm of the UDA was dissolved in late 2001, because its strategy of support for the Good Friday Agreement was at odds with the withdrawal of support for the peace process by the UDA. The significance of this development lies in the implication that opponents of the peace process become increasingly marginalized even within their own communities, but that they at the same time become more radicalized, too. On the other hand, the 2003 elections saw contradictory developments in the two main communities—Sinn Féin and the DUP were returned as the strongest parties. Even though they are both committed to a durable peace in Northern Ireland, they have very different views on how to achieve it. The DUP insists on a renegotiation of the Agreement and a complete disbanding of all paramilitary groups, especially the IRA, while Sinn Féin has campaigned on a platform of full implementation of the Agreement. Little surprise then that compromise between the two parties has yet to be reached.

This is evidence of increasing polarization between the two communities: Nationalists and Republicans remaining committed to the original Agreement of 1998, while the decreasing confidence of Unionists that the Good Friday Agreement provides a workable framework within which the Northern

Ireland conflict cannot only be managed but eventually also be resolved was the basis on which the DUP was able to increase its share in the vote and become the strongest political party in the Unionist community. The current impasse in Northern Ireland, therefore, must not be underestimated in its potential impact for the future of institutional structures of conflict management, with scenarios ranging from minor cosmetic changes to the Good Friday Agreement, to wholesale reform and to a new Anglo-Irish agreement instituting a new form of direct rule. At the same time, the current impasse should not be overestimated in its consequences for the Northern Ireland conflict as a whole. There is no indication whatsoever that any of the parties will resume a campaign of violence in pursuit of its political goals. Thus, the conflict in Northern Ireland at present may remain unresolved, but it is well contained.

NOTES

* The following draws freely and extensively on previous publications, including Wolff 2001a, 2001b, 2002a, 2002b, 2003a and 2003b, 2004 and 2005. I would like to acknowledge the support of the British Academy for conducting fieldwork in Northern Ireland. Thanks are due to the participants of the Fifth International conference of the Ethnic Studies Network in Derry/Londonderry, Northern Ireland in 2001, to Mari Fitzduff, Colin Irwin and John Darby, Brendan O'Leary and Caroline Kennedy-Pipe for comments on earlier drafts of this paper, and to Lucy Marcus. The usual disclaimer applies.

1 A more detailed overview of the various interpretations of the Northern Ireland conflict can be found in McGarry and O'Leary (1996).
2 As part of the Good Friday Agreement, the Irish Constitution has been modified in this respect.
3 The votes both received in the 1974 Westminster elections were cut down to one-third of the results they had achieved in the 1973 assembly elections. Part of the explanation lies in the different voting systems applied in both elections – PR for the assembly and plurality rule for the Westminster elections.
4 Invitations had also been issued to Unionist parties, who decided to boycott the event.
5 This was also facilitated by a shipment of weapons and equipment from Libya.
6 According to RUC statistics, the three years prior to the Anglo-Irish Agreement produced 195 deaths, 2342 injuries, 716 shooting incidents, 607 explosions and 1708 armed robberies. The respective figures for 1986–88 are: 247 deaths (+27 per cent), 3661 injuries (+56 per cent), 1132 shootings (+58 per cent), 661 explosions (+9 per cent) and 2253 armed robberies (+31 per cent). This increase was not necessarily a direct effect of the Anglo-Irish Agreement as O'Leary and McGarry (1993, 270–273) have shown.
7 An inquiry set up to investigate this accusation found evidence that there was a conspiracy within the security forces to pervert the cause of justice, but no charges against anyone were ever brought.
8 It needs to be mentioned, however, that the Irish government continuously consulted with the SDLP, while the British government had no contact with Unionists during the negotiations. This contributed to the strengthening of Unionist fears and the weakening of moderates. At the same time, this Irish policy was not unanimously embraced in the Republic either – both Ian Gow and

Mary Robinson resigned over this issue. (Personal communication from Antony Alcock.)

9   This was part of the permanent institutional framework set up by the Anglo-Irish Agreement.

10   On Thursday 21 October 1993, ten people (nine civilians and one IRA member) were killed when a bomb exploded prematurely in a fish shop on the Shankill Road in Belfast.

11   Part of the reason for the lack of progress was the British insistence that the decommissioning of paramilitary weapons had to precede Sinn Féin's admission to formal multi-party talks. This pre-condition was set by the Tory party after the negative response by Unionists to the Framework Documents. It somehow reflects the wider problems of the Conservative government and its decreasing majority in Westminster (O'Leary 1997, 672).

12   The Conservative Party (by then in office for seventeen years) had suffered for a long time from what O'Leary calls the "talking and not talking to terrorists syndrome". However, under the government of John Major, parts of the Tory elite became more flexible. While they did not effectively exclude the possibility of negotiations with Sinn Féin (before the 1997 elections were called), their initial over-extensive talks about talks and the burdening of the latter with the decommissioning issue did not have a positive impact on the peace process (O'Leary 1997, 672f.).

13   Former US Senator George Mitchell played a major role as chair of the negotiation process. In general, American influence (both the Irish-American lobby and the Clinton Administration), and pressure, on all negotiating parties was among the facilitating factors of the Good Friday Agreement.

14   A more detailed discussion of the Good Friday Agreement can be found in O'Leary (1999).

15   According to Fay et al. (1998) the death toll was 3225.

16   According to O'Duffy (1995, 741f.), "Changes in the intensity and targets of Republican violence can best be explained by three instrumental factors related to political context: strategic objectives, the effects of security policy (upon opportunity structures), and the organisational strength of each paramilitary group."

17   A part of this high number of self-inflicted casualties has also been caused by prematurely exploded bombs and accidents in the production and handling of explosives.

18   This has also resulted in the emergence of splinter groups that have not called ceasefires, such as the Red Hand Defenders.

19   For a specific case study on these three aspects of community relations see Hamilton (1990).

20   One other feature of segregation in Northern Ireland is the maintenance of a confession-based school system with only few opportunities for integrated schooling.

21   Personal communication from Antony Alcock.

22   All data from http://cain.ulst.ac. uk/issues/politics/election/elect.htm. A good overview of party-political developments between 1969 and 1989 is O'Leary and McGarry (1993, 185ff.).

23   Measured in seats won in elections at local, provincial and parliamentary level.

24   Evans and O'Leary (1997, 674) identify two sources of Sinn Féin support – politically the party has benefited from being identified with the "first peace process", demographically Sinn Féin's strength is that a large number (60 per cent) of voters belong to the 18–34 age cohort.

APPENDIX

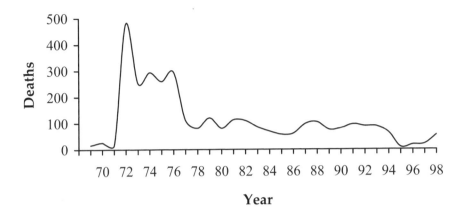

Figure 4A.1 Conflict-related deaths in Northern Ireland 1969–1998

Source: Sutton Index of Deaths

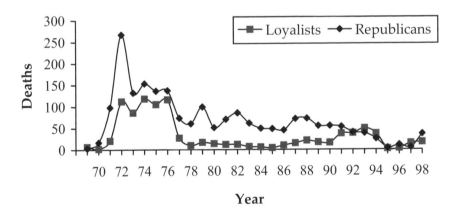

**Figure 4A.2 Conflict-related deaths in Northern Ireland 1969–1998 by
paramilitaries**

Source: Sutton Index of Deaths

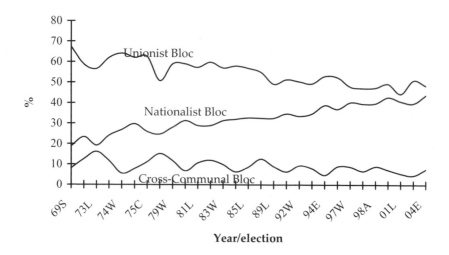

Figure 4A.3 Election performance of the three major party blocs in Northern Ireland 1973–2001

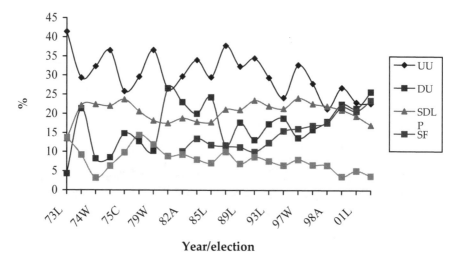

Figure 4A.4 Election performance of major political parties in Northern Ireland 1973–2003

Key for Figures 4A. 3 and 4A.4:

S	Stormont	C	Constitutional Convention
W	Westminster	L	Local
F	Peace Forum	A	Northern Ireland Assembly
E	European		

REFERENCES

Evans, G. and O'Leary, B. (1997), "Frameworked Futures: Intransigence and Flexibility in the Northern Ireland Elections of May 30 1996", *Irish Political Studies* 12, 23-47
Fay, M. T. et al. (1998), "Mapping Troubles-Related Deaths in Northern Ireland 1969–1994" <http://cain.ulst.ac.uk/issues/violence/cts/tables.htm>
Hamilton, A. (1990), *Violence and Communities* (Coleraine: University of Ulster Press)
McGarry, J. and O'Leary, B. (1996), *Explaining Northern Ireland: Broken Images* (Oxford: Blackwell)
O'Duffy, B. (1995), "Violence in Northern Ireland 1969–1994: sectarian or ethno-national?", *Ethnic and Racial Studies* 18:4, 740–771
O'Leary, B. (1995), "Afterword: What is Framed in the Framework Documents", *Ethnic and Racial Studies* 18:4, 862–872
____ (1997), "The Conservative Stewardship of Northern Ireland, 1979–1997: Sound-Bottomed Contradiction or Slow Learning?", *Political Studies* 45:2, 663–676
____ (1999), "The Nature of the British-Irish Agreement", *New Left Review* 233, 66–96
O'Leary, B. and McGarry, J. (1993), *The Politics of Antagonism: Understanding Northern Ireland* (London: Athlone Press)
Sutton Index of Deaths <http://cain.ulst.ac.uk/sutton/>
Wolff, S. (2001a), "Context and Content: Sunningdale and Belfast Compared", in Rick Wilford (ed.), *Aspects of the Belfast Agreement* (Oxford: Oxford University Press)
____ (2001b), "The Road to Peace? Conflict Resolution in Northern Ireland 1972–1998", *World Affairs* 163:4, 163–170
____ (2002a), "The Peace Process in Northern Ireland since 1998: Success or Failure of Post-Agreement Reconstruction?", *Civil Wars* 5 (1)
____ (2002b), "The Peace Process in Northern Ireland since 1998", in Jörg Neuheiser and Stefan Wolff (eds), *Peace at Last? The Impact of the Good Friday Agreement on Northern Ireland* (New York and Oxford: Berghahn)
____ (2003a), "From Sunningdale to Belfast, 1973–98", in Jörg Neuheiser and Stefan Wolff (eds), *Peace at Last? The Impact of the Good Friday Agreement on Northern Ireland* (New York and Oxford: Berghahn)
____ (2003b), *Disputed Territories: The Transnational Dynamics of Ethnic Conflict Settlement* (New York and Oxford: Berghahn)
____ (2004), "The Institutional Structure of Regional Consociations. A Comparative Analysis of Brussels, Northern Ireland and South Tyrol", *Nationalism and Ethnic Politics* 10:4, 387–414
____ (2005), "Between Stability and Collapse: Internal and External Dynamics of Post-agreement Institution-building in Northern Ireland", in Sid Noel (ed.), *From Power Sharing to Democracy* (Montreal and Kingston: McGill-Queen's University Press)

5 The Decline of PKK and the Viability of a One-State Solution in Turkey

MATTHEW ADAM KOCHER

As recently as 1998, the foremost expert on Kurdish history wrote:

> The conflict between the Republic of Turkey and a large part of its Kurdish population continues to be escalating. On both sides moderates have had to yield to hardliners, and the prospects for a peaceful settlement are not very bright. If wisdom does not prevail – and there are as yet no signs that it will – we are likely to witness an ongoing confrontation of increasing violence and brutality in which either the Kurdish secessionist movement is physically destroyed or the social costs of the war become so high to Turkey that the as yet unthinkable alternative, secession, will come to be considered as the best solution (Bruinessen 1998).

Despite the steadily declining battlefield fortunes of the Parti Karkaren Kurdistan (PKK)[1] during the second half of the 1990s, most observers agreed with Bruinessen's assessment and argued for the necessity of a political compromise by the Turkish state.[2] They insisted that the state's single-minded focus on a military response to PKK would only further polarize identity and opinion, turning peaceful civilians into militants.

Developments in Turkey since the late 1990s pose a puzzle for this analysis. As of 2002, the Kurdish Southeast of Turkey is largely pacified. PKK guerrillas have withdrawn across the Iraqi border. Abdullah Öcalan, the PKK leader, languishes in the island prison of Imralı. Emergency rule has been lifted in all but four provinces. For all intents and purposes, PKK is no longer a military presence in Turkey. Moreover, this outcome was achieved without the granting of *any* important concessions by the state.

If violence results from frustrated ethnopolitics, then we should not be seeing what we are seeing in Turkey. What Bozarslan (1996) calls the "policy of *aggiornamento*" should have caused an increase in militancy rather than

93

its decline. Instead, since the capture of Abdullah Öcalan in February 1999, a new political movement has begun to emerge in Turkey that favours electoral competition and non-institutional pressure tactics over violence. Only since the collapse of militancy has the government begun to make hesitant steps toward concessions.

The failure of those with the best area knowledge to foresee these events resulted, I believe, from flawed theory: in particular, a tendency to conflate distinct processes of conflict and violence (Brubaker and Laitin 1998). Violence is neither a natural nor an inevitable consequence of ethnic politics, even when political demands are not satisfied. Organized violence is always the product of organizations designed for violence, and violent organizations are not reducible to the social groups they purport to represent. PKK managed to build an impressive base of both active and passive popular support in the early 90s, but it remained throughout an organization built for war and dedicated to winning compliance and control. PKK lost its war to a determined enemy using an effective counterinsurgency strategy.

The civilian population of the Kurdish region was profoundly affected by the civil war that raged from 1984 to 1999. Many were killed; vast numbers were uprooted from their lands. The effects of insurgency and counterinsurgency on their ethnic identities and political views are difficult to measure, but it would be a caricature to treat the conflict as one that pitted rigid ethnic blocs against each other. Although the civil war appears to have had a polarizing effect on *some* Kurds, that result was not universal. The evidence suggests that ethnic boundaries in Turkey continue to be porous and multifaceted, while ethnicity is only one of the factors that influence political opinion.

The strategy of this volume, disaggregating violence, identity and opinion, is therefore well suited to analysing Kurdish politics, because the effect of Turkish government policy on each component of the ethnic research agenda is distinct. This chapter is divided into three main sections, each addressing one of these three dependent variables. In the first section, I argue that PKK/state violence is best described as a classic rural insurgency, rather than a popular uprising. The state's counterinsurgency campaign was effective in defeating it, and similar violence is unlikely to arise in the future due mainly to rapid urbanization. The second section addresses identity. I argue that, despite the civil war, the boundaries of Kurdish identity are more open than is often appreciated. Although polarization has occurred for some individuals, processes of assimilation continue simultaneously, and further ethnification is not inevitable. In the third section, I address support for Kurdish nationalism by examining returns from three recent elections. Although Kurdish nationalist parties have been competitive, the majority of Kurdish voters favoured rightist and Islamist parties, which suggests that support for nationalism is weaker than usually thought. I conclude by discussing some of the policy implications of this case.

Note on Terminology

The "Kurdish question" is fraught with semantic discord. The state insists that use of the term "Kurdistan" implies an endorsement of secession; Kurdish nationalists argue that terms like "the Southeast" are euphemistic, intended to deny their existence as a distinct group. Similarly, the state argues that calling PKK violence "civil war" legitimates the organization; they prefer "terrorist".

There is no way out of these arguments except to state one's prejudices. I do not believe the legitimacy of ethnonational claims to political status can be decided in ideal terms. A Kurdish state has no more, *or less*, right to exist than states based on any of the other identities that cross-cut or sub-divide Kurdish identity. I concur with Levy (2000, ch. 3), who argues that a generalized right to self-determination is incoherent. When identities overlap and crosscut, granting self-determination to one group *entails* denying it to others.

Given that I do not endorse one side, I use the terms that identify the region interchangeably. Although terror has been part of PKK's (and the state's) repertoire, it has been the predominant tactic of neither. By historical standards, the 5424 civilians reported killed from 1984 to 1999 (US DOS 2000) is extraordinarily low, and suggests selectivity and restraint by both parties to the violence.[3] The violence in south-east Turkey satisfies scholarly definitions of civil war, insurgency, and ethnic violence, and I use all three in ways that are consistent with that literature.

VIOLENCE AND DEMOGRAPHIC SHIFT

In this section, I argue that Turkey is unlikely to return to the violence of the period 1984–99, regardless of the degree to which it accommodates Kurdish nationalist demands. The reason for this is fundamentally strategic, not political. The civil war in Kurdistan was a rural insurgency, not a popular uprising, and while south-eastern Turkey was ideally suited to guerrilla warfare in the early 1980s, it is no longer. The civil war has fundamentally altered the demographics of the region, inducing vast internal migration and rapid urbanization. Insurgency warfare is a rural phenomenon and cannot be resurrected in the new urban landscapes of Kurdish life. Though we will likely continue to see ethno-national political activity in Kurdistan, some of which may overflow non-violent boundaries, the coming years are unlikely to witness a return to generalized violence.

There are two dominant narratives about the Kurdish region prior to the civil war. On the one hand, the region is described as prostrate under state repression (McDowall 2000, 402). The second narrative identifies the region as lawless and neglected by authorities. Yalman (1971, 213) describes the area around Diyarbakir as "[V]ery unsettled. The law is weak and distant. Only tough men can survive the ruthlessness of the struggle. The landlord who is weak loses all he has and may, indeed, have to write off very considerable and valuable property as a total loss." In Yalçın-Heckmann's (1991) description of life in a Kurdish village, relations with the state were arbitrary, but sporadic. Before the civil war, Kurdistan was predominantly rural, with low population density: 62 per cent of the inhabitants lived in villages and there may have been as many as 36 000 settlements of less than 2000 persons (McDowall 2000, 400). These ethnographic accounts suggest that the state was both repressive and weak. Indeed, the two factors may be linked; established states typically use more and more arbitrary violence in regions they control less fully (Ron, 2003).

The civil war inaugurated by the PKK in 1984, was not a spontaneous uprising. The PKK was formed by Kurdish militants who splintered from Turkish Marxist-Leninist youth groups in the mid-1970s. Left–right violence was endemic to urban areas of Turkey in the late 1970s; it largely crosscut the Turkish–Kurdish divide. Öcalan's fledgling organization was in the minority in adopting an ethnic and separatist orientation. The PKK attacked landlords and rightists in the Siverek region in the late 1970s. The organization was largely rolled up following the coup d'etat of 12 September 1980. A small number of activists, including Öcalan, escaped to Syria, where they were supported with sanctuary, weapons and training in a bid to destabilize Turkey. The PKK had no popular base at this time; Öcalan himself admits that Syrian support was crucial to the organization's survival and development (İmset 1992, 25).

The civil war began as a series of cross-border raids staged from sanctuaries in northern Iraq (İmset 1992, 38–41). The initial wave of militants often had few ties to the local inhabitants of the provinces where the insurgency began, coming instead from the original heartland of the PKK in Siverek. After a few tactically disastrous attacks against the security forces, the PKK adopted a strategy of targeting civilians: mayors, schoolteachers and tribal chiefs, anyone perceived as an actual or potential collaborator with the state (Barkey and Fuller 1998, 28; İmset 1992, 34–35, 44, 100).

PKK strategy conformed closely to classic Maoist principles of "revolutionary" war, what statist analysts call "insurgency" (Blaufarb and Tanham 1989). Rather than targeting the state's military forces, insurgency aims to create a climate of insecurity for all but large and well-armed elements of the state, reducing contact between the population and its government and undermining confidence in the state's ability to provide security and enforce its mandate. The ensuing void of authority is filled by insurgent counter-government, which is used to extract the intelligence, manpower, and resources needed for further operations. According to Öcalan, "Before anything else, there is the duty to bring the people to the stage of defending themselves and to make them believe, before anything else, that they need to be defended" (quoted in İmset 1992, 99).

The practice of basing one's logistics network on local production is charitably referred to as "revolutionary taxation", or less charitably as "looting". A sharp distinction between the two is difficult to sustain empirically (Kalyvas 2001b, 103). Villagers in insecure areas may wish to assist the guerrillas, or they may prefer directing scarce resources toward their families. Those who support insurgent goals may prefer that their neighbours shoulder the burden of paying for it. Whether giving to the guerrillas is free or coerced is difficult to determine, since it depends upon unobserved or off-the-equilibrium-path behaviour. A single beating or killing in the past, or the story of a similar incident elsewhere, may be sufficient to induce apparently voluntary compliance in the present.

In this sense, insurgents are no different from the state; both seek compliance from supporters and non-supporters alike. For this reason, students of counterinsurgency have long recognized that defeating insurgent strategy depends upon the state's ability to provide security for the population. Critics of counterinsurgency practice argue that security is a euphemism for control, and that legitimate governments have no need for coercive strategies. But, security and control are opposite sides of the same coin; a state that cannot protect its citizens from the coercion of other parties cannot gain their compliance for itself.

The key role of security explains why insurgency is an almost wholly rural phenomenon (Laqueur 1998, 403–4): defence is much easier when the population is concentrated. The Kurdish case is no exception; throughout the civil war, towns were state strongholds. During the period of its greatest success, the PKK contested the state for control of some district and provincial centres (Barkey and Fuller 1998, 29). However, in the force-on-force encounters that are required to take and hold towns, the PKK suffered dreadful losses (Barkey and Fuller 1998, 28).

The government's control over rural Kurdistan, however, steadily declined throughout the 1980s and early 1990s. Some observers believe that the Turkish military did not take the threat seriously enough during the early years of the insurgency (İmset 1992; Pope and Pope 1997). Consequently, the military stayed "inside the wire," instead of taking the battle to the enemy (Ron 1995). The state's strategy for rural defence mainly involved recruiting tribesmen into a local militia as *köy korucu* or village guards. The *korucu* and their families took the brunt of PKK attacks during this period, and the militia's numbers dwindled as the risks increased (İmset 1992, 100).

In the early 1990s, the state seems to have concluded that static defence of villages was a strategic failure. The security forces, while maintaining the *korucu* system, began driving civilians from their villages. "Evacuation", as this process is euphemistically described, is also a standard element of the counterinsurgent playbook. It aims to disrupt guerrilla logistics by physically removing the population. Evacuation concentrates populations in larger settlements, which can be effectively defended. The government pursued a less expensive variant of this strategy by accelerating existing processes of migration to the cities and towns. Direct action by the state was complemented by "voluntary" migration of people desperate to escape violence and economic collapse.

According to government estimates, 3236 settlements had been cleared in south-east Turkey as of 1999, forcibly displacing 362 915 persons (US DOS 2000, 18).[4] Villages were often destroyed to deny their use by guerrillas and prevent the return of residents. In some documented instances, these evacuations were carried out brutally. Soldiers met resistance with coercion: beatings, rapes and selective instances of extra-judicial killing (Ron 1995). However conducted, being forcibly removed from ancestral villages is a horrifying and life-altering event.

Table 5.1   Rapid urbanization of the Kurdish Provinces, 1990–97

Provinces	% Δ Population 1990–97	% Δ Rural population 1990–97	% Δ Urban population 1990–97
OHAL (13)	14.0	–11.9	44.5
Non- OHAL (67)	11.0	–4.0	20.9
Kurdish (21)	12.8	–10.3	39.8
Non-Kurdish (59)	11.0	–3.4	19.9
Kurdish non-OHAL (8)	11.4	–8.3	34.3

Provinces	% Rural 1990	% Rural 1997	% Δ Rural 1990–97
OHAL (13)	54.2	41.9	–14.0
Non- OHAL (67)	39.6	34.2	–5.4
Kurdish (21)	53.9	42.9	–11.0
Non-Kurdish (54)	38.2	33.2	–5.0
Kurdish non- OHAL (8)	53.7	44.1	–9.5

Source: T. C. Başbakanlık, Devlet İstatistik Enstitüsü

The civil war dramatically altered the demography of the Kurdish region. Table 5.1 presents statistics on the urbanization of Kurdistan that spanned the fiercest periods of violence, when the majority of evacuations took place. Two methods are used to identify the region. First, the 13 provinces that have been part of the emergency region (OHAL) are identified separately. Second, I distinguish 21 provinces that had more than 10 per cent mother-tongue speakers of Kurdish languages in the 1965 census (when language was last officially counted). Turkey identifies as an urban resident anyone who lives in a district centre.

According to the upper half of the table, the absolute size of the rural population in the OHAL provinces plunged by 11.9 per cent from 1990 to 1997, despite population growth of 14 per cent. The population of district centres in the same region jumped by 45 per cent. Simultaneously, the rural population of the rest of Turkey declined by 4 per cent, while urban areas grew by 21 per cent.

A direct comparison with base rates is misleading, however. While rural de-population in the OHAL region proceeded nearly three times faster than in the rest of Turkey, the population of OHAL was growing faster at the same time. Similarly, anecdotal evidence suggests many new migrants to the cities of western Turkey came from the South-east. A similar, though less dramatic, pattern is evident if we consider all 21 Kurdish provinces.

Table 5.1 shows that urbanization in Kurdistan changed dramatically from 1990 to 1997 in relative terms as well. In 1990, a far higher percentage of the population of Kurdistan lived in rural areas than did so in the rest of Turkey. By 1997, the Kurdish region was almost as urbanized as the rest of Turkey had been in 1990. Although urbanization was rapid across Turkey, it was 2–3 times as rapid in Kurdistan. South-east Turkey changed from a majority rural region to a majority urban region in only seven years.

It is impossible to directly test the effects of the civil war, but the data are suggestive. The Kurdish provinces outside OHAL almost certainly suffered much less from evacuation. That these provinces displayed rates of urbanization nearly as high as OHAL suggests that economic decline and general insecurity were more important causes of migration than previously appreciated.

However, even the dramatic statistics in Table 5.1 understate the urbanizing trend in Turkish Kurdistan. While Kurdish residents were moving from the villages to the towns, they were also favouring larger towns. Table 5.2 illustrates this pattern by disaggregating growth rates to the district level in Diyarbakir Province. The table displays percentage growth figures for rural and urban populations and raw figures for cumulative population change.

Districts are listed in increasing order of their 1997 population. First, these data confirm the effects demonstrated in Table 5.1. The absolute size of the rural population declined in all but two districts of Diyarbakir Province from 1990 to 1997, while the urban population grew in 11 out of 14 districts. The only significant rural population *gain* occurred in the district centre, the one town in the province with suburbs. Without this district, rural decline would have been twice as great. In addition, the two largest towns in the province, Bismil and Diyarbakir, accounted for 83 per cent of the total urban growth from 1990 to 1997, while three smaller towns in the province declined in population. In short, urban growth favoured the larger towns in Diyarbakir.

These data probably understate changes in rural concentration in one additional respect. The evacuations targeted high-altitude villages at a rate higher than more accessible settlements in valleys and near roads (Ron 1995, ch. 2). High-altitude villages tend to be smaller, because food production in mountainous areas cannot support high population densities. Small, scattered settlements were also more vulnerable to coercion and taxation by the PKK, and residents may have sought the relative security of larger villages.

The consequences of rural concentration for the PKK were consistent with the counterinsurgency paradigm:

> [F]rom 1996 the PKK found itself increasingly on the defensive, losing access to food and shelter because of the evictions and suffering an increasing level of

Table 5.2 **Rapid urbanization in Diyarbakir Province, 1990–97**

District	% Δ Rural Population 1990–97	District centre 1990–97 Cum. Δ Rural Population	% Δ Urban population 1990–97	District centre 1990–97 Cum. Δ Urban population
Kocaköy	−23.0	−2 567	19.3	819
Çunguş	−20.4	−5 248	5.2	1 022
Hazro	−36.5	−11 058	−25.5	−1 029
Lice	−73.5	−37 101	−20.2	−3 378
Egil	−1.0	−38 729	−7.2	−3 722
Hanı	4.0	−38 050	5.1	−3 194
Kulp	−56.4	−62 323	46.6	291
Dicle	−19.6	−68 322	140.4	7 891
Çermik	−1.7	−68 885	128.1	10 009
Çınar	−0.4	−69 048	56.3	15 684
Erganı	−4.8	−71 022	28.2	26 237
Silvan	−12.1	−77 105	22.8	39 894
Bismil	−15.1	−86 027	154.6	101 469
Province Centre	48.2	−43 737	34.2	231 965
Province Total	−9.0	−43 737	38.6	231 965

Source: T. C. Başbakanlık, Devlet İstatistik Enstitüsü

casualties. By 1996 the estimated number of deaths [total, since 1984] was 20 000. By 1999 they were thought to exceed 35 000. The area dominated by the PKK was unmistakably contracting. It was clear that guerrilla tactics were failing. (McDowall 2000, 442)

Far from forcing the population into the hands of PKK, the vast majority of civilians fled into government-controlled territory. Scholarly and journalistic reports amply attest to the rage that many migrants maintain against the state, but the expected nationalist explosions never materialized.

IDENTITY

In this section I discuss Kurdish identity. This reverses the usual order of presentation, in which violence is treated as the *consequence* of an identity cleavage. Fearon and Laitin (1996) have shown that it is a mistake to assume that identity causes violence; in fact, violence between ethnic groups is rare. In the preceding section, I argued that the rise and fall of the PKK depended on strategic factors that are largely independent of the ethnic identities and opinions of the population. However, if ethnic difference does not cause violence, it remains an open question what effect violence has on the perceptions and identities of the population. Kaufman (1996) has argued that the causes of ethnic violence are irrelevant to the policy question of how violence is to be contained, because violence turns cleavages into chasms, hardening formerly fluid identities into rigid boundaries.

By contrast, I argue that the boundaries between Turkish and Kurdish identity have historically been porous and crosscut by key religious cleavages. Although the civil war has caused ethnic boundaries to rigidify for some people, the surprising fact is that Turkish and Kurdish communities remain quite open to each other and societal-level tensions continue to be quite manageable. The trajectory of ethnic identity in Turkey is difficult to predict, but I argue (in this section and the following one) that the most likely future involves a Kurdish population that remains bilingual and integrated into mainstream political life.

In its broadest understanding, the term "Kurdish" applies to speakers of one of four closely related Indo-Iranian languages (Kurmanji, Sorani, Zaza, and Gurani), or descendants of people so identified who speak other languages (McDowall 2000, 9–10). The number of people who satisfy this criterion is unknown, but some observers place it in the range of 25 million persons (Randal 1999, 16), giving rise to the oft-repeated claim that Kurds are the "world's largest ethnic group without its own state". Broad-definition Kurds are located mainly in contiguous territory within the borders of Turkey, Iraq and Iran, with smaller indigenous populations in Syria and Armenia. Millions live as settled migrants in the cities of western Turkey, and large numbers have emigrated to the developed world, primarily Germany. The number of Kurds in Turkey is a subject of dispute. By a purely linguistic criterion, roughly 13 per cent of the population was Kurdish in the early 1990s (Kirişçi and Winrow 1997). If Turkish-speaking descendants of Kurds are included, the figure is certainly much higher.

The viability of the broad definition as the basis for a political identity, much less an actual state on the territory of Turkey, Iraq, and Iran, is minimal and does not appear to be on anyone's agenda in the region, though it probably has substantial support in the European diaspora. The borders in this region, though artificial, have had a profound effect on political and social identities: "In each of these countries, the modern world was only accessible through the state language; but the Kurds who were literate in Turkish and their fellow Kurds who used Arabic or Persian came to inhabit different symbolic universes" (Bruinessen 1998).

Turkish nation-building is often treated as a failed experiment, largely on the basis of Kurdish evidence, but this is a misunderstanding. In fact, Turkey has been more successful than most twentieth-century states in assimilating a diverse population to a relatively unified collective identity (Cornell 2001). Pre-republican Anatolia was exceptionally diverse. Even discounting non-Muslims, Turkey embraced large numbers of Kurds, Arabs, Laz, Circassians, Albanians, Pomaks and Greek-speaking Muslims. With the exception of Kurdish, these linguistic identities are not so much forgotten as they are politically inconsequential. Most people see no contradiction between being Laz and being Turkish.

Although assimilation is often characterized as forcing people to abandon their identity, this, too, is misleading. According to Bruinessen (1998): "More important, and ultimately much more successful [than violence], however, were the more peaceful means to which nation-building regimes everywhere have had recourse: compulsive general education, general conscription into the army (for males at least) and state-controlled radio and press." His understanding of Turkey is consistent with the literature on European nation-building, which generally treats benefits as more important than sanctions. The success of nation-building is probably attributable more than anything else to the relative openness of the Turkish opportunity structure. The Ruritanians of Gellner's (1983) modernization story found ample room for economic and political integration.

Kurds were no exception: "This difficulty [of assimilating them] was not so much due to the strength of Kurdish nationalism as to the Kurds' sheer numbers and the tribal social structure of their society" (Bruinessen 1998). Turks eagerly point to ethnic Kurds like Türgüt Özal (a former president of Turkey) and Ibrahim Tatlises (a singer and television personality, arguably Turkey's most popular media figure) as evidence of a common identity. Assimilation is often crudely rendered as selling out, but the reality is more complex. For many individuals, assimilation was essentially complete prior to the intense politicization of the 1980s. For others, being Kurdish and Turkish poses no contradiction; their political identity does not supervene on their cultural identity (Barkey and Fuller 1998, 81).

The processes of identity formation and change in Turkey are extremely fluid, and their future direction and magnitude are uncertain. Bruinessen (1998) sees assimilation in full retreat, but he draws heavily on observation of the European diaspora community, whose political dynamics are quite different from those within Turkey. Many activists and scholars believe the counterinsurgency campaign and state harassment of Kurdish politics has radicalized the population along ethnolinguistic lines (Wedel 2000; McDowall 2000; Pope and Pope 1997). There can be no doubt but that they are correct about an important segment of the population. Barkey and Fuller (1998, 82) suggest that ethnic mobilization and assimilation are occurring *simultaneously*.

Indeed, the institutions of nation-building, principally conscription and universal education, are still in place. Turkish national identity also has an autonomous capacity to reproduce and draw converts as well, given the degree to which individual life-chances are linked to the metropolitan identity.

The Kurdish region of Turkey is predominantly a bi- or multilingual region. Compulsory education is conducted entirely in Turkish, and conscription entails that Kurdish men will spend at least 550 days of their lives in an all-Turkish environment. Even in the east, a great deal of commerce, and of course all official discourse with the state, is conducted in Turkish. Consequently, it is unusual to meet Kurdish men who do not speak Turkish with a fairly high level of fluency.

In my judgement, there are formidable obstacles to the development of a literate Kurdish culture in Turkey which result from factors largely outside the state's control. Given the current paucity of Kurdish-language materials, a student trained to read only Kurdish would find little to read; a student trained in Kurdish and Turkish would read mostly Turkish if they read at all. Economic opportunities in Turkey are linked tightly to literacy in Turkish and European languages, especially in the urban areas. When I asked Kurdish informants in Turkey what language they would choose to teach their children if Kurdish became a realistic option, the most common choice was both: Turkish for opportunity, Kurdish for identity.

In addition to the porousness of identity in Turkey, there is a key religious distinction that directly crosscuts the Kurdish/Turkish cleavage. Although the majority of the residents of Anatolia are Sunni Muslims, as many as 30 per cent are members of religious groups that are historically and doctrinally related to Shi'ism (US LOC 1996). By far the largest of these groups is the Alevi, and this name is often used as shorthand for all Shi'ite-derived groups within Turkey. Roughly an equal proportion of Kurds and Turks are Alevi. Their confession was regarded as heretical by the state-monopoly Sunni Islam of the Ottoman Empire. The proclamation of a secular republic in 1925 was widely embraced by Alevis, who stood to gain from Atatürk's abrogation of the official Sunni religious monopoly. Mustafa Kemal is still especially revered among Alevis.

Scholars are divided as to the political consequences of the Alevi identity for Kurdish nationalism. Some believe that Alevi mobilization will further undermine the conceit of a unitary identity in Turkey. Others see the Alevi/Sunni division as weakening the unity of an appeal to Kurdishness.

At a social and cultural level, the Alevi/Sunni cleavage has traditionally been of far greater importance than any linguistic divisions. According to Yalman (1971, 214), in the Kurdish region "[A] Sunni Kurdish-speaker and Sunni Turkish-speaker are much closer to each other in every aspect of their culture and personality than either group is with, for instance, Turkish or Kurdish-speaking Alevi or Bektashi [another Shi'ite-related sect]." Intermarriage between ethnic Turks and Kurds is common; between Sunnis and Alevis, it is rare. The urban violence that convulsed Turkey in the late 1970s, though ideological, broke closely along religious lines. As recently as 1993, an anti-Alevi pogrom in Sivas took the lives of 37 people (Pope and Pope 1997, 324–5); despite the public passions roused by the civil war, there has been virtually no societal-level violence between Turks and Kurds (Cornell 2001). On the other hand, Kurdish Alevis have not been spared by the military's counter-insurgency campaign; Wedel (2000, 191) found

Kurdish Alevi migrants in one Istanbul neighbourhood mobilizing along the linguistic cleavage in response to their perception of state repression.

There is an unfortunate tendency in the literature on Kurdish politics to assume that Kurdishness is a more natural category and the direction that ethnogenesis *should* pursue. In Turkey, Kurdish identity is in at least a three-cornered fight with religious and state-national identity. All three have undoubted appeal. In the following section, I discuss some evidence on public opinion about Kurdish nationalism in south-east Turkey. This information has relevance, albeit more tenuously, for questions of identity, because it tells us something about the degree to which individuals are affected by ethnicity in the formation of opinion.

PUBLIC OPINION

In this section, I use data on voting behaviour as an indicator of Kurdish public opinion. The available evidence, though far from conclusive, suggests that supporters of Kurdish nationalism remain in the minority, even in the south-east, and despite the brutality and dislocation of the civil war. I argue that the Kurdish mainstream remains politically conservative and unwilling to embrace the leftist agenda of Turkey's only Kurdish party.

Public opinion is notoriously difficult to measure in war zones. When identifying combatants it is common, though erroneous, to call armies by the names of the groups they fight for (Kalyvas 2001b, 111). Thus, journalists often say that "the Kurds" have been waging a war for secession. In fact, at least twice as many Kurds were actively employed in the security forces than were members of PKK militias at the height of insurgent mobilization.[5] Of course, the latter is a measure only of *compliance*, not opinion: presumably both Turkish and Kurdish boys would rather have been doing something else. PKK is known to have engaged in kidnapping as a tool of recruitment (İmset 1992, 84–6), and Kurdish families have been subjected to revolutionary surcharges if their sons report for military service (Rosenberg 1994).

In Turkey, only the military claims to have conducted systematic opinion surveys. Their data have not been made available, and their bias is well known. The best-known independent survey of Kurdish opinion during the civil war found substantial support for Kurdish nationalism and very little support for secession, but it had an urban bias and was based on a sample of convenience.[6]

Anecdotal evidence on Kurdish opinion is abounding, but can be extremely misleading. In April 2000 the Istanbul correspondent for a major Western newspaper, who had travelled in and reported from Kurdistan extensively over a period of years, told me: "In the south-east, everyone supports Öcalan." When he was captured in 1999, Kurds staged demonstrations in cities across Turkey and Western Europe. However, "expressions of support", can mean many things. They can mean, "We respect this man who has fought for us", they can mean, "We support his goals and tactics", or they can mean, "We want this man to govern us". There is no necessary connection between these preferences. Most observers believe that very few Kurds in Turkey have ever supported secession, though it is widely believed that Kurdish-language broadcasting and education would be extremely popular. In casual conversations I had while travelling through south-east Turkey, I found people eager to insist that "This place is Kurdistan" (a punishable statement in Turkey), while simultaneously thanking God for the end of a war the Turkish military has so decisively won.

Journalists and travellers are subject to opposing biases. Travellers usually favour security, which means government control. Journalists often seek out controversy and conflict. They have very little interest in "the dog that does not bark", since it makes for poor copy. Nevertheless, in any war zone the absence of battle is far more common than its presence; civilians outnumber both activists and combatants.

All visitors to Turkey are probably subject to a bias in identifying Kurds as well. If one asks to meet Kurds, one is likely to be steered towards nationalists; if one asks "Turks" about their background, one often discovers Kurdish parents or grandparents. I have encountered people who are not entirely sure if they are Kurdish. "Discovering" one's Kurdishness is a common occurrence among Turkish citizens. One Kurmanji-speaking student I met in Istanbul griped to me about the *poseurs* who suddenly find they are Kurdish and seek him out for instruction on what to do.

The bottom line is that we do not know what the Kurds of Turkey believe and what they prefer. At best, we know what some think and want at a particular moment in time. Until systematic opinion studies by independent scholars are permitted, we simply cannot answer this question with any degree of precision.

There is one source of data on public opinion that has been somewhat neglected: election returns. Turkey was rare among states experiencing civil war in holding regular elections throughout the violence. These elections have generally been considered free and fair, though the Kurdish nationalist parties have at times been harassed by Turkish security services (US DOS 2000, 3). In the early- to mid-1990s, several members of Kurdish parties were gunned down in "mystery killings", presumably committed by government-supported contra-guerrillas.

Election data have drawbacks as indicators of opinion. Ideology and ethnicity are only two among many issues that matter to voters. Turkish parties are thought to be exceptionally "personalistic". Most observers think Turkish politics is more venal than in most democracies. It has been argued that Kurdish magnates can deliver their members en masse to political parties. The notion that tribesmen are manipulable has been badly damaged by ethnography (Yalçın-Heckmann 1991) showing that tribal politics involves complex two-way transactions, but bloc voting remains a reality that may undermine the conclusions that can be drawn from studying vote choice in Kurdistan. Nevertheless, electoral data have the benefits of systematicity and low measurement error. They are the best indicators we have regarding Kurdish opinion.

Table 5.3 gives vote share in selected provinces for the parties that garnered 94.2 per cent of the total vote in the 1999 general election. In this analysis I have collapsed together parties that occupy roughly the same ideological space. A single vote share is given for the centre-left Democratic Left Party (DSP) and Republican People's Party (CHP); the True Path Party (DYP) and the Motherland Party (ANAP) are treated as a centre-right bloc. The hard-right National Action Party (MHP), the Islamist Virtue Party (FP) and the Kurdish People's Democracy Party (HADEP) are treated separately. Of these seven parties, only five received seats in parliament; HADEP and CHP failed to meet the 10 per cent electoral threshold. Three groups of provinces are included: the thirteen OHAL provinces, the eight Kurdish provinces not included in OHAL ("other Kurdish provinces"), and four metropolitan areas in western Turkey that are thought to have large Kurdish populations.

Scholars have noted the failure of Kurdish nationalist parties to capture anything close to the presumed proportion of Kurds in the population of Turkey's western cities (Bozarslan 1996a; Bozarslan 1996b; Kirişçi and Winrow 1997). It is widely believed by residents that 20–30 per cent of the population of Istanbul is now Kurdish, but HADEP's best showing out of Istanbul's three electoral precincts in 1999 was 4.7 per cent. Bozarslan (1996a, 152), analysing HADEP's similar performance in the 1995 general election, comments: "This poor showing seems to indicate that the metropolitan cities continue to have an important integrative function that give [*sic*] birth to new political formations."

Table 5.3   Vote share for selected parties, 1999 General Elections (%)

1999 General Election	DYP/ ANAP	FP	MHP	DSP/ CHP	HADEP
Turkey	25.2	15.4	18.0	30.9	4.7
All Kurdish provinces	29.8	19.3	12.2	12.5	19.1
OHAL provinces	29.1	17.3	6.5	10.8	27.0
HADEP Max. (Hâkkari)	27.5	9.9	2.0	10.6	46.1
HADEP Min. (Elazığ)	15.6	24.5	13.6	8.8	4.9
Other Kurd. provinces	30.6	21.5	18.4	14.4	10.5
HADEP Max. (Ağrı)	21.9	12.8	7.7	6.9	33.7
HADEP Min. (Malatya)	13.2	25.3	19.8	20.2	2.3
Major cities	25.9	15.3	12.8	40.5	4.3
HADEP Max. (Adana)	21.2	10.3	23.6	33.9	7.4
HADEP Min. (Antalya)	32.5	6.3	22.3	32.3	2.5

Source: T. C. Başbakanlık, Devlet İstatistik Enstitüsü

However, there is another possibility, namely that urban Kurdish politics reflects long-standing *intra-ethnic* ideological and party loyalties. What is most surprising about these data is that HADEP, the only party with Kurdish nationalist credentials, was unable to muster a majority in *any* province of Turkey. Across the OHAL provinces, only 27 per cent of the electorate chose HADEP, while the secular centre-right and far-right (excluding the Islamist FP) gained a collective 35.6 per cent of the ballot. In the other Kurdish provinces, the party's performance was abysmal: less than 11 per cent supported HADEP, while the right garnered 48 per cent. In this context, HADEP's low level of support in the metropolis is less surprising.

Table 5.4 gives similar data for the 1991 and 1995 general elections. The party system in 1995 was virtually identical, and the electoral results were quite similar. Indeed, Kurdish nationalism did somewhat better in the south-east in 1999 than it did in 1995, but the overall tendency was a stable centre- and far-right majority in Kurdistan. In 1991, HEP (a Kurdish nationalist precursor to HADEP) formed a special electoral alliance with SHP (an ancestor of today's CHP). Though HEP had a distinct corporate identity, its candidates ran on the SHP list. Thus, a vote for SHP could have been the vote of a nationalist or a non-nationalist leftist. SHP did very well in 1991, gaining outright majorities in some provinces of OHAL. In Kurdistan as a whole, however, the right did much better. In short, during the 1990s, a period of Kurdish nationalist efflorescence and secessionist civil war, there was a stable tendency for large numbers of Kurds (probably majorities) to vote for rightist Turkish parties.

Several explanations have been offered for HADEP's poor showing. The party itself claimed widespread intimidation of rural voters, who were supposedly told by security forces to cast blank ballots (*Reuters* 19 April 1999). This allegation is not supported in the data. Although the participation rate in 21 Kurdish provinces (83 per cent) was lower than in Turkey overall (87 per cent), the proportion of valid to total votes in the Kurdish provinces was higher (95 to 94 per cent).

Bozarslan (1996a, b) argues that HADEP's success is confined to a "micro-space" of compact Sunni-Kurmanji settlement. On his account, the party's failure elsewhere is "closely linked to intra-Kurdish ethnic differentiations". This account cannot be rejected, given that many Alevis abjure Kurdish identification. There are reasons to doubt his story also. Bozarslan's reasoning explains why HADEP did worse in some Kurdish provinces than in others, but it cannot explain why Kurdish nationalists underperformed overall. Moreover, Alevism cannot explain support for rightist and Sunni-Islamist parties, which was widespread outside Bozarslan's micro-space, since Alevism is traditionally associated with the left and with suspicion of Sunni dominance.

HADEP's failure to galvanize Kurdish voters is best explained by its leftist identity. The left performed badly across the board in the south-east. McDowall (2000, 397) argues that Kurdistan was an area "hostile to, and dangerous for, radicals of the secular left" as early as the 1950s. DSP and CHP together received only 10.8 and 14.4 per cent in OHAL and the other Kurdish provinces, respectively, at a time when DSP became the most popular party

Table 5.4   **Vote share for selected parties, 1995 and 1991 General Elections (%)**

1995 General Election	DYP/ ANAP	RP[7]	MHP	DSP/ CHP	HADEP
Turkey	38.8	21.4	8.2	25.3	4.2
All Kurdish provinces	32.8	29.1	7.1	9.7	16.2
OHAL Provinces	31.2	26.4	5.1	7.6	24.2
HADEP Max. (Hâkkari)	31.3	6.0	2.2	4.6	54.2
HADEP Min. (Elazığ)	36.0	41.8	6.9	9.8	3.9
Other Kurd. provinces	34.6	31.8	9.1	11.9	7.8
HADEP Max. (/ğdir)	25.2	9.4	15.1	21.2	21.7
HADEP Min. (K.Maraş)	36.4	36.8	10.5	12.0	2.7
Major Cities	38.6	20.8	7.8	26.8	4.0
HADEP Max. (Adana)	34.0	16.7	14.3	26.6	6.7
HADEP Min. (Antalya)	41.2	13.3	12.2	30.0	1.9

1991 General Election	DYP/ ANAP	RP	—	DSP	SHP
Turkey	51.0	16.9	—	10.7	20.8
All Kurdish provinces	45.2	21.8	—	3.3	28.6
OHAL provinces	41.3	19.0	—	1.9	36.5
SHP Max. (Şırnak)	34.2	2.5	—	1.1	61.2
SHP Min. (Elazığ)	52.5	29.3	—	2.4	15.5
Other Kurd provinces	49.4	24.9	—	4.9	20.0
SHP Max. (Kars)	43.9	7.1	—	17.2	31.1
SHP Min. (Erzurum)	50.1	37.0	—	3.4	9.0
Major cities	49.3	14.2	—	14.2	21.7
SHP Max. (Ankara)	46.9	17.6	—	10.4	24.6
SHP Min. (Istanbul)	46.3	16.7	—	17.6	18.8

Source: T. C. Başbakanlık, Devlet İstatistik Enstitüsü

in Turkey. This raises two possibilities: either HADEP monopolized the left vote in Kurdistan, or many Kurds will only vote left for an ethnic party. The data are inconclusive on this question, yet it is clear that Kurdish voters have not shaken off the conservatism that puzzled Bruinessen (1992) in the 1960s.

The 6.5 and 18.4 per cent captured by MHP in OHAL and the other Kurdish regions, respectively, is the most surprising finding. Often known by the name of its militant wing, the Greywolves, MHP long advocated an extreme, racialist Turkism (Çağlar 1990) and has consistently resisted any concession to Kurdish demands. The appeal of MHP to some Kurds was confirmed by one of my informants. An educated young man, raised in the predominantly Kurdish provinces of Ağrı and Adıyaman, he explained that two of his uncles had long-standing ties to MHP. Both were native Kurmanji-speakers, from Ağrı. The votes of ethnic Turks undoubtedly account for some of MHP's support in the east. Nevertheless, determining why individuals cross ethnic cleavages, sometimes to extremes, is a key question for the study of ethnic politics. The most likely explanation is that contemporary MHP support stems from the left–right cleavage of 1970s Turkish politics (McDowall 2000, 411), which was weakly linked to Kurdish ethnicity.

Bruinessen (1992) concluded that the "primordial" loyalties of local tribal and kinship relations explained persistent political conservatism among the Kurds and tended to undermine a broader nationalism. The civil war may have helped to revitalize these solidarities as security-seeking induced individuals to work collectively (Yalçin-Heckmann 1991, 71). The village guard system, in particular, was built largely along tribal lines and tribal leaders have often acted as agents of the state in the recruitment of militia forces.

The rapid urbanization of the past decade is likely to undermine these solidarities, not least because tribes lose something of their security function in urban areas. What sort of new solidarity will emerge is difficult to predict. The evidence on Kurdish vote choice we have available suggests that urban migrants may adopt differing views depending upon where they land: the large urban areas of the east, such as Diyarbakir and Batman are emerging as strongholds of Kurdish political mobilization, while nationalism appears to be fizzling somewhat among migrants to the Turkish milieu of the west.

IMPLICATIONS FOR FUTURE POLICY

Many readers will find the implications of this chapter normatively depressing, because they suggest that states can "win" with repression. In fact, the Turkish case should give policy-makers several reasons for optimism.

First, there is very little that is worse for democracy and human rights than civil war. Although it is common to argue that rebellion results from repression and brutality, in fact the causal arrow points more strongly in the opposite direction. The end of the civil war in Turkey ought to be greeted with relief by anyone whose goal is the protection of human rights, since its continuation would surely have resulted in far more brutality on both sides.

Second, the decline of the PKK suggests that the aftermath of ethnic civil wars need not involve territorial separation of ethnic groups, as Kaufman (1996) has argued. Although the civil war in Turkey involved considerable brutality, it never degenerated to the point where populations were indiscriminately targeted by ethnicity alone. Most Kurds never favoured secession, and most do not favour it now. The PKK never succeeded in creating a *fait accompli*, as other rebel groups like the Kosovo Liberation Army have done. The Turkish case tells us that stable multi-ethnicity can be maintained in the face of ethnic violence.

Third, throughout the civil war, the state and mainstream political parties opposed opening the system to explicitly Kurdish demands. Important political groups in Turkey continue to support their exclusion on the grounds that "concessions" on Kurdish policy will promote secession. If, as I have argued, the production of violence depends on factors that are largely independent of peaceful politics, then suppression of Kurdish politics cannot be justified as a defence against separatism. Kurdish political organizations in Turkey have renounced violence and separatism. The question for the state is the credibility of those claims. If my argument is correct their credibility is high, because violent secession is no longer a realistic option. The state can now maintain its Weberian monopoly on coercion at a low cost, while permitting a more open politics than it has in the past. The Western governments that have generously supported Turkey's campaign against the PKK (Ron 1995, App. B) should make it clear that the indefinite postponement of reform occasioned by civil war is no longer justified.

NOTES

1   The Parti Karkaren Kurdistan, or Kurdish Workers Party, is a militant organization established with the aim of creating an independent, Marxist-Leninist, Kurdish state in Southeastern Turkey.
2   See Barkey and Fuller 1998, 214; Muller 1996, 193; Kirişçi and Winrow 1997, 183, for similar statements.
3   This figure is based on government sources and may be an underestimate. I am unaware of any independent attempt to estimate war deaths in Kurdistan. Even if the true figure is five times greater, this case was far less deadly than insurgencies in, e.g., South Vietnam, Algeria, or Sri Lanka. In civil wars, civilian casualties typically exceed combatant casualties (Kalyvas 2001a, 6), which has not been true in Turkey.
4   This figure is disputed. At the upper bound, a figure of 2–3 million displaced by evacuation is widely touted by human rights groups. The number is too high; if true, it would account for the entire 1990 rural population of OHAL or nearly a third of the total 1990 population of the Southeast.
5   Barkey and Fuller (1998, 47) estimate 5–10 000 PKK guerrillas, plus a militia of 50 000, though it is not clear what years this figure covers. The village guard system was estimated to have 67 000 fighters in 1995 (Ron 1995), of which we can assume nearly all were Kurdish. The military had 410 200 draftees in 1995 (US LOC, 1996). If 20 per cent of the population is Kurdish, and we assume a constant

rate of conscription, there were 82 040 Kurdish conscripts in the Turkish army in 1995.
6   This survey, conducted by Prof. Doğu Ergil for the Turkish Union of Chambers of Commerce and Industry (TOBB), is cited in several sources (Barkey and Fuller 1998; Kirişçi and Winrow 1997), but I have not been able to obtain a copy. My criticisms of the survey are based on personal communication with Professor Ergil.
7   RP stands for "Refah Partisi", or Welfare Party, the Islamist precursor to FP.

REFERENCES

Barkey, H. J. and Fuller, G. E. (1998), *Turkey's Kurdish Question* (Lanham, MD: Rowman & Littlefield Publishers, Inc.)
Blaufarb, D. S. and Tanham, G. K. (1989), *Who Will Win? A Key to the Puzzle of Revolutionary War* (New York: Taylor & Francis New York, Inc.)
Bozarslan, H. (1996a), "Political Crisis and the Kurdish Issue in Turkey", in Robert Olson (ed.), *The Kurdish nationalist movement in the 1990s* (Lexington, KY: University of Kentucky Press)
―――― (1996b), "Turkey's Elections and the Kurds", *Middle East Report* 26:2, 16–19
―――― (2000), "Why the Armed Struggle? Understanding the Violence in Kurdistan of Turkey", in Ferhad Ibrahim and Gülistan Gürbey (eds), *The Kurdish Conflict in Turkey: Obstacles and Chances for Peace and Democracy* (New York: St. Martin's Press)
Brubaker, R. and Laitin, D. D. (1998), Ethnic and Nationalist Violence, *Annual Review of Sociology* 24: 423–52
Bruinessen, M. van (1992), *Agha, Sheikh, and State: The Social and Political Structures of Kurdistan* (London: Zed Books)
―――― (1998), "Shifting National and Ethnic identities: the Kurds in Turkey and the European Diaspora", *Journal of Muslim Minority Affairs* 18:1, 39–52
Çağlar, A. N. (1990), "The Greywolves as Metaphor", in Andrew Finkel and Nükhet Sırman (eds), *Turkish State, Turkish Society* (London: Routledge)
Cornell, S. E. (2001), "The Kurdish Question in Turkish Politics", *Orbis* 45:1, 31–47
Fearon, J. D. and Laitin, D. D. (1996), "Explaining Interethnic Cooperation", *American Political Science Review* 90:4, 715–35
Gellner, E. (1983), *Nations and Nationalism* (Ithaca, NY: Cornell University Press)
İmset, İ. G. (1992), *The PKK: A Report on Separatist Violence in Turkey* (Ankara: Turkish Daily News Publications)
Kalyvas, S. N. (2001a), "Ethnicity and Civil War Violence: Micro-level Empirical Findings and Macro-level Hypotheses", paper presented at the Annual Meeting of the American Political Science Association, 30 August to 2 September, San Francisco
―――― (2001b), "'New' and 'Old' Civil Wars: A Valid Distinction?", *World Politics* 54:1, 99–118
Kaufman, C. (1996), "Possible and Impossible Solutions to Ethnic Civil Wars", *International Security* 20:4, 243–85
Kirişçi, K. and Winrow, G. M. (1997), *The Kurdish Question and Turkey: An Example of a Trans–state Ethnic Conflict* (Portland, OR: Frank Cass & Co., Ltd)
Laqueur, W. (1998), *Guerrilla Warfare: A Historical and Critical Study* (New Brunswick, NJ: Transaction Publishers)
Levy, J. T. (2000), *The Multiculturalism of Fear* (New York: Oxford University Press)
McDowall, D. (2000), *A Modern History of the Kurds*, 3rd Edition (New York: I. B. Tauris & Co., Ltd)

Muller, M. (1996), "Nationalism and the Rule of Law in Turkey: the Elimination of Kurdish Representation during the 1990s", in Robert Olson (ed.), *The Kurdish Nationalist Movement in the 1990s* (Lexington, KY: University of Kentucky Press)

Pope, N. and Pope, H. (1997), *Turkey Unveiled: A History of Modern Turkey* (New York: Overlook Press)

Randal, J. C. (1999), *After Such Knowledge, What Forgiveness? My Encounters of Kurdistan* (Boulder, CO: Westview Press)

Ron, J. (1995), *Weapons Transfers and Violations of the Laws of War in Turkey* (New York: Human Rights Watch)

_____ (forthcoming), *Frontiers and Ghettoes: State Violence in Serbia and Israel* (Ms.: McGill University)

Rosenberg, M. (1994), "On the road: Archaeological Adventures in Anatolia", *Middle East Quarterly* 1:1

US Library of Congress (LOC), Federal Research Division (1996), *Turkey: A Country Study,* Helen Chapin Metz (ed.) (Washington, DC: Federal Research Division, Library of Congress)

US Department of State (DOS), Bureau of Democracy, Human Rights, and Labor (2000), *1999 Country Reports on Human Rights* (Washington, DC: US Department of State)

Wedel, H. (2000), "Migration and Displacement: Kurdish Migrants in Istanbul in the 1990s", in Ferhad Ibrahim and Gülistan Gürbey (eds), *The Kurdish Conflict in Turkey: Obstacles and Chances for Peace and Democracy* (New York: St. Martin's Press)

Yalçın-Heckmann, L. (1991), *Tribe and kinship among the Kurds* (Frankfurt am Main: Verlag Peter Lang)

Yalman, N. (1971), "On Land Disputes in Eastern Turkey", in Girdhari L. Tikku (ed.), *Islam and its Cultural Divergence* (Urbana, IL: University of Illinois Press)

PART II
LINGUISTIC DIVERSITY

6 Language Rights as an Integral Part of Human Rights – A Legal Perspective

FERNAND DE VARENNES

Does not the sun shine equally for the whole world? Do we not all equally breathe the air? Do you not feel shame at authorizing only three languages and condemning other people to blindness and deafness? Tell me, do you think that God is helpless and cannot bestow equality, or that he is envious and will not give it? (Constantine the Philosopher {Cyril}, ninth century AD)[1]

European countries operate today on the basis of shared, common values. These comprise the rule of law, democracy, human rights, including the rights of persons belonging to minorities, tolerance and a pluralistic society. They are values that are widely accepted from Organisation for Security and Co-operation in Europe (OSCE) documents to Council of Europe treaties, as well as part of the political criteria for admission of new states to the European Union. The observance of these values is no longer a matter of choice, but a political and – in the case of human and minority rights – legal imperative. As stated in the 1990 Charter of Paris for a New Europe "the rights of persons belonging to national minorities must be fully respected as part of universal human rights". The promotion of tolerance and pluralism is also an important component of these shared values.

Minorities have numerous rights in relation to language. They can be based on international or European treaties which are legally binding documents. A number of rights found in international law and in Council of Europe treaties are also repeated in documents from the OSCE and other organizations. While these latter examples do not for the most part involve legally binding documents, they do represent at the very least political and moral obligations. Perhaps more importantly, they reflect a generalized consensus as to what are the human rights of minorities and on the standards that are applicable in the area of language.

The purpose of this paper is to make the link between language rights and human rights. There is often the mistaken view that the rights of minorities, or language rights, are part of a new generation of rights, or are collective in nature. This perception is both unfortunate and erroneous: unfortunate because it tends to consider language rights as less deserving than "real" human rights, and wrong because it fails to understand the actual sources of these rights. To put it simply, most – if not all – of what are called today language rights derive from general human rights standards, especially non-discrimination, freedom of expression, right to private life, and the right of members of a linguistic minority to use their language with other members of their community. All of these are "authentic", individual human rights as generally recognized in international law.

The error which is too often perpetuated is, as this chapter will attempt to demonstrate, simply based on the failure to see the larger picture of the phenomenon which has emerged in the last 10 or 20 years: that the treaties and other documents dealing with the rights of linguistic minorities are but a more detailed enumeration of the consequences of general human rights in specific situations. Just as there are many documents and treaties which have provided more detail as to the consequences of general human rights in specific sectors of society such as women and children, for example, there now is a process providing more detail as to the consequences of general human rights in another specific sector of society – minorities.

There is not in the present state of international law or under European treaties an unqualified "right to use a minority language" or "right to language". This should be clear from a close examination of relevant treaties, but also of the decision of the European Court of Human Rights in the *Belgian Linguistic Case*. There are a number of basic human rights and freedoms that affect the issue of language preferences and use by members of a minority or by the State.

PRIVATE USE OF MINORITY LANGUAGE

One way to approach these matters is to begin by explaining how and why language rights are to a large degree based on pre-existing individual human rights, and by focusing on the content of the rights of minorities which you find in a treaty like the Council of Europe's *Framework Convention on the Protection of National Minorities*, though not in any way exclusive to it.

In almost all treaties or language right documents, there is a distinction made between the private use of a language by individuals and the use of a minority language by public authorities. It is a useful distinction to make conceptually, because it will help to show that what one may assume are "language rights" or "rights of minorities" are also at the same time simply the manifestation, the application of fundamental individual rights such as freedom of expression and others in the private realm.

On the issue of language rights in the private sphere, state conduct which prevents or controls the use of a language in private activities can be in breach of existing international human rights such as the rights to private and family life, freedom of expression, non-discrimination or the right of persons belonging to a linguistic minority to use their language with other members of their group.

Of course, the right to privately use a minority language is a minority right or language right contained in the Council of Europe's *Framework Convention on the Protection of National Minorities* and other documents such as the OSCE-sponsored *Oslo Recommendations regarding the Linguistic Rights of National Minorities*, but these minority or language rights are additionally based on freedom of expression and other individual human rights.

It may help, and indeed be more convincing, to give a few precise examples. All language or minority treaties essentially recognize that individuals have the right to have their name or surname in their own language. This is a minority or linguistic right, but it is also a basic human right. This right is clearly recognized in international law as a part of the right to private life.[2] In one of its decisions, the United Nations Human Rights Committee has made it clear that the notion of privacy includes:

> ... the sphere of a person's life in which he or she can freely express his or her identity, be it by entering into relationships with others or alone. The Committee is of the view that a person's surname [and name] constitutes an important component of one's identity and that the protection against arbitrary or unlawful interference with one's privacy includes the protection against arbitrary or unlawful interference with the right to choose and change one's own name.[3]

Public authorities cannot interfere with this right arbitrarily or unlawfully, and the Committee has indicated that a restriction on the right to choose one's name would have to be reasonable to satisfy this requirement. A state cannot prevent an individual from having a name or surname which is not in an official language or not contained on a prescribed list. Names and surnames constitute a means of identifying persons within their families and the community, and as such are an inseparable part of private life.

Another relevant example, especially in the European context, is when a government authority bans the private use of a minority language in public areas (such as banning individuals from having a private conversation in their language in public streets, or banning its use in a public park and so on). Such attempts are breaches of freedom of expression, would in all likelihood be a form of discrimination based on language, and would certainly be contrary to Article 27 of the UN's *International Covenant on Civil and Political Rights* if they restrict the use of a minority language by individuals who are members of such a minority. This is once again a minority or language right in a number of European treaties and documents, but it is first and foremost a manifestation of an existing, fundamental human right.

Essentially, all of the provisions in the *Framework Convention for the Protection of National Minorities*; the *Central European Initiative for the Protection of Minority Rights*; the *Oslo Recommendations regarding the Linguistic Rights of National Minorities*, and the many, many similar documents on minority or language rights which deal with the private use of a minority language, are examples of the direct application of general human rights provisions, mainly freedom of expression, non-discrimination, right to private life and the rights of members of a linguistic to use their own language with other members of their group.

The freedom for private individuals to use a minority language in private correspondence or communications, including in private business or commercial correspondence, by telephone or electronic means; to have private displays such as outdoor commercial signs and posters in a minority language; to use a minority script on posters, commercial signs and so on of a private nature; the freedom to print in a minority language; the freedom to use a minority language in the conduct of private business and economic activities; even the right to create and operate private schools teaching in a minority language, are all language rights. But their very nature is anchored, they originate, from existing human rights.

These examples are important to make especially in the European context, because there is a tendency of describing language rights in relation to "national minorities", and that is both dangerous and incorrect. All of the examples that have been given up to now on the private use of minority languages, based as they are on human rights such as freedom of expression and so on, are not limited to national minorities. Any individual, whether their language group is "national" or not, has freedom of expression, has the right to private life, has the right to non-discrimination, and has, as confirmed by the United Nations Human Rights Committee, the right to use their language with other members of their linguistic group. These rights are not restricted to national minorities nor to citizens, as may be the case in Europe under some of the treaties of the Council of Europe.

USE OF MINORITY LANGUAGE BY PUBLIC AUTHORITIES

Once again, it may be conceptually easier to explain the relationship between human rights and the language rights dealing with the use of a minority language by public authorities by making a distinction between two categories of language use: one can be identified as language rights in relation to the fairness of judicial proceedings, and the other with the general use of minority languages by public officials.

It is a well-established language right that when an individual does not understand the language used in criminal court proceedings, or the language used in a criminal accusation, that public authorities must use the (usually minority) language this person understands. This first example of the right to have public authorities use a minority language is recognized as a minority or language right in treaties such as the *Framework Convention for the Protection of National Minorities*, the *European Charter for Regional or Minority Languages*, and many, many other documents at the level of the OSCE and the UN that are simply too numerous to name.

These two rights are universally recognized in international law and found in most treaties dealing with human rights, usually linked to the principle of a fair trial. Any accused, including persons belonging to linguistic minorities, whether they are citizens or not, has the right to an interpreter in criminal cases for translation of proceedings, including court documents, if they do not understand the language used in criminal proceedings. The right to be informed promptly in a language one understands is similarly universally recognized in international law as a basic linguistic right based on a fundamental human right.

The above describes much of the content that most people would have always assumed were simply minority rights: in fact, they are all the application of fundamental human rights. That leaves but one category of language rights for which a connection with fundamental human rights has not been shown. This is the category involving the general use of minority language(s) by public authorities. It is an area of major concern, because it covers many matters such as public education using a minority language as medium of instruction, public radio and television broadcasting in a minority language, use of minority languages by public officials in the provision of services to the public (and therefore a major source of employment for individuals within the civil service) and so on

One thing is now clear: public authorities have an obligation to use the language of minorities in appropriate circumstances, such as where numbers and geographic concentration of the speakers of a minority language make it a reasonable or justified arrangement. These language or minority rights are now well-accepted European standards: from a legal point of view, they are contained in two treaties of the Council of Europe, the *Framework Convention on the Protection of National Minorities* and the *European Charter for Regional or Minority Languages.*

The right to have public authorities use a minority language where reasonable or justified is also referred to in an increasingly large number of resolutions, declarations and other documents in the Council of Europe, the EU (where respect for minority rights is now part of the political criteria for admission of new States to the EU), the Organization for Security and Co-operation in Europe, and the United Nations. These confirm the widespread acceptance of these rights as fundamental political commitments in addition to legal obligations.

This right in relation to the use of a minority language by public officials is quite variable. It is not a right to a language, it is not a right which appears every time there is a minority language or a demand to use a minority language, it is only a right which arises, essentially, when there are substantial speakers or sufficient speakers of a language who demand a certain type of public service in their language. It actually means that where the numbers of speakers of a minority language are too low, or it is too onerous to use a minority language in a certain type of public service, it is not a violation of a language or minority right for public officials not to use this language.

In other words, in some situations the various relevant conditions make it reasonable, or if you prefer justified in pursuit of a legitimate objective, for public authorities not to use a minority language in their activities and services. But if the numbers of speakers are substantial enough, as the term is used in the *Framework Convention on the Protection of National Minorities,* then it would be unreasonable or unjustified for public officials not to use to the appropriate degree and level the minority language in their activities.

This minority or language right uses the same basic approach as is guaranteed in international law from the application of the general prohibition of discrimination as to language, as contained in Article 26 of the *International Covenant on Civil and Political Rights*, and under the new *Protocol No. 12 to the Convention for the Protection of Human Rights and Fundamental Freedoms.*[4]

It is no coincidence that the same type of test is involved in determining the situations where public officials must use a minority language and the situations involving non-discrimination: just as has been shown, most language or minority rights in the private sphere involve fundamental human rights such as freedom of expression and the right to private life: in the area of the use of a minority language by public officials, what is involved in most cases is the proper application of non-discrimination based on language. This can also be shown with the *Belgian Linguistics Case* which was handed down by the European Court of Human Rights. This decision has more often than not been deemed to signal that there is no right to state education in a minority language under the European Convention, even in combination with the principle of non-discrimination. In fact, that is not quite correct. The European Court of Human Rights actually indicated that non-discrimination based on language did not automatically guarantee to all minorities such a right. What was meant was that there might be situations where the denial of education in a minority language could possibly be discrimination on the basis of language, but that the linguistic policies in the area of education in Belgium were, for the most part, not unjustified in the circumstances, and therefore not discriminatory. But that conversely meant that had the language policies in education been deemed unjustified, there would have been a situation of discrimination, and some rearrangement of the language policies in relation to public education would have been necessary.

It may help to give a few examples of what constitutes this language or minority right in relation to the use of a minority language by public officials, and then end with an explanation as to why the linkage of these rights as an integral part of human rights has significant consequences in the European context. Where public authorities at the national, regional or local levels face a sufficiently large number of individuals who use a particular language, the authorities must provide an appropriate level of service in this language.

For example, in the case of local districts and their administration where minorities are concentrated, local authorities should generally provide for an increasing level of services in their language as the number of speakers of a particular language increases. Beginning at the lower end of what will be called a "sliding-scale model", public officials should at the very least have official documents and forms available in appropriate areas where there is a low, though sufficient number of speakers of a minority language. As the number progressively get higher, in addition to bilingual or minority language documents, public officials would have to accept and respond to applications in a minority language.

At the very top of the scale, there would have to be some kind of bilingual administration in districts where a minority language is used by a very high percentage of the population. This means that there would have to be a sufficient number of public officials who are in contact with the public in place to respond to the use of the non-official or minority language, and even that in these areas the minority language be used as an internal and daily language of work within public authorities. So the principle, based on the relevant treaty provisions or non-discrimination, would apply to all activities relating to "administrative or public authorities", all areas of state involvement, including the judiciary, state education, state-provided health services, public broadcasting and so on.

For example, where a sufficient number of students of a linguistic minority are concentrated territorially, it would be unreasonable – and in all likelihood be a breach of non-discrimination – for a state not to provide an appropriate degree of use of their language as medium of instruction in public schools. The degree of use of a minority language will vary according to what is reasonable, appropriate or practical in each situation: the extent of demand for such instruction, the level of use of the minority language as medium of instruction, the state's ability to respond to these demands and so on. This follows the same sliding-scale model as described earlier.

SIGNIFICANCE OF LINKING LANGUAGE RIGHTS AS PART OF HUMAN RIGHTS

The Council of Europe has two major treaties dealing with language, and even the EU is increasingly recognizing language rights, so what useful purpose is served by trying to link language or minority rights with human rights? Such a linkage is still necessary because of the two main weaknesses of both the *Framework Convention for the Protection of National Minorities* and the *European Charter for Regional or Minority Languages*.

The first main weakness is the tendency to limit language rights to national minorities, while leaving unclear what is a national minority. The second weakness is the almost complete absence of any recourse for individuals whose rights are not respected.

While it is true that both treaties have made an invaluable contribution to our understanding of language and minority rights by spelling out their content in greater detail, it is unfortunate that they seem to suggest that only citizens have language rights if by national minorities is meant a traditional, historical minority on a state's territory. It is however clear, especially when using the concept of the private use of language, that such a view is wrong. As you will remember, most of the language or minority rights dealing with the private use of a language are based on freedom of expression. Freedom of expression is not limited, in European or international law, to citizens, so it is obviously clear that we cannot limit language rights in the private sphere to national minorities. The Council of Europe treaties do not actually say this, but unfortunately a number of people in Europe and elsewhere seem to believe that only national minorities have language rights since only they are specifically referred to in these treaties. That is, as my example shows, clearly wrong. But linking language rights to specific human rights, as can be done in most if not all cases, does provide for the possibility for those individuals who may not be considered to be national minorities to use the human rights approach and to use mechanisms to have their rights respected, especially in the area of private language use with its emphasis on freedom of expression and other rights.

The second weakness, and in my view an even more serious one, is the lack of any individual remedies. States which have ratified the *Framework Convention for the Protection of National Minorities* or the *European Charter for Regional or Minority Languages* have reporting obligations, and their compliance will be examined by committees of experts, but that is essentially all. States are not subjected to a judicial or quasi-judicial body which can investigate claims of violations of the treaties. There will not be decisions or judgments which will be issued as to whether or not a government is in violation of the Charter or Convention. This is of course much, much weaker than what you have under the *European Convention on Human Rights*, where you have a court that can hand down judgments, and the UN which has a Committee under the *International Covenant on Civil and Political Rights* which can hand down communications in response to complaints by individuals that their rights are not being respected.

And this is where, once again, the significance of linking language rights with human rights becomes apparent. The absence of any individual judicial recourse under the *Framework Convention for the Protection of National Minorities* and *European Charter for Regional or Minority Languages* can be corrected, to some degree, by using those treaty mechanisms which do permit the adjudication of individual complaints.

The language rights of individuals involving freedom of expression, the right to private life, non-discrimination, the right to freely use a minority language with other members of the minority and so on, can in appropriate cases be raised either before the European Court of Human Rights or the UN Human Rights Committee, even if individuals have no direct recourse under the *Framework Convention for the Protection of National Minorities* or the *European Charter for Regional or Minority Languages*.

LINGUISTIC RIGHTS, STABILITY AND MULTICULTURAL DEMOCRACIES

> [T]he Imperial City has endeavoured to impose on subject nations not only her yoke, but her language, as a bond of peace ... but how many, great wars, how much slaughter and bloodshed have provided this unity. (Saint Augustine, The City of God {c. 410})

There is finally an additional consideration to keep in mind in relation to the value and position of language rights in democratic societies. The genesis of language rights from internationally recognized human rights provide a form of legal control which gives to minorities a legitimate mechanism to deal with the main matters of contention within multicultural societies – including language preferences – in a way which helps to avoid past discriminatory practices by state authorities.

States, contrary to what is sometimes presented as a theoretical *acquis*, are not simply the sum of the preferences of all of their citizens. On the contrary, try as much as they may, states can never be entirely neutral in ethnic terms. As others have pointed out persuasively in this book, democracy cannot simply amount to a majoritarian winner-takes-all sum game in linguistic, religious or cultural terms. It is on the contrary undeniable that to ignore language rights, and other rights of minorities affecting religious and cultural differences, can have serious consequences and even lead to a deficiency in legitimacy of state institutions and conflict:

> In the distribution of power within their structures, states inevitably reflect the dominant groups within civil society (by class and interest, as well as ethnic derivation). [M]any states invest their national personality with the cultural attributes of the leading ethnic community. Even in countries with predominantly civic forms of nationalism, such as the United States, the argument that different communal segments (racial in this instance) were neutrally treated would be impossible to sustain historically. States are thus asked – figuratively speaking – to leap out of their own skins, to transcend their own cultural nature.[5]

By providing for language rights along the lines described in this chapter, state authorities are in fact creating a balance that seeks to avoid state preferences in linguistic choices (as well as other cultural attributes) that would disproportionably or unreasonably impact on segments of their population, and therefore provide for an approach more consistent with principles of tolerance, coexistence and integration. Integration in this sense does not mean trying to eliminate or deny human differences such as language, but rather taking them into account and accommodating them to the extent possible and practical so that individuals may be able to participate in the life of the community to which they belong as well as of the larger national community.

This balancing of interests is in essence found in documents referred to earlier such as the UN's *Declaration on the Rights of Persons Belonging to National or Ethnic, Religious or Linguistic Minorities*, the *Oslo Recommendations Regarding the Linguistic Rights of National Minorities*, and the Council of Europe's *Framework Convention on the Rights of National Minorities*. They are all part of a process to increase understanding and respect for human rights which are anchored upon principles of tolerance, coexistence and integration. It is in this spirit that the rights of linguistic and other minorities must be understood.

This and other rights represent an attempt to reach a proper balance between the different interests of individuals who belong to minorities and those of the State. They do not involve a loss of sovereignty or threat to unity. On the contrary, they may help avoid tensions and conflicts involving language issues in a number of countries.

Generally speaking though, the point is still the object of some disagreement. It could be suggested that the dynamics of tension leading up in some cases to actual violent conflicts involving language – such as Macedonia, Sri Lanka, Bangladesh and many others – occur not where language compromises are made or rights are recognized, but where they have been avoided, suppressed or ignored in countries where a major segment of the population is composed of a linguistic minority. Countries likely to be the setting for conflicts are those where members of ethnic groups feel that they are being discriminated against, treated unfairly, or denied rights and opportunities allowed to members of the majority.[6]

CONCLUSION

Unius linguae uniusque moris regnum imbecille et fragile est. (St. Stephen)[7]

Europe is without any doubt at the forefront of developments in the area of language or minority rights. The Council of Europe's treaties such as the *European Charter on Minority or Regional Languages* and the *European Convention on the Rights of National Minorities* are clarifying the content of the rights of minorities, in much the same way as treaties for specific groups such as women and children have evolved at the international level. There are also many other documents and other instruments which follow the same general principles, from OSCE to EU documents, as well as bilateral treaties. Despite differences in wording, emphasis or even perspective, all tend to confirm the same basic minority rights in the area of language.

What is unfortunately sometimes, even perhaps often, forgotten is that these language or minority rights are not an exception to, or a weaker type of, human rights. Not only are they an integral part of human rights – which many documents from the Council of Europe and the European Union tend to confirm – they are more importantly mostly based on such fundamental human rights as freedom of expression and non-discrimination.

This understanding of the nature of language rights must be emphasized because of the mistaken belief that only certain categories of individuals such as national minorities have language rights. As most clearly demonstrated with the example of private use of a minority language, this is false: the language rights based on freedom of expression are available to any individual, not restricted to those who belong to a national minority category.

Finally, understanding the human rights origins of language rights may also help avoid one of the central weaknesses of the *European Charter on Minority or Regional Languages* and the *European Convention on the Rights of National Minorities*. Individuals whose language rights are violated by governments have no direct recourse available to them under either treaty.

This failure to give individuals a direct route of redress can be avoided by using the available procedures for judicial redress that are available under the *International Covenant on Civil and Political Rights* or the *European Convention for the Protection of Human Rights and Fundamental Freedoms* and the human rights guarantees which are at the root source of most language or minority rights, especially freedom of expression and non-discrimination.

NOTES

1   Quoted in Fishman, Joshua A. (ed.) (1968), *Readings in the Sociology of Language* (The Hague: Mouton and Co. N.V. Publishers), p. 589
2   *Coeriel and Aurik v. Netherlands*, United Nations Human Rights Committee, Communication No. 453/1991, UN Doc. CCPR/C/52/D/453/1991 (1994); *Burghartz v. Switzerland*, European Court of Human Rights, judgment of 22 February 1994, 16213/90 [1994] ECHR 2
3   *Coeriel and Aurik v. Netherlands*, supra, Paragraph 10.2.
4   See de Varennes, Fernand (1996), *Language, Minorities and Human Rights* (The Hague: Martinus Nijhoff), chapter 4 for a detailed discussion of this issue
5   Young, Crawford (1994), *Ethnic Diversity and Public Policy: An Overview*, Occasional Paper No. 8, World Summit for Social Development, United Nations Research Institute for Social Development: Geneva
6   de Varennes, Fernand (2000), *Minority Rights and the Prevention of Ethnic Conflicts*, Working Paper, United Nations Working Group on the Rights of Minorities, UN Doc. E/CN.4/Sub.2/AC.5/2000/CRP.3, Geneva.
7   Macartney, C. A. (1968), *National States and National Minorities* (New York: Russell and Russell)

BIBLIOGRAPHY

de Varennes, F. (1996), *Language, Minorities and Human Rights* (The Hague: Martinus Nijhoff)
de Varennes, F. (2000), *Minority Rights and the Prevention of Ethnic Conflicts*, Working Paper, United Nations Working Group on the Rights of Minorities, UN Doc. E/CN.4/Sub.2/AC.5/2000/CRP.3, Geneva
Fishman, J. A. (ed.) (1968), *Readings in the Sociology of Language* (The Hague: Mouton and Co. N.V. Publishers)
Macartney, C. A. (1968), *National States and National Minorities* (New York: Russell and Russell)
Young, C. (1994), *Ethnic Diversity and Public Policy: An Overview*, Occasional Paper No. 8, World Summit for Social Development, United Nations Research Institute for Social Development: Geneva

7 Protecting Linguistic Minorities – The Role of the OSCE

SALLY HOLT & JOHN PACKER

LANGUAGE IN THE OSCE FRAMEWORK

As a security organization the Organization for Security and Co-operation in Europe (OSCE) derives its interest in language issues from a conflict-prevention perspective. The protection of the rights of persons belonging to national minorities, including their linguistic rights, constitutes a key element within the framework of the OSCE's overall approach of "comprehensive security" (which recognizes the interdependence of issues of military and political security, economic and environmental well-being, and respect for human rights) and "cooperative security" which is grounded in the commitment of all States to cooperate within a framework of open, democratic societies with free market economies, based on the rule of law and respect for human rights. It is important to note from the outset that all OSCE participating States have voluntarily accepted that human rights are a legitimate concern to all participating States and that they do not belong exclusively to the internal affairs of the State concerned.[1] Furthermore, all OSCE States have bound themselves to respect not only express OSCE commitments, but all relevant international law irrespective of its source. The existence and functioning of the OSCE institutions is the product of consensus decision-making – neither standards nor institutions are imposed. The work of the OSCE institutions which often reaches significantly into the specific regulatory and practical affairs of participating States therefore proceeds from assumptions of common interests and cooperation.

OSCE and Conflict Prevention

Disputes over language use and the rights of persons belonging to linguistic minorities have emerged as among the most common sources of conflict in many OSCE States. As the principal OSCE institution mandated in July 1992 specifically to prevent conflicts in situations involving minority issues, the High Commissioner on National Minorities (HCNM) has been engaged, in cooperation with other OSCE institutions, in a number of situations that have threatened to destabilize certain regions of Central and Eastern Europe and the former Soviet Union. While the roots of disputes and the particular historic circumstances may differ, the status of the mother tongue and the regulation of the use of language are particularly contentious elements that tend to polarize parties like no other.

So why are issues surrounding language so charged? Part of the answer lies in the symbolic function of language and its centrality to notions of identity, both as a source of individual self-identification and as a crucial element in the collective cultural identity of many communities (especially in Europe).[2] Of course "identities" are complex and changeable, with different elements becoming more important depending on the contexts and the nature of interactions encountered therein. In a depoliticized context, "national" identity in the sense of ethnic (or even purported "racial") characteristics may take a backseat.[3] This element comes to the fore when the sense of identity – whether individually or collectively – feels threatened in some way. Any threat (real or perceived) to the use of language, such as inadequate opportunities to learn or use one's own language in public or in private, is interpreted as tantamount to a threat to the very identity of those involved, thus provoking understandably strong and defensive reactions. This entanglement of issues of language with such a sensitive phenomenon as identity provides fertile ground for conflicts.

Further to its implications for identity, language also functions as a tool of social organization. Choices made by States in the use of language – especially in the public sphere of governance – have a bearing on access to important public goods, and constitute either a means to or obstacle in the way of social integration (Packer 2001, 258). Problems arise when persons or groups feel that they are being excluded from certain processes or opportunities in the public sphere – including access to an equitable share of the State's resources – derived from their lack of knowledge of the State language(s). Disputes may arise over access to, *inter alia,* public services and facilities, employment or economic opportunities, and prestigious positions within the State. Fundamentally in some States, language is also a key factor affecting access to citizenship (in particular through language requirements in the naturalization process) which in itself is key to full participation and integration within the State.

The role of the OSCE as a security organization, and specifically of the HCNM as an instrument of conflict prevention, is not to address questions of identity per se. Indeed, it is the experience of the HCNM that although questions of identity often help to explain the context of a dispute they seldom, in themselves, represent the root of the problem. A minority/ majority may be concerned about the protection of identity, but usually in relation to a particular issue or set of issues. The HCNM, therefore, seeks to direct disputing parties towards the solution of concrete issues and away from the rather nebulous and volatile concept of identity. By focusing on specific substantive questions – on policy, legislation and governmental practice – parties are able to frame their concerns in a subject-oriented rather than national(ist)-oriented way (see Kemp 2001, 119).

Integrating Diversity

It is the task of the democratic State to provide the framework within which each individual can be free to maintain and develop his or her identity pursuant to a "social contract" which both legitimizes and sustains the State in that same task for the benefit of others. In doing so the State has a responsibility to ensure an even-handed (as opposed to a completely neutral "hands-off") approach in responding to competing claims – including matters of culture and identity – with the aim of ensuring equal respect for all (see Carens 2000, 12). While no liberal democratic regime can ever be culturally neutral – since every State has to make choices regarding, for example, the language(s) to use for government, the courts and in public education – cultural particularism should be kept strictly to a minimum (see Carens 2000, 11).

The creation of new States (or the restoration of their sovereignty) in post-Cold War Europe, including post-Soviet State formation, has been accompanied in many areas by national and ethnic revivals. Thus, the OSCE has paid particular attention to problems of diversity, especially linguistic diversity. The objective promoted by the OSCE is one of "integrating diversity", that is, the simultaneous maintenance of different identities and the promotion of social integration. This implies a pluralist, multicultural model of societal organization based on the principle of non-discrimination (as opposed to an assimilationist or exclusivist approach). A common fear is that support for integration within the State will in fact lead to its disintegration. The OSCE approach informs that the reverse is true. Specifically, the HCNM's experience is that "a minority that has the opportunity to fully develop its identity is more likely to remain loyal to the State than a minority who is denied its identity" (van der Stoel 2000, 209).

Within the framework of integrating diversity, as informed by international standards, the State is entitled and indeed obliged to seek integration in accordance with the principles of equality and non-discrimination.[4] This is a matter of balancing general and particular interests and wills. Distinctions and preferences must constitute a *proportionate balance* between the different interests in accordance with respect for the dignity of the individual and the protection of their rights – most relevantly the rights to freedom of expression and association. As de Varennes observes, in order to determine whether such preferences (in this case linguistic ones) are discriminatory, various factors must be taken into account, including a State's demographic, historical and cultural circumstances: what is reasonable in the context of one State may not be in another (De Varennes 1993, 8).

Furthermore, States have an obligation (in accordance with paragraph 33 of the Copenhagen Document) to encourage conditions for the promotion of identity that goes beyond mere protection and requires special or "positive" measures to ensure equal enjoyment and development of the rights of minorities in fact as well as under law. Crucial in this regard are the language and educational policies of the State concerned (see Eide 1999, 322). Persons who have the official language of the State as their mother tongue (usually the numerical majority) are automatically advantaged over those who speak a minority language. The privilege of the State language must therefore be balanced by adequate compensatory measures aiding persons belonging to linguistic minorities. At the same time, the international instruments for the protection of minorities provide that the exercise of positive rights shall neither impinge on the rights of others,[5] nor shall they in any way compromise the territorial integrity of the State.[6]

Accordingly, in practice, in OSCE States (Estonia, Georgia, Latvia, the former Yugoslav Republic of Macedonia, Moldova, Slovakia and Ukraine among others) where language regulation has been a source of tension, the HCNM stresses that, while he remains aware of and sensitive to the historical experiences of past repression, there is a need to balance efforts to preserve and promote the language of the majority with measures to ensure the maintenance and development of the languages of persons belonging to minorities. At the same time, the HCNM reminds minorities that as members of the larger society of the State, they also have interests and even certain obligations to learn and use the language(s) of the State.

While learning the State language promotes intra-State cohesion in general, it also benefits linguistic minorities in terms of their integration into society and their access to public goods. This has been so particularly in cases where knowledge of the State language is required in order to facilitate access to citizenship (for example, as is the case in the Baltic States, see Cilevičs in this volume). In many newly-independent States of the former Soviet Union, where a substantial part of the population may not speak the designated State language to any degree of proficiency, there is a need for adequate educational opportunities for persons belonging to minorities to gain or improve command of the State language(s). In response to such needs the OSCE HCNM and Missions have consistently encouraged the development of training programmes (for example, the State Language Training Programme in Latvia and similar programmes in Moldova and the former Yugoslav Republic of Macedonia (fYROM)) aimed at enabling persons who according to the law must use the State language, or who would wish to do so for their own benefit.

Some Remarks Regarding States' Practice

Practice amongst OSCE participating States varies considerably in terms of the constitutional and legal recognition and protection of minority languages.[7] Within the OSCE area, a number of newly-independent States have elevated selected language(s) to enjoy official status over others – in some cases directly inverting the hierarchy imposed under the previous regime, and thereby signalling the dominance of those for whom the official language is the mother tongue. In the Baltic States and elsewhere, the objective of the titular communities or so-called "State-forming nations" has been to enact the real and symbolic restoration of the language(s) spoken by the majority to primacy as the sole official languages of the State in a process of "cultural recovery".

While some States make no provision for languages other than the dominant State language, other States make provision for minority languages to a greater or lesser degree including in their Constitutions. For example, the Georgian Constitution provides for the additional official use of Abkhazian in the Abkhaz region. Similarly, Tajikistan has enshrined minority language rights for Tajik, Russian and Uzbek speakers in its Constitution. Other Constitutions (for example, those of Uzbekistan and Ukraine) embody a wider, more liberal approach to language issues whereby the State guarantees to respect, protect and create the conditions for the free development of all minority languages.[8]

De jure protection does not, however, guarantee equality in practice and so OSCE documents expressly include the need for *effective* implementation of OSCE commitments. The 1999 Istanbul Summit Declaration, for instance, emphasizes the requirement that laws and policies regarding the linguistic rights of persons belonging to national minorities at all levels conform to applicable international standards.[9] Even where constitutional protection exists, failure to enact and implement language legislation can create uncertainty on the part of linguistic minorities as to the content and extent of the rights granted to them, leading to anxiety and creating tensions.

Failure to adopt regulations for the swift implementation of existing laws can have a similar effect. In 1996, for example, the HCNM recommended that the implementation of the Romanian Law on Education be expedited in order to address the uncertainty and fears of the Hungarian minority.[10] Similarly, on the adoption of the State Language Law in Slovakia, the HCNM encouraged the rapid adoption of a law on minority languages as a counter-balance in order to avoid a legal vacuum on issues such as the use of minority languages in official communications.[11] In addition, the need to promote more *understanding* of relevant legislation regarding minority rights has also been an issue, in Kazakhstan for example (see Kemp 2001, 275). This last element is crucial insofar as there frequently exists a considerable gap between widely held "folk" beliefs about the rules of language, which can contribute to distrust and resentment between linguistic groups, and the reality in law (see Kontra 1999, 89-93).

Even where good laws exist at a national level, reluctance or inability to implement them at local public administration level can generate problems. In the fYROM, for example, there was a dispute at the Pedagogical Faculty of the principal university in Skopje in 1998 as the Dean refused to implement a special law ensuring instruction in the Albanian language with a view to meeting the practical need to train a sufficient number of Albanian-language instructors to fill posts in Albanian-language schools throughout the country (see Packer 2001, 268).

The Oslo and Hague Recommendations

It was in order generally to assist policy- and law-makers in developing and implementing good policies and laws in the areas of minority education and language rights that the HCNM facilitated the elaboration of two sets of general recommendations by a group of independent internationally-recognized experts for use in all OSCE participating States and beyond. Where, in the High Commissioner's experience, the international standards for protection of minorities lack clarity in some areas in terms of their content which leaves them open to interpretation and possible inconsistencies on application, the aim of *The Oslo Recommendations Regarding the Linguistic Rights of National Minorities* (1998)[12] and *The Hague Recommendations Regarding the Education Rights of National Minorities* (1996)[13] is to provide States with some guidance in finding appropriate accommodations for their minorities in the spheres of education and language that fully respect the letter and spirit of the internationally agreed standards. As such, the Recommendations represent an expert interpretation of binding, legal obligations and political commitments. Aimed at use in all OSCE participating States and beyond, they provide a clear framework within which States can develop law and policy tailored to their own cultural and linguistic context. Endorsed by the HCNM and available in several languages, they have been: circulated widely; the subject of seminars organized by the HCNM; discussed in the Permanent Council and at the 1999 OSCE Summit meeting in Istanbul; and generally become a reference among OSCE participating States (see Packer 2001, 262).

Survey of State Practice

In 1996, the HCNM also initiated a survey of OSCE participating States' practice concerning the linguistic rights of persons belonging to national minorities within their jurisdictions. Information was sought on four fundamental aspects of linguistic rights: the official status of languages; communication with administrative and judicial authorities; language in educational curricula; and access to public media in a minority language. The resulting comparative study, the *Report on the Linguistic Rights of Persons Belonging to National Minorities in the OSCE Area* issued in March 1999, provides an analytical summary of States' replies (mainly received in the course of 1997 and 1998 thus reflecting laws and practices in force at that time) grouped not only according to the questions asked but from the perspective of relevant international standards.[14] In doing so, the HCNM sought not only to document the range and variety of common States' practice, but also to indicate those options which met or surpassed minimum international standards — thereby indicating "best" practices upon which States could draw in developing or reforming their own regimes for the protection of the linguistic rights of minorities.

ROLE OF OSCE INSTITUTIONS IN ADDRESSING SPECIFIC LANGUAGE-RELATED ISSUES

This section highlights some recurring issues related to language arising in the OSCE context, providing the reader with a survey of the practical application of OSCE values through the work of the OSCE institutions in addressing specific language-related issues. It does not seek to provide a comprehensive survey of every issue that has arisen in the OSCE States in which the HCNM, Missions and other OSCE institutions are involved, but rather to provide an insight into the interventions of OSCE institutions in practice.

OSCE Institutions[15]

As the main OSCE institution mandated specifically to prevent conflict arising out of disputes between majority/minority groups, the HCNM has raised minority language issues as outlined below in many aspects of his work. He has done so through quiet diplomacy with the States concerned and has elaborated specific recommendations, communicated through formal exchanges of letters with governments, aimed at helping States to adopt policy and law in line with international standards. To this end, they usually refer to specific policies, laws and administrative practices and tend to be precise and detailed in substantive terms. The OSCE and other international standards to which the States have voluntarily subscribed serve as the principal framework of analysis and provide the basis for these recommendations.[16] These exchanges, although neither specifically foreseen by the mandate nor initially expected to become public, formed a mainstay of the first HCNM's engagement with States.[17] The written recommendations reflected the overall problem-solving, solution-oriented approach of the first HCNM, who sought politically viable solutions based on detailed (often legal) analysis within the framework of OSCE values and international standards. The HCNM has also raised minority language issues in many other aspects of his work including through direct personal contacts with various interlocutors, at seminars and round-tables conducted behind closed doors, through confidential exchanges of correspondence which may include specific recommendations, as well as in his confidential periodic reports to the Chairperson-in-Office and the Permanent Council of the OSCE (a practice the second HCNM has continued), in exchanges with inter-governmental organizations and in consultations with independent experts (see Packer 2001, 258).

In most situations where he is involved the HCNM's office maintains regular contacts with OSCE Missions and other field operations. While the OSCE Missions predominantly carry out their functions according to their own specific mandates which include minority languages to varying degrees,[18] they also provide valuable support to the HCNM, particularly in following up on his recommendations by means of monitoring, maintaining direct contacts, contributing analyses and performing tasks (see Packer 2001,

263). The work of both the OSCE Office for Democratic Institutions and Human Rights (ODIHR) and the OSCE Representative on the Freedom of the Media also have a bearing on minority language issues to some degree (as described below).

Much of the HCNM's attention has been directed towards the challenges of facilitating *social integration*. These varied according to the context and particulars of the situation be they relating to matters of policy, law, implementing regulations, public administration, institutional development or public information and popular perception. In the Baltic States he was particularly involved in the process of amending the State Language Law in Estonia and the elaboration of implementing Decrees pursuant to the 1999 State Language Law in Latvia. Minority-related language and education issues were also a matter for discussions with a number of States such as Ukraine and Russia (where the HCNM undertook a comprehensive survey on minority language education opportunities), in Slovakia (in relation to training for minority language teachers) and Romania (where reforms were introduced to facilitate minority language education and teacher training at tertiary level – a matter which had long been the subject of dispute). In Moldova, in addition to engagement with matters of minority language education, the HCNM also expressed reservations about language regulation in the private sphere, particularly with regard to the prescription of the state language as a means of communication in the electronic media.

The HCNM has maintained active engagement in language issues ranging from the constitutional and legislative protection of minority languages and the implementation of laws, to support for practical projects aimed at achieving a fair balance between the interests and needs of different linguistic groups represented within society. Even where general laws which protect the linguistic rights of minorities are in place, the crux of the matter lies in the implementation. Thus, for example, following Estonia's adoption of the Law on Language in 2000 the HCNM focused attention on the elaboration of the subsidiary regulations for practical implementation. Similarly, in Latvia the HCNM on several occasions expressed concern that the State Language Law be implemented in strict conformity with its various provisions.[19]

This concern for practical effect is borne out in two subjects of HCNM attention in recent years, as follows:

Official language certificates

Persistent problems concerning acceptable forms of *proof* of linguistic proficiency required for various reasons existed (such as naturalization, access to employment and other positions in public office and so on). In Estonia there was concern that up to 40 000 individuals who already held language certificates issued before July 1999 (when changes to the old system of testing entered into force) and which were due to expire on 1 July 2002 would not automatically have their certificates renewed, but would have to pass a new test. This was problematical, not least because the basic level of proficiency in the Estonian language under the new system was higher than under the old system. It was also administratively unnecessary, and was unfair to those persons who through personal effort, financial cost and evident good will had passed the previous tests and were being required to pass a new test merely because the State had chosen to change its system. As such, the HCNM repeatedly expressed to the Estonian authorities his misgivings about this renewed testing. In a letter to the Estonian Minister of Foreign Affairs in May 2001, the HCNM expressed his conviction that a solution could be found to make re-testing unnecessary and that such an approach would promote greater and better integration of society.[20]

In Latvia, progress on a similar issue of re-testing was made in November 2001 when amendments were adopted to the secondary language legislation, precluding the State Language Centre from rechecking the knowledge of individuals who already possess a legally obtained State Language Proficiency Certificate. The time for reissuing a lost certificate was also reduced.[21] The recognition of Latvian language exams passed by students for graduation as a valid test for purposes of naturalization was also favourably resolved in June 2001. This was in accordance with previous HCNM recommendations for a unified system (that is, with the Naturalization Board) to ease the bureaucratic process and act as a positive sign to the young non-citizen population[22] (as was achieved in Estonia, where secondary school and civic exams were recognized for naturalization purposes in 2001).

Tension-reducing projects

Since 2001, the Office of the HCNM has provided the Parliament and Government of Georgia with several comments on the Draft Law on the State Language. The HCNM viewed the State Language Law as an important element in social integration in Georgia, and called on the Government to follow it up with "a comprehensive programme to promote the knowledge and use of the State language throughout the country".[23] In this respect, the HCNM offered advice, technical assistance and financial support. Specifically, the HCNM aimed several language projects at alleviating the linguistic isolation of the Armenian-speaking population of the Samtskhe-Javakheti region, in the hope that they might participate more in Georgia's civic, economic and political life. In keeping with the HCNM's standard approach to promoting integration, efforts to improve the fluency of persons belonging to national minorities in the State language were coupled with provisions to promote the minority languages as well. Projects include: teaching the Georgian language to local civil servants; improving the instruction of Georgian as a second language in local schools; and providing high school graduates with Georgian language training so they may attend Georgian universities. At the same time, the HCNM supported a project to rebroadcast news programmes from the Georgian capital in the Armenian language which is the dominant language in the region.

A host of projects were developed under the umbrella of the multi-sector "Conflict Prevention and Integration Programme for Samtskhe-Javakheti". Designed in 2002 and initiated in spring 2003, the Programme takes a coordinated approach to addressing the economic, social and political isolation of the region and attendant immediate problems with a number of language-related and other capacity-building initiatives aimed at promoting the inclusion and integration of the region and its population into Georgian society. In addition, Georgian language training for civil servants in the area aimed to help integrate the local public administration into the institutions of the State as a whole.

Public/Private Divide

Issues arise in relation to both the "public" and "private" spheres and particularly at their point of intersection, raising difficult questions of the balance between legitimate public interests and the protection of human rights (see Packer 1999, 312). Activities in the private sphere may be subject to regulation by the State in the interests of protecting *inter alia* national security, public order, public health or morals, or the rights and reputations of others. The State could, for example, require the use of an official language *alongside* the minority language in the activities of private groups or organizations in the keeping of financial records and other official documentation. Any restrictions by the State made purportedly in the public interest must be proportional to the aim sought. Unwarranted interference (specifically the imposition of language preferences) by the State in the private sphere is often a major source of dispute between governments and linguistic minorities. Attempts to do so may fall foul of a number of well-established rights in international law, including the right to family and private life, freedom of expression and non-discrimination, as well as the norms of international labour law.

In the public sphere, issues arise in situations where persons belonging to national minorities seek the use of their own language in a wide range of activities involving State authorities, including the provision of public services. While there is a public interest in ensuring coherent and effective administration, it should be noted that multilingualism in public affairs is both possible and common practice in many States and in certain fields allowing minorities to use their mother tongue is a matter of ensuring access to justice (for example, in communication with the judiciary).

Whereas a State can adopt any official language(s) it chooses, there are situations where it would be unreasonable and therefore discriminatory *not* to allow the use of other languages in the provision of public services or in the sphere of public administration *in addition* to the State language. This applies typically (though not exclusively) under certain conditions, that is in areas where minorities are "traditionally" present or are concentrated in "substantial numbers" and where there is a "sufficient demand".[24] In some cases such a provision is also a matter of public interest. With regard to health services, for example, consultation provided in a language that the individual understands ensures good diagnosis and appropriate treatment – which may have wider, public health implications.

In practice, difficulties have arisen in terms of defining what proportion of the population constitutes "significant numbers". In Slovakia, for example, the threshold percentage of persons belonging to a national minority needed in order for a community to provide minority language services (10 per cent or 20 per cent) was a bone of contention between ethnic Slovak and Hungarian parties in the governing coalition of 1998 (see Kemp 2001, 125). Although percentage minimums appear necessary, it is most important that decisions are reasonable, that the specific situation of minorities is taken into consideration and that creative solutions are sought (see Siemienski 1999, 353).

The HCNM has been involved in ensuring that procedures for the monitoring of compliance with the provisions of State language laws are in keeping with the letter and spirit of the law. In Latvia, the HCNM gave advice during the elaboration of the Code on Administrative Violations. In May 2001 he reiterated concerns (initially expressed in a formal letter in November 2000) about proposed amendments to the Code, particularly with regard to: provisions for the penalization of organizers of public events who fail to ensure interpretation into the State language; excessive fines for employers who sign a contract with a person who should possess linguistic proficiency, but who does not hold a certificate issued by the State Language Centre; as well as general penalization of incorrect use of the State language. As the HCNM has recalled on several occasions, such penalties could only apply in situations involving a legitimate public interest (such as public health or safety) and then only to the extent necessary to achieve this aim.[25] More generally, the HCNM has supported efforts to train inspectors of the responsible agency for implementation, the State Language Centre. In 2001 the HCNM's Office assisted the now closed OSCE Mission with its proposal to elaborate a legal manual for the Inspectorate aimed at clarifying the limits of the provisions of the law; notably, requirements should not be imposed on private activities without legitimate public interest. An understanding between the High Commissioner and the Head of the State Language Centre was reached on its application.[26] Specifically, to assist the inspectors in applying the Language Law, in early 2003 the HCNM engaged a Latvian and an international legal expert to develop a practice manual for use by the Inspectors. This work continued in 2004.

Resources

The fact that State obligation is linked to specific territorial and other limiting criteria reflects the concerns of States about potentially open-ended spending commitments and potential shortages of minority language speakers to provide such services if the obligation to do so were absolute.[27] Given the political sensitivities of "fragile majorities" combined with competing demands on limited resources, particularly in transitional economies, the majority is often reluctant to see resources expended on the promotion of the cultural and linguistic rights of persons belonging to minorities. Inequality in the distribution of State resources thus becomes a major point of dispute – particularly in the realms of culture and education. Access to cultural subsidies for the Hungarian minority under the Mečiar Government in Slovakia, for example, constituted a source of tension. The OSCE approach, informed as it is by the principle of non-discrimination, advises that while resources will always be limited, it is important to ensure that those which are available be used in an equitable fashion and to maximum effect – that is, to the benefit of the largest number of persons and groups. In particular, cost-effectiveness and transparency are key in ensuring acceptance among majority opinion for minority language policies.[28] It is worth noting, in addition, that relatively simple and inexpensive ways can often be found to facilitate minority language use in, for example, communication with the State.

Even where the political will exists, sometimes States simply cannot afford to implement desirable policies aimed at accommodating minority demands. In Georgia, for example, serious economic constraints on the authorities have made it difficult to overcome the lack of educational materials for minority language schools across the country (see Packer 2001, 267). In specific cases the OSCE Missions and the HCNM have both intervened to facilitate funding for various desirable policy-making endeavours. In Kyrgyzstan, for example, new textbooks for Uzbeki schools were provided with the assistance of the Foundation on Inter-Ethnic Relations.[29]

Public Administrative Authorities

The extent and conditions under which State authorities may have an obligation to allow the use of non-official minority languages in addition to the State language(s) in contacts with official authorities in the conduct of governance (for example, in organs of local self-administration) has been the source of controversy in many OSCE participating States. This right is particularly significant for persons belonging to linguistic minorities since it both ensures that they are able to understand the policies that affect them, and that they may express their own views and become actively involved in civil life.[30] In Bosnia and Herzegovina, for example, use of language in official communications, including documentation and official settings (such as meetings), has been a constant source of disputes (see Packer 2001, 264).

All OSCE States are committed to "endeavour to ensure that persons belonging to national minorities … have adequate opportunities … wherever possible and necessary for its [the mother tongue's] use before public authorities."[31] According to both the Copenhagen Document and the Framework Convention,[32] where national minorities need to communicate with governmental institutions, typically though not exclusively in areas where they live traditionally or in substantial numbers, the government should make every effort to make this possible. At the same time, both instruments recognize that financial and other constraints may come into play.[33]

The issue of the use of minority languages in official communications with governmental officials and bodies has arisen frequently in OSCE States. Some, like Tajikistan, have taken the step of guaranteeing in their Constitutions minority language rights, including access to administrative services and courts in areas where minority language groups live in substantial numbers (see Packer 2001, 269). By contrast, in Slovakia the use of minority languages in official communications was a major source of dispute between the ethnic Hungarian minority and the Meçiar Governments in the Slovak Republic between 1993 and 1998. During this period the HCNM consistently argued for the restoration of the rights of minorities to use their languages in official communications and, specifically, against proposals by the Government to oblige a translation in the State (that is, Slovak) language to be included in every such communication (which, the HCNM argued, would rob the right of its meaning).[34] Subsequent to the change in Government in 1998, the issue was resolved the following year with provision now made for minorities to use their language in communications with public administrative organs and in organs of local self-administration in those municipalities where they constitute at least 20 per cent of the population.[35] In Romania in this regard, a significant development was the passage in January 2001 of a law on public administration that allows for the official use of minority languages in communities where the speakers make up at least 20 per cent of the population. Some States, such as Croatia, guarantee the official use of minority languages and script together with the State language where persons belonging to minorities constitute more than 50 per cent of the population in a municipality.[36] The obvious shortcoming of the aforementioned provisions lies in the fact that minority protection is not usually extended in official relations beyond the municipal framework, which means to the exclusion of minorities that are not territorially concentrated.

With regard to communication with judicial authorities, as a matter of due process the State is obliged to provide interpretation for those who do not understand the language of the Court in criminal proceedings.[37] The protection afforded, however, requires the use of the individual's own language only if they understand no other; it does not permit a member of a minority to choose the language to be used (see Dunbar 2001, 105). With respect to the use of the mother tongue in non-criminal court proceedings, the OSCE has not reached consensus on standards to this effect, although other international standards do allow for a "sliding-scale" approach dependent upon the particular circumstances.[38]

Positive developments took place in Romania and Estonia in 2001 with the adoption, respectively, of the Law on Local Public Administration (February 2001) and the Local Government Organization Act (December 2001) which, taking into account HCNM and OSCE Mission concerns, allow for the official use of minority languages in line with relevant international standards. The HCNM continued his engagement with the two Governments on issues of implementation, including reform of the public administration in Romania.

In Latvia, while changes to the Constitution on 9 May 2002 stipulated the required use of the Latvian language at the local level, this does not preclude the use of other languages. However, Latvian legislation neither specifically provided for nor facilitated the use of minority languages as required according to paragraph 34 of the OSCE Copenhagen Document. In this connection, there were significant calls from the Russian-speaking minority community for such opportunities at least at the local level.[39] This has been the subject of HCNM discussions with the Government of Latvia.

In terms of practical implementation, in 2004 the HCNM began a project in Georgia to establish legal information centres in three districts of the predominantly Armenian-speaking Samtskhe-Javakheti region to provide the local population with information about their civil rights in a language that they understand. At the same time, local civil servants received language education in the Georgian language to enhance their communications with authorities in Tbilisi.

In Kyrgyzstan in April 2003, the HCNM focused on promoting multilingual education and the integration of ethnic minorities into law enforcement agencies. In meetings with officials, he argued that efforts on both fronts would do much to promote integration.[40]

Public Office and the Electoral Process

Political representation through access to positions of public office and to the electoral process is a key to ensuring the effective participation of minority language-speakers in public life. In a number of OSCE States language issues have arisen both in terms of the linguistic proficiency of candidates for public office, and of the proceedings of the electoral process. The work of the ODIHR on elections and democratization is especially relevant in this regard. In relation to OSCE election-related commitments, as reflected principally in the 1990 Copenhagen Document,[41] there is no specific mention of language requirements, although issues arise in relation to the principle of non-discrimination, the freedom of expression and voter understanding of election processes and political platforms (see Packer 2001, 272).

In view of the importance of democratic processes open to all citizens, effectively disenfranchising or excluding individuals from standing for office because they do not speak the official language would most likely constitute an unreasonable, and therefore discriminatory, restriction (see De Varennes 2001, 27); in fact, Article 25 of the ICCPR stipulates a much more precise and rigorous standard insofar as "no distinction" is to be made with regard to the right to stand for elected office.[42] The rationale underlying this standard is not only to protect the individual's right to seek to be elected, but also the more fundamental interest to ensure the freedom of the electorate to choose their representatives and, thereby, that the will of the people shall be the basis of the authority of government in the State.[43]

The concern about elections foreseen by the United Nations in 1966 in adopting the precise text of Article 25 as part of the ICCPR appears today remarkably astute. In practice, States do act to prevent individuals not proficient in the official language(s) from standing for election to official posts. For example, in early 1999 the presidential election in Kazakhstan drew criticism from the ODIHR insofar as candidate registration required the passing of a Kazakh language test that was considered to be arbitrary and gave rise to public mistrust of the process.[44] Likewise, language proficiency requirements for presidential candidates of the Kyrgyz Republic, including the establishment of a special Language Commission for purposes of testing candidates, effectively resulted in elimination of representatives of certain political groups; this also drew criticism from ODIHR.

The question of linguistic requirements (of the highest proficiency) to stand for elected office was a significant aspect of the HCNM's engagement in both Estonia and Latvia. In fact, both ODIHR and the HCNM (as well as the EU[45]) expressed concern about the effective restrictions on the right of citizens to seek office and of the voters' right to decide who they deem most suitable to represent their interests (regardless of their command of language), in contravention of international obligations.[46] The HCNM has stressed throughout the underlying democratic principle that the will of the people shall be the basis of the authority of government; should the electorate so choose, they should be free to elect persons who enjoy their confidence but who may not, in the opinion of others, possess relevant or desirable skills, much less purported "proficiencies". The critical matter is that the elected person is deemed by the electorate to represent them (irrespective of how well).[47]

In Estonia, amendments in 1998 to the Laws on Parliamentary Elections, Local Elections and the State Language, which tightened the linguistic requirement to stand for elected office to the *Riigikogu* (Parliament) or local government council, led both ODIHR and the HCNM to express concerns about the effective restrictions on the right of citizens to seek office, in contravention of both Estonia's international obligations and her own Constitution.[48] In November 2001, Estonia acted to abolish these requirements, satisfied with the stipulation of the Estonian language as the sole language of the *Parliament*; the HCNM issued a welcoming statement in response.[49]

Progress in Latvia on this issue was slower, following the HCNM's December 2001 analysis (at the request of the Latvian authorities)[50] which found that those provisions of the election legislation stipulating the highest Latvian language proficiency for persons standing for office both in the *Saeima* (Parliament) and also to elected councils of self-government were in line neither with international human rights standards nor with the Latvian Constitution. At the same time, the President of Latvia made a strong recommendation to the Latvian Parliament to remove the restrictions, with leading Statesmen (including US Secretary of State Colin Powell, US President George W. Bush and NATO Secretary General Lord Robertson) issuing similar statements. The case for their removal was further strengthened by the 9 April 2002 judgment of the European Court of Human Rights in the *Podkolzina v. Latvia* case. The Court found the re-examination of the language proficiency of a deputy candidate (who already held a state language certificate to the highest proficiency), and her subsequent removal from the electoral list, to be in contravention of Article 3 of Protocol 1 of the European Convention on Human Rights.[51] Following pressure from the HCNM and others throughout the spring of 2002,[52] amendments to the Latvian Election Laws were finally adopted on 10 May 2002. In response, the HCNM issued a positive statement welcoming the abolition of the Latvian language proficiency requirement for persons standing for elections at the national and municipal levels.[53]

Still, the HCNM continued to watch that no obstacles remained in practice.

The use of language in the national parliament was also a source of contention in Macedonia, where representatives of the Albanian minority sought the possibility for Albanian-speaking parliamentarians to speak their mother tongue during debates.[54] As in the Baltic States, discussions were complicated by a fear on the part of the majority community that the possibility for the use of languages other than the majority language would lead to effective bilingualism in parliament and, as a result, diminishment of the language of the titular community. In response, the HCNM stressed in his meetings with Government officials that, through the use of interpretation, it is possible to allow for the use of minority languages while maintaining the principle that parliamentary discussions will take place in the State language (that is, without negative effect for the majority).

As regards the election process generally, the ODIHR Election Observation Handbook states that "in multilingual societies, observers should note whether the election administration has made any effort to facilitate voting of those citizens who may not speak the language of the majority".[55] Subsequently developed *Guidelines to Assist National Minority Participation in the Electoral Process* clearly state that the use of any language should not be prescribed or proscribed in the electoral process; they recommend the monitoring and assessment of language requirements concerning: design, print and dissemination of ballots; voter education/information campaigns (including access to the media in a minority language); political party registration and promotion materials; and State language laws affecting voter/candidate registration.[56] In 1999, for example, the ODIHR Election Observation Mission in Estonia noted that the Estonian regulations on language use interfered with the ability of some candidates to communicate with parts of the electorate by limiting the language on campaign posters and related materials only to the State language.[57] Regarding voter registration, the OSCE Mission in Kosovo reported that the majority of Kosovo Turks did not participate in the process for the October 2000 municipal elections because the Turkish language was not used in the registration process.[58] As a result, provisions to accommodate the need for the use of the Turkish language to facilitate participation of this community in Kosovo-wide elections in 2001 were developed.[59]

Language-related problems have also arisen with respect to political associations and parties which, while generally deemed to operate in the private sphere (and not therefore subject to language restrictions), are subject to regulation where they intersect with the public sphere, for example in the broadcasting of political messages on public media or in the registration process. In 1998 in Macedonia, for example, an ethnic Albanian political party was refused registration by a court of registration partly on the ground that its seal was bilingual and thus said to be unconstitutional since the State language is Macedonian written in Cyrillic Script – causing significant political controversy (see Packer 2001, 268).

Employment in the Public and Private Spheres

With regard to non-elected public positions, the HCNM and other relevant OSCE bodies have urged a balanced ethnic composition of personnel in various branches of the public service such as governmental departments, the military and police in various States where such an imbalance has caused tension.[60]

Issues of State language proficiency have also arisen with regard to certain jobs in both public and private sectors. In Latvia in 1998, the HCNM was instrumental in persuading the Latvian President to reconsider an amendment to the labour code which would have empowered the State Language Inspectorate to require employers to terminate contracts of those employees who did not meet language requirements stipulated under Latvian law. In 2000, this time in connection with implementation of the State Language Law, the HCNM expressed concern over the penalization of employers who would engage persons who should have State language proficiency, but do not have proof of this proficiency from the State Language Centre (as opposed to other sources of proof).[61] In Estonia, the HCNM expressed concern regarding a Governmental decree adopted in May 2001 implementing the Estonian Language Law with regard to employment in the private sector, where he felt regulations were overly intrusive. Implementation decrees pertaining to the language requirements for employment in the public and private spheres (as stipulated in the Law on Language) continued for a long time to be the subject of informal discussion between Estonian authorities and experts from the HCNM's office. While the decree was elaborated in consultation with the Office of the HCNM, concerns remained over the imposition of language requirements for two categories in particular: in private educational institutions, and for sales and service personnel in private enterprises.[62] In this context, both the HCNM and other international actors articulated their concerns that implementation of the Language Law should be conducted under strict adherence to the principle of proportionality in safeguarding public interests.[63] The HCNM addressed the Estonian Foreign Minister in a letter in June 2001 seeking assurances that his interpretation would be the one guiding the implementation of the Act and the decree by the implementing agency. The Estonian authorities responded by clarifying that employers in the sales and services sector would have the responsibility but also the choice to determine who exactly among their workers (that is, not *all* employees) should have a basic knowledge of the Estonian language. The same applies in the education sector.

When regulating in this area, the HCNM has stressed to States like Latvia, which adopted a similar implementing decree in August 2000,[64] that State language proficiency requirements must be directly and convincingly connected with specific legitimate public interests.[65] Lists of professions requiring a high level of proficiency in the State language should therefore be kept to a minimum so as to avoid discrimination.[66]

Regarding proficiency in the State language for various positions in the private sector, the HCNM again addressed matters arising in policy, law and practice in Estonia and Latvia. The HCNM also questioned the practice in

Latvia of fining an employer whose employees are required to be proficient, but who do not hold a proficiency certificate. Since there are other forms of proof of proficiency than possession of a State-issued certificate (the most obvious being graduation from a Latvian language educational establishment), the requirement of only the certificate issued from the State Language Centre was viewed to be discriminatory.

Concerns have persisted regarding proposals to extend the imposition of language requirements (of a State language proficiency certificate) in the private sphere to include professions such as hairdressers and shop assistants – professions and jobs which were previously removed from the implementing decree as not serving legitimate public interests.

Another closely related matter is whether the whole population possess the linguistic proficiencies required for employment of various kinds, whether in the public service or in private employ but where legitimate public interests stipulate a linguistic proficiency. Unless the whole population enjoys access to education of such a kind as ensures them such proficient, they will not enjoy equal access to employment. Obviously, speakers of non-official languages (typically minorities) are disadvantaged in this regard. Accordingly, the HCNM has sought in such places as Estonia, Latvia, Georgia, Macedonia, Moldova, Kazakhstan and Kyrgyzstan to promote better State language education in minority language schools with a view to increasing the opportunities for subsequent employment in public positions and in private positions with legitimate public interest among persons belonging to minorities.

Citizenship

The HCNM has also encountered language issues in relation to stipulations made by Citizenship Laws and naturalization procedures. Most notably, the HCNM's engagement in the Baltic States focused on the persistent problem of the large number of Stateless persons in these countries, constituting an unparalleled percentage of the total population.[67]

Specifically, in Latvia, the HCNM in cooperation with the OSCE Mission sought to stimulate the slow naturalization process by overcoming obstacles of language testing and procedural requirements (such as the so-called window system which restricted applicants according to date of birth) and also, through a greater pace of naturalizations, to promote social integration (see Packer 2001, 260). In order to promote public awareness regarding naturalization procedures and so encourage applications, the HCNM requested the Foundation on Inter-Ethnic Relations to prepare a pamphlet in both the Estonian and Russian languages (since non-Latvian-speakers – mainly Russian-speakers – comprise the overwhelming majority of the Stateless population). The Mission, for its part, monitored the work of the Naturalization Board and sought simplification and other improvements in the language tests for naturalization. In particular, the Mission monitored and encouraged the work of the National Programme for Latvian-Language Training, including efforts to find funding for this crucial programme. Prior to its closing at the end of 2001, the OSCE Mission encouraged and secured foreign funding for free language training for 2000 persons through the Latvian Naturalization Board in order to prepare these persons to pass the language test forming part of the naturalization process; it is remarkable that demand outstripped the available places by a ratio of 10 to 1.

The slow rate of naturalization and the need to maintain and accelerate momentum was a central theme of the HCNM's discussions with the Latvian authorities.[68] In April 2001 the HCNM suggested improvements in the administrative procedure to encourage non-citizens to apply and to speed up the process for those who do. The fee for naturalization (which remained one of the main obstacles for non-citizens, particularly from rural communities[69]) was reduced in June 2001.[70] Problems with the recognition of Latvian language exams of students on graduation from basic school were likewise resolved in June 2001 following HCNM persistence.

Similarly, in Estonia the HCNM's central recommendations focused on the need to set reasonable linguistic standards and develop a proactive public information campaign (in the language of the target group) aimed at clarifying requirements, in particular to dispel fears about their level of difficulty. He also encouraged the Government to address concerns regarding, amongst others: opportunities to retake the language test; measures to reduce the risk of different interpretations and practices by the officials concerned; and the rate of examination fees.[71] Since 2001, when the rate of naturalization stabilized around the figure of 3000 per annum, the HCNM's concerns centred on the fees for the State language test necessary for naturalization (and employment) purposes, as well as the need for governmental steps to facilitate language instruction for those wishing to naturalize. In sum, the HCNM's recommendations have always been specific and reasoned, for example stressing the importance of an effective system of language instruction with qualified instructors, modern teaching materials and methods, and expanded use of the mass media.[72]

Economic/Commercial Sphere

Freedom of expression extends to the right of persons belonging to minorities (as to all other persons) to use their own language in private activities, including in the private display of signs, posters and so on, of a commercial nature.[73] This does not, however, exclude the possibility for the State to require some use of an official language in private commercial enterprises where a legitimate public interest may be invoked — such as the furtherance of workplace health and safety or consumer protection or in dealings with the public authorities in accounting, taxation or other processes.[74] However, such a requirement may only ever stipulate the additional use of an official language: it may never expressly or in effect prohibit the use of (an)other language(s). Thus, requirements must be both pursuant to a legitimate public interest and be proportionate to the specific aim sought such that, for example, a requirement would be in violation of international standards should it require *all* employees (without distinction, or without specific justification) of a private enterprise to speak an official language (see De Varennes 2001, 16).

The extent of permissible State interference in the private sphere raises practical, administrative and other issues relating to economic efficacy. The State should take into account the practical effects of their requirements in order to ensure that they do not make unrealistic and discriminatory demands on owners of private enterprises. In 1997, for example, the HCNM criticized a Latvian draft law which stipulated the use of the State language within all enterprises (companies), including meetings of directors and staff.[75] Similarly, in July 1999 the OSCE Mission in Moldova informed the HCNM of proposed amendments to the Moldovan Law on Commercial Advertising effectively prohibiting advertising in the Russian-language (or any other language than the State language); when the Government moved in the autumn of 1999 to adopt the amendments, the HCNM wrote to the Foreign Minister recommending withdrawal of the proposed amendment on the argument that it contradicted the freedom of expression.[76] While the Foreign Minister did not share the HCNM's assessment – arguing the need to take account of the country's "specific situation, also characteristic for other states from former soviet space" – the exchange initiated an on-going dialogue with the Government about the regulation of language in general in Moldova.[77]

Provision of Public Services

The extent to which the State is required to accommodate the desire of persons belonging to national minorities to use their own language in the public sphere has arisen frequently vis-à-vis the provision of key services in the fields of health, social services and education. The use of the minority mother tongue is particularly important in the areas of health and social services where individuals must be able to express themselves clearly and fully. This right might extend in certain situations (at least in regions and localities where minorities are present in significant numbers and where they have expressed a desire for it) beyond the right to address and receive a reply from the authorities in the minority language, to include the right to receive services in that language (see Packer & Siemienski 1999, 345). Of course, the provision of services in a national minority language may have substantial resource implications. However, as persons belonging to minorities often point out, as taxpayers their needs should be taken into account according to the principles of equality and non-discrimination. Indeed, from the perspective of need, it may well be that special measures are required exactly for smaller groups who otherwise would be disadvantaged and normally would not comprise a sufficient economic base to generate their own financially justified "demand". In fact, economic and financial considerations are arguably over-stated in these cases; careful recruitment policies (for example, engaging bilingual staff) in the relevant services can often respond satisfactorily to particular needs.

Education

Perhaps nowhere has the question of the State funding of services provoked more debate than in the sphere of education. Education and the extent to which an education system allows the use and development of minority languages is crucial for minorities, both in its implications for cultural continuity and for access to employment and other opportunities within the State. The UN Committee on the Rights of the Child has clearly indicated that education should aim to promote respect for each child's own cultural identity, language and values, along with the national values of the country in which the child is living; this requires a balanced approach, reconciling a wide range of values, crossing religious, ethnic and cultural boundaries.[78] In addition, the promotion of understanding, tolerance and friendship as a component of education is important insofar as children may play a unique role in bridging differences that have historically separated groups from one another in their wider social environment.

Issues arise in both public and private spheres as regards the teaching *of* and teaching *through* the medium of the minority language at all levels (pre-school, primary, secondary, vocational, and tertiary) as well as the content of the curriculum, the training of teachers, the monitoring of performance, and the recognition and provision of qualifications in the minority language. In particular, the question of State obligations regarding the funding of private educational institutions set up by minorities in an effort to meet their own linguistic and educational needs has been a source of contention in many States.

The principle that minorities should, where possible, be provided with adequate opportunities for instruction of or in their mother tongue (without prejudice to the learning of the official language or the teaching in this language) is established in OSCE and other international standards.[79] To this end, they are entitled to set up and to manage their own private educational and training establishments.[80] States are often resistant to the creation of such parallel institutions and argue that, where they do exist, they should be privately funded. While there is no formal obligation on States to provide funding to private minority language educational establishments, paragraph 32.2 of the Copenhagen Document stipulates that such institutions have the right to "seek voluntary financial and other contributions as well as public assistance ...".[81] In situations where the State already provides assistance to private schools, then minority educational facilities would be entitled to similar support in accordance with the principle of non-discrimination (see De Varennes 2001, 28).

Nowhere is the argument more heated over the funding of minority language education than at tertiary level. The situation in Macedonia shows how this issue can stir nationalist feelings. Here, the question of official State recognition and funding of the "underground" Albanian language University in Tetevo (created without prior consultation with, or the consent of, the State authorities) has constituted one of the key demands of the minority Albanian-speaking population and is inextricably linked to the very process of State-building in the fYROM.[82] Indeed, while certainly not the only issue of concern, the Albanian community mobilized around the question of a minority university to the extent that it strained majority–minority relations to breaking point. At various points since the HCNM's involvement in 1993, the issue threatened to erupt into violence. In his efforts to promote dialogue and accord between the parties, the HCNM consistently urged the Government to accommodate the legitimate Albanian aspirations for improved access to higher education in the mother tongue, while appealing to the Albanian community to pursue their aims through available legal channels. Specifically, he was instrumental in brokering the compromise that led to adoption of the Law on Higher Education on 25 July 2000 which allows for higher education in minority languages, thus making it possible to establish a new private higher educational institution, the South Eastern Europe University (SEE University) located at Tetevo, which offers a curriculum mainly in the Albanian language with courses also in the Macedonian, English and other European languages. Under the HCNM's guidance a business plan was developed and an International Foundation established to plan and oversee the project, funding for which was secured from several OSCE States, the EU Commission and the Soros Foundation.[83] Commitment to this project continued even against the backdrop of escalating hostilities in the region at various times and which, in July and August 2001, necessitated the suspension of construction work in Tetevo.[84] The SEE University officially opened its doors on 20 November 2001 at a ceremony attended by both the first and second HCNMs, Mr Ekéus and Mr van der Stoel, the latter of whom is also chairman of the university's international advisory board.[85] Mr Ekéus joined the Board in March 2002. The SEE University has since thrived, with a 2004–2005 enrolment of some 5000 students in five faculties. Students have already successfully graduated. In January 2004 a law on establishing a new (third) State university in Tetevo was adopted. At the request of the Macedonian authorities the HCNM provided assistance to the Maticna Commission which was established by the Government to carry out the preparatory work for setting up the new institution; the HCNM also supported an independent expert to advise on a range of matters.

In addressing demands for separate State funded minority-language institutions in Macedonia and elsewhere, the HCNM has encouraged parties to explore different options available for promoting minority language education, including the possibility of enhancing existing institutions to accommodate the linguistic needs of minority groups. Such an approach avoids the potential risk of creating separate institutions leading not to integration but to linguistic "ghettoization". In Romania, for example, while the Hungarian minority was calling for re-establishment of the Hungarian University in Cluj, the HCNM urged parties to consider options other than the restoration of an exclusively Hungarian institution. Options proposed by various parties included: establishing a university with Hungarian and German lines of study, establishing separate Hungarian faculties within the existing Babes-Bolyai University (BBU) in Cluj-Napoca, or developing the concept of multiculturalism at BBU by adapting its curriculum and introducing a better ethnic mix of staff. The last option was eventually facilitated by the adoption of a new Law on Education in 1999, which also allowed the possibility of the development of a private Hungarian University. Similarly, in Macedonia, the HCNM looked into the possibility of providing Albanian language courses at existing Pedagogical Faculties in Skopje and Bitola (see Kemp 2001, 187). Significantly, one of the preconditions of the current agreement on the SEE University requires a close and institutionalized cooperation with the Saint Cyril and Methodius University in Skopje. The HCNM was also instrumental in encouraging access for Albanian-speaking students to Macedonian-speaking higher education through the setting up of a Transition Year Programme providing Albanian-speaking students in the fourth year of secondary school with specialized training in the State language aimed at raising their success in Macedonian language State examinations for entrance to institutions of higher education. The programme became active in all seven Albanian-language gymnasia, co-taught by ethnic Albanian and ethnic Macedonian instructors.[86]

Questions of State intervention and funding in education also raise issues of design and control. While the State has a right and responsibility to ensure that all educational institutions are established and maintained in accordance with the law, and may impose certain requirements (such as the learning of the official language(s) up to a certain level),[87] the HCNM has cautioned against the imposition of "unduly burdensome legal and administrative requirements regulating the establishment and management of educational institutions, whether private or public".[88]

Whether incorporating linguistic diversity into existing institutions or setting up new educational establishments, assuring minorities a degree of control over the design and implementation of decisions that directly affect them is key. In Romania, for example, particular emphasis was placed on the need for changing decision-making structures at the BBU in order adequately to safeguard the interests of especially the Hungarian-speaking minority.[89]

Linguists recognize that along with other design and implementation issues, the content of curricula can have a profound effect on the levels of success in protecting the rights of linguistic minorities (see Dunbar 2001, 111). Where possible, the HCNM has encouraged the development of alternative textbooks, particularly in subjects relating to language, history and culture, to develop the curriculum. ODIHR activities and projects have also touched upon language issues in this regard, with the sponsoring, publication and distribution of the first Roma-Macedonian dictionary which has been instrumental in fostering integration while contributing to the preservation of Roma identity. Such steps facilitate parental choice as foreseen in Article 5, as well as in Articles 28 and 29 of the Convention on the Rights of the Child, Article 13 of the International Covenant on Educational, Social and Cultural Rights, and recommendation 7 of The Hague Recommendations regarding the Education Rights of National Minorities.

At the primary and secondary levels, linguistic minorities frequently raise concerns regarding the quality of minority language education and the need for more teachers, specifically the lack of State-funded facilities to train teachers who could offer instruction in minority languages. Accordingly, the HCNM has encouraged and supported teacher-training projects and programmes in a number of places, including Latvia and Moldova. In a similar vein, the HCNM has encouraged and supported the improvement of teaching of the majority language (usually the official or State language) in minority-language schools since quality language instruction as a second language is critical for the future social, economic and political mobility of the individual children and also for the future social stability of the country as a whole.

The HCNM has also assisted States in addressing logistical problems of, for example, physical accessibility related to the provision of minority language education. In Ukraine, where the Crimean Tatar minority are geographically dispersed and children have experienced problems getting to or integrating into mainstream schools, the HCNM has encouraged the development of "home schools" whereby individuals are provided with support to enlarge their homes to accommodate classes and local teachers are contracted to provide instruction in the Tatar, Ukrainian and Russian languages (see Kemp 2001, 227). In another case, the HCNM has supported the Spillover Mission in Macedonia which facilitated communication between donors and communities seeking funds to improve the infrastructure of their schools which is doubly strained in those schools with parallel (Albanian and Macedonian) teaching shifts.

In the period of 2001–2002, the importance of language use in education as a major concern of the HCNM was manifest in the reciprocal concerns of Russia and Ukraine that "their" minorities living in the respective other State enjoy adequate opportunities for mother-tongue education. Pursuant to an invitation received in 2000, and following a fact-finding mission by a group of international experts, the HCNM communicated recommendations to the Foreign Ministers of both countries in January 2001.[90] His main concerns related to the legal guarantee of parental choice and the need to inform parents about the possibilities for setting up minority language classes in schools, as well as the balance of Ukrainian/Russian language teaching in schools, with a view to ensuring adequate opportunities for learning the Russian language in Ukrainian schools and vice versa. In this connection, the HCNM encouraged the parties to sign (Russia) and ratify (Ukraine) the European Charter for Regional or Minority Languages.

Matters of education were also preoccupying in Moldova where the HCNM expressed concern about the situation of schools in Transdniestria which sought to teach children the Moldovan and Romanian languages in the Latin script, against the wishes of the effective powers in Tiraspol who insist instead that the Cyrillic script be used, notwithstanding applicable Moldovan law or the wishes of the parents. The HCNM closely monitored the situation together with the Moldovan Government, the OSCE Mission to Moldova and the United Nations High Commissioner for Refugees (UNHCR).[91] Unfortunately, the powers in Tiraspol forcefully closed down the schools in 2004 on the heels of an HCNM visit and in the face of HCNM appeals.

Tertiary education and, specifically, the training of minority language teachers has also long been an issue in Slovakia. In the autumn of 2000 and early in 2001, the HCNM, together with two internationally recognized experts on higher education, visited Constantine the Philosopher University in Nitra to discuss ways of improving the training of teachers in minority languages. A visit in January 2002 confirmed the view that there needed to be established a separate faculty with instruction in the Hungarian language.

In terms of facilitating the learning of the State language for persons belonging to minorities, the HCNM and OSCE Missions have consistently encouraged the development of training programmes (for example, the State Language Training Programme in Latvia and similar programmes in Moldova and in Macedonia) aimed at enabling persons who according to the law must use the State language, or who would wish to do so for their own benefit. However, a number of States suffer from a lack of qualified teachers of the State language (as a second language for minorities). In October 2000, the Office of the High Commissioner, in cooperation with the OSCE Mission to Moldova, the Moldovan Government and a local NGO, began a project for training teachers of the Moldovan language. The project was designed to improve the teaching methods of those who teach Moldovan as a second language and is aimed at teachers of the fifth to ninth grades in schools which have large numbers of pupils from minority communities.[92]

In the Baltic States of Estonia and Latvia, the HCNM has stressed that the reform schedules with regard to the transformation of minority Russian-language secondary education systems (that is, so that the majority of teaching will take place in the State languages) should accommodate minority language instruction through adequate financial and material support from the government to ensure the preparation of teachers and schools for the transformation. Where they would not be prepared in time, then the HCNM advocated a delay of implementation of the transformation until such time as they would be objectively ready. During a visit to Estonia in March 2004, the HCNM stressed the need for careful preparation – especially the careful training of teachers – as key to the successful implementation of the minority education reform.[93] The HCNM has argued for flexibility in implementation to ensure that different regions and individual schools are able to undertake progressive reform at a pace related to their specific conditions and preparedness. In this connection, the HCNM has also stressed the need for dialogue with the affected students, their parents and teachers in order to gain broad acceptance of the process. This was especially needed in Latvia where the reform process met substantial opposition from the Russian minority.[94] The HCNM expressed his intention to remain engaged in dialogue on these issues and to offer his advice on the implementation of the reform, which was to begin in September 2004. In response to his concerns, in Latvia a Consultative Council on Minority Education was established under the auspices of the Ministry of Education in order to take into account the views of minority schools' representatives on the implementation of the reform.[95]

Separately, the Latvian Government adopted regulations on the language of instruction in minority schools on 13 May 2003. The new regulations stated that 60 percent of the curriculum of minority schools must be taught in Latvian, although each school may determine which classes will be in the Latvian language and which in the minority language. The HCNM expressed no objection to Latvia's plan and said he hoped it would make graduates more competitive in the job market.[96]

The HCNM has also contributed modestly but constructively to peaceful development in other countries. For example, in conjunction with the Federal Ministry of National and Ethnic Minorities in Serbia and Montenegro, in 2003–2004 the HCNM supported a group of experts in assisting the Government in reforming school curriculum in order to make it relevant to students belonging to all ethnic groups. In Georgia, during a visit in March 2003 the HCNM met with officials of the Autonomous Republic of Abkhazia with a view to their guaranteeing Georgian-language education in the Gali District where Georgian-speakers predominated.

In Central Asia, the importance of the involvement of minority representatives in decision-making processes, especially on issues that have a direct impact on them and their communities, is further reflected in a multilingual education project which the HCNM supported in Kyrgyzstan. A working group comprising representatives of government, national minorities and NGOs was established to develop practical recommendations for the promotion of integration through educational policy and practice that take greater account of, in particular, the needs of the Uzbek minority. The education situation of ethnic Uzbeks has also drawn the attention of the HCNM in Kazakhstan. In September 2003 he initiated a project in the southern part of the country to help Uzbek schools prepare their students for the State examination, which must be taken either in Kazakh or Russian and is a prerequisite for higher education in Kazakhstan. Extra-curricular Kazakh or Russian language training for final year students, as well as plans for in-service training in methodology and languages for school teachers from Uzbek schools, were designed to improve the overall quality of the teaching, help students to overcome language barriers and so improve their chances of admittance to higher education and ultimately their employment prospects. The first students to benefit from this project took their tests in June 2004.

The Media

Engagement of the OSCE Representative on Freedom of the Media in various OSCE States since the first Representative (Mr. Freimut Duve of Germany) took up office in 1998 focused mainly on the independence of the media and constraints on journalistic freedom.[97] Freedom to use (minority) languages in the media is also an issue in many OSCE States, which so far has been addressed primarily by the HCNM. Following the OSCE's Supplementary Human Dimension Meeting on Freedom of Expression held in Vienna in March 2001, the HCNM and the Representative on Freedom of the Media cooperated in studying issues in this field.[98]

There is no doubt that the freedom of expression guarantees not only the right to impart and receive information, but the right to do so in the chosen medium, including language and form.[99] As far as private operations are concerned, it is difficult to imagine a convincing basis which could interfere (in particular by prohibiting) with the language of the media as the vehicle of communication; there would seem to be no legitimate public interest that would justify either restricting or requiring a choice of language in this way.[100] However, legitimate public interests may justify restrictions on the *content* of communications.[101] It is also to be acknowledged that the State may regulate with regard to licensing and registration where a legitimate public interest may be invoked, in the use of radio bands for example (indeed, regulation is essentially required in this field). Furthermore, the State may act in these fields on the basis of a public interest to promote various activities or to provide various services, including government owned/run broadcasting.[102] In Moldova, Ukraine and elsewhere, the HCNM, while acknowledging the legitimacy of promoting the State language (through the dedication of resources, and so on), has stressed that this should not be achieved through the proscription of alternative (private) broadcasting.[103]

Both the OSCE Representative on the Freedom of the Media and the HCNM have addressed the issue of the freedom of the use of (minority) languages in the predominant media, both broadcast and print, in Moldova, following the adoption of legislation prescribing a substantial amount of programming in the State language even in *privately* owned and operated media. In 2000, restrictive measures in the Moldovan Law on Audio-Visual Broadcasting were introduced stipulating that at least 65 per cent of all broadcasts even on private stations had to be in the State language, leading to the suspension of the licenses of a number of private radio stations. The HCNM requested that the Moldovan Parliament amend the relevant article of the law to bring it into line with international standards (specifically, freedom of expression); amendments were subsequently made, but still failed to comply with the standards.[104]

Neither freedom of expression in general nor more specific provisions of minority-related instruments[105] impose an obligation on States to provide resources for minority media — private or public. The principle of non-discrimination, however, implies that an *equitable* share of State resources should go to support such activity.[106] Furthermore, with regard to the provision of minority language programming in the public media, international standards imply that where there are a substantial number of persons belonging to a (linguistic) minority they should be given access to a share of broadcast time in their own language on publicly-funded media commensurate with their numerical size and concentration.[107] In practice, the HCNM has encountered a number of situations whereby legislation in the field of media failed to make express provision for minority-language programming (for example, the subsequently amended 1999 Croatian Telecommunications Law). On occasion, the HCNM raised these issues: for example, the need for adequate airtime for public radio and television in the Slovak language in the Republic of Hungary.[108]

The effect of this issue on inter-ethnic relations is reflected in the agreement of April 2001 in Macedonia that State television would provide programmes in minority languages as a measure to build confidence between the ethnic Macedonian and ethnic Albanian communities.[109] Reactions to such restrictions were voiced in several other countries including notably Croatia, Latvia and Ukraine.

At the March 2001 Supplementary Human Dimension Meeting on Freedom of Expression and, later in the same month, in the OSCE Permanent Council, the HCNM, along with the OSCE Representative on Freedom of the Media, was requested by a number of delegations to address this subject through further work. In order to respond to these concerns, towards the end of 2001 the HCNM initiated two parallel, complementary processes aimed, first, at clarifying the concrete situation with regard to State practice across the OSCE and, second, at clarifying the specific content of relevant international standards.

With a view to cataloguing the breadth of State practice across the OSCE region, the HCNM commissioned the Programme in Comparative Media Law and Policy at the Centre for Socio-Legal Studies of Oxford University's Wolfson College and the Institute for Information Law at the University of Amsterdam to carry out a survey; the report with their findings was published in spring 2003.[110] As for clarifying international standards, a set of guidelines on the use of minority languages in the broadcast media was prepared through a process of consultations with a group of independent experts. These *Guidelines on the Use of Minority Languages in the Broadcast Media*[111] were launched at a conference in October 2003 in Baden bei Wien, Austria.[112]

In terms of practical measures, the HCNM has stimulated and provided concrete aid and assistance in the Samtskhe-Javakheti region of Georgia for rebroadcasting Georgian-language news programmes in the Armenian language in order to make the information more accessible to the region's inhabitants who do not yet speak well the Georgian language and so do not understand the news from their capital. As such, access to news in a language they understand not only meets their obvious linguistic needs, but it promotes their integration within the State.

CONCLUSION

As the previous discussion shows, the general thrust of the HCNM's activities in support of the protection of minority language rights and the broader accommodation of linguistic diversity within plurilingual societies has generally remained the same during the past decade. However, two more recent developments can be discerned. Firstly, particular attention has been given to the use of minority languages in the broadcast media. This is important because in the information age the media are not only a means of communication but also a principal carrier of culture, offering tremendous opportunities to constitute an active language community on a daily basis as well as to defuse tensions over language as technologies increasingly make it possible and affordable to use many languages and communicate simultaneously across the same space. Secondly, the HCNM's initial attention to situations in Central and Eastern Europe has turned mainly to the countries of the former Soviet Union. This is partly due to developments within Europe, notably EU enlargement and its extending reach through stabilization and association agreements which stipulate protection of minorities and also changes within the EU itself in terms of the Charter for Fundamental Rights and the prospective new EU Constitution which incorporate standards of minority protection and maintenance of cultural (including linguistic) diversity.

The HCNM did briefly venture West with activity in Northern Ireland and with regard to Roma/Gypsies/Travellers. Significantly, there have been calls for the HCNM to address the challenges posed by what are sometimes called "immigrant" or "new minorities" and their linguistic needs, interests and aspirations (not that Turkish, Arabic or other such languages are at all "new" to Europe). Notable among these were those of the OSCE Parliamentary Assembly which in 2004 called twice upon the HCNM "to initiate a comprehensive study of the integration policies of established democracies and analyse the effects on the position of new minorities."[113] While this fits well with the HCNM's work and is wholly consistent with all he has argued (indeed, it is hard to imagine which institution would be better placed to carry out this evidently important study), it can be doubted that there is the same political will among OSCE States to address in a similar way this growing part of their populations, that is, their own increasing diversity. Certainly, there seems an apparent need and also an opportunity for leadership such that the HCNM could share accumulated experience and contribute independent, impartial and expert services to the common good.

What is indisputable is that the complexity of societies shows no sign of diminishing and the common interest in accommodating it remains high both within and among States. This is not only so for those immediately interested and affected, but for the wider societies which in fact are not bounded by political frontiers – indeed, which are less and less so. In various fields and to varying degrees, all States regulate regarding the use of language and Europe certainly has a long history of providing opportunities for the use of the mother tongue in various aspects of public life. Since States can never be completely neutral in this regard, good governance should seek to find a suitable balance between competing interests and desires. There are many ways to accommodate the use of various languages within the same State, including in public administration. While solutions need to be found that are suited to the specificities of each situation, guidelines on how States may achieve this can be found in OSCE commitments and other international standards (as further supplemented by the Oslo Recommendations and the OSCE HCNM's 1999 Report on the Linguistic Rights of Persons Belonging to National Minorities in the OSCE Area). Careful practical implementation of these standards will lead to good policies, laws and practice at every level of governance.

NOTES

1   See the 1991 Document of the Moscow Meeting of the Conference on the Human Dimension of the (then) CSCE in Bloed 1993, 606.
2   Prior to recent enlargement, an estimated 40–50 000 000 EU citizens spoke a language other than the main official language of the State of which they are citizens; see O Riagain 2001, 33. The number grew substantially with enlargement.
3   For a presentation of research conducted into the self-articulation of identity in the South African context which found individuals defining themselves in terms of personality traits, institutional, familial/social and regional identities over and above "race", see Carrim 2000.
4   See Eide 1999, 322. The principle of non-discrimination is enshrined in, *inter alia*, the following standards: The 1948 Universal Declaration of Human Rights (UDHR), Article 2; the 1966 International Covenant on Civil and Political Rights (ICCPR), Articles 2(1) and 26 which provides guarantees beyond those rights set out in the instrument itself; the 1950 European Convention for the Protection of Human Rights and Fundamental Freedoms (ECHR), Article 14 (along with Protocol 12 additional to the ECHR); the Council of Europe Framework Convention for the Protection of National Minorities (Framework Convention), Article 4(1); the Document of the Copenhagen Meeting of the Conference of the CSCE (Copenhagen Document), paragraphs 31 and 32; and the 1992 United Nations Declaration on the Rights of Persons Belonging to National or Ethnic, Religious and Linguistic Minorities (UN Minorities' Declaration), Articles 3(1) and 4(1). In addition, dedicated anti-discrimination instruments are important, such as the 1965 International Convention on the Elimination of All Forms of Racial Discrimination.
5   See Dunbar 2001, 118. See, for example, Article 8(1) of the United Nations Minorities' Declaration, and Article 20 of the Framework Convention.
6   As paragraph 37 of the Copenhagen Document makes clear: "None of these commitments [that is, specified minority rights] may be interpreted as implying any right to engage in any activity or perform any action in contravention of the purposes and principles of the Charter of the United Nations, other obligations of international law or the provisions of the [Helsinki] Final Act, including the principle of territorial integrity of States."
7   For a survey and analysis of OSCE States' practices regarding the linguistic rights of minorities, see the HCNM's March 1999 *Report on the Linguistic Rights of Persons Belonging to National Minorities in the OSCE Area* (hereafter "Linguistics Report").
8   The Uzbek Constitution (in Article 4) prescribes that Uzbek is the State language, but at the same time obliges the State to "ensure a respectful attitude toward the languages, customs and traditions of all nationalities and ethnic groups living on its territory, and create the conditions necessary for their development". Similarly, Ukraine's Constitution (in accordance with a recommendation of the HCNM) guarantees the free development, use and protection of Russian and other languages of national minorities in Ukraine, as well as guaranteeing the right of citizens to receive instruction in the native tongue or to study the native language in State and communal educational establishments and through national cultural societies.
9   The 1999 Istanbul Summit Declaration at para. 30.
10   See OSCE HCNM letter to HE Mr Teodor Melescanu, Minister for Foreign Affairs of Romania, 26 February 1996, OSCE doc. REF.HC/6/96, available at <http://www.osce.org/documents/hcnm/1996/04/2742_en.pdf>.

11   Although when a Law on the Use of Minority Languages was adopted in 1999, the HCNM expressed his regret that his proposal to clarify the legal relationship between the two laws was not included. See OSCE HCNM letter to H. E. Mr Janos Martonyi, Minister for Foreign Affairs of Hungary, 11 August 1999.

12   The Oslo Recommendations are reproduced, together with some scholarly analysis of the related subject matter, in a special issue of the *International Journal on Minority and Group Rights* 6:3 (1999).

13   The Hague Recommendations are reproduced, together with some scholarly analysis of the related subject matter, in a special issue of the *International Journal on Minority and Group Rights* 4:2 (1996/97).

14   The full texts of the replies form an Annex to the HCNM's report which is available from the Office of the HCNM in The Hague.

15   For basic information on the OSCE, its institutions and their mandates and work see: the OSCE Handbook and other relevant documentation (for example Fact Sheets, monthly Newsletter, and so on) available from the OSCE's Documentation Section (Rytirska 31, CZ-110 00 Prague, Czech Republic, e-mail: quest@osceprag.cz); the OSCE Yearbooks prepared by the Institute for Peace Research and Security Policy at the University of Hamburg; as well as Bloed 1993 and 1997; Rotfeld 1996; Ghebali 1996; Bothe, Ronzitti, Rosas 1997 and Cohen 1999.

16   It is to be noted that, beginning with Principle X of the *Helsinki Final Act* signed on 1 August 1975 by the Heads of State or Government of the then 35 participating States, all OSCE participating States have committed themselves to "fulfil in good faith their obligations under international law, both those obligations arising from the generally recognized principles and rules of international law and those obligations arising from treaties or other agreements, in conformity with international law, to which they are parties". It is also to be noted that a wide variety of relevant obligations arise from the fact that all OSCE participating States are members of the United Nations, 46 OSCE States are members of the Council of Europe, 17 OSCE States are members of the Central European Initiative, 25 OSCE States are members of the European Union, 12 OSCE States are members of the Commonwealth of Independent States, and 11 OSCE States are members of the Council of Baltic Sea States – all of which (not to mention sub-subregional organizations and arrangements or bilateral treaties) bind OSCE participating States to a fundamentally consistent body of essentially repeated obligations.

17   Unfortunately, the second HCNM appears to have largely discontinued the practice and thus reduced substantially its effectiveness; NB, there have been relatively few exchanges since July 2001 (when the second HCNM took up his mandate) and none posted on the OSCE website or otherwise made public since spring 2001.

18   For a description and analysis of the concept and mandates of OSCE Missions, including accounts of the work of selected ones, see Rosas and Lahelma 1997, 167–190.

19   He did so, for example, in response to the publication of an interview with the Director of the State Language Centre (the responsible body for implementation) in which she stated that she considered the Language Law to be an "enemy" of the Latvian language; see OSCE HCNM Letter to HE Mr Indulis Bērziņš, Foreign Minister of the Republic of Latvia, 15 June 2001.

20   OSCE HCNM Letter to HE Mr Toomas Henrik Ilves, Minister of Foreign Affairs of the Republic of Estonia, 25 May 2001 (hereinafter "HCNM Letter to Ilves, 25 May 2001").

21 Letter to the OSCE HCNM from HE Mr Indulis Bērziņš, Foreign Minister of the Republic of Latvia, 12 December 2001 (hereinafter "Bērziņš Letter to HCNM, 12 December 2001").
22 OSCE HCNM Letter to Bērziņš, 13 April 2001.
23 See, for example, Speech of the HCNM, Joint OSCE-HCNM-UNDP Conference "Promoting Integration and Development in the Samtskhe-Javakheti Region of Georgia", 19 November 2002, available at: <http://www.osce.org/documents/hcnm/2002/11/464_en.pdf>.
24 For applicable standards regarding the rights of persons belonging to national minorities to use their own language in dealing with public authorities, in the public display of local names, and to receive instruction in that language, see: the Framework Convention, Articles 10(2), 11(3) and 14(2); and The European Charter for Regional or Minority Languages (European Language Charter), Articles 8, 9 and 10. Paragraph 34 of the Copenhagen Document, while not making explicit reference to geographic concentration, tradition or numbers, stipulates that States should "endeavour ... wherever possible" to ensure that persons belonging to national minorities enjoy adequate opportunities to use their mother tongue before the public authorities and to be taught in this language.
25 See, for example, OSCE HCNM Letter to Bērziņš, 13 April 2001.
26 OSCE HCNM Report to the Permanent Council, 7 March 2002.
27 See Dunbar 2001, 112. Although, as Dunbar notes, while some argue that the more territorially concentrated and more assertive the minority, the greater their entitlement to positive measures should be, one could equally argue that the relative weakness and marginalization of a minority group would justify more, not less extensive measures of support.
28 See the European Centre for Minority Issues 2000, The Flensburg Recommendations on the Implementation of Policy Measures for Regional or Minority Languages, at para. 9, available at <http://www.ecmi.de/34/2004/10/07/Evaluating-Policy-Measures-for-Minority-Languages-in-Europe.php>.
29 A non-governmental organization established on the HCNM's initiative when he began his mandate in 1993, but legally and financially independent, in order to fund initiatives and projects to enhance the effectiveness of the HCNM. The Foundation was dissolved in 2000 and its assets and activities were incorporated into the Office of the HCNM.
30 The Linguistics Report, *supra*, n. 9, at p. 12.
31 The Copenhagen Document, para. 34.
32 The Framework Convention, Article 10(2).
33 The Linguistics Report, *supra*, n. 9, at p. 13.
34 OSCE HCNM letter to the Minister for Foreign Affairs of the Slovak Republic, HE Mr Juraj Schenk, 24 August 1995, OSCE doc. REF.HC/9/95, available at <http://www.osce.org/documents/hcnm/1995/10/2749_en.pdf>.
35 Having consistently urged Slovakia over the years to clarify the specific rights of persons belonging to national minorities to use their languages in accordance with the Slovak Constitution and international standards, the HCNM welcomed the introduction of a Law on the Use of Minority Languages which was finally adopted in July 1999; see OSCE HCNM Press Release of 19 July 1999, "High Commissioner Welcomes Restoration of Use of Minority Languages in Official Communications in Slovakia", available at <http://www.osce.org/item/5119.html>.
36 See the 1991 Constitutional Law on Human Rights and Freedoms and the Rights of National and Ethnic Communities and Minorities in the Republic of Croatia, as cited in Packer 2001, 265.

37 ECHR, Articles 5(2) and 6(3); ICCPR, Article 14(3); and the Framework Convention, Article 10(3).

38 The European Language Charter in Article 9, for example, allows for an increase in the use of minority languages in criminal, civil and administrative tribunal proceedings where "the number of residents ... justifies the measures". The same approach is embodied in Recommendations 18 and 19 of the Oslo Recommendations.

39 See, for example, the Appeal of Latvian NGOs on Minority Policies in Latvia, Minelres Archive, at <http://www.riga.lv/minelres/archive.htm>.

40 See OSCE HCNM Press Release, "OSCE High Commissioner on National Minorities visits Kyrgyszstan", 22 April 2003, available at: <http://www.osce.org/news/generate.pf.php3?news_id=3216>.

41 Regarding elections see Chapter I of the Copenhagen Document (more especially paras. 5.1, 5.2 and 7 with all its sub-paragraphs).

42 See the views of the UN Human Rights Committee adopted on 25 July 2001 in the case of *Ignatane v. Latvia* (Communication No. 884/1999), UN Doc. CCPR/C/72/D/884/1999.

43 As de Varennes observes: "The relatively simple truth is that if someone not proficient in the official or dominant language is elected, it is either because that person represents many people who are in the same situation or, in any event, because the electorate indicated that with their votes their confidence in his or her ability to represent their interests in the legislature. If anything, such election is evidence of the social reality in that constituency. It should only be set aside for the most clear and pressing reasons which would (and should) in all likelihood be extremely rare, if at all possible" (De Varennes 2001, 317).

44 See Report of the ODIHR Election Assessment Mission, 5 February 1999, available at <http://www.osce.org/documents/odihr/1999/02/1263_en.pdf>.

45 See, for example, EU statement in response to Ambassador Hertrampf, Head of the OSCE Mission to Estonia, Permanent Council No. 345, 28 June 2001, OSCE Doc. PC.DEL/484/01 (hereinafter "EU statement, 28 June 2001").

46 The conclusion that a language proficiency of any kind for a candidate for election is incompatible with international law is supported by the View adopted by the UN Human Rights Committee on 25 July 2001 that Article 25 of the ICCPR secures to every citizen the right and the opportunity to be elected at genuine periodic elections without any of the distinctions mentioned in Article 2, including language. The Committee found a violation of Article 25 exactly in such a case; see *Ignatane v. Latvia* (*supra*, note 44).

47 See OSCE HCNM Letter to HE Mr Indulis Bērziņš, Foreign Minister of the Republic of Latvia, 17 December 2001 (hereinafter "HCNM Letter to Bērziņš, 17 December 2001").

48 See OSCE HCNM letter of 19 December 1998 addressed to HE Lennart Meri, President of Estonia, calling upon the President not to promulgate the adopted Laws; the letter is reproduced in Rob Zaagman, *Conflict Prevention in the Baltic States: The OSCE High Commissioner on National Minorities in Estonia, Latvia and Lithuania*, ECMI Monograph #1, April 1999, at Annex 4. Notwithstanding this appeal, the Laws were promulgated and subsequently criticized by ODIHR when observing the next elections.

49 See the Statement by the OSCE HCNM of 22 November 2001 welcoming the Estonian Parliament's abolition of the linguistic requirements to stand for elected office; OSCE doc. HCNM.GAL/6/01, available at <http://www.osce.org/item/6571.html>.

50 HCNM Letter to Bērziņš, 17 December 2001, in response to the request of Minister Bērziņš in his letter to the HCNM of 12 December 2001.

51 ECHR App. No. 46726/99.
52 Following the *Podkolzina v. Latvia* judgment, the HCNM issued a statement reiterating his support for the intention of the Latvian Government to amend the election laws by removing linguistic requirements to stand for elected office, as a necessary condition in a functioning democratic society; see "High Commissioner Supports Amendments to the Election Laws in Latvia", 11 April 2002, OSCE Doc. HCNM.INF/3/02, available at <http://www.osce.org/item/6655.html>. The EU also expressed the expectation that the Latvian Electoral Law be amended as soon as possible by the abolition of language requirements for candidates; see EU statement of 7 March 2002.
53 OSCE HCNM Press Release, "Statement on Adoption of Amendments to Latvian Election Laws", 10 May 2002, OSCE Doc. HCNM.INF/4/02, available at <http://www.osce.org/item/6705.html>.
54 To this end, they made reference to the 1991 Provisional Book of Regulations of the Assembly of the then Socialist Republic of Macedonia which allowed for this possibility.
55 See *The ODIHR Election Observation Handbook*, Fourth Edition, April 1999.
56 See "Guidelines to Assist National Minority Participation in the Electoral Process", ODIHR, Warsaw, March 2001, particularly Addendum III on Integrating Minority Issues into ODIHR Election Observation. The Guidelines, elaborated jointly by experts under the auspices of ODIHR, HCNM and the International Institute for Democracy and Electoral Assistance (IDEA), expand upon Recommendations 7–10 of the "Lund Recommendations on the Effective Participation of National Minorities in Public Life" which were elaborated in September 1999 by independent experts upon request of the HCNM. For the full text of the Lund Recommendations, see <http://www.osce.org/documents/hcnm/1999/09/2698_en.pdf>; see also *Helsinki Monitor*11:4 (2000), pp. 45–61, with an explanation in Packer 2000.
57 See Report of the ODIHR Election Observation Mission, 7 March 1999, available at <http://www.osce.org/documents/odihr/1999/03/1427_en.pdf>.
58 Restricted report on file with the authors.
59 OSCE Mission in Kosovo Proposal for an operation plan for Voter Services (Registration) and a Kosovo-wide Election in 2001, restricted OSCE Doc. SEC.GAL/61/01, 3 May 2001.
60 See, for example, the HCNM's Statement on Inter-Ethnic Issues in fYROM, 9 November 1998; <http://www.osce.org/press_rel/1998/11/828-hcnm.html>.
61 OSCE HCNM letter to HE Ms. Ingrida Labucka, Minister of Justice of Latvia, 29 November 2000.
62 In this respect, the HCNM expressed his regret that the adopted text "has neither taken into account all my recommendations nor fully reflects the results of consultations with experts in my office", see HCNM Letter to HE Mr Henrik Ilves, Minister of Foreign Affairs of Estonia, 25 May 2001.
63 Ibid. The EU likewise stressed the need for a "liberal interpretation of the principles of justified public interest and of proportionality in its implementation", see EU Statement of 28 June 2001.
64 "Regulations of the Cabinet on the Proficiency Degree in the State Language Required for the Performance of the Professional and Positional Duties and the Procedure of Language Proficiency", Implementing Decree No. 296, 22 August 2000.
65 OSCE HCNM letter to HE Ms. Ingrida Labucka, Minister of Justice of Latvia, 4 August 2000.

66   OSCE HCNM Statement regarding the adoption of regulations implementing the Latvian State Language Law, 31 August 2000, available at <http://www.osce.org/hcnm/item_1_5273.html>.

67   In Estonia, Stateless persons still constitute about one-seventh of the total population, while in Latvia they constitute about one-fifth of the total population.

68   See, for example, 8(4) *OSCE Newsletter* (2001), News from the High Commissioner on National Minorities, "HCNM Urges Acceleration of Naturalization Process in Latvia".

69   See OSCE HCNM Letter to HE Mr Indulis Bērziņš, Foreign Minister of the Republic of Latvia, 13 April 2001(hereinafter "HCNM Letter to Bērziņš, 13 April 2001").

70   Delegation of Latvia, reply to the statement by the Permanent Representative of the Russian Federation to the OSCE at the Meeting of the OSCE Permanent Council, 20 February 2002, OSCE Doc. PC.DEL/101/02.

71   CSCE Communication No. 124, Prague, 23 April 1993, available at <http://www.osce.org/documents/html/pdftohtml/2728_en.pdf.html>.

72   "Recommendations of 9 March 1994 on the question of the implementation of the Estonian Law on Aliens", CSCE Communication No. 20, Prague, 14 June 1994 (includes response from the Minister of Foreign Affairs), available at <http://www.osce.org/documents/html/pdftohtml/2707_en.pdf.html>.

73   The UN Human Rights Committee in *Ballantyne, Davidson and McIntyre v. Canada* (Communication Nos. 359/1989 and 385/1989, 31 March 1993) clearly stated its view that the freedom of expression applies to any commercial activity and signs, rejecting the argument that commercial expression is somehow not worthy of protection under Article 19 of the ICCPR; for more on this point, see De Varennes 1994, 177.

74   Consistent with international standards, the Oslo Recommendations, in para. 12 of the Explanatory Note, make reference to a number of areas where a private enterprise could be required to accommodate the official language(s) of the State.

75   See OSCE HCNM letter to HE Guntis Ulmanis, President of Latvia, 10 November 1997.

76   See OSCE HCNM letter to HE Mr Nicolae Tabacuru, Foreign Minister of the Republic of Moldova, 2 November 1999, available at <http://www.osce.org/hcnm/documents/recommendations/moldova/1999/2-10-1999.html>.

77   For the response of the Foreign Minister, see his letter of 31 March 2000; available at <http://www.osce.org/hcnm/documents/recommendations/moldova/2000/31-3-2000.html>.

78   See the UN Committeee on the Rights of the Child, General Comment No. 1 (17 April 2001) on Article 29(1): The Aims of Education, UN Doc. CRC.GC/2001/1.

79   The Copenhagen Document, para. 34 provides that: "The participating States will endeavor to ensure that persons belonging to national minorities notwithstanding the need to learn the official language or languages of the State concerned, have adequate opportunities for instruction in their mother tongue, as well as, wherever possible and necessary, for its use before public authorities, in conformity with applicable national legislation." The Framework Convention contains a similar provision in Article 14 applicable under certain circumstances, that is, in areas inhabited, traditionally or in substantial numbers, by persons belonging to national minorities, if there is sufficient demand.

80   The Copenhagen Document, para. 32.2; the Framework Convention, Article 13.

81   The parallel provision of the Framework Convention, Article 13(2), makes it clear that this right does not imply any financial obligation on the State.

82   In this context it should be noted that problems of interethnic character in Macedonia are grounded to a large extent in the assertions of Albanians that they are not a "national minority", but one of the founding "peoples" of the State; see Siemienski 2001, 188.

83   For more on the SEE University, see <http://www.see-university.com>.

84   See SEE University Foundation, Annual Report 2001, for a historical account of the university's development.

85   OSCE HCNM Press Release, "South Eastern European University Opens in Tetevo, Former Yugoslav Republic of Macedonia", 20 November 2001, OSCE Doc. HCNM/INF/3/01; available at <http://www.osce.org/hcnm/item_1_6421.html>.

86   OSCE HCNM Statement on Inter-Ethnic Issues in fYROM, 9 November 1998; <http://www.osce.org/press_rel/1998/11/828-hcnm.html>.

87   See: 1960 UNESCO Convention against Discrimination in Education, Article 2; 1966 International Covenant on Economic, Social and Cultural Rights, Article 13 (3); the Framework Convention, Article 14 (3); the Copenhagen Document, para. 34; and the European Language Charter, Article 8(1).

88   "The Linguistic and Education Rights of National Minorities and their application in Moldova", Keynote speech by Max van der Stoel, Chisinau, 18 May 2000. The HCNM was referring to the teaching of Moldovan in the east of the country (also known as Transdniestria) which has a large Russian-speaking population; for the full text of his speech, see <http://www.osce.org/hcnm/documents/speeches/2000/index.php3>.

89   See, for example, OSCE HCNM letter to HE Mr Andrei Marga, Romanian Minister of Education and Rector of the Babes-Bolyai University, 30 March 2000; available at <http://www.osce.org/documents/hcnm/2000/03/2745_en.pdf>.

90   For the HCNM's full recommendations, see OSCE HCNM Letters to HE Mr Igor Ivanov, Minister of Foreign Affairs of the Russian Federation and HE Mr Anatoly M. Zlenko, Minister for Foreign Affairs of Ukraine, 12 January 2001; available at <http://www.osce.org/documents/hcnm/2001/01/2746_en.pdf>.

91   8(9) *OSCE Newsletter* (2001), News from the High Commissioner on National Minorities, "High Commissioner Supports Inter-ethnic Initiatives in Moldova".

92   OSCE Annual Report 2001.

93   "Key to social integration is dialogue, OSCE High Commissioner says after Estonia visit", OSCE Press Release, 19 March 2004; available at <http://www.osce.org/hcnm/item_1_8157.html>.

94   See, for example, OSCE HCNM Press Release of 27 February 2004, available at <http://www.osce.org/hcnm/item_1_8109.html>.

95   Delegation of Latvia, reply to the HCNM Rolf Ekéus at the Permanent Council Meeting No. 383, 7 March 2002, OSCE Doc. PC.Del/142/02.

96   RFE/RL Newsline Vol. 7, No. 90, Part II (14 May 2003).

97   The activities and interests of the Representative on Freedom of the Media are reported publicly on an annual basis in the *Freedom and Responsibility Yearbooks* available through the OSCE secretariat in Vienna or the OSCE Documentation Section in Prague or at <http://www.osce.org/fom/publications.html>.

98   See: Supplementary Human Dimension Meeting on Freedom of Expression: New and Existing Challenges, Final Report, 29 March 2001, OSCE Doc. PC.DEL/204/01/Corr.1; and The Representative on Freedom of the Media, Mr Freimut Duve, Report to the Permanent Council, 5 April 2001, OSCE Doc. FOM/GAL/9/01. For supporting statements, see: US Mission to OSCE Statement on Freedom of Expression delivered to the Permanent Council, 5 April 2001, OSCE Doc. PC.DEL/243/01; and EU Statement in Response to Mr Duve, the OSCE Representative on Freedom of the Media, Permanent Council No.331, 5 April 2001, OSCE Doc. PC.DEL/228/01.

99   For a comprehensive discussion of the inter-relationship between language and the freedom of expression, see De Varennes 1994, 163-186.

100   On this question, see Packer 1996, 501–522, arguing that there is essentially no basis for a derogation from certain minority rights (including, by extension, language as a vehicle of communication, as distinguished from its content, under either Article 19 of the ICCPR or Article 10 of the ECHR).

101   Oslo Recommendations, para. 12 of the Explanatory Note.

102   See *supra*, note 107.

103   See, for example, OSCE HCNM letter to Mr Taniuk Les Stepanovovych, Chairman of the Ukrainian Parliamentary Committee on Culture, 28 May 2001.

104   See OSCE HCNM letter to HE Mr Nicolae Tabacuru, Foreign Minister of the Republic of Moldova, 22 September 2000.

105   That is, the Framework Convention (Article 9) and the European Language Charter (Article 11(2)).

106   See Oslo Recommendations 7 and 9.

107   See Article 9(1) of the Framework Convention and Oslo Recommendation 9.

108   See OSCE HCNM letter to the Minister for Foreign Affairs of the Republic of Hungary, HE Mr László Kovács, 26 February 1997, OSCE Doc. REF.HC/5/97; available at <http://www.osce.org/documents/hcnm/1997/05/2721_en.pdf>.

109   8(5) *OSCE Newsletter* (2001), News from the High Commissioner on National Minorities, "Concerns Over Former Yugoslav Republic of Macedonia Remains a High Priority for HCNM".

110   See Tarlach McGonagle, Bethany Davis Noll and Monroe Price (eds), "Minority-Language Related Broadcasting and Legislation in the OSCE", April 2003. This (over 500 page) survey can be obtained in hard copy from the Institute for Information Law at University of Amsterdam or the Office of the HCNM in The Hague; it can also be accessed electronically at <http://www.ivir.nl/staff/ mcgonagle.html> or <http://pcmlp.socleg.ox.ac.uk/minority-languages.pdf>.

111   The Guidelines were initially available in English and Russian from the Office of the OSCE HCNM or, in electronic form, on the HCNM's website at <http:// www.osce.org/hcnm/documents/recommendations/>. The Guidelines are also reproduced with an introductory article by John Packer and Sally Holt in 15(2) *Helsinki Monitor* (2004), 103-26.

112   The Baden Conference proceedings are available in a special issue of the journal *Mercator Media Forum* 8 (2005).

113   Edinburgh Declaration of the OSCE Parliamentary Assembly and Resolutions adopted at the Thirteenth Annual Session, 5–9 July 2004, para. 71, available at <http://www.oscepa.org/admin/getbinary.asp?FileID=531>. This appeal was a reiteration of an initial call made by the Parliamentary Assembly at its Third Winter Meeting held in Vienna in February 2004.

REFERENCES

Bloed, A. (ed.) (1993), *The Conference on Security and Co-operation in Europe: Analysis and Basic Documents, 1972–1993* (Dordrecht: Martinus Nijhoff Publishers)

Bloed, A. (ed.) (1997), *The Conference on Security and Co-operation in Europe: Basic Documents, 1993-1995* (The Hague: Kluwer Law International)

Bothe, M., Ronzitti, N. and Rosas, A. (eds) (1997), *The OSCE in the Maintenance of Peace and Security; Conflict Prevention, Crisis Management and Peaceful Settlement of Disputes* (The Hague: Kluwer Law International)

Carens, J. H. (2000), *Culture, Citizenship, and Community: a Contextual Exploration of Justice as Evenhandedness* (Oxford/New York: Oxford University Press)

Carrim, N. (2000), "Critical Anti-racism and Problems in Self-articulated Forms of Identities", *Race, Ethnicity and Education* 3(1): 25–44

Cohen, J. (1999), *Conflict Prevention in the OSCE; An Assessment of Capacities* (The Hague: Netherlands Institute of International Relations Clingendael)

De Varennes, F. (1993), "Derechos Humanos y Lengua: La Situatión especial de los Pueblos Indígenas", contribution to XI Congreso, Instituto Indigenista Interamericano Managua, Nicaragua, 22–26 November 1993.

De Varennes, F. (1994), "Language and Freedom of Expression in International Law". *Human Rights Quartely* 16(1): 163–186

De Varennes, F. (1999), "Equality and Non-discrimination: Fundamental Principles of Minority Language Rights", *International Journal on Minority and Group Rights* 6(3): 307–318

De Varennes, F. (2001), "The Linguistic Rights of Minorities in Europe", in Snezana Trifunovska (ed.) (2001), *Minority Rights in Europe: European Minorities and Languages* (The Hague: T.M.C.Asser Press), 3–30

Dunbar, R. (2001), "Minority Language Rights in International Law", *International and Comparative Law Quarterly* 50, 90–120

Eide, A. (1999), "The Oslo Recommendations Regarding the Linguistic Rights of National Minorities: An Overview", *International Journal on Minority and Group Rights* 6(3): 319–328

Ghebali, V.-Y. (1996), *L'OSCE dans l'Europe post-communiste, 1990-1996; Vers une identité paneuropéenne de sécurité* (Bruxelles: Etablissements Emile Bruylant)

Kemp, W. (ed.) (2001), *Quiet Diplomacy in Action: the OSCE High Commissioner on National Minorities* (The Hague/Boston/ London: Kluwer Law International)

Kontra, M. (1999), "'Don't Speak Hungarian in Public!' – A Documentation and Analysis of Folk Linguistic Rights", in Miklós Kontra, Robert Phillipson, Tove Skutnabb-Kangas and Tibor Várady (eds) (1999), *Language: A Right and a Resource* (Budapest: Central European University Press), 81–97

O Riagáin, D. (2001), "All Languages Great and Small: A Look at the Linguistic Future of Europe with Particular Reference to Lesser Used Languages", in Snezana Trifunovska (ed.) (2001), *Minority Rights in Europe: European Minorities and Languages* (The Hague: T.M.C.Asser Press), 31–42

Packer, J. (1999), "Editor's Note", *International Journal on Minority and Group Rights* 6(3): v–vi

Packer, J. and Siemienski, G. (1999), "The Language of Equity: The Origin and Development of the Oslo Recommendations Regarding the Linguistic Rights of National Minorities", *International Journal on Minority and Group Rights* 6(3): 329–350

Packer, J. (2000), "The origin and nature of the Lund Recommendations on the Effective Participation of National Minorities in Public Life", *Helsinki Monitor* 11(4): 29–45

Packer, J. (2001), "The Protection of Minority Language Rights through the Work of OSCE Institutions", in Snezana Trifunovska (ed.) (2001), *Minority Rights in Europe: European Minorities and Languages* (The Hague: T.M.C.Asser Press), 255–274

Packer, J. (1996), "United Nations Protection of Minorities in Time of Public Emergency: The Hard-Core of Minority Rights", in Daniel Prémont (ed.), *Non-Derogable Rights and States of Emergency* (Brussels: Etablissements Emile Bruylant), 501–522

Rosas, A. and Lahelma, T. (1997), "OSCE Long-Term Missions", in Michael Bothe, Natalino Ronzitti and Allan Rosas (eds) (1997), *The OSCE in the Maintenance of Peace and Security; Conflict Prevention, Crisis Management and Peaceful Settlement of Disputes* (The Hague: Kluwer Law International), 167–190

Rotfeld, A. D. (ed.) (1996), *From Helsinki to Budapest and Beyond: Analysis and Documents of the Organization for Security and Co-operation in Europe, 1973–1995* (London: Oxford University Press)

Siemienski, G. (2001), "Le Haut Commissaire aux Minorités Nationales de L'Organization Pour La Coopération et la Sécurité en Europe (OSCE): Le Langage du Compromis", *Termonigramme: La Protection des Minorités Linguistiques* 95–96, 183–200

Siemienski, G. (1999), "Report on the Vienna Seminar on the Linguistic Rights of National Minorities". *International Journal on Minority and Group Rights* 6(3): 351–358

Van der Stoel, M. (12 April 2000, Antalya), "The Protection of Minorities in the OSCE Region", address at a Seminar at the OSCE Parliamentary Assembly, in Wolfgang Zellner and Falk Lange (eds) (2001), *Peace and Stability through Human and Minority Rights; Speeches by the OSCE High Commissioner on National Minorities* (Baden-Baden: Nomos Verlagsgesellschaft), 207–212

8 Language Legislation in the Baltic States

BORISS CILEVIČS

In this chapter, I examine the development of language legislation in three Baltic states – Estonia, Latvia and Lithuania – after the restoration of their independence. Thus, I describe the regulations determining the status of the state language and the languages of national minorities, as well as governing the use of languages in elected bodies, before public authorities, in media, in education and in employment. Having identified possible inconsistencies with the provisions of the international instruments on minority rights and having analysed the main features of the language policies in the Baltic states, I propose a theory concerning the main factors affecting the formation of these policies.

All three Baltic states regained their independence after the collapse of the USSR in 1991 put an end to a half-century-long Soviet annexation. For Estonia and Latvia, the period of pre-war independence was rather short, and the processes of state- and nation-building had been far from completed. After the Second World War, Estonia and Latvia experienced large-scale immigration of a predominantly Slavic population. Although sizable ethnic Russian minorities were present in the Baltics for centuries, in the late 1980s, the proportion of ethnic Estonians in the total population of Estonia dropped to 62 per cent and of ethnic Latvians in Latvia to 52 per cent. In Lithuania, the proportion of ethnic Lithuanians remained at approximately 80 per cent.

These demographic changes brought about a substantial alteration of the linguistic situation. Although the use of the Baltic languages was formally permitted in different areas, as is evident in the parallel system of public education in Russian and in the Baltic languages from kindergarten to university level, and the relatively generous financing for the publication of Baltic literature and the development of arts, the overall sphere in which they functioned was severely curtailed. In the areas of state government, transport, industry, military, public safety and security only the "imperial" language, Russian, was allowed for official use. This situation could be described as "diglossia", or asymmetrical bilingualism with clear domination of one language, and gradual suppression of another.

This asymmetry was also manifested in the language proficiency of the Baltic residents in the Soviet period. In 1989, only 22.3 per cent of ethnic Russians in Latvia had proficiency in the Latvian language (Kamenska 1995). In Estonia and Lithuania, the corresponding figures were 13.7 per cent and 33.5 per cent.[2] By the 1990s, this situation had changed considerably: in 1995, already 55.8 per cent of ethnic Russians claimed fluency in the Latvian language (Druviete 1998).

However, as the years passed, the progress in this field slowed substantially: for the population census conducted in Latvia in 2000, 58.5 per cent of ethnic Russians said they were proficient in Latvian.[2] Overall, the proportion of people in Latvia able to speak Latvian (81.7 per cent) was less than those able to speak Russian (84.4 per cent).[3] More recent surveys reveal that these data have not changed since then.[4]

After the restoration of independence, development of the new linguistic legislation became one of the major challenges for the restored states. It is important to note that the states themselves were not acting alone in this field. Although Russian-speaking minorities, poorly mobilized and largely disenfranchized due to restrictive citizenship legislation (the so-called "legal continuity" concept)[5] could hardly have a serious impact on shaping of the new language legislation, external actors were much more actively involved. International organizations, the OSCE, the Council of Europe, and later the European Union played an important role in the shaping of the new language legislation. Russia also played a role, though limited, in this process.

This paper will briefly describe the main features of the linguistic legislation developed in the Baltic states since the late 1980s, and will analyse the main factors, trends and controversies in this field.

DEVELOPMENT OF LINGUISTIC LEGISLATION AFTER THE RESTORATION OF INDEPENDENCE

The language issue was a central factor behind the mass mobilization for the drive for independence of the Baltic states in late 1980s. Domination by the Russian language gave rise to widespread concerns about the "imminent extinction" of Latvian, and slogans aimed at the protection of language were actively supported by a great majority of ethnic Latvians.

Even before the very idea of independence appeared explicitly on the public agenda, the Supreme Soviets (Soviet-time parliaments) of three Baltic states had adopted special declarations assigning Estonian, Lithuanian and Latvian languages the status of "state language" for the corresponding republics. Furthermore, special language laws were adopted in all three Baltic countries in 1989: the Language Law of the Estonian SSR adopted 18 January 1989, the Decree on the Lithuania SSR Official Language Usage adopted 25 January 1989 and the Republic of Latvia Language Law adopted 5 May 1989. These laws essentially had a dual nature: while the aim of asserting the position of the newly re-established state languages was more than apparent, the role of Russian, the official language of the then superior state structure, had to be secured in order to avoid an overly hostile reaction from the Moscow authorities, who still maintained at that moment control over the situation in the Baltics.

However, soon after the restoration of independence de facto, the language legislation in all three Baltic states underwent substantial changes resulting in the adoption of completely new language laws: the Estonian Language Act of 21 February 1995, the Lithuanian Law on the State Language of 31 January 1995, and the Latvian State Language Law of 21 December 1999.

In the case of Latvia, substantial amendments to the 1989 Language Law which tightened its regulations considerably had already been adopted by 1992, two months before its scheduled entry into force. Many provisions of the law were made more restrictive than its former incantation and increasingly excluded the use of other languages in public administration and, in many cases, even in the private domains as was for example the case for public information of a private nature.

In Latvia, the new State Language Draft Law also appeared in 1995, but its adoption had to be delayed considerably because of harsh criticism directed at it by the OSCE High Commissioner on National Minorities and other international organizations. As a result of protracted debate, conducted both in public and behind the scenes, some provisions of the new State Language Law appeared to be even more liberal than those in force before its adoption. In particular, the new law allowed, under certain conditions, the use of other languages in public information of a private nature and at public gatherings. Simultaneously, however, the possibility to submit individual applications or complaints to state or municipal institutions in English, German and Russian envisaged by the Law of 1992, had been eliminated.

Meanwhile, numerous other acts adopted since 1990 incorporated several essential provisions relevant to language use. In the next chapters, the principal rules for the use of languages in different areas in the Baltic countries will be outlined.

STATUS OF LANGUAGES AND RECOGNITION OF MINORITY LANGUAGES

The status of the state languages has been enshrined in the Constitutions of all three Baltic states: in Article 14 of the Constitution of the Republic of Lithuania, Article 6 of the Constitution of Estonia and Article 4 of the *Satversme* - Constitution of Latvia.[6] The Constitutions of all three Baltic states refer to the minority language in the following, very general way:

> Persons belonging to ethnic minorities have the right to preserve and develop their language and their ethnic and cultural identity. (Article 114 of the Latvian Constitution)

> Citizens who belong to ethnic communities shall have the right to foster their language, culture and customs. (Article 37 of the Lithuanian Constitution)

The Constitutions do not spell out any specific rights beyond the broad statements cited above. There are, however, a few exceptions: the Estonian Constitution, for example, guarantees the right to use minority languages in education (Article 37 paragraph 4) and before public authorities in localities where at least half of the permanent residents belong to an ethnic minority (Article 51 paragraph 2).

The Language Act of Estonia explicitly mentions the notion of minority language in the following terms:

> § 2. Foreign language.
>
> For the purposes of this Act, any language other than Estonian is a foreign language. A language of a national minority is a foreign language which Estonian citizens who belong to a national minority have historically used as their mother tongue in Estonia.

In contrast, the State Language Law of Latvia does not mention minority languages, except for the "Liv" language,[7] which is not, however, defined as a minority language:

> Article 5. For the purpose of this Law, any other language used in the Republic of Latvia, except the Liv language, shall be regarded as a foreign language.

However, in other pieces of Latvian legislation, minority languages are explicitly referred to, thus creating certain inconsistency in the legal framework which regulates the use of languages.

The Law on the State Language of Lithuania does not mention minority languages at all. Thus, one can say that minority languages are marginally recognized in the legislation governing the Baltic states.

Some clauses relevant to the use of minority languages have been incorporated into special laws regarding national minorities. For example, Article 1 of the Law on Ethnic Minorities of Lithuania adopted 23 November 1989, stipulates:

> The Lithuanian SSR ... shall guarantee to all ethnic minorities residing in Lithuania the right to freely develop, and shall respect every ethnic minority and language.

The Estonian Law on Cultural Autonomy, adopted 26 October 1993, provides:

> Members of a national minority have the right: ... to use their mother tongue in dealings within the limits established by the Language Law. (Article 4)

The Law about the Unrestricted Development and Right to Cultural Autonomy of Latvia's Nationalities and Ethnic Groups (adopted 19 March 1991) envisages that:

> The Republic of Latvia government institutions should promote the creation of material conditions for the development of the education, language and culture of the nationalities and ethnic groups residing within Latvia's territory. (Article 10)

Thus, at the level of declarations, the presence of minority languages is recognized and some formal safeguards enshrined in the national legislation. However, more detailed regulations and concrete mechanisms for the implementation of these declared rights are either ineffective or non-existent. Thus, the declarative constitutional provisions are not legally enforceable.

However, the amendments to the Latvian Law on the Constitutional Court which took effect on 1 July 2001 permit an individual to bring a case before the Constitutional Court, and several actions questioning the compatibility of some legal provisions with those contained in the Constitution have been initiated. In 2001 the Constitutional Court recognized that the practice of "Latvianization" of personal names and surnames is in compliance with the Constitution.[8] The privacy of personal life in this case is:

> limited in order to protect the right of other residents of Latvia to use the Latvian language within the whole territory of the country and to protect the democratic system of the state.

In another case of 2003, the Court declared the language quotas for private broadcasting media unconstitutional.[9] The Law on Radio and Television stipulated that broadcasting in languages other than Latvian could not exceed 25 per cent of the total broadcasting time on private TV and radio. As of October 2004, the Court is yet to consider the case concerning the switch to Latvian as the main language of instruction in state-supported secondary schools for minorities.

USE OF LANGUAGES IN LEGISLATURES AND ELECTED MUNICIPAL BODIES

Legislatures in all three Baltic states must perform their functions using only the state language. As for municipal bodies, Article 52(2) of the Estonian Constitution permits the use of the language of the majority of the permanent residents:

> in localities where the language of the majority of the population is other than Estonian … for internal communication to the extent and in accordance with procedures determined by law.

Article 11 of the 1995 Language Act stipulates:

> In local governments where the majority of permanent residents are non-Estonian speakers, the language of the national minority constituting the majority of the permanent residents of the local government may be used alongside Estonian as the internal working language of the local government on the proposal of the corresponding local government council and by a decision of the Government of the Republic.

However, in practice, this provision has never been implemented, as the national Government has rejected all proposals of the kind received thus far (Jarve 2000).

The Lithuanian Law on Ethnic Minorities of 1989 stipulates in Article 4:

> In offices and organizations located in areas serving substantial numbers of a minority with a different language, the language spoken by that minority shall be used in addition to the Lithuanian language.

In Latvia, all municipalities must work in the state language only, regardless of how many persons belonging to minorities reside in a given locality. Although no language requirements ever existed in Lithuania for candidates running in parliamentary and municipal elections, in Estonia and Latvia these requirements were established by law. In Estonia, the regulations determined language requirements for all candidates elected to the national or local legislature; however, they were silent with regard to procedures designed to ensure such requirements. Corresponding laws in Latvia stipulated more exigent requirements: persons who could not demonstrate the highest level of proficiency in the state language could not stand for elections.

Of more substance, the amendments to the *Riigikogu* (Estonian Parliament) Election Act adopted in December 1998 explicitly required that all elected members of Parliament are proficient in the Estonian language.[10]

Identical amendments were simultaneously made to the Local Government Council Election Act. As mentioned above, the legislation did not include a framework of formal procedures by which the language requirements can be implemented. Nevertheless, in at least two cases, governmental bodies responsible for the implementation of the language legislation have initiated court proceedings aimed at preventing the individuals elected at the municipal level from sitting due to an alleged failure to comply with the language requirements. The court proceedings, however, were not completed before the following elections or, consequently, the expiration of the mandates of the individuals involved.

In Latvia, the language requirements for the candidates running for office in both Parliament and municipal councils were more detailed. Persons were not eligible to run in elections and should not be included in the list of candidates if they "have not mastered the state language to the highest (third) level of competence" (Article 5 paragraph 7 of the *Saeima* (Latvian Parliament) Election Law of 25 May 1995; Article 9 paragraph 7 of the Election Law on City and Town Councils, District Councils and Pagasts Councils of 13 January 1994).

When registering as candidates, persons who have graduated from a school that provides instruction in a language other than Latvian had to attach to the list of candidates a copy of the certificate of the highest (third) knowledge level of the State language (Article 11 paragraph 5 and Article 17 paragraph 4, respectively). Moreover, even where a person possessed the required certificate, the State Language Inspectorate could assess the person, and if the language inspector concluded that the candidate's language proficiency did not correspond to the highest knowledge level, the candidate was to be removed from the list of candidates.

This occurred during the municipal elections held in 1997 and 2001, and during the parliamentary elections held in 1998. In some cases, the removal of the candidate from the list resulted in the lodgement of individual complaints to the UN Human Rights Committee and the European Court of Human Rights. The plaintiffs claimed that the universal right to be elected, which cannot be restricted on the basis of language, had been violated. For one of the complaints lodged, the UN Human Rights Committee found that Articles 2 and 25 of the International Covenant on Civil and Political Rights had been contravened.[11] In another case based on similar facts the European Court of Human Rights decided in 2002 that there was a violation of Article 3 of the Protocol No.1 of the European Convention on Human Rights.[12]

Following the above-mentioned developments, as well as under pressure of the OSCE strongly backed by NATO and other international actors, the language requirements have been abolished both in Estonia and Latvia in 2002. However, abolition was accompanied by the adoption of other "compensational" amendments aimed at strengthening the positions of the state language. Thus, in Latvia the constitutional amendments were adopted which stipulated that all elected MPs must swear, *inter alia*, to strengthen … Latvian language as the sole state language. Other amendments stipulated at the constitutional level that Latvian is a sole working language in both parliament and municipalities. Besides, Article 104 (provides the right to address submissions to State or local government institutions and to receive a materially responsive reply) was supplemented with the provision that "everybody has the right to receive answers in Latvian".[13]

RIGHT TO USE MINORITY LANGUAGE(S) BEFORE PUBLIC AUTHORITIES

The Language Act of Estonia stipulates:

> In oral communication with public servants and employees of state agencies and local governments, persons who are not proficient in Estonian may, by agreement of the parties, use a foreign language which the public servants and employees understand. If no agreement is reached, communication shall take place through an interpreter and the costs shall be borne by the person who is not proficient in Estonian. (Article 8)

Further, under certain circumstances, the limited right to use a minority language before public authorities is guaranteed by law:

> In local governments where at least half of the permanent residents belong to a national minority, everyone has the right to receive answers from state agencies operating in the territory of the corresponding local government and from the corresponding local government and officials thereof in the language of the national minority as well as in Estonian. (Article 10 paragraph 1 of the same law)

However, in practice, implementation and invocation of this provision are not common.

According to Article 9 of the Lithuanian Law on the State Language:

> All the transactions of legal and natural persons of the Republic of Lithuania shall be conducted in the state language. Translations into one or more languages may be attached to them.

Only foreign individuals and organizations are permitted to transact in other languages. However, this provision exists alongside Article 4 of the 1989 Law on Ethnic Minorities mentioned above. Thus, a discretionary margin for interpretation is left open to officials.

In Latvia, in addition to Latvian, the Language Law of 1989/92 allowed applications to public officials to be made in English, German, and Russian. Civil servants were given the choice of answering in either Latvian or the language used in the application. However, the 1999 State Language Law abandoned such a liberal approach. According to Article 10 of this law:

> State and municipal institutions, courts and agencies belonging to the judicial system, as well as state and municipal enterprises (or companies) shall accept and examine documents from persons only in the state language.

Documents in other languages should be accepted only "if they are accompanied by a translation verified according to the procedure prescribed by the Cabinet of Ministers or by a notarized translation". However, several instances of exception to this rule arise: documents issued in the territory of Latvia before the date on which this law comes into force, as well as documents received from abroad, need no translation; nor do statements submitted to the police, medical institutions, or rescue services or the like in emergency situations.

Thus, the right to use minority language when dealing with public authorities is severely restricted, particularly in Latvia. After the new State Language Law took effect on 1 September 2000, several cases were reported where individuals had made complaints regarding the effective denial of the basic rights guaranteed by Latvian law as a result of the provisions of Article 10.[14] The individuals involved were not sufficiently fluent in Latvian to prepare a complaint concerning abuse by the police or local authorities, to complete applications to social security office, or to make submissions of similar importance. Nor did they have adequate funds to pay for the required translation and/or certification which meant that their applications were not accepted by public institutions.

Therefore, the restriction of the use of minority language before public authority, endorsed even at the constitutional level (see above about the new wording of Article 104 of the Latvian Constitution) might cause effective denial of implementation of certain essential rights formally guaranteed by law.

PROFESSIONAL AND OCCUPATIONAL LANGUAGE REQUIREMENTS

The language laws of all three Baltic states prescribe obligatory proficiency in the state language for employees in certain fields. Provisions enshrined in the earlier versions of Latvian and Estonian language laws caused protracted controversy in that the new laws extended the application of the language requirements to include employees working in the private sector. Only after the OSCE High Commissioner on National Minorities and the European Commission became actively involved was a compromise achieved.

Thus, Latvian State Language law requires that all employees of state and municipal institutions, courts and judicial agencies, state and municipal enterprises and companies in which the state or a municipality holds the largest share of the capital have knowledge of the state language. Employees of private institutions, organizations and enterprises, as well as people who are self-employed, must use the state language if their activities relate to legitimate public interests such as public safety, health, morals, health care, protection of consumer rights and labour rights, workplace safety and public administrative supervision or if they "perform certain public functions" envisaged by law or other normative acts (Article 6).

The Estonian Language Act contains very similar provisions (Article 5). However, the Lithuanian Law on the State Language mentions private institutions only implicitly in the following terms:

> Heads, employees and officers of state and local government institutions, offices, services, as well as heads, employees and officers of the police, law-enforcement services, institutions of communications, transportation, health and social security and other institutions providing services to the population... (Article 6)

Legislators in all Baltic states, influenced by the international organizations, also incorporated the principle of proportionality into clauses contained in their respective laws: that is, the language restrictions established by law had to be supported by a legitimate public interest and had to be proportionate to the stated objectives. The Latvian State Language Law, for example, contains the following clause:

> [government employees] must know and use the state language to the extent necessary for the performance of their professional and employment duties.

In practice, attempts to reconcile the principle of proportionality with the push to broaden as much as possible the scope of professions subject to language requirements has resulted in the adoption of detailed governmental regulations. These regulations stipulate the degree of proficiency in the state language required, testing procedures and the lists of the professions and occupations in which the specified level of language proficiency is required. Concerns have been expressed regarding the risk that the principle of proportionality has been interpreted too broadly and has resulted in the imposition of excessive language requirements, particularly in the private sphere.

Initially, three levels of language proficiency were introduced in Latvia – basic, intermediate and advanced. However, regulations adopted in August 2000 by the government of Latvia replaced this system with six levels.

The complex and voluminous content of these regulations and the adoption of numerous amendments and interpretative documents make a more comprehensive analysis of the regulations in this paper impossible. However, a brief analysis reveals that almost all medium-ranking and high-ranking officials and state servants are required to have the highest level of language proficiency. That is, a successful career in any area of public service or state sector or in the legal professions presupposes perfect knowledge of the state language. It should be noted that, in addition to these regulations, other pieces of legislation also include language requirements for particular professions. For example, the Latvian Law on Education stipulates that all teachers employed in state or municipal educational institutions must have the highest level of command of the Latvian language (Article 50 of the Education Law of 1998).

As a consequence of the introduction of these language requirements many hundreds of thousands of people have had to take exams to prove their command of the state languages. Moreover, these requirements have impacted heavily on reshaping the representation of native speakers of titular languages and Russian-speakers in the state and municipal sector: today Russian-speakers are vastly under-represented in the state sector and are employed mostly in the private sphere.[15]

LANGUAGES IN MEDIA

No language restrictions exist in any of the Baltic states in the field of printed media. However, the situation regarding the electronic media in Estonia and Latvia is markedly different.

Article 25 of the Estonian Language Act requires that, during broadcasts, "foreign language text shall be accompanied by an adequate translation into Estonian". However, radio broadcasts "which are aimed at a foreign language audience" are explicitly exempted from this requirement (paragraph 3). Moreover, paragraph 2 of Article 35 of the 1994 Broadcasting Act requires that at least one of the two Eesti Raadio (public radio) channels air "in a foreign language". This clause used to be interpreted as implying broadcasts in the language of the largest Russian minority. However, paragraph 4 Article 25 of the Estonian Language Act, introduced as an amendment in 1997, limits the volume of foreign language news programmes and live foreign language programmes on both public and private television which can be broadcast without translation into Estonian under paragraph 2, to no more than 10 per cent "of the volume of weekly original production". In Latvia, the share of broadcasts on private radio and television channels in languages other than Latvian had not to exceed 25 per cent of the total amount of daily broadcasting (Article 19 of the Radio and Television Law of 1995). This provision was in force until the Constitutional Court has declared it null and void in 2003.[16] As for public television and radio, the first channel must broadcast exclusively in the state language, whereas the same law allows for up to 20 per cent of broadcasting in minority languages on the second channel (Article 62 of the same law). However, these language limitations are not extended to cable and satellite TV.

In practice, the legal constraints of the kind are dubious to say the least in the limits that they place on freedom of expression, as they effectively prevent minorities from establishing their own electronic media. The restrictions placed on radio broadcasting are particularly detrimental as, in contrast to television broadcasting where a compromised solution can be achieved through dubbing or subtitling (although this obviously places broadcasters under additional financial burden), no technical means of translation are available for radio broadcasts.

Although there were no administrative proceedings reported in Estonia in respect to the above-outlined limitations, in Latvia several cases are known where private broadcasters were punished through fines or temporary suspension of their broadcasting licences for violation of the language quotas. Moreover, in at least one case where a violation was established, the corresponding supervisory body, National Radio and TV Council, demanded the outright cancellation of the broadcasting licence.

USE OF LANGUAGES IN EDUCATION

Access to education in minority languages remains the most controversial language issue in the Baltic states. The Lithuanian legislation is the most liberal in this regard. Article 10 of the Law on Education of 1991 declares that:

> The language of instruction at Lithuanian schools of the Republic of Lithuania shall be Lithuanian.

However, it continues:

> Populous and compact communities of ethnic minorities in the Republic of Lithuania shall be provided facilities for having public or maintained pre-school institutions, schools of general education and lessons in the mother tongue.

Classes, optional courses and Sunday schools are envisaged by law for small and non-compact minorities. In Estonia, the use of languages in general schools is determined in the main by Article 9 of the Basic Schools and Upper Secondary Schools Act of 1993. In basic schools, that is grades 1 to 9, "any language may be the language of instruction", such language of instruction ultimately determined by the corresponding municipality. However, in the upper secondary schools, grades 10–12, the legislation stipulates that the language of instruction be Estonian. The transition to secondary education in which instruction is to be provided exclusively in Estonian was initially scheduled for introduction in the year 2003, but was later postponed until 2007. An important amendment to this law was adopted in 2000 in that a clause was introduced defining the notion of "language of instruction" as follows:

> The language of instruction is the language in which at least 60 per cent of the teaching on the curriculum is given.

Thus, in secondary schools, up to 40 per cent of all curricula can be taught, in principle, in a minority language. Another essential amendment was adopted in 2002, allowing postponement of the transition to instruction mainly in Estonian by request of school boards supported by corresponding municipalities.

In vocational schools in Estonia, the language of instruction is Estonian. However, the Minister of Education can decide on the use of other languages as languages of instruction under Article 18 of the Vocational Educational Institutions Act of 1998.

In Latvia, the provisions for acquiring education in minority languages are the most stringent. Article 9 of the Law on Education of 1998 permits education in languages other than Latvian only in the following cases:

1. at private education institutions;
2. at state or municipal education institutions which implement education programs of national minorities. The Ministry of Education and Science shall determine the subjects of these programs which have to be taught in the state language;
3. at education institutions prescribed by special laws.

Thus, the law establishes mandatory bilingual education in primary schools (grades 1–9), and the share of curricula offered in the minority language may vary significantly, depending on the decisions of the Ministry of Education.

Transitional provisions of this law stipulated that, beginning in the year 2004, secondary schools as well as all vocational schools must change to teaching exclusively in Latvian. In other words, the complete elimination of state and municipally financed minority language secondary education was scheduled for 2004. This provision has attracted considerable protest from a number of minority NGO and minority-based political parties. In 2003, large-scale protest campaigns began, including mass rallies with participation of many thousands. The unwillingness of the authorities to reconsider this provision before the proposed deadline caused significant tensions. Finally, in 2004 the controversial provision was amended: as of September 1, 2004 at least 60 per cent of curricula in state-supported secondary minority schools are to be taught in Latvian. However, minority NGOs claim that it is not enough, and that severe restriction of the curricula in the mother tongue leads to substantial deterioration of the quality of education and endangers preservation of the minority children's identity.

Paragraph 2 of Article 59 of the Latvian Law on Education has also been a matter of concern. This provision envisages possible subsidies from the state budget for private schools, however only those private educational institutions which "implement state-accredited education programs in the state language" are eligible for these subsidies. Thus, minority private schools cannot claim subsidies unless they change to providing instruction in the Latvian language.

Finally, mention should be made of a number of specific aspects concerning the viability of minority schools. First, the training of teachers requires comment. All state-funded university education, according to the law, must be conducted in the state language. In addition, the law requires that all teachers in the state and municipal educational institutions have perfect proficiency in the state language. These regulations effectively prevent many potential teachers from being employed in municipal schools, and create an artificial shortage of the staff. Second, regarding the availability of training materials, the Ministry of Education does not allow use of many textbooks published outside of Latvia, while the scope of textbooks and manuals published within Latvia in minority language is limited, and they are not always of comparable quality.

CONCLUSIONS: MAIN FEATURES OF THE LANGUAGE POLICIES IN THE BALTIC STATES

The historical and political upheavals of the last century – the loss and restoration of independence, considerable changes to the demographic situation and the emergence of widespread asymmetrical bilingualism – predetermined stringent language policies in the Baltic states. Even a brief and incomplete overview of the language legislation clearly reveals that the higher the proportion of speakers of Russian in a given population, the more rigorous the linguistic containment policy: the language legislation is visibly more liberal in Lithuania, a country with a strong ethnic Lithuanian majority of more than 80 per cent, more severe in Estonia and the most restrictive in Latvia, the most ethnically diverse Baltic state.

The citizenship policies in Estonia and Latvia have contributed a great deal to the development of the language legislation. Both states adopted the so-called "legal continuity" approach, where only those residents who had possessed Estonian/Latvian citizenship before the annexation of 1940 and their direct descendants were "automatically" recognized as citizens after the restoration of independence. Thus, a considerable majority of the Russian-speakers – all those who arrived in Estonia or Latvia after the Second World War – did not receive citizenship and were supposed to acquire it through a process of naturalization with rather demanding conditions, a process which has so far brought modest results. Therefore, without voting rights, the majority of the Russian-speakers in both Latvia and Estonia had little opportunity to have any input into the formulation of the linguistic legislation drafted in the 1990s.

In summary, several major trends in the language politics in the Baltic states can be identified:

- *Protection of the state languages.* A common challenge faced by the languages spoken by a relatively small number of people has, in the case of Estonia and Latvia, been aggravated by the undermining during the Soviet period of the positions held by the titular languages through diglossia and the exclusion of these languages from some important areas, like military affairs, industry and transport. The restoration of independence brought about a massive "invasion" of English and other foreign languages. Harsh language legislation is seen as a tool for preserving the titular languages and ensuring their competitiveness, or as combating "linguistic Darwinism", as one leading linguistic expert in Latvia described it.

- *Strengthening statehood.* In the Baltic states, languages also perform very important symbolic functions. The undisputed domination by the titular languages is perceived as one of the main attributes of sovereignty, and, conversely, statehood is seen largely as a tool to protect the language. Under these circumstances, promotion of minority languages is often seen as a manifestation of disloyalty. Hence, legislators are usually reluctant to resort to this kind of action.

- *Emphasizing new geopolitical orientation.* Promotion of the titular languages is linked with an ulterior purpose: the eradication of Russian as a symbol of the eradication of Russia's domination. Efforts to join the European Union and NATO might seem to be undermined symbolically if Russian – "the language of oppressors" – is practised too widely. While some language purists are now hostile towards the more dangerous invader – American English – most Balts are inclined to tolerate the vast presence of Western languages (although knowledge of them is not yet common), and are much less tolerant towards Russian.

- *Ensuring political domination.* During the dismantling of the Soviet government system and the formation of new state bureaucracies, severe and allegedly excessive language requirements ensured pivotal advantages for native-speakers of the titular languages (largely ethnic Balts), and excluded the absolute majority of Slavs.[17] Nationalistically minded political groups did not conceal their more ambitious goal: that of promoting the emigration of Slavs, termed "voluntary repatriation". Liberalization of the linguistic legislation might increase competitiveness of minorities. In the eyes of many of those who belong to the Baltic political élites, this might jeopardize the role of their states as the guarantors of the survival and domination of the titular nations within their historical territories.

In addition to these internal factors, external influences have also played an essential role in shaping language policies in the Baltic states. Nation and state-building, interrupted by the forced incorporation into the Soviet Union in 1940, resumed in 1990 under completely different conditions: a framework of international organizations actively monitored the human rights situation in the restored independent Baltic countries. Although this monitoring was not always consistent and free from purely political considerations, inter-governmental organizations became important actors in the creation of language policies. Lithuania, Latvia and Estonia were eager to achieve full recognition and accession to international organizations. Hence, they were compelled to consider foreign advice, even in cases where such recommendations clearly ran contrary to the preferences of their own political élites.

All of these often competing factors determined the main trends of the linguistic policies and the development of the language legislation which can be briefly and somewhat superficially summarized as follows:

- The state languages are mostly promoted through legislative restrictions, such as language requirements for employment and the prescription of mandatory use of the state languages in various areas, and through punitive measures such as the establishment of governmental bodies responsible for monitoring the implementation of the language legislation and punishing those who breach it.
- In the meantime, positive instruments of the language policy, such as free state language training for the speakers of minority languages, remain very limited. It is revealing that despite establishment of the ambitious National Language Training Programme in Latvia,[18] it was catered from foreign donors, and only since 2000 the money from the state budget began to be allocated for this Programme. Similarly, only once (in 2003) was a certain amount of funds allocated from the state budget for free Latvian language training for naturalization applicants; all other state language training projects were financed by international organizations and foreign governments. As a result, free Latvian language training is not available for the majority of the adult residents;
- While minority languages are explicitly or implicitly recognized, their practice tends to be legislatively limited to certain "designated areas": activities of special "ethnic cultural societies", religious practices, and inter-personal or family relations;
- There have been extremely emotional and politicized, even irrational, reactions to the language issues which is due to their perception as issues of crucial importance for the development of the re-established statehood.

The array of the linguistic legislation which has emerged as a result of these trends, is usually evaluated as being "essentially in conformity" with the international obligations of the Baltic states.[19] However, serious criticism has also been directed at several provisions. Indeed, compatibility of some regulations with the norms of the basic human rights instruments is more than doubtful. Judgments of the European Court of Human Rights, as well as opinions of the UN Human Rights Committee, helped to eradicate some provisions of this kind, in particular, language restrictions for deputy candidates.

Other provisions appear to be incompatible with the Framework Convention for the Protection of National Minorities and may give rise to serious allegations of discriminatory treatment of persons belonging to linguistic minorities. Prohibition of the use of minority languages before public authorities, which may, in some cases, lead to effective denial of constitutionally guaranteed rights, is perhaps the most obvious example; take for example prison inmates who do not have sufficient command in the state language and who, for obvious reasons, have no access to professional translation and notaries' services.[20] Another serious problem is related to lack of legislation to envisage guarantees for use of minority language in healthcare. As more young doctors, who received their education after 1990 and speak poor or no Russian, begin working, many patients, particularly elderly people, will encounter serious difficulties in communicating with the medical staff. However, the curtailment of use of minority language in state-funded schools in Latvia and Estonia remains potentially the most explosive issue in the field of the language politics.

Strategies aimed at the integration of the societies[21] have been recently declared to be official state policies in Estonia and Latvia. This declaration clearly marks a substantial shift in the attitude of these states concerning their minorities to a more liberal and balanced approach. Meanwhile, it remains to be seen how these declarations will be implemented in reality; for example, how the idea of the "integration on the basis of the state language" will be interpreted. So far several minority organizations have criticized the documents on integration for not taking into consideration important proposals put forward by minorities, for insufficiently accounting for minority rights standards and anti-discrimination measures, and have concluded that the integration concept is actually aimed rather at the forced assimilation of minorities.

Despite growing bilingualism and efforts aimed at the integration of their respective societies, Estonia, Latvia, and, to a much lesser extent, Lithuania, remain deeply divided along linguistic lines. To cope effectively with this problem and to ensure the peaceful and democratic development of the Baltic states, the efforts aimed at protection and promotion of the state languages must be reconciled with the legitimate concerns and interests of their sizeable Russian-speaking minorities – a task that Estonia and Latvia have so far failed to fully resolve.

Constructive dialogue within the states is a necessary prerequisite for this kind of compromise. Thus far, internal dialogue has often been replaced with dialogue with, on the one hand, the OSCE, the Council of Europe and the European Union, and with the Russian Federation on the other. Significant cooperative efforts are required from both the titular political élites and the minority leaders. In addition, a consistent approach and permanent involvement is required from international organizations if this goal is to be achieved. Finally, further development of a free market economy, and restraint of unnecessary intervention on behalf of the state, in particular, into the use of languages in the private sphere, will undoubtedly facilitate the achievement of reasonable and compromised solutions.

NOTES

1 Jamestown Foundation, <http://www.amber.ucsf.edu/homes/ross/public_html/ russia_/ruslang.txt> (website consulted on April 15, 2005).
2 RFE/RL Newsline, 10 April 2001.
3 RFE/RL, ibid.
4 The Baltic Institute of Social Science, 2004, <http://www.lvavp.lv/user_images/ documents/apt_2003_atskaite.doc>.

5 Latvia and Estonia were the only two post-Soviet states who rejected the so called "zero option" of citizenship. Not all persons who lawfully resided within their territories at the moment of the restoration of independence were recognized as citizens. Only those who had possessed the citizenship of pre-war Latvia and Estonia before annexation and their direct descendants were recognised as such. Those who entered after the Second World War were defined as foreigners who had to apply for residence permits (in Estonia), or as "non-citizens", an entirely new legal status introduced by a special law (in Latvia). This "restorationist" concept resulted in factual deprivation of the political rights of approximately one-third of the population of Latvia, and secured the political domination by the ethnic Latvians: their share in the citizenry appeared to be approximately 80 per cent although they only comprised a little over 50 per cent of the total population).

6 All legal texts are quoted after the collection of minority related national legislation at the MINELRES website: <http://www.minelres.lv/NationalLegislation/Estonia/estonia.htm>,   <http://www.minelres.lv/NationalLegislation/Latvia/latvia.htm>, <http://www.minelres.lv/NationalLegislation/Lithuania/lithuania.htm>.

7 The Livs are small indigenous Finno-Ugric group numbering approximately 200 members in 2000.

8 Judgment of the Constitutional Court of the Republic of Latvia, Case No. 2001-04-0103, 21 December 2001, <http://www.minelres.lv/NationalLegislation/Latvia/Latvia_ConstCourt2001_English.htm>.

9 Judgment of the Constitutional Court of the Republic of Latvia, Case No. 2003-02-0106, 5 June 2003, <http://www.satv.tiesa.gov.lv/upload/2003-02-0106E.rtf>.

10 "2-1.Language requirements: The oral and written knowledge of Estonian of a member of the Riigikogu shall enable him or her to participate in the work of the Riigikogu, which means:
    to understand the content of legislation and other texts;
    to present reports on agenda items and express his or her opinion in the form of a speech and a comment;
    to make inquiries, pose questions and make proposals;
    to communicate with electors, respond to appeals and petitions, and answer inquiries."

11 Views of the Human Rights Committee under article 5, paragraph 4 of the Optional Protocol to the ICCPR, Seventy-second session, 25 July 2001, Communication No.884/1999, *Ignatane v Latvia*, <http://www.minelres.lv/un/cases/UNHRC_Ignatane_2001.html>.

12 Chamber Judgment in the case *Podkolzina vs Latvia*, 9 April 2002, <http://www.echr.coe.int/Eng/Press/2002/apr/PR%20Podkolzina%2009042002E.htm>.

13 Bulletin "Minority Issues in Latvia", No. 49, <http://www.minelres.lv/MinIssues/info/2002/49.html>.

14 See, for example, Annual Report of the National Human Rights Office 2000. Riga, 2001.

15 See for example A. Pabriks (2002), "Occupational representation and ethnic discrimination in Latvia", <http://www.politika.lv/polit_real/files/lv/SFL_Pabriks_eng.pdf>.

16 Judgment of the Constitutional Court of the Republic of Latvia, Case No. 2003-02-0106, 5 June 2003, <http://www.satv.tiesa.gov.lv/upload/2003-02-0106E.rtf>.

17 For further details concerning the ethnic aspect of the formation of the new elites in the Baltic states, see: Steen 1994.

18 See <http://www.lvavp.lv/>.

19 See, for example, OSCE High Commissioner on National Minorities "Statement regarding the adoption of regulations implementing the Latvian State Language

Law", 31 August 2000, <http://www.osce.org/item/5273.html>; and "Statement regarding the adoption of amendments to the Law on Language by the Estonian Parliament", 15 June 2000, <http://www.osce.org/item/4859.html>.
20 See Human Rights in Latvia in 2000, Latvian Centre for Human Rights and Ethnic Studies, <http://www. minelres/.lv/count/latvia/hrlatvia2000final.htm>.
21 See <http://www.np.gov.lv/lv/faili_lv/SIP2.rtf>; <http://www.lsif.lv>; <http://www.meis.ee/index.php?lang=eng>.

REFERENCES

Druviete, I. (1998), *Latvian language policy in the context of European Union. Brief summary* (Riga: Academy of Science Institute of the Latvian Language)
Jarve, P. (2000), "Language Legislation in the Baltic States: Changes of Rationale?", paper presented on the Panel "Language Laws: Nation-Building, Ethnic Containment, or Diversity Management?" at the ASN 2000 Convention, New York, 13-16 April 2000
Kamenska, A. (1995), *The state language in Latvia: Achievements, problems and prospects* (Riga: Latvian Center for Human Rights and Ethnic Studies)
Steen, A. (1994), *Recruitment and Expulsion: The New Elites in the Baltic States* (Oslo: University of Oslo. Department of Political Science), working paper 09/94

9 Language Rights in South Africa: an Adequate Level of Minority Protection?

KRISTIN HENRARD

A theme which gains increasing prominence both in international and in South African parlance is "unity in diversity". In the sphere of language and language rights this translates itself in the recognition of the importance of a language for cross-community communication, a kind of lingua franca, while at the same time protecting and promoting the separate (linguistic) identities of the various population groups in a state through language rights. The latter pole of protection and promotion of diversity is furthermore important in view of substantive or real equality concerns and of true democracy. Indeed, the exclusive use of one language in a multilingual society impedes equal access to government services (including education, health service and public services) and equal access to political participation for those groups who do not speak that one language.

These statements seem to confirm what is developed by de Varennes in this book, namely the fact that language rights are protected and promoted through individual human rights in combination with the prohibition of discrimination (interpreted in a way which protects true, substantive equality). In view of ongoing developments in case law, more particularly in terms of the European Convention of Human Rights with its exemplary function towards other (regional) systems of human rights, this holds true, at least to some extent. The various jurisprudential openings towards state obligations to achieve substantive equality, if need be by differential treatment[1] and the ongoing development of positive state obligations of states should be highlighted in this respect.

However, it cannot be denied that in addition to these individual human rights, minority rights are generally acknowledged to be necessary to obtain an adequate level of minority protection, also as regards linguistic rights. Since the special needs of minorities are often not sufficiently catered for by general human rights, their right to identity and the principle of substantive equality seems to call for "special" measures for members of (linguistic) minorities. In this respect two essential pillars of minority protection can be distinguished: more specifically the pillar of individual human rights in combination with the prohibition of discrimination, and the pillar with special measures for member of minorities (Henrard 2000, 8–13).

Of course, minority rights are human rights, more specifically a set of category specific human rights (like the rights of children, of detained persons and so on) and hence human rights and minority rights cannot that neatly be disentangled. This is *inter alia* visible in Article 27 ICCPR (International Covenant on Civil and Political Rights), the most basic provision of minority rights in international law, which forms part of a general human rights treaty. Similar straddling provisions concerning language rights can be found in the South African post-apartheid constitution's Bill of Rights. Furthermore, provisions (in treaties and in national law) concerning language use and status of languages should also be taken into account when studying "language rights". Arguably, it is less important how a certain provision or regulation is qualified (as human right or minority right or ...), and most attention should go to the actual interpretation and implementation which goes along with it.

Nevertheless, it has to be acknowledged that numerous language rights are to be found in minority rights instruments. Especially important, in view of the preceding statement, is that the increasing prominence of minority rights is reflected not only in ongoing refinements at the level of (quasi) standard setting,[2] but also and especially in significant developments at the level of supervision.[3] Despite initial apprehension about its possible impact, the supervisory practice of minority specific conventions decidedly constrains the at first sight extensive state discretion, hence contributing to stronger levels of minority protection, also as concerns language rights.[4]

The theme "unity in diversity" is often put forward in South Africa, as it is going through a massive transformation process in the post-apartheid era. In view of the divide-and-rule strategy of the apartheid regime, nation-building and the focus on unity is crucial. It is equally essential that South Africa's high population diversity and the concomitant multitude of linguistic identities are fully respected and promoted after decades of neglect and devaluation during apartheid. Furthermore, concerns of substantive equality and true democracy are of vital importance to South Africa because of apartheid's systemic discrimination against the non-white population.

As will be developed below, South Africa made a very promising start concerning "unity in diversity" with the adoption of its first fully democratic constitution in 1996. Indeed, several of its provisions reveal a move towards decoupling of political and cultural identity, also as related to the status of languages and language rights.[5] However, the more concrete elaboration of language policies and language rights as well as their actual implementation has been riddled with problems, mainly due to a lack of political will on the side of the authorities.[6] Nevertheless, certain painstakingly slow developments can be highlighted.

This paper will be divided into seven parts and will focus on the way in which and the degree to which linguistic minorities are protected in South Africa. First, a brief analysis of the minority concept and its application to the South African situation will be undertaken. Second, historical developments in South Africa relevant to the focus of this article will be discussed. Third, an overview of the constitutional negotiations will be given and the ensuing constitutional provisions will be analysed. It can be pointed out already here that even though some of these provisions form part of the Bill of Rights, at least one of them can appropriately be qualified as a minority rights provision, while the most basic provision on the status of languages is situated in a different chapter of the Constitution altogether, more specifically chapter 1 on the Founding Provisions. After a brief analysis of the certification judgements of the Constitutional Court of South Africa, a succinct overview is presented in the fifth part of the overall practice and policy development since the adoption of the Constitution. Finally, the South African experience is examined against the background of international and European standards pertaining to language rights for minorities. Here various significant developments (since the first version of this article) in the spheres of both individual human rights and minority rights will be highlighted, which will entail a more critical evaluation of the current South African situation.

DEFINITION OF THE MINORITY CONCEPT AND ITS APPLICATION TO THE SOUTH AFRICAN POPULATION

Although there is no generally accepted definition of the minority concept (Thornberry 1991, 164) it is possible to distinguish certain essential components, some of which are objective and others subjective, (Deschênes 1986, 289) which contribute to a better understanding of the minority concept. The objective components of the minority concept can be listed as possessing ethnic, religious or linguistic features which are different from those possessed by the rest of the population, comprising a minority position numerically as compared to the rest of the population, that is comprising less than 50 per cent of the total population, and fulfilling the so-called "non-dominance" requirement, namely that the minority should not have a dominant position over the rest of the population. The subjective component refers to the collective wish of the minority group to preserve and develop its own, separate identity.

The reference in the above definition to "the rest of the population" implies that the reference point does not have to be one monolithic bloc but can itself consist of several population groups. Thus, the minority concept can be applied in plural societies where there is no clear majority population. This understanding also colours the meaning of the non-dominance requirement: non-dominance does not necessarily imply being subordinate or oppressed, it merely denotes that the group concerned is not dominant. It is precisely in situations in which the numerical minority rules the state that the need for this third criterion becomes apparent: the criterion of non-dominance denies the qualification "minority" to such groups which are obviously not in need of special protection (Ramaga 1992, 104). A case in point was that of the Afrikaner minority during apartheid.

It should be noted that the nationality requirement for the members of a population group, which used to be considered an essential component before the group would be considered a minority, has been met with mounting criticism (Nowak 1993, 488–489).[7] The Human Rights Committee has also explicitly rejected the nationality requirement in its General Comment on Article 27 ICCPR.[8]

On the basis of the above extrapolation, the following working definition of the minority concept can be formulated:

> a minority is a group numerically smaller than the rest of the population of the state. The members of this non-dominant group have ethnic, religious or linguistic characteristics different from those of the rest of the population and show, even implicitly, a sense of mutual solidarity focused on the preservation of their culture, traditions, religion or language. (Henrard 2000, 48)

It is of particular importance to underline that, following the above working definition, all population groups in a plural society that are less numerous than the rest of the population of the society concerned (thus less than 50 percent of that population), that have separate, distinct characteristics and the wish to preserve these, can be considered "minorities" in so far as they are non-dominant (Capotorti 1991, 96).

The application of this definition to South Africa, using *inter alia* the results of the census conducted in 2001,[9] reveals that all population groups of South Africa that can be distinguished on linguistic grounds constitute minorities, with the possible exception of the English language group (Sacks 1997, 681). The most numerous linguistic group in South Africa is the Zulu, comprising 24 per cent of the national population, while Ndebele is spoken by only 1.6 per cent of the national population. In view of the increasing dominant status of English (lingua franca) in the public domain, the population group possessing English as mother tongue might be considered as no longer able to fulfil the non-dominance requirement of the minority concept. It follows that it is possible to question whether the English-speaking group can be afforded linguistic minority status.

South Africa is in any event characterized by an enormous diversity as to languages. The current general provision on languages contained in the South African Constitution (section 6, 1996 Constitution) reveals that in addition to Afrikaans, English and indigenous languages (Khoi, Nama, San, Sepedi, Sesotho, Setswana, Siswati, Tshivenda, Xitsonga, isiNdebele, isiXhosa and isiZulu), there are several other European and Asian languages spoken in South Africa (German, Greek, Portuguese, Hindi, Gujarati, Tamil, Telegu, Urdu, Arabic, Hebrew and Sanskrit). Furthermore, it is clear from the wording of section 6 that this list of languages is not exhaustive in that it refers to "all languages commonly used by communities in South Africa including ...". Moreover, whereas all language groups are scattered throughout the territory, most of them do have relative territorial concentrations in a certain province or in certain provinces. Striking examples in this regard are the

Eastern Cape which consists of over 80 per cent Xhosa's and Kwazulu-Natal which comprises almost 80 per cent Zulu's.[10]

RELEVANT HISTORICAL EVENTS AND DEVELOPMENTS

Historically, the battle between the two groups of colonizers, namely those speaking English and Dutch (later Afrikaans), and the ensuing language regulations, has enduring legacies for contemporary linguistic policies and regulations. The old struggle (see *inter alia* the Great Trek[11] in the 1830s and the Anglo-Boer War[12] 1899–1902) still forms the ideological foundation for Afrikaner nationalism and the source of the strong emotional reactions from a sector of the Afrikaner population towards rules which, purportedly aimed at multilingualism, they consider to be a veiled attempt to move towards English lingua franca.

Since the union of South Africa in 1910, South Africa has had two official languages, namely Dutch (later Afrikaans) and English, which have equal status in public business as reflected in the bilingual public service (Davenport 1991, 231). The result of such an arrangement meant that the development and promotion of the indigenous languages and the Indian languages was simultaneously neglected, thus giving these languages an inferior status (Currie looseleaf, 37.1; Hankoni Kamwendo 2004, 4).

Further, it should be emphasized that the language policy regarding education has been and remains today a very sensitive issue in South Africa. During apartheid, the policy regarding the African population was constructed in such a way as to promote ethnic identity while hampering proficiency in the official languages in order to limit access to employment (Desei and Taylor 1997, 169). It can even be argued that "the language-in-education plan"[13] became a central component of apartheid education. The principle of mother-tongue education was "conveniently applied to further the political interests of division amongst all communities" (Heugh 1995, 42). Moreover, the sudden change from the mother-tongue medium of instruction to the double medium or "50/50 policy" (English/Afrikaans) caused a great deal of educational disadvantage among African students (Heugh 1995, 43). Students were simply not able to grasp the meaning of what was written in the syllabus because of the language hurdle. This difficulty was compounded by the fact that the shift away from mother-tongue education to Afrikaans and English occurred at a stage when the students did not have adequate proficiency in these two languages.

CONSTITUTIONAL NEGOTIATIONS AND ANALYSIS OF THE RELEVANT PROVISIONS OF THE 1996 CONSTITUTION OF SOUTH AFRICA

The transformation process began with President de Klerk's speech on 2 February 1990. Subsequently several attempts at negotiation between the apartheid government (National Party), the ANC and several other political parties can be identified. An important issue for all sides to the negotiations was the process envisaged for achieving a constitution to govern the post-apartheid, democratic South African State. For the National Party Government it was important to be able to secure a certain level of protection in the future and limit the damage incurred as a result of relinquishing power. For the ANC, however, it was crucial that "the Constitutional Assembly should be bound as little as possible by the non-elected negotiating forum" (De Villiers 1994, 38).

Eventually a two-stage process was agreed upon. The first stage entailed the drafting of an interim Constitution by the negotiating political parties before any democratic election. That Constitution would govern the country during the period covering the first democratic elections and during negotiations leading up to the adoption of the so-called "final" Constitution. As Chaskalson and Davis have identified, "in order to give greater comfort to all parties, it was agreed that the final Constitution could not erode the fundamental values and principles contained in the interim Constitution. Agreement was reached on a series of 34 Constitutional Principles with which the final Constitution had to comply" (Chaskalson and Davis 1997, 340). Constitutional Principle XI is of particular relevance to the focus of this article as it requires the protection and promotion of the diversity of cultures and languages. The ensuing discussion will be limited to an analysis of the 1996 (final) Constitution and its implementation, although incidental reference to the interim Constitution will be made.

Two issues that remained outstanding until the very last moment concerned the provision in the chapter on "founding provisions" concerning the status of languages[14] and a provision in the Bill of Rights regarding the right to education, more particularly language in education. As argued above, it seems less important to focus on the qualification of a certain right as human right or minority right, or even a right pertaining more to the use of languages and less on language rights. Hence, the focus will be on the implications of these provisions, which is also visible in the last part where the relevant international provisions span individual human rights, minority rights and rights pertaining to the use of languages.

The sensitivity in South Africa pertaining to the languages and language rights has to be analysed in the context of the history of apartheid as well as the dominant position of English as lingua franca, despite the proclamation contained in the 1993 or interim Constitution that the State had to promote the equal use of the 11 official languages.

The proclamation in the chapter on Founding Provisions of 11 official languages (section 6(1) 1996 Constitution) has important symbolic value, particularly for the speakers of the nine African languages, who were formerly deprived of such status.[15] It is nevertheless striking that the 1996 Constitution no longer has the equal treatment of the 11 official languages as an objective, albeit distant, but "merely" the equitable treatment and parity of esteem of these languages (section 6(4) 1996 Constitution). "Equitable" treatment can be interpreted as strengthening the internal reference to subsection 2 and the need expressed by that clause for positive measures by the state to elevate the status of the indigenous official languages. "Equitable" makes explicit that there is, in view of the "history of official denigration and neglect" of these indigenous languages, a need for differential and preferential treatment and not merely formally equal treatment (Currie looseleaf, 37.5). However, "equitable treatment" can also be understood as an acknowledgment that not all 11 official languages should or can be used in all official domains for all official functions and purposes, which is in line with theories of functional multilingualism.[16] "Parity of esteem" would then imply that "considerations of practicality aside, a sincere attempt must be made to ensure that particular languages do not dominate while others are neglected" (ibid., 37.6). Even though the wording of section 6 seems primarily focused on the diversity pole of "unity in diversity", it can equally be argued that the goals of the language policy enshrined in the Constitution include the promotion of national unity within the country's linguistic diversity (Hankoni Kamwendo 2004, 8).

The National Party strongly favoured the retention of the non-diminishment provision contained in the interim Constitution, which ensured that the status of Afrikaans (and English) would not be reduced as compared to the pre-1994 situation. For the ANC it was vital that the constitutional possibility should exist to improve the indigenous languages by reducing the status of Afrikaans so as to reach an equitable use of and status for all 11 official languages. Ultimately, the National Party was only prepared to agree that the non-diminishment provision be dropped on condition that the section dealing with "use of language for purposes of government" at the national and provincial levels would require that more than one language be used. The party felt that such a provision would at least go some way to countering its greatest fear, namely that only English would be used at these levels.

Finally, when compared to the 1993 Constitution, the 1996 Constitution modifies the Pan South African Language Board's (PANSALB) obligations in two respects. The overall mandate of the Board remains "to provide for the recognition, implementation and furtherance of multilingualism in the Republic of South Africa, and the development of previously marginalized languages".[17] However, it was seen as important to include three highly marginalized indigenous languages, namely Khoi, Nama and San, among the languages that needed to be promoted and further developed alongside the official languages. Secondly, there is no longer a development requirement regarding "(i) all languages commonly used by communities in South Africa, including German, Greek, Gujurati, Hindi, Portuguese, Tamil, Telegu and Urdu; and (ii) Arabic, Hebrew, Sanskrit and other languages used for religious purposes in South Africa" (section 6(5) 1996 Constitution). This second change was justified on the basis that it would affect languages that were mainly spoken in Europe and Asia and which were already sufficiently developed. In view of the scarce resources and multiple transformation projects in South Africa, it seems reasonable to focus the funds for the promotion of multilingualism on the indigenous languages, which are, in any event, numerous. This view is further supported by the Board's remaining obligations to promote and ensure respect for "all languages commonly used by communities in South Africa". The establishment of PANSALB can only be welcomed as it amounts to a measure of institutional support for the multilingual goals of the Constitution.

These provisions of section 6 of the 1996 Constitution are clearly aimed at promoting multilingualism and indirectly providing numerous forms of special protection for (members of) the corresponding language groups, most of which qualify as linguistic minorities. It can already be noted here that this method of indirectly protecting linguistic minorities is comparable to the approach of the European Charter for Regional or Minority Languages of the Council of Europe, which similarly does not give rights to speakers of minority or regional languages but is focused on the languages and their use per se (see below).

Three other provisions of the 1996 Constitution are relevant to the issue of minority language rights, two of which belong to the Bill of Rights, the third one forms part of the chapter entitled Institutions Supporting Democracy. The latter provision and one of the Bill of Rights have resulted from multiple negotiations initially focused on a "right to self-determination for a community sharing a common language and cultural heritage". Eventually, broader concerns were taken on board and a three-dimensional agreement was reached requiring:

1. a provision in the Bill of Rights guaranteeing cultural rights such as Article 27 ICCPR, the most basic international norm concerning minority rights (section 31);
2. a provision creating a Commission for the Protection and Promotion of the Rights of Cultural, Religious and Linguistic Communities (section 185 of the 1996 Constitution, part of the Chapter on Institutions Supporting Democracy); and
3. a provision concerning self-determination for communities sharing a common cultural and language heritage (section 235).

The similarities between section 31 of the 1996 Constitution,[18] which forms part of the Bill of Rights, and Article 27 ICCPR are indeed striking, notwithstanding the fact that the concept "community" is used instead of "minority", and "ethnic" is replaced by "cultural". This different terminology was felt more appropriate because the ICCPR concepts are too tainted by apartheid ideology and practices to be used in the post-apartheid constitution. Nevertheless, it can be argued that the most pragmatic way to deal with the difficulties of definition of the term "community" is to see it as doing more or less the same work as the term it substitutes for Article 27's "minority" (Currie looseleaf, 35.16). Similarly, the term "ethnic" should be viewed as having a meaning more or less concurrent to the concept of "cultural" (ibid., 35.12). The wording of section 31 clearly supports the diversity pole of "unity in diversity", while the prohibition to deviate from the other provisions of the Bill of Rights in section 31(2) strives to maintain adequate "unity" as well.

Section 185, providing the institutional complement to section 31, equally reflects "unity in diversity" considerations. While constitutional provisions are necessarily vague, and many references are made to the need for further "national legislation", the primary objects of the Commission outlined in section 185(1) stress the importance of promoting national unity while guaranteeing respect for linguistic diversity.

The second provision of the Bill of Rights which requires special attention from a minority rights perspective is the provision on the right to education (section 29 of the 1996 Constitution). This provision also proved very contentious because of the issues of language in education and single medium institutions. From a certain point of the negotiations onwards, the National Party insisted on a right to single medium institutions in the public education sector, which they considered a crucial means of maintaining the Afrikaner language. The ANC, however, was not open to any such concessions as it considered a right to such type of educational institutions a return to apartheid practices (ibid., 35.6–35.7). Eventually, the National Party agreed to a considerably diluted version of its original proposal in the provision on the medium of instruction:

> Everyone has the right to receive education in the official language or languages of their choice in public educational institutions where that education is reasonably practicable. In order to ensure the effective access to, and implementation of, this right, *the state must consider all reasonable educational alternatives, including single medium institutions*, taking into account:
> (a) equity;
> (b) practicability; and
> (c) the need to redress the results of past racially discriminatory laws and practices [emphasis added].[19]

The factors which the state is to take into account when implementing the right to receive education in the official language or languages of choice have some if not significant potential for the realization of single medium Afrikaans institutions. Although the final factor contained in the above provision does not seem to support the concept of single medium Afrikaans institutions, as such institutions were mostly advantaged rather than disadvantaged by the past racially discriminatory laws and practices, this might be balanced out in certain circumstances by the "equity" factor, for example in areas where the majority of the people speak Afrikaans. Once again the vague formulations of the Constitution are open to multiple interpretations and seem to allow for different modes of more concrete implementation; hence the importance to assess the on-going policy development and actual implementation (see below).

CERTIFICATION JUDGEMENTS AS RELATED TO THE 1996 CONSTITUTION OF THE CONSTITUTIONAL COURT

The Constitutional Court had to certify, in accordance with section 71 of the interim Constitution, whether the 1996 Constitution complied with the 34 Constitutional Principles before the latter Constitution could come into effect. In the first Certification Judgement the Court held that:

the NT [new text, referring to the 1996 Constitution] cannot be certified as it stands because there are several respects in which there has been non-compliance with the Constitutional Principles ... Yet, in general and in respect of the overwhelming majority of its provisions, the CA [Constitutional Assembly] has attained that goal [of measuring up to predetermined requirements].[20]

Of particular relevance is an analysis of the answers of the Constitutional Court as regards objections raised concerning the language-related clauses enumerated above. An objection was raised that none of the Indian languages spoken in South Africa were given the status of "official language". The Court, however, rejected the argument and emphasized that:

the object of Constitutional Principle XI is to provide protection for the diversity of languages, not the status of any particular language or languages. The granting of official status to languages is a matter within the sole responsibility of the Constitutional Assembly, and it is the Constitutional Assembly's considered determination in that regard that is reflected in New Text 6(1).[21]

The Court also remarked that linguistic diversity is recognized and promoted by the other subsections of section 6. For example, the Pan South African Language Board is required "to promote and ensure respect for ... Gujurati, Hindi, Tamil, Telegu, Urdu ... and Sanskrit ...",[22] which are the principal Indian languages spoken in South Africa (Currie looseleaf, 37.3).

A further complaint about the language clause was related more specifically to the status of Afrikaans, which was allegedly diluted under the 1996 Constitution due to the dropping of the non-diminishment provision. In view of the fact that no Constitutional Principle prohibited the status of Afrikaans being altered, the Court rejected this complaint and added that:

in any event, the [New Text] does not reduce the status of Afrikaans relative to the [interim Constitution]: Afrikaans is accorded official language status in terms of [New Text] 6(1). Affording other languages the same status does not diminish that of Afrikaans.[23]

The absence of a non-diminishment provision does imply a reduction of the constitutional rights of that language since 1910. This is not, however, unreasonable or unjust, also in view of the overall requirement that all official languages should be treated equitably and with "parity of esteem". Of related concern was the provision obligating national and provincial governments to use at least two official languages as languages of government which, despite its underlying intention, does not guarantee that this will include Afrikaans (Currie looseleaf, 37.7). Arguably the Court considered that Afrikaans should not always be among the languages for governmental purposes in all provinces and at national level for it to be treated equitably and with parity of esteem.

The two objections levelled against section 29 New Text, targeted the fact that the right to education in the language of choice was reduced under the 1996 Constitution. In response, the Court emphasized that its task is not to compare the new text with the interim Constitution but with the 34 Constitutional Principles. However, it did point out that the relevant subsection contained in the 1996 Constitution imposes a clear objective duty on the state to implement the right to receive education in the official language or languages of choice in so far as that would be "reasonably practicable", whereas that duty did not exist under the interim Constitution.[24] Consequently, according to the Constitutional Court the language clauses of the 1996 Constitution did not have to be amended in order to comply with all 34 Constitutional Principles. The amended version of the Constitution was eventually certified by the Constitutional Court and came into effect 4 February 1997.

IMPLEMENTATION OF THE RELEVANT CONSTITUTIONAL PROVISIONS

Section 6 of the 1996 Constitution: Status of Languages Spoken in South Africa

The constitutional framework concerning the accommodation of South Africa's linguistic diversity is rather promising in that it provides a basis for the enhanced empowerment (Sachs 1994, 2) and political participation, as well as equal access to services (Reagan 1995, 320), for the speakers of the 11 official languages. Furthermore, the importance of promoting and ensuring the respect of the other languages spoken in the country is acknowledged (section 6(5)). Simultaneously, the improved constitutional recognition of several of the indigenous languages contributes to the achievement of the principle of substantive equality, which is so vital in the new South Africa.

Although the Constitution recognizes 11 official languages, the actual content of the official language policy is only determined by specific regulation of language use in interactions between the state and the subjects (Currie looseleaf, 37.3–37.4). As already briefly mentioned above, the Constitution includes a subsection on language use for "purposes of government" (subsection 3) which indicates the factors that should be taken into account when devising such policy at national, provincial and local level. "Purposes of government" include the determination of languages of record, journals, proceedings in Parliament, bills, laws (Du Plessis 1998, 276–284) and notices of general public importance. At the national and provincial level, at least two official languages must be employed for the purposes of government, which could be viewed as an indication of the perceived need to counter the move towards English-only practices. Further, there are also certain considerations such as "usage, practicability, expense, regional circumstances and the balance of the needs and preferences of the population".

Currie writes that the usage factor:

> would clearly justify the use by a provincial government of only the principle languages of a region for purposes of legislation and administration. It would also justify the national government formulating a policy of using only the principal languages of a region for the purposes of administrative services in that region. (Currie looseleaf, 37.11)

These considerations can be related to the use of the "sliding-scale" approach and imply a recognition of the practical constraints in a multilingual country. Indeed, it "will all too often be practically and financially impossible to provide every type of government service in each of the official languages everywhere" (ibid., 37.13). The sliding-scale approach would imply that the higher the degree of concentration of speakers of a language in a particular area and the more important a government service for the population, the more pronounced the state/provincial obligation to provide services in that language would be. An analogous approach would be valid for the municipal level, although the only factors explicitly mentioned as relevant for the determination of the policy for language use for purposes of government at that level are "usage and preferences of their residents" (ibid., 37.12). The fact that municipalities are allowed to use only one official language for purposes of government seems to open the door for "English only" practices but can also be understood as the ultimate confirmation of the sliding-scale approach in the sense that at municipal level it is more common to find strong concentrations of one particular language which would exactly correspond to the "usage and preferences of their residents". Furthermore and as already referred to above, the language stipulations of South Africa's Constitution, more particularly the qualifying conditions concerning language use for purposes of government, recognize the principle of functional and demographic differentiation. Indeed, different languages can be allocated to different domains and levels of official capacity without (necessarily) contradicting the spirit of constitutional multilingualism (Webb 2003, 5).

The Pan South African Language Board undeniably provides a degree of institutional support for the language policy as outlined in the Constitution. The Board's functions encompass advising government, making proposals on language policy and investigating complaints concerning language rights. The overall goal of the Board is the promotion of multilingualism. However, due to a lack of governmental and departmental support, the Language Board has not been in a position to contribute a great deal to the achievement of a multilingual policy in post-apartheid South Africa. Nevertheless, PANSALB did manage to establish national and provincial language committees as well as lexicographical units (Webb 2003, 4). These bodies provide an important institutional substratum, which is especially important for the indigenous languages, since these require further development.[25] The Language Board's activities (including its on-going practice of dealing with complaints concerning language use) and difficulties suggest that the practice regarding language issues in South Africa is rather disappointing. This is exacerbated by the shift towards English lingua franca in the public domain.

The actual practice regarding language use for purposes of government and other related public functions falls well short of the promising constitutional principles contained in the 1996 Constitution. African languages are seldom employed in public administration at national level and hardly anything has been done so far to raise the status and use of the indigenous official languages.[26] African languages are occasionally used for Acts of Parliament and in provincial and local administration and they are used in a certain amount of public broadcasting, but English is clearly dominant and omnipresent.

There is, consequently, a rather uniform complaint about the dominant status of English as lingua franca and the concomitant negation of meaningful multilingualism as demanded by the Constitution. Certain public institutions and national departments are trying to develop language policies which contribute to the right of identity of the various linguistic groups in South Africa while taking practical constraints and considerations of nation-building into account.[27] Nevertheless, it cannot be denied that overall there seems to be a de facto denial of several constitutional principles concerning the status of languages and multilingualism.

The Language Directorate at the Department of Arts, Culture, Science and Technology was so far not entirely satisfied with the distinctive language policy proposals made by the government departments and parliament prior to the adoption of a clear national framework policy and act in this regard. In general, the lack of intergovernmental cooperation and the perceived subtext of stamping out Afrikaans are regarded as negative aspects. Furthermore, the tendency to proclaim a single homogeneous position is far less optimal then a more flexible approach taking fully account of South Africa's high degree of linguistic diversity.

The Language Plan for South Africa, developed by the Language Directorate, is envisaged to become an important tool for the effectiveness of multilingualism in South Africa and has, as its central principles, language equity and widespread language facilitation services. The latter would contribute to equal access to all spheres of South African society – particularly to public administration – for all South Africans. The Plan is balanced in that it takes the practical and other resource constraints sufficiently into account by advocating functional multilingualism, which would entail a functional differentiation of the official languages, as explained above.

However, the lack of political will to make multilingualism a reality on the ground in the public sphere manifested itself *inter alia* by the extremely slow development of that Language Plan, the ensuing Language Bill and the disappointing delivery rate. Only six years after the coming into force of the 1996 Constitution was the Action Plan approved by Cabinet, more specifically in March 2003. This long delay is even more glaring when one considers that the principle of multilingualism and the designation of 11 official languages were already enshrined in the 1993 Constitution. In this respect it should also be highlighted that even though the Language Bill was accepted by Cabinet in March 2003, by October 2004 it has still not been discussed by the portfolio committee or discussed by parliament. As a matter of fact, it is not even put on the parliamentary agenda. It seems that certain cabinet members are not fully satisfied with the accepted bill. In other words, problems concerning political will once again interfere with the finalization of a multilingual policy which can proceed to the implementation phase.

The South African Language Bill,[28] which forms a substantial part of this Action Plan, translates the constitutional provisions into more concrete policy decisions that reflect the concern to realize unity in diversity, promote the equitable use of the 11 official languages and ensure redress for the previously marginalized indigenous languages while promoting equitable access to government services. The Bill applies to all government structures (at all levels of government) but also sets out to encourage and support private enterprises to develop and implement their own language policies in accordance with the national language policy framework. However, it should immediately be noticed that "encouraging and supporting" does not guarantee compliance, while overall the supervision of this Bill is entrusted to agencies (PANSALB, the language units in national departments and so on – see below) lacking the power to bring transgressors to court.

Be that as it may, it is to be welcomed that the Bill proclaims the principle that communication with the public should be in the language of the citizen's choice (article 2(c)), which is not only empowering for these citizens but also contributes to equal access to government services. Concerning government publications the principle of functional multilingualism is to be observed: while all comprehensive government communication should be published in all official languages, other national government documents should be published in at least six official languages selected from six categories, more specifically English, Afrikaans, the Nguni languages, the Sotho languages, Venda and Tsonga. As regards the mutually intelligible languages of the Nguni and the Sotho group an internal rotation principle is to be followed. Furthermore a language code of conduct for public officials should be developed as well as a strategy for the development of the previously marginalized languages. Each department of the national and provincial governments should also establish language units to monitor policy implementation and ensure the promotion of multilingualism.

Even though the Language Bill contains a plan of action and implementation for selected core activities of this most laudable plan, it has been criticized for not being explicit enough regarding the specific strategies that should be adopted to reach the strategic goals, which would (further) impede actual realization (Webb 2003, 6–7).

Considering the lack of political will to get the Language Bill enacted, it is not surprising that the actual delivery of the Language Plan is painstakingly slow and disappointing. By October 2004, of the three structures the Plan proposed to implement the overall policy it proclaims, only one, the National Language Forum, is actually established and is functioning. The forum meets four times a year and provides a platform for deliberation on policy matters pertaining to language use. Since the national language bill (and the underlying policy) is not yet finalized it was to be expected that not much harmonizing has been achieved so far. Furthermore, of the 12 mechanisms proposed by the Language Plan, only three are operative. The mechanisms in question, terminology development for the indigenous languages, translation and editing were already present in the Department of Arts and Culture since 1994. The remaining mechanisms which have not yet materialized are: language technology, a language code of conduct, a directory of language services, language audits and surveys, language awareness campaigns, the telephone interpreting service for South Africa, an information databank, the development of sign language and language learning and finally budgeting. Notwithstanding that the drawn-out policy process has resulted in promising ideas, strategies and so on, the actual delivery rate seems to confirm that the necessary political will to realize multilingualism is simply not present (sufficiently) in South Africa.

Nevertheless, it needs to be pointed out that some provincial and local governments and even some state departments have begun developing language policies in line with the Bill, because they realize that when it becomes law they need to be ready. Still, some provinces do not even have draft policies in place and want to await the finalization of the national legislation (whose content might still change). So far only the Western Cape has devised and implemented a language policy, the contents of which are captured in the Western Cape Provincial Languages Act.[29] At the municipal level, the metropolitan councils of Tshwane and Cape Town have progressed quite impressively.[30]

Overall, the finalization of an appropriate language policy and its effectuation on the ground necessitates well-thought-through decisions attempting to strike an appropriate balance between the accommodation of linguistic diversity, the promotion of previously disadvantaged indigenous languages and real equal access to government services on the one hand and concerns of national unity, the need for cross-community communication and limited resources on the other. Similar considerations apply to the language in education policy, which is an important component of an overall education policy. The policy regarding language in education has important repercussions not only for the degree to which linguistic identities are protected and promoted (Tabory 1980, 185) but also for the overall development students can realize (Skutnabb-Kangas 1981, 118–119) Indeed, ample research results identified the importance of being taught in one's mother tongue (at least in the first years of study) to be able to achieve an optimal level of cognitive and emotional development (de Varennes 1996, 121, 185). The latter is of vital importance for one's studies at secondary and tertiary level and hence also one's future career (Alexander 2004, 5).

Language in Education: Section 29(2) of the 1996 Constitution

A particularly sensitive issue with regards the right to education is the policy concerning language of instruction, as exemplified by the constitutional negotiations on the relevant subsection. The relevant constitutional sections are not only the non-discrimination clause (section 9(3) and (4)), which prohibits direct or indirect discrimination on the basis of language, but also that part of the section on the right to education which states that:

> everyone has the right to receive education in the official language or languages of their choice in public educational institutions where that education is reasonably practicable. (Section 29, 2, first sentence of the 1996 Constitution)

In 1997 the national ministry of education proclaimed *Norms and Standards regarding Language Policy published in terms of Section 6(1) of the South African Schools Act, 1996*.[31] The basic principles of this document should be set against the background of the *Language in Education Policy* produced by the same department in 1997, which underscored the importance of multilingualism and additive bilingualism in education and imposes an obligation on the schools to promote multilingualism.[32] These national Norms and Standards can be considered a genuine attempt to realize as much as possible the individual student's choice concerning the medium of their instruction, while taking resource and other practical constraints duly into account.[33] The Norms and Standards make explicit what is meant by "where reasonably practicable"[34] and, overall, take into account such things as local conditions, the need to coordinate the policy choices at regional level, and the need for a minimum number of students asking and/or willing to follow education in that language.[35]

Although this policy seems rather progressive, and provide openings towards mother tongue education, especially in light of the Language in Education Policy, the principles can, nevertheless, be criticized regarding several of its components. It can be argued that the numerical criteria[36] are so elevated that they de facto exclude the possibility of instruction in one of the smaller official languages, such as Venda or Ndebele. More generally, little attention is paid to the way in which African languages should be promoted and developed, as is demanded by section 6(2) of the 1996 Constitution. Furthermore, no attention is paid at all to non-official languages, even though some of them, such as the Indian languages have a significant territorial concentration in Kwazulu-Natal.

It should also be noted that in the end the governing body of each public school determines the schools policy on medium of instruction. However, this "choice", as is the individual choice of each student, is socially and politically constrained in the sense that social, political and market forces are free to play a decisive role in the decision process. In the context of the asymmetric power relations between the South African languages, this liberal model inevitably leads to an overwhelming choice for English as medium of instruction, on the sides of both students/parents and governing bodies of schools. This choice is indeed greatly influenced by the legacy of apartheid's indoctrination about the lack of value of indigenous languages and the perception of the absolute power of English. Although the African communities do wish to hold on to their languages, they have the impression that they can only "make it" in their careers if they have been taught in English, even though such impressions are incorrect. Language awareness campaigns organized by the National Department of Education and of Arts and Culture are specifically aimed at countering these internalized negative perceptions about the African languages and their value in future life (Desei 1998, 5).

Nevertheless, also in view of the ongoing reality that English dominates as medium of instruction on the ground, a more comprehensive directive on how governing bodies should go about deciding their language policies is necessary (Webb 2003, 7). In this respect it is to be welcomed that the new Minister of Education, Naledi Pandor, has announced in her 2004 budget speech that she favours mother tongue education in the first three years. This would not only empower the students to develop to the full extent of their capacity but would at the same time significantly contribute to the restoration of esteem for and respect of the indigenous languages.

Despite the laudable constitutional principles as regards language policy in general and language in education policy in particular, and the promising albeit slow policy developments, the actual practice reveals an overpowering dominance of English in official contexts. Hence, there is an urgent need for more directive government policies, with concrete measures aimed at countering the dominance and perceived supremacy of English.[37]

Minority Rights *sensu stricto* and Language, including the "Minorities" Commission

As discussed above, section 31 of the 1996 Constitution of South Africa is very similar in its formulation and intent to Article 27 ICCPR, and can thus be identified as a minority rights provision *sensu stricto*. In view of apartheid's abuse of the minority rights discourse, it is certainly remarkable to have such a constitutional provision relatively soon after the official abolition of apartheid. There are, however, differences in formulation evident in the text of the Constitution, which can be explained by sensitivities due to apartheid's legacy in this regard. However, due to the strong similarities between section 31 of the Constitution and Article 27 ICCPR, it can nevertheless be argued that one can rely on the General Comment pertaining to Article 27 ICCPR, and perhaps also on the UN 1992 Declaration on the Rights of Persons belonging to National or Ethnic, Religious and Linguistic Minorities, as interpretative guidelines to establish a more precise content of section 31.[38]

In this respect, it should be noted that the UN Declaration contains in Article 1 a confirmation that states have certain positive obligations as regards their minorities, even though these do not seem that extensive when compared with more detailed provisions contained in the same Declaration. The Human Rights Committee in its General Comment on Article 27 ICCPR also seems to require not only positive measures of protection,[39] but also positive measures in certain circumstances in order to protect the identity of a minority and "the rights of its members to enjoy and develop their culture and language and to practise their religion in community with the other members of their group".[40] The following argument can thus be made in favour of positive state obligations in certain circumstances regarding the "communities" of section 31 of the 1996 Constitution:

> The s. 31 right requires for its exercise the existence of an identifiable community practising a particular culture or religion or speaking a particular language. Therefore, if as a result of state action or inaction that community loses its identity, if it's absorbed without trace into the majority population, the individual right of participation in a cultural or *linguistic* community will be harmed. Section 31 therefore certainly requires non-interference with a community's initiatives to develop and preserve its culture. In addition, it is likely that it requires positive measures by the state in support of vulnerable or disadvantaged cultural, religious and *linguistic* communities that do not have the resources for such initiatives. (Currie looseleaf, 35.18 [emphasis added])

Only further implementation of this constitutional section will reveal to what extent this position is effectively followed in South Africa. By October 2004, however, implementing legislation does not appear to be on the cards at all and, presumably will not be for the near future. The slow development of legislation concerning the section 185 Commission for the Promotion and Protection of the Rights of Cultural, Religious and Linguistic Communities attests to the significant amount of time which may be required before such legislation is framed.

Whereas the formulation of section 185 seems to imply a stronger recognition of the group dimension of these "communities" or minorities, in that it refers to rights of these communities as such and not to rights of the members of these communities, the eventual Act establishing the "Communities" Commission (Act 19 of 2002) does not bear this out. The Act remains quite vague and does not give many further indications about the kind of protection (linguistic) minorities can expect in South Africa. It certainly does not provide any indication about the kind of specific rights that flow from section 31 of the Constitution.

Article 4 enumerates the primary objectives of the Commission, including the promotion of respect for the rights of communities and of tolerance and national unity. Part 5 of the bill on the functions and powers of the Commission does not convey a strong commitment to minority protection as these are confined to monitoring, investigating, researching, educating, lobbying, advising and reporting on any issues concerning minorities, without imposing any obligation on government to take these activities into account. Further, although the Commission is empowered to deal with complaints by linguistic minorities, there is no further clarification as to what this can entail. Consequently, the Commission does not seem to have any enforcement powers. The Act also stipulates that the Commission should convene annually a national consultative conference, which is supposed to provide a forum for the consideration of recommendations made by the Commission, the evaluation of progress in South Africa with the promotion of respect for the rights of linguistic communities and the furthering of national unity and tolerance among linguistic communities. The Act also refers to the possibility of the establishment of so-called "cultural councils" for a community or communities. However, no further criteria are stipulated regarding the establishment and recognition of these councils. Consequently and in view of the obscurity surrounding these councils, it does not seem likely that they will become a reality in the near future.

It should be highlighted that the Act obliges the Commission to cooperate with other constitutional institutions and organs of state where the functions of the Commission overlap with those of such other constitutional institutions or organs of state.[41] This encouragement of coordination and cooperation among various bodies with mandates pertaining to language rights and language communities can only be welcomed since this will diminish the occurrence of mutual inconsistent policies or unnecessary duplications. Regarding linguistic minorities, both the Pan South African Language Board and the South African Human Rights Commission appear relevant bodies in this respect.[42]

Since April 2004 the Commission is finally established but so far its contribution to the protection of linguistic minorities in South Africa is hard to gauge. Nevertheless, it seems fair to say that the slow pace of its establishment underscores the de facto reluctance of the current government to engage seriously with minority protection issues.

INTERNATIONAL FRAMEWORK REGARDING LANGUAGE RIGHTS FOR MINORITIES

The existing international framework regarding language rights for members of minorities is not extensively developed and is relatively weak. Nevertheless, there have been several meaningful developments over the last years at the level of both standard-setting and supervision (interpretation and enforcement) which carry substantial potential to enhance minority protection levels. Even though most explicit language rights pertain to the domain of minority rights *sensu stricto*, the supervisory practice of at first sight language-neutral provisions of human rights conventions reveals that these also have certain implications for linguistic minorities and their language rights.

Standards

When screening general human rights conventions like the ECHR, the ICCPR and the ICESCR for explicit language rights, very few can be identified.[43] In so far as language is considered explicitly it concerns contacts with public authorities and courts within the criminal system, and is limited to a language one understands, not the mother tongue or the language of choice. Even though one could relate this to the principle of true or substantive equality, which is crucial for minority protection purposes, the predominant concern is safeguarding the rights of defence of the suspect. Even the prohibition of discrimination did not use to offer much protection for linguistic minorities in the traditional jurisprudence of the supervisory bodies, like the European Court of Human Rights and the Human Rights Committee.[44] The domain of regulations pertaining to language use was one of the glaring examples where individual human rights (in their traditional interpretation) simply were not sufficient to address the special needs and disadvantages of linguistic minorities. It is thus not surprising that most language rights provisions developed in terms of minority specific rights.

When turning to the minority specific provisions, Article 27 ICCPR, the most basic provision in international law regarding minority rights, is not particularly helpful in that it merely states that persons belonging to linguistic minorities shall not be denied the right to use their own language. Nor is the General Comment of the Human Rights Committee regarding Article 27 ICCPR very informative on the more precise content of Article 27 rights for members of linguistic minorities. Paragraph 5.3 of this General Comment merely establishes that the right of linguistic minorities to use their own language is valid both in private and in public and should be distinguished from other language rights of the ICCPR. This requirement of distinction does not clarify the content of Article 27 itself.

The UN Declaration on the Rights of Persons belonging to National or Ethnic, Religious and Linguistic Minorities is inspired by the provisions of Article 27 ICCPR (preamble, paragraph 4) and arguably further illuminates the meaning of Article 27, while also containing provisions which go beyond Article 27 (Schulte-Tenckhoff and Ansbach 1995, 66). Especially in respect to the latter it should be acknowledged that a UN Declaration is not legally binding on the member states of the UN. Whereas Article 2(1) of the Declaration reformulates Article 27, Article 1(1) explicitly recognizes the right to linguistic identity of minorities, which is only implicit in Article 27 ICCPR (De Varennes 1996, 149; Thornberry 1991, 141). Furthermore, Article 4 contains two paragraphs with language-related provisions, namely paragraph 2 and 3. Paragraph 2 stipulates that states shall take measures to create favourable conditions to enable persons belonging to minorities to develop their language. Although prima facie promising, this provision is so vague and open-ended that it does not impose much of a real obligation on states. Paragraph 3 contains even more loopholes as it reads: "states *should* take *appropriate measures* so that, *wherever possible*, persons belonging to minorities have *adequate opportunities to* learn their mother tongue *or* to have instruction in their mother tongue" [emphasis added]. The use of formulations such as "wherever possible", "adequate opportunities" and the use of the verb "should" rather than "shall" to reflect states' obligations inevitably concede a wide margin of discretion to states (Karagiannis 1994, 218). In other words, these provisions tend to be formulated in such a cautious way that states can easily argue that they comply (Benoît-Rohmer 1996, 23).

On a pure textual level, similar arguments can be made in relation to other relevant international and European instruments. The UNESCO Convention on the Elimination of Discrimination in Education indicates in Article 2(b) that the establishment or maintenance of separate educational systems or institutions for linguistic reasons would not amount to prohibited discrimination. This implies that states can allow separate educational institutions in certain circumstances but does not oblige them to do so. In Article 5(1)(c)[45] however, the contracting states do agree to allow members of national minorities to establish and maintain, in certain circumstances and under certain conditions, their own educational institutions in which lessons can be taught in the minority language. Still, the overall effect of numerous restrictions is to heavily restrict the recognition of the right with the effect that "they enable each state to frustrate the operation of the clauses referred to by, for example, invoking discretionary considerations of national educational policy or the need to avoid compromising sovereignty" (Capotorti 1976, 8–9).

At the European level, reference should first of all be made to the 1995 Framework Convention for the Protection of National Minorities and the 1992 European Charter for Regional or Minority Languages. Both these Council of Europe instruments are legally binding for the contracting states and contain several provisions on language rights. The most striking feature of the Framework Convention is that, although it is the first international treaty with a general protection regime for minorities (Benoît-Rohmer 1998, 145), it concedes a very wide measure of discretion to the contracting states as it consists of vague programmatic provisions and includes numerous escape clauses (Klebes 1995, 93–94). Regarding language rights, Articles 10 and 14 are of special importance. Article 10[46] guarantees the right to use the minority language. However, its second paragraph, concerning the right to use this language in communication with the public authorities, is very strongly qualified (Klebes 1995, 95). Not only is the right contingent on a high geographic concentration of members of the linguistic minority but it is also weakened by discretionary phrases such as "where such a request responds to a real need" and "as far as possible". Consequently, the actual implications of this provision seem prima facie rather weak.

Article 14[47] regarding the right to learn the minority language and to be taught or receive instruction in a minority language is equally cautiously formulated. Moreover, the states do not appear to have an obligation to take positive measures regarding the right to learn the minority language. The right to instruction in a minority language in particular is very tentatively phrased. Indeed, states are not obliged but merely encouraged to provide this service (Fenet 1995, 180), since they can also opt to "endeavour to ensure that members of national minorities have adequate opportunities to receive education of their minority language". Together with the requirement of territorial concentration, Article 14, § 2 also contains vague conditions such as "as far as possible" and "within the framework of their education system", which seem to be easily open to abuse by states.

The European Charter for Regional or Minority Languages is remarkable in that it does not grant any rights to speakers of certain (minority) languages or to certain linguistic groups but is instead focused on the languages themselves. Nevertheless, promoting the use of minority languages undeniably protects and promotes the identity of linguistic minorities albeit in an indirect way (Schumann 1994, 93). A second important feature of the Charter is the fact that, certain general principles in Article 7 aside, the contracting states can under certain minimum conditions choose their obligations à la carte (De Varennes 1997, 156). The states ratifying the Charter commit themselves to a greater or lesser extent[48] to protect and promote the use of regional or minority languages in the domain of education (Article 8), judicial authorities (Article 9), administrative authorities and public services (Article 10), access to the media (Article 11), as well as the domain of cultural, economic and social activities (Articles 12 and 13). The high level of discretion which seems left to states is further confirmed by the apparently free choice by each state to what languages, spoken in its territory, the Charter will apply (Benoît-Rohmer 1998, 146).

While the text of the Charter makes one wonder about its actual contribution to minority protection in view of its high flexibility as regards the content of state obligations (Blair 1994, 59–60), the Explanatory Report on the Charter reveals already that the contracting states do not have a boundless discretion. Indeed, the states may not choose arbitrarily between the options contained in the Charter but should do so "according to the situation of each language".

Arguably this reflects a sliding-scale approach in that it would imply that "the larger the number of speakers of a language, and the more homogeneous the regional population, the 'stronger' the option which should be adopted" (ibid., 59–60). This approach seems particularly meaningful for a multilingual country like South Africa and its influence can indeed be identified in some of the South African policy documents regarding language use, such as the Norms and Standards governing Language Policy in Education.

Prior to considering the supervisory practice in terms of (some of) the preceding instruments, certain recent developments as regards (quasi) standard setting should be highlighted. When the OSCE established the High Commissioner on National Minorities (HCNM) in 1992, this institution was decidedly not meant to engage in standard setting but was supposed to be an instrument of conflict prevention at the earliest possible stage. Through his experiences with numerous disputes between minorities and governments, the HCNM identified certain recurrent themes, in which language often took centre stage. While he is no supervisory mechanism, he uses the international standards to which the states concerned are bound. Hence the HCNM considered it useful to commission a group of international experts to devise recommendations on these themes, which clarify the content of the rights concerned in the OSCE region.

Three out of four of the sets of recommendations that have ensued so far concern, at least in part, language rights, more specifically The Hague Recommendations regarding the Education Rights of National Minorities (October 1996, paragraphs 11–18), the Oslo Recommendations regarding the Linguistic Rights of National Minorities (February 1998) and the Guidelines of the Use of Minority Languages in the Broadcast Media (October 2003). Even though these Recommendations as such are not legally binding, the fact that they are based on the existing international standards provides them a considerable level of de facto authority. While these recommendations warrant a more in-depth discussion, suffice it here to indicate that the interpretation put forward by the experts is on the strong side. These strong interpretations concomitantly curtail state discretion, imbued as they are with substantive equality considerations. .

Secondly, it should be pointed out that even though the European Union's focus on minority protection was initially mainly confined to third states and candidate countries, there was already from the 1980s some explicit attention for minority languages (de Witte 2002, 485–486). Because of the lack of a clear competence basis in the treaties concerning the promotion of minority languages, most activities in favour of minority languages now appear as spin-offs of strategies aimed at language learning to facilitate the free movement of persons and so on A striking example in this respect was the Commission's Action Plan 2004–2005 of July 2003, entitled "Promoting Language Learning and Linguistic Diversity" (COM (2003) 449 final). The Action Plan purports to adopt a new approach not only regarding language learning but also concerning the promotion of linguistic diversity with special attention for minority languages. However, a closer study of the Action Plan reveals that it is focused on the promotion of language learning, as related to the promotion of free movement of persons and services and hence the common market rationale. In other words, the promotion of linguistic diversity, and of minority languages more specifically, seems predominantly a spin-off, a more marginal matter.[49] The Constitution adopted in June 2004 mentions for the first time the respect for minorities as one of the foundational values of the EU (article I-2), and article II-23 obliges the Union to promote linguistic diversity. Nevertheless, the fact remains that there is still not a clear competence base for EU policies and legislation on minority languages. Hence, mainstreaming of linguistic diversity concerns, with reference to existing standards of other organizations, and particularly the European Language Charter,[50] is probably the most that can be expected in the near future (de Witte 2004, 18–20).

Supervision[51]

A first important development that can be noted in terms of general human rights conventions is the espousal of substantive or real equality considerations by supervisory bodies. While traditionally the prohibition of discrimination was predominantly understood in terms of formal equality, the European Court of Human Rights (ECHR) decidedly opened the door for substantive equality reasoning in its *Thlimmenos v Greece* judgement of 6 April 2000 in which it underscored that

> the right not to be discriminated against in the enjoyment of the rights guaranteed under the Convention is also violated when states without an objective and reasonable justification fail to treat differently persons whose situations are significantly different. (para. 44)

Similar progressive readings of the prohibition of discrimination have also led the Human Rights Committee (HRC) to be more sensitive towards the "special" needs of minorities, also as regards language rights.[52] This is exactly the reading that people like De Varennes and Morawa put forward when arguing that several of the "special" measures that linguistic minorities strive for can be obtained on the basis of the prohibition of discrimination.

Secondly, the ECHR furthermore seems to be attaching more weight to the parents' convictions about the benefits of a certain medium of instruction for their children. Even though its reasoning is not framed in terms of the importance of mother tongue education for the cognitive development of students and the related substantive equality considerations, it does conclude that the failure to provide education in a certain language "must be considered in effect to be a denial of the substance of the right at issue" (paras 277–278). Arguably a continuation of this line of jurisprudence might eventually include more explicit minority (language) rights considerations, as already happened in the seminal case of *Chapman v UK*.

A third development that can be gleaned from both the jurisprudence of the ECHR (*Podkolzina v Latvia* of 9 April 2002) and the HRC (*Ignatane v Latvia* of 25 July 2001) is a growing sensitivity to problems encountered by linguistic minorities, more particularly when these are related to rights to political participation. Even though states have a certain discretion to impose linguistic requirements for election candidates, the proportionality principle should be respected, necessitating (at least) objective and fair procedures and legal certainty. States have apparently not an unlimited discretion in the way in which and the degree to which they impose linguistic requirements for certain public functions. The possibilities for linguistic minorities to participate more fully in the political life of the state in which they find themselves appears concomitantly strengthened. Needless to mention that fully guaranteeing the rights of political participation of all citizens is also of crucial importance in South Africa.

Finally, it should be noted that special interest for linguistic issues and the rights of linguistic minorities is also visible in the practice of the supervisory bodies of the International Covenant on Economic, Social and Cultural Rights, the Convention on the Rights of the Child and the Convention on the Elimination of All Forms of Discrimination. Mother tongue education for members of minorities is for example strongly advocated[53] and concern is expressed about the lack of possibilities for minorities to use their language in dealings with public authorities.[54] This growing attention for minority (linguistic) issues in various bodies arguably augurs well for an enhanced protection of minority language rights, through a significant reduction of state discretion and a clear focus on substantive equality.

The assessment of the supervision of minority rights instruments will be confined to the Framework Convention for the Protection of National Minorities and the European Charter on Regional or Minority Languages of the Council of Europe. At the level of the UN and the OSCE there are no legally binding instruments entirely devoted to minority rights, while the views of the HRC in terms of Article 27 ICCPR have not been particularly ground-breaking.[55] While a more in-depth analysis is done elsewhere,[56] I will suffice here with discussing the broad lines of the most important developments, paying special attention to language rights.

It has been pointed out on numerous occasions that both the Framework Convention and the Language Charter are formulated in such a way as to leave extensive discretion to the contract parties. This manifests itself for the former by the inclusion of numerous escape clauses and for the latter in a broad choice model of state obligations (Dunbar 2001, 107–119). The monitoring mechanisms for both instruments at first sight consolidate the intrinsic weakness of the instruments as the final word is given to a political body, more specifically the Committee of Ministers of the Council of Europe, excluding judicial supervision. However, the actual practice has revealed unexpected and rather impressive developments. Not only have the independent expert bodies that are meant to advise the Committee of Ministers adopted far-reaching interpretations of the provisions and a critical attitude towards the contracting states, the Committee of Ministers actually tends to follow these assessments of and recommendations by these independent experts.

An important theme highlighted by the Advisory Committee (AC) of the Framework Convention is that full, real equality requires the adoption and implementation of special measures for persons belonging to minorities.

This is in line with the opening towards substantive equality considerations at the level of individual human rights. More specific themes pertaining to language rights that are noticeable in the monitoring practice include the strict scrutiny of regulations on language use as regards public authorities. The AC is critical about certain numerical thresholds and also critically reviews whether the different minority languages each get a fair share of the overall broadcasting time. Mother tongue education is furthermore strongly promoted as well as the related accompanying measures of recruiting staff, providing language training and having adequate textbooks. Finally, it should be underlined that the AC also considers the actual practice and does not stop at reviewing the legal and policy framework.

A similar pattern emerges in the practice of the Committee of Experts in relation to the Language Charter. Also the Committee of Experts significantly circumscribes the at first sight broad state discretion of contracting states regarding its regulations of language use in the various domains of public life, without however ignoring the inherently flexible system of the Language Charter. The Experts furthermore do not limit their review to legal standards but also take actual practice into account.

While most language rights are to be found in minority specific instruments, it cannot be denied that the interpretation of human rights standards, and especially the prohibition of discrimination, has evolved to such an extent as to provide an essential level of protection of language rights for members of minorities. Furthermore, the supervision of the binding instruments devoted to minority rights or the use of minority languages has revealed that the ensuing state obligations are not as weak as they may seem at first sight. Even though judicial or quasi-judicial procedures are lacking, the ongoing review in terms of the Language Charter and the Framework Convention arguably impress on states a sense of obligation to guarantee a use of minority languages which is reasonable in the circumstances.

EVALUATION OF THE SOUTH AFRICAN NORMS AND THEIR APPLICATION IN LIGHT OF THIS FRAMEWORK

As the preceding analysis of the South African situation has revealed, it seems that in theory, at the level of policy decision-making, South African policies and regulations are in line with the international (and European) standards of relevance to minority protection. However, several recent developments both at the level of human rights and at the level of minority rights, increasingly constrain the at first sight broad discretion of states in this respect and reflect a heightened minority consciousness. Hence, it is not inconceivable that criticisms can be voiced vis-à-vis. existing policies, such as the norms and standards pertaining to language in education.

Furthermore, it can be argued that the current practice in South Africa would not pass muster in terms of the international framework because the supervisory bodies also evaluate whether the actual practice satisfies the international norms. Indeed, in terms of actual practice, the picture in South Africa is considerably less positive, which is mainly determined by a lack of political will. The latter is also the main reason why even ten years after the abolition of apartheid and the proclamation of multilingualism in the 1993 Constitution, the South African Language Bill, which sets out to effectuate this policy, is still not enacted. It remains to be seen how the actual adoption and implementation of this Bill will turn out. It can in any event be noted that several linguists keep calling for more resolute governmental actions and programmes to counter the shift towards English lingua franca in the public domain and to improve to some extent the status of the indigenous (official) languages.

NOTES

1   See the discussion *infra* on ECHR, *Thlimmenos* v *Greece*, and to some extent *McShane* v *the UK*. For an analysis of broader (then language rights) developments pertaining to minority protection in terms of the ECHR, see Geoff Gilbert (2002), 'The Burgeoning Minority Rights Jurisprudence of the ECHR', *Human Rights Quarterly* 24.

2   Reference should be made to the various Roma specific standards (as well as institutions) that are gradually emerging in various intergovernmental organizations, and also to the various sets of recommendations made by experts commissioned by the HCNM. Especially the latter focus extensively on language issues, as will be elaborated upon *infra*.

3   See *infra* for a brief review of the supervisory practice under the Framework Convention for the Protection of National Minorities and the European Charter on Regional or Minority Languages.

4   In addition to the increasing prominence of minority rights concerns generally via the accession process, the European Union has been active in promoting linguistic diversity to some extent by promoting minority languages. In the latter respect, a brief reference will be made *infra* about the Action Plan of the Commission entitled 'Promoting Language Learning and Linguistic Diversity: an Action Plan 2004–2006', COM (2003) 449 final

5   Specifically relevant for languages is section 6 on the status of languages, proclaiming 11 official languages, and section 31 concerning the rights of persons belonging to (*inter alia*) linguistic communities. The Bill of Rights also provides a certain opening towards a legislative recognition of marriages and systems of personal law (s. 15(3)), while section 211 provides a similar opening towards a place for customary law in the national legal system.

6   Neville Alexander, 'Language Policy and Language Planning in the New South Africa', UCT, Cape Town, 2003, 3. See also Rajeshwari V Pandharipande (2002), 'Minority Matters: Issues in Minority Languages in India', *IJMS* 4:2, 224–226.

7   See also the various contributions in the report of the NHC's roundtable conference of 20 October 2003 on *New Minorities: Inclusion and Equality*, Netherlands Helsinki Committee.

8   HRC, General Comment 23 on article 27 ICCPR, § 5.2. See also HRC, General Comment 15, The Position of Aliens under the Covenant, § 7.

9   Census 2001: Primary Tables South Africa, Statistics South Africa, 2002.

10 Vic Webb, *Language in South Africa: The Role of Language in National Transformation, Reconstruction and Development*, University of Pretoria, 74.

11 From the mid-nineteenth century the Dutch speaking Afrikaners in the Cape faced a twin assault on their cultural and spiritual values in the form of the so-called

"liberal tendency" and intensified British cultural imperialism. Examples of the latter include the requirement of verbal English skills in order to gain employment in the civil service and the abolition of Dutch as medium of instruction in the public schools. The Great Trek was made by a group of about 15 000 Afrikaners, escaping British rule in the Cape and eventually resulted in the creation of two Boer republics to the north, namely the Transvaal and the Orange Free State. See Giliomee 1989, 21 and Pelzer 1980, 6.

12 Ongoing tensions between the two Boer and the two British republics and attempts to expansion led eventually to the Anglo-Boer War. The war lasted for three years and resulted in strained relations between the two groups which has ongoing implications in the twenty-first century. Notably the British concentration camps for the Afrikaner women and children resulted in a great deal of resentment on the part of the Afrikaners. See Pelzer 1980, 6.

13 The language in education plan of the Apartheid era refers primarily to choice as to the medium of instruction for the distinctive population groups. In concrete terms, it meant that all the population groups received mother tongue education, which after a few years switched to double medium Afrikaans/ English (the precise number of years of mother tongue education shifted over time).

14 Section 6, 1996 Constitution:
The official languages of the Republic are Sepedi, Sesotho, Setswana, SiSwati, Tshivenda, Xitsonga, Afrikaans, English, isiNdebele, isiXhosa and isiZulu.
Recognizing the historically diminished use and status of the indigenous languages of our people, the state must take practical and positive measures to elevate the status and advance the use of these languages. (a) The national government and provincial governments may use any particular official languages for the purposes of government, taking into account usage, practicality, expense, regional circumstances and the balance of the needs and preferences of the population as a whole or in the province concerned; but the national government and each provincial government must use at least two official languages. Municipalities must take into account the language usage and preferences of their residents. The National government and provincial governments, by legislative and other measures, must regulate and monitor their use of official languages. Without detracting from the provisions of subsection (2) all official languages must enjoy parity of esteem and must be treated equitably. A Pan South African Language Board established by national legislation must promote, and create conditions for the development and use of all official languages; the Khoi, Nama and San languages; and sign language; and promote and ensure respect for all languages commonly used by communities in South Africa, including German, Greek, Gujarati, Hindi, Portuguese, Tamil, Telegu and Urdu; and Arabic, Hebrew, Sanskrit, and other languages used for religious purposes in South Africa.

15 The actual implementation and measures taken to give meaning to the status of official language will be discussed *infra*.

16 This can be related to Pandharipande's theory that the functional load of languages in combination with their transparency are crucial factors in determining their sustainability. In so far as a certain language has almost a one-to-one relation to a certain function, this would be ideal for its maintenance (Pandharipande 2002: 224–226).

17 Cf. Long title of the Pan South African Language Board Act, No 59 of 1995.

18 Section 31, 1996 Constitution:
Persons belonging to a cultural, religious or linguistic community may not be denied the right, with other members of that community –to enjoy their culture,

practice their religion and use their language; and to form, join and maintain cultural, religious and linguistic associations and other organs of civil society. The rights in subsection (1) may not be exercised in a manner inconsistent with any provision of the Bill of Rights.

19 Section 29(2) 1996 Constitution.
20 First Certification Judgement of the National Constitution, § 31.
21 Ibid, § 211.
22 Ibid, § 210.
23 First Certification Judgement of the National Constitution, § 212.
24 First Certification Judgement of the National Constitution, § 81.
25 Vic Webb, 'Language Policy Development in South Africa', paper presented at the 2002 World Congress on Language Politics, unpublished but on file with the author, pp. 3 and 11.
26 There are certain initiatives at some universities, but this occurs at the instigation of the universities themselves without any guidance from government. Some work is being done to establish dictionaries in the nine indigenous official languages by the Language Directorate of the Department of Arts, Culture, Science and Technology, but this work is developing very slowly. Further, the Language Plan for South Africa with more concrete principles pertaining to language use in the public sphere is still not finalised.
27 The language policy proposals in the Department of Defense for example, suggested that English would be the "thread language" or the lingua franca for general communication, command, control and coordination as well as training, while the other official languages would be used as "link languages" where the situation so warranted or demanded it.
28 The long title of the bill reflects nicely the unity in diversity theme as well as the link with democracy, equal access to services and so on, and reads as follows: "Bill to provide for an enabling framework for promoting South Africa's linguistic diversity and encouraging respect for language rights within the framework of building and consolidating a united, democratic South African nation, taking into account the broad acceptance of linguistic diversity, social justice, the principle of equal access to public services and programmes, respect for language rights, the establishment of language services at all levels of government, the powers and functions of such services and matters connected therewith."
29 Email from Anne Marie Beukes, professor at Rand Afrikaans University, 2 June 2004.
30 Email from Vic Webb, professor at the University of Pretoria, 7 October 2004.
31 Government Gazette, 4 August 1997.
32 Language in Education Policy in terms of section 3(4) (m) of the National Education Policy Act, 1996, *Government Gazette*, 4 August 1997, §§ 4.1.5., 4.1.6. and 5.3.1.
33 Ibid., *inter alia* § 5.4.4. "The provincial department must explore ways and means of sharing scarce human resources. It must also explore ways and means of providing alternative maintenance programmes in schools or school districts which cannot be provided with or offer additional languages of teaching in the home languages of learners."
34 Norms and Standards, § 5.4.3: "It is reasonably practicable to provide education in a particular language of learning and teaching if at least 40 on Grade 1 to 6 or 35 in Grades 7 to 12 learners in a particular grade request it in a particular school."
35 Norms and Standards, § 5.3.2: "Where there are less than 40 requests in Grades 1 to 6, or less than 35 requests in Grades 7 to 12 for instruction in a language in a given grade not already offered by a school in a particular school district, the head of the provincial department of education will determine how the needs

of those learners will be met, taking into account ... 5.3.2.2. the need to achieve equity; 5.3.2.3. the need to redress the results of past racially discriminatory laws and practices; 5.3.2.4. practicability ...".

36 See Note 22 *supra*.

37 Vic Webb identified the following as tasks to be performed for the effective implementation of linguistic pluralism in South Africa: the need to develop the indigenous languages and the need for adequate formal measures for the protection of minority languages and ethnolinguistic diversity (Webb 2003: 11–14).

38 In so far as the two Council of Europe instruments of relevance to minority protection have the same goal of protecting the (linguistic) identity of minorities against forced assimilation, their principles and the related supervisory practice can also be taken into consideration. See in this respect also section 39(1)(b) of the 1996 Constitution which instructs courts, tribunals or forums when interpreting the Bill of Rights to consider relevant international law. See *infra* for further information about the current stance and practice in terms of international law.

39 HRC, General Comment on article 27 ICCPR, § 6.1.

40 Ibid., § 6.2.

41 Section 22(2) of the draft bill.

42 See also the Language Bill, section 9 on cooperation which stipulates that the national or provincial language units or any other organ of state involved in the implementation of this act shall respect the mandate of PANSALB and shall liaise and cooperate with any other public or private body which has the capacity to facilitate the implementation of the Act so as to avoid duplication of activities and services.

43 For a more elaborate discussion of language rights in the ECHR, see Henrard 2000: 125–128.

44 See *inter alia* Eur. Ct HR, case relating to certain aspects of the laws on the use of language in education in Belgium, 23 July 1968; Eur. Ct HR, *Inhabitants of Alsemberg and Beersel* v *Belgium*, 26 July 1963; Eur. Comm. HR, *X v Austria*, 10 October 1979. Regarding the ICCPR see the elaborate analysis in Joseph, Schultz and Castan 2000: chapter 23 and especially the discussions of indirect discrimination 533–536 and 538.

45 Article 5(1)(c) UNESCO Convention on the Elimination of Discrimination in Education:
The State Parties to this Convention agree that : ...
It is essential to recognize the right of members of national minorities to carry on their own educational activities, including the maintenance of schools and, depending on the educational policy of each State, the use or the teaching of their own language, provided however: that this right is not exercised in a manner which prevents the members of these minorities from understanding the culture and language of the community as a whole and from participating in its activities, or which prejudices national sovereignty; that the standard of education is not lower than the general standard laid down or approved by the competent authorities; and that attendance at such schools is optional.

46 Article 10, § 2 Framework Convention: In areas inhabited by persons belonging to national minorities traditionally or in substantial numbers, if those persons so request and where such a request corresponds to a real need, the Parties shall endeavour to ensure, as far as possible, the conditions which would make it possible to use the minority language in relations between those persons and the administrative authorities.

47 Article 14 Framework Convention: § 1. The Parties undertake to recognize that every person belonging to a national minority has the right to learn his or her

minority language. § 2. In areas inhabited by persons belonging to national minorities traditionally or in substantial numbers, if there is a sufficient demand, the Parties shall endeavour to ensure, as far as possible, and within the framework of their education systems, that persons belonging to those minorities have adequate opportunities for being taught the minority language or for receiving instruction in the minority language.

48 The articles of the European Charter for Regional or Minority Languages are too extensive to quote here.

49 See in this respect K. Henrard, 'An Investigation into the desirable and Possible Role of the Language Charter in Expanding on article 22 of the EU's Charter of Fundamental Rights', <http://www.ciemen.org/mercator>, under mercator publications.

50 In this respect it should certainly be highlighted that the Commission already explicitly encouraged in its Action Plan national and regional bodies to give special attention to measures to assist those language communities, whose numbers of native speakers is in decline from generation to generation, and this "in line with the principles of the European Charter for Regional or Minority Languages" (at p. 12).

51 For a more in-depth analysis of the latest developments concerning supervision of minority protection instruments see K. Henrard (2005), 'An Ever Increasing Synergy towards a Stronger Level of Minority Protection between Minority Specific and Non Specific Instruments', *European Yearbook on Minority Issues 2003–2004*.

52 See *Waldman v Canada*, views of 3 November 1999 and as regards language rights *J.G.A. Diergaardt et al v Namibia*, views of 25 July 2000, para 10.10. See also Morawa 2002: 9.

53 *Inter alia* CESCR/C, Concluding Observations on Guatemala, 2003, para 27; CERD/C, Concluding Observations on Albania, 2003, para 6; CRC/C, Concluding Observations on Georgia, 2003, para 71.

54 *Inter alia* CESCR/C, Concluding Observations on Estonia, 2002, para 57; CERD/C, Concluding Observations on Ghana, 2003, para 20.

55 For a more in-depth discussion of the views of the HRC in terms of Article 27 ICCPR, see K. Henrard (2004), "Charting the Gradual Emergence of a More Robust Level of Minority Protection; Minority Specific Instruments and the European Union", *Netherlands Institute of Human Rights* (NHRQ) 22:4.

56 Ibid, and K. Henrard (2005), 'An Ever Increasing Synergy towards a Stronger Level of Minority Protection between Minority Specific and Non Specific Instruments', *European Yearbook on Minority Issues 2003–2004*.

REFERENCES

Alexander, N. (2004), *Language Policy: The Litmus Test of Democracy in Post Apartheid South Africa* (University of Cape Town)
Bakker, E. and Bomers, J. (eds) (2003), *New Minorities: Inclusion and Equality*, Roundtable conference 20 October 2003 (The Hague: NHC)
Benoit-Rohmer, F. (1996), *The Minority Question in Europe: Towards a Coherent System of Protection of National Minorities* (Strasbourg: Council of Europe)
—— (1998), "Le Conseil de l'Europe et les Minorités Nationales", in K. Malfliet and R. Laenen (eds) *Minority Policy in Central and Eastern Europe: The Link between Domestic Policy, Foreign Policy and European Integration* (Louvain: KULeuven)
Blair, P. (1994), *The Protection of Regional or Minority Languages in Europe* (Fribourg: Institut du Fédéralisme)

Capotorti, F. (1976), "Protection of Minorities under Multinational Agreements on Human Rights". *Italian Yearbook on International Law*, 3–32
_____ (1991), *Study on the Rights of Persons belonging to Ethnic, Religious or Linguistic Minorities* (New York: United Nations)
Chaskalson, M. and Davis, D. (1997), "Constitutionalism, the Rule of Law, and the First Certification Judgement: Ex Parte Chairperson of the Constitutional Assembly in Re: Certification of the Constitution of the Republic of South Africa 1996. 1996 (4) SA 744 (cc)". *South African Journal of Human Rights*, 430–445
Currie, I. (Loose leaf), "Official Languages", ch. 37.1–37.15 in M. Chaskalson et al. (eds), *Constitutional Law of South Africa* (Kenwyn: Juta)
_____ (Loose leaf), "Minority Rights: Education, Culture and Language", ch. 35.1–35.35 in M. Chaskalson et al. (eds), *Constitutional Law of South Africa* (Kenwyn: Juta)
Davenport, T. R. H. (1991), *South Africa: A Modern History* (Toronto: University of Toronto Press)
Deschenes, J. (1986), "Qu'est-ce qu'une Minorité", *Les Cahiers de Droit*, 255–291
Desei, Z. and Taylor, N. (1997), "Language and Education in South Africa", in D. Coulby, J. Gundara and C. Jones (eds), *Intercultural Education – World Yearbook of Education 1997* (London: Kogan Page), 169–177
Desei, Z. (1998), "*Enabling Policies, Disabling Practices*", paper presented at the Tenth World Congress of Comparative Education Societies (Cape Town, 16 July, 1998), unpublished but on file with the author
De Varennes, F. (1996), *Language, Minorities and Human Rights* (The Hague: Kluwer)
_____ (1997), "Ethnic Conflicts and Language in Eastern European and Central Asian States: Can Human Rights Help Prevent Them?", *International Journal on Group and Minority Rights*, 135–174
_____ (2001), "Language Rights as an Integral Part of Human Rights", *International Journal on Multicultural Societies* 3:1, 15–25
De Villiers, B. (1994), "The Constitutional Principles – Content and Significance", in B. De Villiers (ed.), *Birth of a Constitution* (Kenwyn: Juta)
De Witte, B. (2002), "Politics versus Law in the EU's Approach to Ethnic Minorities", in J. Zielonka (ed.), *Europe Unbound: Enlarging and Reshaping the Boundaries of the EU* (Palgrave)
_____ (2004), "The Constitutional Resources for an EU Minority Protection Policy", in G. Von Toggenburg (ed.), *The Protection of Minorities and the enlarged European Union* (Budapest: LGI Books)
Dunbar, R. (2001), "Minority Language Rights in International Law", *International Comparative Law Quarterly* 50, 90–120
Du Plessis, L. M. (1998), "*Statutory Multilingualism and Textual Conflict under the 1996 Constitution*" (Tydskrif vir die Hedendaagse Romeins-Hollandse Reg), 276–284
Eide, A. (1996), *Comprehensive Examination of the Thematic Issues Relating to Racism, Xenophobia, Minorities and Migrant Workers*, Working Paper for the UN Working Group on Minorities, UN Doc. E/CN.4/Sub.2/1996/30
Fenet, A. (1995), "Europe et les Minorités", in A. Fenet et al. (eds), *Le Droit et les Minorités: Analyses et Textes* (Brussels: Bruylant)
Giliomee, H. (1989), "The Beginning of Afrikaner Ethnic Consciousness", in L. Vail (ed.), *The Creation of Tribalism in Southern Africa* (Berkeley: University of California)
Hankoni Kamwendo, G. (2004), *South Africa's Post Apartheid Language Policy: Some Encouraging and Worrisome Trends* (University of Helsinki)
Henrard, K. (2000), *Devising an Adequate System of Minority Protection: Individual Human Rights, Minority Rights and the Right to Self-Determination* (London: Kluwer)

Heugh, K. (1995), "From Unequal Education to the Real Thing", in K. Heugh et al., (ed.), *Multilingual Education for South Africa* (Johannesburg: Heinemann)

Holt, S. and Packer, J. (2001), "OSCE Developments and Linguistic Minorities", *International Journal on Multicultural Societies* 3:2, 107–134

Joseph S., Schultz, J. and Castan, M. (2000), *The International Covenant on Civil and Political Rights: Cases, Materials and Commentary* (OUP)

Karagiannis, S. (1994), "La Protection des Langues Minoritaires au titre de l'Article 27 du Pacte International relatif aux Droits Civils et Politiques", *Revue Trimestrielle de Droits de l'Homme*, 195–222

Klebes, H. (1995), "The Council of Europe's Framework Convention for the Protection of National Minorities – Introduction", *Human Rights Law Journal* 16, 92–105

Morawa, A. (2002), "Minority Language and Public Administration: A Comment on Issues Raised in Diergaardt et al v Namibia", ECMI Working Paper 16, <http://www.ecmi.de/doc.public_papers>

Nowak, M. (1993), *The UN Covenant on Civil and Political Rights: Commentary on CCPR* (Kehl: NP Engel)

Pandharipande, R. V. (2002), "Minority Matters: Issues in Minority Languages in India", *International Journal on Multicultural Societies* 4:2, 217–237

Pelzer, A. N. (1980), *Die Afrikaner Broederbond: Eerste 50 Jaar* (Cape Town: Tafelberg)

Ramaga, P. V. (1992), "Relativity of the Minority Concept", *Human Rights Quarterly*, 104–119

Reagan, T. G. (1995), "Language Planning and Language Policy in South Africa: A Perspective on the Future", in R. Meshtrie (ed.), *Language and Social History: Studies in South African Sociolinguistics* (Cape Town: David Phillips)

Sachs, A. (1992), *Language Rights in the New Constitution* (Johannesburg: South African Constitution Studies Centre)

_____ (1994), *Advancing Human Rights in South Africa* (Cape Town: University Press)

Sacks, V. (1997), "Multiculturalism, Constitutionalism and the South African Constitution", *Public Law*, 672–69

Schulte-Tenckhoff, I. and Ansbach, I. (1995), "Les Minorités en Droit International", in A. Fenet et al. (eds), *Le Droit et les Minorités: Analyses et Textes* (Brussels: Bruylant)

Schumann, K. (1994), "The Role of the Council of Europe", in Miall, H. (ed.), *Minority Rights in Europe: The Scope for a Transnational Regime* (London: Pinter)

Skutnabb-Kangas, K. (1981), *Bilingualism or Not: the Education of Minorities* (Clevedon: Multilingual Matters)

Tabory, M. (1980), "Language Rights as Human Rights", *Israel Yearbook on Human Rights*, 167–223

Thornberry, P. (1991), *International Law and the Rights of Minorities* (Oxford: Clarendon Press)

Webb, V. (2002), "Language Policy Developments in South Africa", Presentation at World Congress on Language Policies, unpublished but on file with the author

_____ (2003), "The Sustainability of South Africa's Pluralist Language Policy", Presentation at the International Seminar of Applied Linguistics in a Global World, New Delhi, unpublished but on file with the author

_____ (2004), "The Non-Promotion of the Indigenous Languages of Africa: Why? A Language Planning Perspective", Presentation at Adalest III, Malawi. 4 September 2004, unpublished but on file with the author

10 The Impact of Language Policy on Endangered Languages

SUZANNE ROMAINE

Over the past 10 000 years various forces such as the spread of agriculture, European colonization, the industrial revolution and now globalization have propelled some few languages – all Eurasian in origin – to expand. The speakers of the ten largest languages such as English, Chinese and so on make up half the world's population, and this figure is increasing. Mandarin Chinese with some 900 million speakers is spoken by more people than any other language in the world. Today an Indo-European language – English, French, Spanish or Portuguese – is the dominant language and culture in every country in North, Central and South America. The 100 largest languages account for 90 per cent of all people, with the remaining 6000 or so languages confined to 10 per cent of the world's most marginalized peoples, who have generally been on the retreat for several hundred years. The majority of these smaller languages may be at risk (Nettle and Romaine 2000).

Fewer than 4 per cent of the world's languages have any kind of official status in the countries where they are spoken. A small minority of dominant languages prevail as languages of government and education. English is the dominant de facto or official language in over 70 countries; French has official or co-official status in 29. The fact that most languages are unwritten, not recognized officially, restricted to local community and home functions, and spoken by very small groups of people reflects the balance of power in the global linguistic market place. Campaigns for official status and other forms of legislation supporting minority languages often figure prominently in language revitalization efforts, despite the generally negative advice offered by experts on their efficacy. As Fishman (1997, 194) has pointed out, endangered languages become such because they lack informal intergenerational transmission and informal daily life support, not because they are not being taught in schools or lack official status. Nevertheless, because official policies banning or restricting the use of certain languages have been seen as agents of assimilation, if not also by some such as Skutnabb-Kangas (2000) as tantamount to acts of genocide, it is no wonder that hopes of reversing language shift have so regularly been pinned on them. Skutnabb-Kangas (2000, 312), for example, maintains that "unsupported coexistence mostly ... leads to minority languages dying".

Nevertheless, we have here a good example of unwarranted and simplistic conclusions being drawn about causal relationships between language and policy, if not outright confusion of policy and planning. As Benton (1999, 23) so aptly puts it, "there is a difference between permission to speak, and actually speaking". Basque speakers in Spain's Basque Autonomous Community (BAC) have been hesitant to use their language in relations with the administration not because they are not allowed to, but because they have difficulty in doing so. A long history of dealing with officialdom in Spanish and lack of education in Basque leaves most ordinary people unfamiliar with the newly coined terminology used in this domain (Gardner 1999).

Likewise, McCarty and Watahomigie (1998, 321) observe that:

> in practice, language rights have not guaranteed language maintenance, which ultimately depends on the home language choices of native speakers. Such decisions are notoriously difficult for extra-familial institutions to control, even when those institutions are community controlled.

Nettle and Romaine (2000, 39–40) warn in a similar vein that:

> conferring status on the language of a group relatively lacking in power doesn't necessarily ensure the reproduction of a language unless other measures are in place to ensure intergenerational transmission at home ... conferring power on the people would be much more likely to do the trick.

Looking to schools and declarations of official status to assist endangered languages is much like looking for one's lost keys under the lamp-post because that is where the most light appears to shine rather than because that is where they have been lost. Just as it is easier to see under the lamp-post, it is far easier to establish schools and declare a language official than to get families to speak a threatened language to their children. Yet only the latter will guarantee transmission. This points to the negligible impact of official language policies on home use. Strubell (2001, 268) notes that "the way people bring up their families – including the language they choose – is not for the authorities to decide". In any case, these acts fall short of what is required in practical terms if the language is to survive in spoken everyday use.

Many language-policy statements are reactive ad hoc declarations lacking a planning element. The Native American Languages Act (NALA) of 1990 is one of the most explicit statements on language ever issued by the United States Congress, yet it is a classic example of a policy with no planning dimension. Among other things, NALA states that "the United States has the responsibility to act together with Native Americans to ensure the survival of these unique cultures and languages" and "to preserve, protect and promote the rights and freedom of Native Americans to use, practice and develop Native American languages". As Schiffman (1996, 246) observes, now that the languages are practically extinct and pose no threat to anyone, we can grant them special status. Those who think that NALA is a pro-active policy rather than a recommendation lacking means of enforcement just because it is written and carries the grand name of "act" deceive themselves. However, this does not mean that policy is totally useless. As Lucas (2000) points out in a quite different context (that of assessing the legal status of Hawaiian), the 1978 state constitutional amendments declaring Hawaiian and English as the state's official languages may provide language advocates with the tools to compel the state to take various measures to support Hawaiian, but they must be tested in court. No state courts have yet interpreted the legal implications of these provisions.

In this chapter I examine some of the obstacles faced in evaluating language policies and some examples of weak linkages between policy and planning which render ineffective most policies aimed at assisting endangered languages.

EVALUATING POLICIES AND THE FALLACY OF AUTONOMY

The ideal way to evaluate language policies in a systematic fashion would be to control all the independent variables but one, and examine the consequences. Needless to say, in practice, things are otherwise. Evaluation of the efficacy of policies is made difficult, if not impossible, by the existence of almost as many variables as there are polities and policies as well as the lack of congruence between the sociolinguistic condition of the group in question and the language policy (see Schiffman 1996, 26, and Spolsky 2004). A plethora of interlocking factors make it difficult to discern any direct relationship. Bourhis (2001, 114), for example, says that "cause and effect relationships are difficult to establish when evaluating the impact of language policies on language behaviour and language shift".

At first glance, a number of typologies of language policies appear to offer some guidance through the entangled thicket (see for example Cobarrubias 1983, Skutnabb-Kangas 2000), but upon closer examination we are forced to conclude that language policy is not an autonomous factor. As Conversi (1997, 1) puts it in a different context, "no country's politics exists independently of its culture". What is ostensibly the "same" policy may lead to different outcomes, depending on the situation in which it operates. Strubell's (1999, 27–8) comparison of the status of Catalan in Catalonia and Valencia is an insightful case in point. He concludes that "the same degree of devolution granted to Catalans and Valencians ... has not led to the same increase – or rather recovery – in the use of the (same) language" (1999, 26).

Carrington (1997, 88) furthermore notes how change of status can be used as a political instrument to neutralize those pressing for recognition of their language by reducing the rallying power of their cause. Amery (2000, 231) suggests that Australia's adoption of a

> softer approach to language and culture by the federal government may be a trade-off for their hardline stance on land matters – a partial compromise which directs some additional resources to those areas which do not pose a direct threat to the economic interests of the rich and powerful.

After years of suppressing the indigenous languages of New Caledonia, France provided financial support to encourage their use in education. This was clearly part of an attempt to promote peace with militant Kanaks who have long struggled against French control, and to mitigate anti-French sentiment in advance of a referendum on independence.

Elevation in status of a previously unrecognized or unsupported minority language or efforts to extend its use to new domains may also trigger backlash from speakers of the dominant language, as in Spain where Spanish nationalists have protested against legislation in Catalonia requiring knowledge of Catalan for certain jobs. In the Basque Autonomous Community, similar efforts to "normalize" the use of Basque in education and government through legal measures prompted battles over the rights of individuals. The 1982 Basic Law for Normalizing Basque Language Use made the right to use Basque an individual rather than a territorial right. The declaration of officiality, however, was challenged by the Spanish Constitutional Court, which declared that it could not affect bodies of the Spanish Government operating in the BAC. More recently in December 2000, the Navarre Government passed an Autonomous Decree regulating the use of Basque in public administrative bodies. One result is that knowledge of Basque has ceased to be a requirement for many public-service positions. The government has justified the decree as a corrective measure in face of discrimination suffered by Spanish speakers. Meanwhile, bilingual road signs, advertisements and other public notices are being replaced with Spanish monolingual ones (Peña 2001, 9). Yet another example comes from Peru, where Quechua was made co-official with Spanish in 1975, with provision made for Quechua to be taught at all levels from 1976, and from 1977 for it to be used in court actions involving Quechua speakers. Again, resistance from the Spanish-speaking majority made implementation difficult, and it has fallen far short of its ambitions.

Magga and Skutnabb-Kangas (2001, 26) underline similar difficulties in implementing the provisions of the Saami Language Act passed in 1992 in Norway, which designated certain areas as Saami administrative districts. Many of the municipalities outside these districts withdrew services in Saami, claiming that the law did not require them. Even in traditional Saami areas, where there may be one Norwegian speaker in a class, it is assumed that all teaching must be done in Norwegian. When teachers have used Saami in such contexts, allegations of discrimination against Norwegians ensued. Magga and Skutnabb-Kangas attribute such actions to a culture clash between the Saami community's collective right to develop their language and the right of individual Norwegian speakers. The choice to use Saami is thus politicized and restricted territorially.

Fishman (1991, 84) writes of the damage, both locally and beyond, done by previously disadvantaged language activists who become "cultural imperialists" themselves within their newly dominated networks. When Quebec francophones adopted various legislative measures designed to protect French, in particular a requirement for newcomers to learn it and direct financial incentives to increase the birth rate, anglophones felt threatened. Bill 101 mobilized anglophones to mount legal challenges and to boycott Montreal stores with French monolingual signs; by 1988 the Canadian Supreme Court ruled that the legal requirement for French-only signs contravened both the Quebec and Canadian Charter of Rights and Freedoms. Quebec's linguistic laws also stirred up much negative feeling among anglophones outside the province as well as outside Canada. Bourhis (2001, 133) observes how the English Only movement in the US regularly uses controversial features of Quebec language laws to justify its campaigns against minority language maintenance. Nevertheless, he sees democratically adopted language laws as necessary tools allowing modern states to harmonize class and ethnic conflicts (see also Kymlicka 1995, 2000).

In proposing such measures, Quebec's francophones sought no more than to guarantee for themselves similar "rights" to control their own reproduction that anglophone Canadians have felt unnecessary to state as policy because they were implicit in practice anyway. Quebec anglophones, in particular, benefited from the provision of a state-financed English-medium education system ranging from pre-kindergarten through university, to an extent rarely granted a linguistic minority elsewhere (except perhaps to the Swedish-speaking minority in Finland). What amounted to an affirmative action plan for Quebec anglophones passes unnoticed because it is regarded as "normal". In this way, all nations unavoidably promote and support the languages sanctioned for use in education, at the same time as they marginalize other languages denied the same public space.

This reminds us not to overlook the fact that policy is implicit even if no specific mention is made of language. Probably most majority languages dominate in many domains where they have only de facto and no legal status. As Fishman (2001a, 454) comments:

> even the much vaunted "no language policy" of many democracies is, in reality, an anti-minority-languages policy, because it delegitimizes such languages by studiously ignoring them, and thereby, not allowing them to be placed on the agenda of supportable general values.

Proponents of what is sometimes called "benign neglect" ignore the fact that minorities experience disadvantage that majority members do not face.

Advocates of minority languages have repeatedly stressed that demographically weak languages need firm proactive policies in order to survive and thrive (see for example Strubell 1999, Skutnabb-Kangas 2000). Yet the legal approach to reconciling status differences in languages with equality in a world where majority rights are implicit, and minority rights are seen as "special" and in need of justification, is fraught with difficulty. Magga and Skutnabb-Kangas (2001, 31) emphasize that "equality is misunderstood if it leads to an equal division of time and resources between a minority and a majority language". As Hickey (2001, 466–7) has observed in connection with Irish immersion pre-schools, "equal treatment of different children does not necessarily mean the same treatment is given to each child". Thus, there is an important distinction between legislating equal use of languages and guaranteeing equitable treatment of their speakers, a point to which I return below in my discussion of South Africa's post-apartheid language policy.

In assessing the impact of Quebec's protective legislation, Bourhis (2001, 115) says that the 1996 census suggests increasing intergenerational shift towards French since 1971, although the change can be largely attributed to allophones (that is, those whose native language is neither French or English) adopting French as their home language. In addition, unfavourable reaction to Bill 101 led to anglophone out-migration.

Schiffman (1996) says that we cannot assess the chances of success of policies without reference to culture, belief systems and attitudes about language. The idea that linguistic rights need protection has never been part of American culture, and so they have not been seen as central to American courts unless allied with more fundamental rights such as educational equity, and so on (1996, 216, 246). Elsewhere, however, even international courts have opined that there is no basic human right to education in one's own language. UNESCO's (1953, 6) much-cited axiom "that the best medium for teaching is the mother tongue of the pupil ..." did not lead to any widespread adoption and development of vernacular languages as media of education. The nation-state remains the most critical unit of analysis because it is the policies pursued within national boundaries that gives some languages (and their speakers) the status of majority and others that of minority language. The majority of countries in the world operate either de facto or de jure as monolingual states in recognizing only one language for use in education. This means that in most parts of the world schooling is still virtually synonymous with learning a second language. Skutnabb-Kangas (2000) maintains that education for minorities in many parts of the world still operates in ways that contradict best practices. She estimates that fewer than 10 percent of the world's languages are used in education.

In 2004 UNESCO published a new position paper on languages and education reflecting the changing global context for education in a multilingual world language (King and Schielmann 2004). Acknowledging that issues of identity, power and nationhood are closely linked to the use of specific languages in the classroom, the recommendations reaffirmed the value of mother tongues, the need to preserve the languages and the ethnic identities of small language groups, and the role of English as the lingua franca and the language of instruction in countries where English is not a native language. These concerns grew out of recognition of education as an important reflection of cultural diversity in a rapidly changing world. The UNESCO position paper also endorsed many of the recommendations that have come out of the debate about linguistic human rights (see Chapter 4, this volume).

Although a basic right to education cannot function equitably unless the child understands the language of instruction, this is of little use to groups whose nationalities and languages do not "officially" exist (as is the case with the Kurds and Kurdish in Turkey) or to groups whose language has been so eroded by shift that their children do not speak it. A case in point · is that of Hawaiian, where the state Board of Education's official position is that Hawaiian immersion schools constitute a programme of choice and not of right within the public school system. Hence it has refused to recognize an affirmative duty to provide adequate funding for Hawaiian-medium schools for children desiring education through the medium of Hawaiian. While not all states are actively seeking the eradication of minorities within their borders, they have pursued policies designed to assimilate minorities into the mainstream or dominant culture. It was not too long ago that minority children in countries like Australia, the United States, Britain and Scandinavia were subject to physical violence in school for speaking their home language. Often the education of these children entailed removing them from their parents and their own cultural group. Such schooling produced a collective sense of shame about native languages and identities.

It is not surprising that demands for some form of bilingual education emerge when a group feels it is being discriminated against on other grounds. In a study done of 46 linguistic minorities in 14 European countries, the clearest link to emerge between language and schooling is that a minority language which is not taught tends to decline (Allardt, 1979). Kymlicka and Patten (2003, 7) claim that one reason why there has been a general reluctance to view policies of official bilingualism as rights rather than as pragmatic accommodations is that public institutions in the most powerful western nations, UK, US, France and Germany, have been monolingual for a century or more with no significant movement towards challenging the hegemonic position of the majority language. Despite evidence of growing rather than decreasing diversity in many education systems, in some countries the trend has been not towards recognition of the need for policy and planning, but the imposition of ever more centralized provision and greater intolerance of diversity. There are important differences between "tolerance rights" and "promotion rights". Most democracies provide for freedom of government interference in private language use, but many are reluctant to make legal provision for promotion of languages in the public sector other than the dominant language(s).

WEAK LINKAGES

Although Fishman (2001a, 478) admits that conclusive evidence is lacking at both the state and international level to evaluate the efficacy of policies, he believes that "there is no reason to be overly optimistic in either case, because a lack of priorities and linkages seems to characterize the entire legalistic approach". He does, however, advocate monitoring certain "litigious climates" surrounding languages such as Maori and Frisian in order to gauge the likelihood and the circumstances needed for legislation, and various other legal measures to be able to make a practical difference in language revitalization efforts. Even if such actions do make a difference, Fishman warns that they must still be distinguished from the possible effects of the conventions and treaties adopted by international agencies and organizations lacking the power to enforce their resolutions.

A good example of weak linkages is the European Charter for Regional or Minority Languages, created to provide a legal instrument for the protection of languages. Although it specifies no list of actual languages, the languages concerned must belong to the European cultural tradition (which excludes "migrant" languages), have a territorial base, and be separate languages identifiable as such. The terms of reference are deliberately vague in order to leave open to each member state how to define cultural heritage and territory. Thus, each state is free to name the languages which it accepts as being within the scope of the charter (see the *IJMS* issue on "Lesser Used Languages and the Law in Europe" 2001*a*; and Ó Riagáin 1998, 2001, for information in the status of languages in the European Union and a summary of legislation relating to minority languages). The UK, for example, which ratified the treaty in March 2001, does not include Manx and Cornish. The effectiveness of any initiatives on the supranational level can always be undermined by individual states unless there is some way of guaranteeing the implementation of language-related measures on a supranational level. The only institutions with authority to regulate language policies exist within the political bodies of individual states, and the European Union has generally avoided taking any action that would interfere with national laws or policies concerning linguistic minorities, or for that matter with laws concerning its national languages. Moreover, the charter does not grant rights to speakers or minority language groups, but to languages.

Despite the fact that Greece is signatory to many international covenants and treaties on human rights, as well as a member of the European Union, it voted against the European Charter for Regional or Minority Languages in 1992. In July 1995 Sotiris Bletsas, a member of the minority Aroumanian (Vlach) community, was arrested after he distributed publications of the European Bureau for Lesser Used Languages which mentioned the existence of the Aroumanian language and four other minority languages in Greece (Arvanitika, Macedonian, Turkish and Pomak). The police obliged him to make a statement saying that he was Greek. As a result of charges brought by Mr Haitidis, a right-wing Member of Parliament of the New Democracy party, Bletsas was convicted under Article 191 of the Greek Penal Code which states that dissemination of false information could create fear and unrest among Greek citizens and damage the country's international relations. The European Court of Human Rights had already ruled that this article was in violation of the European Convention on Human Rights, but an Athens court gave Bletsas a 15-month sentence (suspended) and a fine. After several postponements of his appeal, much international pressure, and concern expressed to the Greek Government by the EU Commissioner for education and culture, among many others, Bletsas was finally acquitted in December 2001 by unanimous decision of the Athens Three-Member Appeal Court (see <http://www.eurolang.net> for coverage of this case). Meanwhile, Turkey, an aspiring member of the European Union, still maintains that it has no minorities.

Most European nation-states still apply one set of rules to the national language and another to minority languages within their boundaries, and often in addition apply differing standards to indigenous and non-indigenous minorities (see Romaine 1998). Similarly, New Zealand has progressed in its treatment of Maori language issues, while it has lagged behind in recognition of the rights of migrant Pacific-islander communities.

Differing practices within different regions of the same country, and with respect to different minority groups, add a further dimension to the vexed problems of evaluation and implementation. Although Article 6 of the Italian constitution is a clause pertaining to linguistic minorities which states that the republic protects linguistic minorities by special laws, many minorities do not benefit from any special provisions. There are approximately one million speakers of Sardinian, which has no official recognition, despite the fact that Sardinia is an autonomous region governed by special statutes. However, the region of Trentino/Alto Adige (Südtirol), governed by a Special Statute giving equal status to German and Italian, guarantees the right to education in the mother tongue for Germans in the province (from nursery to higher level).

The effects of policy proposed at the national level can thus be complex, depending on political structures. In Australia, for example, the 1990 National Language Policy did not really challenge the dominance of white anglophone society after centuries of assimilation and restrictive immigration practices (see Romaine 1991 and 1994). Fishman (2001*a*, 479) offers a more recent, but equally pessimistic assessment, and Lo Bianco and Rhydwen (2001, 417) say that community language maintenance has been relegated to a subordinate status with insufficient resources to sustain the few token acclamations remaining in the policy.

Clyne (2001, 386) points out how individual states subsequently developed vastly different policies, and chose different priority languages. Lo Bianco and Rhydwen (2001, 404) explain how the "second languages policy" of the Northern Territory Government's Department of Education serves only as a recommendation to schools and does not cover the specific needs of Aboriginal communities. Neither do its Social and Cultural Education guidelines cover the kinds of programmes that Aboriginal people want to implement. The lack of strong policy support has meant that Aboriginal language and culture programmes have not achieved a secure place in the schools. In 1998 the Northern Territory abandoned public funding for indigenous bilingual education, which had originally been established by the Commonwealth Government when education in the Northern Territory was under its jurisdiction.

Lo Bianco and Rhydwen (2001, 418–19) conclude that policy can lead to change in the ongoing trend of attrition and extinction if control of resources and the means for decision-making, as well as the institutional domains where language socialization occurs, are in the hands of those affected. They doubt whether Aboriginal Australians will be given the space for self-determination and regulation to a sufficient degree.

Benton and Benton (2001) contrast the Kura Kaupapa Maori (a special category of New Zealand state schools with a Maori language and culture orientation) with the Ataarangi movement aimed at the Maori language needs of whole families, which works through homes rather than schools. Because the latter receives no government support, it is not subject to government controls. Attempts to manage the Kura Kaupapa Maori at government level have been divisive. The Council governing these schools lobbied the House of Representatives in 1998 for a bill to require schools seeking designation as Kura Kaupapa Maori to subscribe to a particular set of philosophical principles. Not all communities favoured this move, prompting Benton and Benton (2001, 436) to comment that it remains to be seen whether what were originally independent schools will come under the ideological control of a group selected by the state to enforce a "legislatively defined" Maori world view.

Returning to NALA as an instance of weak linkage between policy and implementation, we can see that it also illustrates how lack of federally mandated language planning has led to a hodgepodge of policies potentially in conflict with state, local or other federal rules. Legislation in Arizona and Hawaii provides at least two examples.

Hawaii is the only state with an official language in addition to English. Article XV, Section 4, states that "English and Hawaiian shall be the official languages of Hawaii". A second amendment (Article X, Section 4) contains a provision "to revive the Hawaiian language, which is essential to preservation and perpetuation of Hawaiian culture". Lucas (2000, 13) mentions two cases involving legal claims brought under the auspices of NALA, both initiated by native Hawaiians. In *Tagupa* v. *Odo* (1994), attorney William Tagupa refused to give his deposition in English, despite his fluency in the language, on the grounds that Article XV, Section 4, of the state Constitution and NALA prohibit federal courts from mandating that deposition testimony be made in English.

In rejecting Tagupa's claim, the federal district judge argued that the intention of NALA was directed at increasing the use of Native American languages in education and not at judicial proceedings in federal courts. He also quoted President Bush's remarks on signing NALA into law to the effect that it was construed as a "statement of general policy" and should not be understood as conferring "a private right of action on any individual or group" (Lucas 2000, 26 fn. 76). Moreover, the judge opined that allowing deposition in Hawaiian would be contrary to the Federal Rules of Civic Procedure, which mandate the "just, speedy and inexpensive determination of every action", because additional costs and delays would be needed to appoint an interpreter.

In 1996 the Office of Hawaiian Affairs (OHA) brought a case against the Department of Education claiming that the department's failure to provide sufficient financial and technical support for the Hawaiian immersion programme was a violation of both state law and NALA. The state removed the suit from state court to federal court, where the same federal district judge who ruled against Tagupa also ruled against OHA. He said that NALA does not create affirmative duties on the states but merely evinced a federal policy to encourage states to support Native American languages. In 2000 the Department of Education and OHA reached an out-of-court settlement which provided an additional US$7.5 million to the immersion programmes under a 2:1 funding partnership, with the state to spend up to a million dollars a year for the next five years.

In November 2000, 63 per cent of Arizona voters passed Proposition 203 to end bilingual education and replace it with one year of untested English immersion marketed with the slogan "English for the children".

The proposition was spearheaded by Ron Unz, who portrays himself as a strong believer in assimilation, and backed a similar successful initiative in California in 1998 (Proposition 227). Seeing Proposition 203 as an attack on the languages spoken by Arizona's Indian tribes, Arizona State Senator Jack Jackson, a member of the Navajo nation, requested an Attorney General's opinion about whether the proposition applied to the Navajo. In February 2001, then Attorney General Janet Napolitano gave her opinion that it did not apply to any Arizona Indians living on or off reservations. She invoked "principles of tribal sovereignty" and NALA's provision that "the right of Native Americans to express themselves through the use of Native American languages shall not be restricted in any public proceeding, including publicly-supported education programs" (Reyhner 2001, 23).

In Nigeria, also, weak linkages prevent most schools from implementing the National Policy on Education, which stipulates that pupils' mother tongues be used in the lower levels of public education. More importantly, no government sanctions are applied to schools that do not follow the policy. Indeed, 80 per cent of African languages lack orthographies (Adegbija 2001) making it difficult to contemplate their effective use in schools. In Senegal, six African languages (Mandingo, Diola, Peul/Poular, Serer, Soninke and Wolof) have been declared official, but little effort has been made to use them in education. Various factors inhibit implementation, such as lack of funding for materials development, teacher training, parental anxiety about their children's acquisition of the dominant language, along with fear among the elite of losing their status gained through education in the colonial language. Brenzinger (1998, 95) estimates that fewer than 10 per cent of African languages are included in bilingual education programmes, with the result that more than 1000 African languages receive no consideration in the education sector.

As Bamgbose notes (1991, 100–1) "the paradox of mother tongue education in many African countries is that while it is negligible at the primary level, it seems to flourish at university level". It is possible in Nigeria, for example, to take a degree in Hausa, Yoruba and Igbo. International aid agencies, colonial regimes, former and current, often tie aid packages to economic, social and educational policies that support and maintain the colonial language. One result is that many minority languages have more status outside their territories than within them, as is evidenced in the fact that Quechua is taught in universities in the United States and elsewhere.

The new democratic regime in South Africa has recognized the linguistic reality of multilingualism that had been ignored under apartheid. Henrard (2001 and this volume) points to a difference between the 1993 Interim Constitution containing a proclamation promoting the state's "equal use" of eleven official languages (among them nine indigenous languages plus the colonial languages Afrikaans and English) and the 1996 Constitution aiming at "equitable treatment" and "parity of esteem" of the official languages. The need for differential and preferential treatment of the indigenous languages, given the past history of denigration and discrimination, was recognized in the stipulation that the state must take practical and positive measures to elevate their status and advance their use. More specifically, the national government and provincial governments must use at least two official languages. Nevertheless, this case also shows the difficulty in attempting to enforce equality of use and status legislatively among a number of languages unequal in social practice. Despite the Constitutional Court's proclamation to the contrary, the elevation in status of nine previously unrecognized indigenous languages has had the practical effect of diminishing the status of Afrikaans, just as the National Party feared. In practice, the public life of the country has actually become more monolingual (Webb 1998). Afrikaans, which no longer enjoys legal and political protection as a language co-official with English, has experienced dramatic losses, one of the most visible in the area of television, where it formerly shared equal time with English. The new broadcasting time is now more than 50 per cent for English, while Afrikaans, Zulu and Xhosa get just over 5 per cent each. Although greater emphasis is to be given to languages heretofore marginalized and more than 20 per cent of broadcasting time is supposed to be multilingual, in practice this time has been taken up mostly by English. Similarly, the South African National Defence Force, which formerly used Afrikaans, declared in 1996 that English would be the only official language for all training and daily communication. The demand for English among pupils and parents also works against implementing multilingualism in education (Kamwangamalu 1998).

These examples show that without additional measures to support teacher training, materials development and a variety of other enabling factors, policy statements which merely permit, encourage or recommend the use of a language in education or in other domains of public life cannot be very effective. Political ideology drives policy in particular directions, creating various divergences between stated policy and actual practice. Lo Bianco and Rhydwen (2001, 416–17) point out how in Australia the low achievement of Aboriginal children in English literacy is used to justify eliminating bilingual education, just as it is in the United States.

Gardner-Chloros (1997, 217) writes that lawyers agree that "the only way to guarantee fundamental rights effectively is to restrict declarations as to what these rights consist in to the most basic and incontrovertible one". In other words, it is pointless to think that "grand declarations of policy ... would be effective if they are not tied to a – preferably existing – legal instrument with an effective machinery for reinforcement". An interesting case of a grand declaration with no such ties is Eritrea's 1995 declaration *not* to recognize an official language. Thus, President Isayas Afewerki (Brenzinger 1998, 94):

> When we come to the question of language as a means of instruction in schools, our principle is that the child should use its mother tongue or a language chosen by its parents in the early years of its education, irrespective of the level of development of the language.
>
> Our policy is clear and we cannot enter into bargaining. Everyone is free to learn in the language he or she prefers, and no one is going to be coerced into using this or that "official" language.

In the case of Hawaiian, however, Lucas (2000, 17–19) suggests that a strategic opportunity lies in Article XII, Section 7, of the state Constitution, which enjoins the state to "protect all rights, customarily and traditionally exercised for subsistence, cultural and religious purposes". The Hawaii State Supreme Court has already held that this imposes an affirmative duty to protect and perpetuate traditional and customary practices. Although Lucas is doubtful whether this article would create a means of forcing increased funding of immersion schools, language activists might get the court to recognize the speaking of Hawaiian as a traditional and customary practice.

The case made for Maori under the provisions of the Treaty of Waitangi is instructive. In 1974 a largely decorative amendment to the Maori Affairs Act "officially" recognized the Maori language as "the ancestral language of the population of Maori descent". While it allowed the Minister of Maori Affairs to take such steps as were considered appropriate to the encouragement of the learning of the language, it had no practical effect until five years later, when it became clear that this statement meant nothing in the courts when an appellant claimed the right to address the District Court in Maori and was refused. The High Court upheld the ruling on the basis of the Pleadings in English Act of 1362, which became part of New Zealand law by virtue of the English Laws Act of 1858 when the New Zealand legislature adopted all the laws of England in force on 14 January 1840. Ironically, the 1362 statute was passed at a time when the official language of court proceedings in England was French. The High Court's decision came as a disappointment to those activists who had seen legislation as a way of strengthening the position of Maori. It was not until 1987 that an act made Maori an official language of New Zealand and established Te Taura Whiri i Te Reo Maori (the Maori Language Commission).

Maori activists have seen the efficacy of linking the struggle for language rights with natural resource management and preservation provisions guaranteed to them in the Treaty of Waitangi of 1840 signed by Maori chiefs and the British. In 1975 the Waitangi Tribunal was created to consider Maori grievances over breaches of the treaty. Although the British regard Maori assent to the treaty as the basis for their sovereignty over New Zealand, there are numerous complicating factors surrounding the treaty and its language which make its interpretation and legal status fraught with difficulties. The terms of the Maori version of the treaty guaranteed to the Maori *te tino rangatiratanga o ratou wenua o ratou kainga me o ratou taonga katoa*, which could be translated as "the full authority of chiefs over their lands, villages, and all their treasures". Maori activists interpret this as a guarantee rather than cession of Maori sovereignty and have pressed land claims as well as support for the Maori language. The Crown acknowledged Maori claims that the treaty obliged it not only to recognize the Maori language as a part of the country's national heritage and a treasured resource on a par with lands but to actively protect it. We have here another instance in which legislation and practices at one level (the English Laws Act) are in conflict with those at another (the Treaty of Waitangi). Recognition that the Crown had broken its promise required affirmative action rather than passive tolerance. As Benton (1985) said in testimony before the tribunal, "rights which cannot be enforced are illusory, and protection which cannot sustain life is no protection". This points to the need for strong linkages between language policy and economic planning, which have generally been lacking. Benton (1999, 7), for example, recognizes that the revitalization of the Maori language is primarily a matter of sustainable cultural and economic development.

Unfortunately, potential sources of support for Maori language activities have felt that tribal resources should not be used to subsidize what is regarded as state responsibility under the terms of the treaty. Benton and Benton (2001, 439) write that if it could be shown that supporting Maori increased tribal monetary wealth, Maori Trust Boards and land corporations might feel more inclined to give it priority.

TIMING: TOO LITTLE TOO LATE?

Much probably depends on the timing of policies and legislation. Planning in many domains, linguistic or otherwise, faces inevitable charges of "too little too late". Few communities are concerned about language transmission when all is proceeding normally, and even when it is not, various factors impede recognition of the impending loss and its consequences. In Quebec, however, Bourhis (2001, 105, 111) says that language planners were well placed to intervene in the 1970s in favour of French with strong intergenerational transmission on their side, even though a sociolinguistic analysis would have led to the conclusion that such planning was unnecessary. More than 80 per cent of the population had French as a mother tongue and more than three-quarters were monolingual French speakers. Moreover, francophones controlled most of the provincial administration, even though they lacked control of the major business and financial institutions. It was the threat to French survival in the long term in the face of declining birth rate and increased immigration of anglophones and others likely to assimilate to the anglophone population that provided the ideological impetus to mobilize. In many other cases, however, where erosion is painfully evident, communities may not recognize or wish to confront the impending loss, or feel that other concerns are more pressing.

One can contrast the case of Quebec with that of Irish, with its far weaker demographic base for reproduction of the language, where similarly aggressive legislative policies in favour of Irish have not significantly reversed language shift. Only 18 per cent (actually an overestimate) of the population was reported to be Irish-speaking in the 1926 census, just after the foundation of the Irish state. The newly independent government in 1922 promoted policies directed at altering the linguistic market, to enhance the social and legal status of Irish by declaring it the national language, to maintain it where it was spoken, and to extend its use elsewhere. Irish was required in public administration, law and media, domains in which it had not been used for centuries. Ó Riagáin (1997, viii), however, says that the problem was not the small demographic base, but rather the social distribution of Irish, confined as it was to peripheral rural communities. The state had hoped, not unreasonably, that by supporting the agricultural sector, it would support Irish, whose speakers were primarily engaged in farming.

Meanwhile, schools were supposed to replace English with Irish as a medium of education. The policy of Gaelicizing the schools was increasingly effective from the 1920s up to the 1950s, at which point just over half the state primary schools were offering an immersion programme of a full or partial type (that is, teaching all or part of the curriculum through Irish to children whose mother tongue was English). Subsequently, the amount of bilingual or all-Irish education declined. Public opinion polls conducted in the 1960s indicated that compulsory Irish instruction was not popular. Even in the 1930s many teachers were opposed to teaching English-speaking children through the medium of Irish (Ó Riagáin 1997, 19, 31).

By the early 1960s, when it was clear that supporting agriculture was not working to stem out-migration and the viability of farming, economic policy shifted to encourage small industry and the export market. By the 1970s, however, when more young people began to look towards education for upward mobility, state language policies had shifted so that Irish ceased to be a compulsory subject in public examinations at the end of secondary schooling. Hence, incentives for achieving Irish competence were weakened at a time when they were needed. In the earlier period, relatively few young people were affected by the incentives for Irish built into the education and civil service sectors. Ó Riagáin's analysis underlines a disjunction between economic policy and language policy before the 1960s and after the 1970s.

Over the past few decades the thrust of policy, in so far as there is any explicit statement of it, has been towards maintenance rather than restoration. Official rhetoric has shifted meanwhile to talking of survival rather than revival. Today the largest proportion of Irish speakers is to be found among those between 10 and 20 years old. Ó Riagáin's (1997, 283) sobering assessment, based on his examination of a century of language policy in Ireland, reveals how timing enters into the equation in another sense too:

> Language patterns are but aspects of highly complex social systems. They are the outcome of slow, long-term processes. If language policies are to have any significant impact, they will require resources on a scale which has not been hitherto realized. Effective language policies will and must affect all aspects of national life and will have to be sustained for decades, if not forever.

FACTORS OTHER THAN LEGAL STATUS

The deficiencies in the formulation and implementation of policy examined by Ó Riagáin are by no means unique to Ireland, but are typical of language-planning experiences more generally. They point back again to the autonomy fallacy. Skutnabb-Kangas (2000, 303) concludes that there is an urgent need for more research before we can start understanding the importance of various factors in supporting or not supporting the world's languages.

Factors other than legal status are often more important. Again, Ó Riagáin (1997, 170–1):

> the power of state language policies to produce intended outcomes is severely constrained by a variety of social, political and economic structures which sociolinguists have typically not addressed, even though their consequences are profound and of far more importance than language policies themselves.

Carrington (1997, 88) comments that "real status is achieved when official action confirms an already existing situation in which significant objectives of official recognition are already operationally in place". As an example, he cites the granting of official status to Papiamento in 1985 in the Netherlands Antilles, which came long after the language was used in newspapers, signs and so on. Likewise, Gardner (1999, 86) comments that laws regulating language matters are often limited "to sanctioning what has already become reality or enabling what sociological dynamics could potentially make reality. What it cannot do in a reasonably democratic society is fulfil a coercive [sic] function in any major way". Any policy for language, especially in the system of education, has to take account of the attitude of those likely to be affected.

Ó Riagáin (1997, 174, 279) notes that while the compulsory element in pre-1973 policies enhanced the practical or economic value of Irish, many people opposed them. Although support for Irish was ostensibly high, the public was not prepared to back policies that would discriminate strongly in favour of Irish and could potentially alter the linguistic landscape. In his view, the major constraint on policy development was the absence of sustained public support and not state action per se (Ó Riagáin 1997, 23).

Strubell (2001) suggests a similar lack of support in Catalonia, while as far as Basque is concerned, Gardner (1999, 85–7) argues that the need for a monolingual heartland is paramount, but legally unobtainable. At the same time, he stresses that "granting monolingual official status to a minority language ultimately affects prestigious but relatively marginal uses of the language. Declaration by decree of a monolingual enclave cannot ensure its existence in practice". He concludes that the problem is not the limits imposed by present laws, but lack of proper awareness of priorities by language planners and Basques more generally (1999, 88). As recent legislation in Navarre illustrates, language rights are not timeless declarations, but are time-limited, subject to shifting political regimes.

Evidence from various quarters indicates that grass-roots initiatives are often more effective than top-down directives. A case in point is the PROPELCA (Projet de Recherche Opérationnelle pour l'Enseignement des Langues Camerounaises) project in Cameroon, one of the best-documented and most complete examples of a literacy programme which includes materials development, a teacher-training programme and evaluation (Gerbault 1997). The project's working principle was to use local languages as instruments for scientific and technical training, rather than to maintain languages per se. Teacher training began in 1981 as an experimental programme in two Roman Catholic schools; by 1986 there were eleven experimental schools in four different provinces teaching in four of Cameroon's 236 languages.

Although the pedagogical approach and its development by local specialists has been exemplary in sub-Saharan Africa, Gerbault (1997, 182) says that it has met with lack of involvement of official institutions typical of this part of the world. Only private institutions and local communities have supported the programme, even though the project workers have recommended that existing practices of using Cameroonian languages for the first three years of primary school should be made official.

Meanwhile, there had been a remarkable recent rise in entirely voluntary Irish-medium schooling in Ireland with over 150 all-Irish primary and secondary schools, and more than twice that number of all-Irish pre-schools. In Northern Ireland, a deliberately created community in Shaw's Road in urban Belfast, where parents who were not native speakers of Irish, has succeeded in raising children who are (Maguire 1991).

CONCLUSION: THE PROOF IS IN THE PUDDING

My assessment of the efficacy of policy in assisting endangered languages has perhaps been unduly pessimistic in an effort not to minimize the complexity and enormity of the task. In his reappraisal of the scene ten years after his 1991 book, Fishman (2001*a*, 478–9) observes that none of the dozen individual cases studied in the late 1980s and early 1990s has experienced "dramatic successes". Naturally, there are many reasons why that is the case, as the individual chapters show, so it would be hard to pinpoint policy as the unique cause or source of either success or failure. Indeed, Fishman's (2001*a*, 480) overall conclusion is an ambiguous one: although the general climate of opinion on threatened languages has improved "in an amorphous and largely still ineffectual sense", the prospects for reversing language shift have not improved much and have even deteriorated.

This does not mean that advocates of linguistic diversity should abandon the struggle to obtain legal measures at all levels supporting languages. On the contrary, we must redouble our efforts. However, we must do so in the knowledge that without well-focused action on a variety of other fronts, these will not guarantee maintenance. It is political, geographical and economic factors that support the maintenance of linguistic and cultural diversity. Holistic ecological planning of the kind advocated by Nettle and Romaine (2000) works towards international, regional and national policies that empower indigenous peoples and promote sustainable development. This is the key to preserving local ecosystems essential to language maintenance. Because the preservation of a language in its fullest sense ultimately entails the maintenance of the group that speaks it, the arguments in favour of doing something to reverse language death are ultimately about preserving cultures and habitats.

Finally, however, the proof is always in the pudding. In the interests of justice, it is incumbent on liberal democracies to accommodate cultural and linguistic diversity to the fullest extent possible. Kymlicka (1995) argues that respecting minority rights is essential for enlarging the freedom of individuals, a cornerstone of liberal democracy. The issue of language rights has begun to receive serious international discussion within the last decade (see, for example, Skutnabb-Kangas et al. 1994; Benson et al. 1998; Skutnabb-Kangas 2000; *International Journal on Multicultural Societies* 2001*a*, 2001*b*). Although survival cannot depend on legislation as its main support, legal provisions may allow speakers of endangered languages to claim some public space for their languages and cultures from which we can all benefit.

REFERENCES

Adegbija, E. (2001), "Saving threatened languages in Africa: A case study of Oko", in J. A. Fishman (ed.) (2001*b*), 284–308
Allardt, E. (1979), *Implications of the ethnic revival in modern industrial society. A comparative study of the linguistic minorities in western Europe* (Helsinki: Societas Scientararium Fennica)
Amery, R. (2000), *Warrabarna Kaurna! Reclaiming an Australian Language* (Lisse: Swets and Zeitlinger)
Bamgbose, A. (1991), *Language and the Nation: The Language Question in Sub-Saharan Africa* (Edinburgh: Edinburgh University Press for the International African Institute)
Benson, P., Grundy, P. and Skutnabb-Kangas, T. (eds) (1998), Special issue on Language Rights, *Language Sciences* 20:1
Benton, R. (1985), Testimony. Waitangi Tribunal, Department of Justice, Wellington, New Zealand
—— (1999), *Maori Language Revitalization* (Final Report, Wellington, New Zealand)
Benton, R. and Benton, N. (2001), "RLS in Aotearoa/New Zealand 1989–1999", in J. A. Fishman (ed.) (2001*b*), 423–51
Bourhis, R. Y. (2001), "Reversing language shift in Quebec", in J. A. Fishman, (ed.) (2001*b*), 101–42
Brenzinger, M. (1998), "Various ways of dying and different kinds of death: Scholarly approaches to language endangerment on the African continent", in Kazuto Matsumura (ed.), *Studies in Endangered Languages. Papers from the International Symposium on Endangered Languages Tokyo November 18–29 1995* (Tokyo: Hituzi Syobo), 85–100
Carrington, L. D. (1997), "Creoles and other tongues in Caribbean development", *Journal of Pidgin and Creole Languages* 8, 125–35
Clyne, M. (2001), "Can the shift from immigrant languages be reversed in Australia?", in J. A. Fishman (ed.) (2001*b*), 364–91
Cobarrubias, J. (1983), "Ethical issues in status planning", in Juan Cobarrubias and Joshua A. Fishman (eds), *Progress in Language Planning: International Perspectives* (Berlin: Mouton), 41–85
Conversi, D. (1997), *The Basques, the Catalans and Spain* (London: Hurst)
Fishman, J. A. (1991), *Reversing Language Shift. Theoretical and Empirical Foundations of Assistance to Threatened Languages* (Clevedon, UK: Multilingual Matters)
—— (1997), "Maintaining languages. What works and what doesn't", in Gina Cantoni (ed.), *Stabilizing Indigenous Languages* (Flagstaff, Ariz.: Northern Arizona University), 186–98
—— (2001*a*), "From theory to practice (and vice versa): Review, Reconsideration and Reiteration", in J. A. Fishman, (ed.) (2001*b*), 451–83
—— (ed.) (2001*b*), *Can Threatened Languages Be Saved? Reversing Language Shift, Revisited: A 21st Century Perspective* (Clevedon, UK: Multilingual Matters)

Gardner, N. (1999), *Basque in Education in the Basque Autonomous Community* (Vitoria-Gasteiz: Eusko Jaurlaritzaren Argitalpen Zerbitzu Nagusia)

Gardner-Chloros, P. (1997), "Vernacular literacy in new minority settings in Europe", in Tabouret-Keller et al. (eds), 189–221

Gerbault, J. (1997), "Pedagogical aspects of vernacular literacy", in Tabouret-Keller et al. (eds), 142–85

Henrard, K. (2001), "Language rights and minorities in South Africa". *International Journal on Multicultural Societies* 3:2, 85–105

Hickey, T. (2001), "Mixing beginners and native speakers in minority language immersion; Who is immersing whom?", *Canadian Modern Language Review* 57:3, 443–74

International Journal on Multicultural Societies 3:1 (2001a), Lesser Used Languages and the Law in Europe

International Journal on Multicultural Societies 3:3 (2001b), The Human Rights of Linguistic Minorities and Language Policies

Kamwangamalu, N. M. (1998), "Preface: Multilingualism in South Africa", *Multilingua* 17:2/3: 119–25. Special issue on Aspects of Multilingualism in Post-Apartheid South Africa

King, L. and Schielmann, L. (eds) (2004), *The Challenge of Indigenous Education: Practice and Perspectives* (Paris: UNESCO)

Kymlicka, W. (1995), *Multicultural Citizenship* (Oxford: Oxford University Press)

Kymlicka, W. and Patten, A. (eds) (2003), *Language Rights and Political Theory* (Oxford: Oxford University Press)

Lo Bianco, J. and Rhydwen, M. (2001), "Is the extinction of Australia's indigenous languages inevitable?", in J. A. Fishman (ed.) (2001b), 391–423

Lucas, P. F. N. (2000), "E ola mau kākou i ka 'ōlelo makuahine: Hawaiian language policy and the courts", *Hawaiian Journal of History* 32, 1–28

Magga, O. H. and Skutnabb-Kangas, T. (2001), "The Saami languages. The present and the future", *Cultural Survival Quarterly* 25:2, 26–31, 51.

Maguire, G. (1991), *Our Own Language: An Irish Initiative* (Clevedon, UK: Multilingual Matters)

McCarty, T. and Watahomigie, L. (1998), "Indigenous community-based language education in the USA", *Language, Culture and Curriculum* 11:3, 309–25. Special issue on Indigenous Community-Based Education, edited by Stephen May

Native American Languages Act. (1990) PL 101–407 (Washington, DC, United States Congress)

Nettle, D. and Romaine, S. (2000), *Vanishing Voices. The Extinction of the World's Languages* (New York: Oxford University Press)

Ó Riagáin, D. (ed.) (1998), *Vade-Mecum. A guide to legal, political and other official international documents pertaining to the lesser used languages of Europe* (Brussels: European Bureau for Lesser Used Languages)

—— (2001), "The European Union and lesser used languages", *International Journal on Multicultural Societies* 3:1, 35–45

Ó Riagáin, P. (1997), *Language Policy and Social Reproduction. Ireland 1893–1993* (Oxford: Oxford University Press)

Peña, J. L. M. (2001), "Bilingualism under threat in Navarre. Navarre government language policy", *Contact Bulletin* 17:2, 8–9 (Brussels: European Bureau for Lesser Used Languages)

Reyhner, J. (2001), "Cultural survival vs. forced assimilation: the renewed war on diversity", *Cultural Survival Quarterly* 25:2, 22–5

Romaine, S. (1991), "Introduction", *Language in Australia*, 1–24 (Cambridge: Cambridge University Press)

—— (1994), "From the fish's point of view", *International Journal of the Sociology of*

Language 110, 177–85

—— (1998), "Language contact in relation to multilingualism, norms, status and standardization", in Unn Royneland (ed.), *Language Contact and Language Conflict* (Volda, Norway: Volda College), 9–25

Schiffman, H. (1996), *Linguistic Culture and Language Policy* (London: Routledge)

Skutnabb-Kangas, T. (2000), *Linguistic Genocide in Education – or Worldwide Diversity and Human Rights?* (Mahwah, NJ: Lawrence Erlbaum Associates)

Skutnabb-Kangas, T. and Phillipson, R. in collaboration with Mart Rannut (eds) (1994), *Linguistic Human Rights. Overcoming Linguistic Discrimination* (Berlin/New York: Mouton de Gruyter)

Spolsky, B. (2004), *Language Policy* (Cambridge: Cambridge University Press)

Strubell, M. (1999), "Language, democracy & devolution in Catalonia", in Sue Wright (ed.), *Language, Democracy and Devolution in Catalonia* (Clevedon, UK: Multilingual Matters), 4–39.

Strubell, M. (2001), "Catalan a decade later", in J. A. Fishman (ed.) (2001*b*), 260–84

Tabouret-Keller, A., Le Page, R. B., Gardner-Chloros, P. and Varro, G. (eds) (1997), *Vernacular Literacy. A Re-Evaluation* (Oxford: Oxford University Press)

UNESCO (1953), *The Use of Vernacular Languages in Education*. Monograph on Fundamental Education VIII (Paris: United Nations Educational, Scientific and Cultural Organization)

Webb, V. (1998), "Multilingualism as a developmental resource: Framework for a research program", *Multilingua* 17:2/3, 125–54. Special issue on Aspects of Multilingualism in Post-Apartheid South Africa

PART III
RELIGIOUS DIVERSITY

11 The Resurgence of Religious Movements in Processes of Globalization – Beyond the End of History or the Clash of Civilizations

SHMUEL N. EISENSTADT

The contemporary resurgence of religion is often regarded as confirming the well-known thesis of a coming "clash of civilizations". This article offers an alternative perspective by putting fundamentalist and communal-religious movements into the context of large-scale social transformations, especially the restructuration of the classical model of the nation-state and the increased global interconnectedness allowing for new interpretations of the cultural programme of modernity as it has developed in Western Europe. Fundamentalist and communal-religious movements, drawing simultaneously on the religious dimension of Axial civilizations and on the Jacobin dimensions of modernity, are indeed very modern, even if they do not accept the premises of the Enlightenment, but they challenge the West's claimed monopoly on modernity. New potential for conflict at a global level therefore arises from the multiplication of different, yet presumably universalistic, interpretations of modernity rather than from the confrontation of different civilizations.

A far-reaching resurgence of religious movements has recently taken place in the contemporary world. The most visible manifestations of this resurgence are, firstly, the development and thriving of fundamentalist movements, demonstrated in particular by Muslim fundamentalism in Turkey and some Arab countries, by Muslim diasporas in Europe and in the United States, by various Jewish groups, and by evangelical movements in the United States and Latin America; and, secondly, the emergence of national-communal movements in South and Southeast Asia, India and Sri Lanka. This resurgence of religious movements has entailed a reconstruction of the religious dimension far beyond what has been envisaged in the classical cultural and political programme of modernity and of the classical model of the modern nation-state.

Such reconstruction calls into question some arguments of post-Cold-War intellectual debates – especially those that proclaim, from definite yet often opposing vantage points – the possibility that the modern project, that is, the classical programme of modernity as it has developed for the last two centuries, is exhausted. In one version of such arguments, most prominently promulgated by Francis Fukuyama (1992), the thesis is defended that we are witnessing the "end of history", meaning that the ideological premises of modernity with all their inherent tensions and contradictions have become almost irrelevant, paradoxically allowing the rise of multiple postmodern visions. From this perspective the resurgence of religious movements is, on the whole, seen as a temporary "aberration".[1] Another version claims that the exhaustion of the modern programme is indicated by a coming "clash of civilizations", to use the terminology of Samuel P. Huntington's highly influential contribution (Huntington 1993, 1996). In his view, Western civilization – the apparent epitome of modernity – is supposed to be confronted in often hostile terms by other civilizations, especially by the Muslim and to some extent by the so-called Confucian civilizations. Huntington considers that the current resurgence of religious movements confirms the interpretation that within these civilizations traditional, fundamentalist, anti-modern and anti-Western values are predominant.

However, a closer look at the resurgence of religious movements suggests that both these interpretations, while pointing to important developments, fail to capture some of their most salient features. Of special importance in this context is the fact that, alongside these religious movements, many ethnic and separatist movements or groups, which have often become closely connected with the former, have developed on the contemporary scene. Concomitantly, new types of social settings or sectors have emerged, important illustrations thereof being new diasporas and minorities. The best known among such new diasporas are the Muslim immigrant minorities – especially in Europe and to some extent in the United States. Parallel developments, yet with significant differences, are to be found among the Chinese and possibly the Korean diasporas in East Asia, in the United States, and in Europe, as well as among Jewish communities, especially in Europe. Further illustrations of these new types of minority are the Russian diasporas in some of the former Soviet Republics, especially in the Baltic States and in parts of Central Asia, where the former ruling class became a minority with strong orientations to the old motherland and to some of the ideals of the defeated Soviet regime. Finally, one may think of Jewish communities which, coming to Israel from former Soviet Republics, also seem to develop a strong attachment to aspects of both the Soviet regime and Russian culture.

Moreover, and paradoxically enough, the religious movements referred to above even share some very important characteristics with those movements which developed a decade or two earlier, especially with the so-called "new" social movements, ranging from the students' movements of the late 1960s and early 1970s, through the feminist to the contemporary ecological movements, all of which have promulgated secular, postmodern themes that at first glance seem contrary to those of the fundamentalist and religious-communal movements but do in fact share some important characteristics with them.[2] This paper explores the characteristics of these religious movements in some detail, in order to provide an alternative interpretation of current social transformations, one that goes beyond the theses of both the end of history and of a coming clash of civilizations.

RESURGENCE OF FUNDAMENTALIST AND COMMUNAL-RELIGIOUS MOVEMENTS AND THE TRANSFORMATION OF THE CLASSICAL NATION-STATE

The common denominator of many of the new movements is that they do not see themselves as bound by the strong homogenizing cultural premises of the classical model of the nation-state – especially by the places allotted to them in the public spheres of such states. They all entail the resurrection, or rather reconstruction, as it were, of hitherto subdued identities – ethnic, local, regional and transnational – and their movement into the centres of their respective societies, often also into the international arena.

It is not that they do not want to be domiciled in their respective countries; indeed part of their struggle is to become integrated, but on rather new terms compared with classical models of assimilation. They aim to be recognized in the public spheres, in the constitution of civil society, and in relation to the state as culturally distinct groups promulgating their collective identities, and not to be confined to the private sphere. They do indeed make claims – as illustrated among others in the recent debate about *laïcité* in France – for the reconstruction of new public spaces as well as of the symbols of collective identity promulgated in respective states (see Gauchet 1998). But, at the same time, while the identities proclaimed in these movements and settings are often very local and particularistic, they also tend to be strongly transnational or trans-state, often connected with broader civilizational frameworks rooted in the great religions – Islam, Buddhism and different branches of Christianity – but reconstructed in modern ways. All these movements, including the resurgent religious movements, constitute part of a wider picture attesting to a far-reaching transformation of the characteristics of the hitherto major political actor in the internal and international arenas alike – the classical nation-state.

The central new development regarding the place of religion is thus that religious identity, which was in the classical model of the nation-state delegated or confined to private or secondary spheres, has become transposed into the public political and cultural arenas, thereby becoming a central, autonomous component in the constitution of collective identities. Such transposition does not however entail a simple return of some traditional forms of religion but rather a far-reaching reconstitution of the religious component.

The movements and sectors mentioned above have also become active on the international scene. Many of the separatist, local or regional settings, as well as ecological movements, for example, have developed direct connections with transnational frameworks and organizations such as the European Union or the United Nations. But it is above all the various religious, especially fundamentalist, movements – Muslim, Protestant, Jewish – that have become very active on the international scene through very intensive networks of communication.

MODERNITY AND THE RESURGENCE OF FUNDAMENTALIST AND COMMUNAL-RELIGIOUS MOVEMENTS

There can be no doubt that all these developments denote far-reaching changes or shifts from the model (or models) of the modern nation-state, in that they attest to the reconstruction of its major structural characteristics and to the weakening of its ideological hegemony. But do they also signal the end of history, the end of the modern programme – epitomized in the development of different "postmodernities" – and above all in the retreat, as it were, from modernity to the fundamentalist and communal-religious movements that have been portrayed – and in many ways have also presented themselves – as diametrically opposed to the cultural programme of modernity?

A closer examination of these movements, especially of the fundamentalist and to some extent also of the communal-religious ones, presents a much more complex picture. It indicates their distinctly modern Jacobin characteristics and their promulgation of distinct visions of modernity formulated in the terms of the discourse of modernity, and their attempts to appropriate modernity on their own terms (see, for example, Göle 1996). While extreme fundamentalist movements promulgate ostensibly anti-modern, or rather anti-Enlightenment, themes, yet they paradoxically share many Jacobin revolutionary components – sometimes in a sort of mirror-image way – with the communist movements, the carriers of the most extreme alternative model to the pluralistic Western model of modernity. With these they particularly share the attempts to establish a new social order, rooted in the revolutionary universalistic ideological tenets, in principle transcending any primordial, national or ethnic units and new socio-political collectivities. Both the communist and the fundamentalist movements – mostly, but not only in the Islamic world – have been international or transnational in orientation, activated by very intensive networks, which have facilitated the diffusion of the social and cultural visions they promulgated, most notably their universalistic messages, and at the same time have continually confronted them with other competing visions (Eickelman and Anderson 1999).

Whereas the communal-religious movements, such as those which developed in Indian and in some South and Southeast Asian societies, do not exhibit such extreme Jacobin characteristics, they are in ideological and in some institutional dimensions similar to the fascist movements of the early twentieth century; like the latter they emphasize the primacy of primordial constructions of collective identity, very often defined in Romantic terms. Unlike the fascist movements they do, however, promulgate very strongly the religious component in the construction of their national identity (see Juergensmeyer 1994). In all these ways these movements and their programmes constitute part and parcel of the modern political agenda.

REINTERPRETATIONS OF MODERNITY – THE LARGER CONTEXT

Such attempts to appropriate and interpret modernity in autonomous terms have not been confined to the fundamentalist or communal-national movements. They constitute part of a set of much wider developments that have been taking place throughout the world, in Muslim, Indian and Buddhist societies, seeming to continue, yet in a markedly transformed way, the confrontations between different earlier reformist and traditional religious movements that developed throughout non-Western societies. In these movements the basic tensions inherent in the modern programme, especially those between the pluralistic and totalistic tendencies, between utopian or more open and pragmatic attitudes, between multifaceted as against closed identities, are played out more in terms of traditions grounded in their respective Axial religions than in those of the European Enlightenment – although they are greatly influenced by the latter and especially by the participatory traditions of the Great Revolutions, most notably by their Jacobin orientations or components.[3]

Some very significant parallels can also be identified between these various religious movements, including the fundamentalist movements with their apparently extreme opposites: the different postmodern ones with which they often engage in confrontation over hegemony among different sectors of society. Concomitantly, all these movements share the concern, which constituted a basic theme of the discourse of modernity from its beginnings in Europe, about the relations between their identities and the universalistic themes promulgated by the respective hegemonic programmes of modernity, and today above all the concern about the relation between such authentic identities and the presumed American cultural and political ideological hegemony. At the same time in most of these movements – the religious and postmodern ones – this fear of erosion of local cultures and of the impact of globalization and its centres is also connected with an ambivalence towards these centres, giving rise to a continual oscillation between cosmopolitanism and various particularistic tendencies. Within all these different movements there develop different combinations of different cultural themes and patterns, and they continually compete about which presents the proper answer to the predicament of cultural globalization (see Friedman 1994; Hannerz 1992; Marcus 1993; Smolicz 1998).[4]

The continuing salience of the tensions between pluralist and universalist programmes, between multifaceted and closed identities, and the continuing ambivalence towards new major centres of cultural hegemony, attest to the fact that, while going beyond the model of the nation-state, these new movements have not gone beyond the basic *problématique* of modernity, which in fact constitutes a central component in their discourses. They all are deeply reflexive, aware that no answer to the tensions inherent in modernity is final – even if each in its own way seeks to provide final, incontestable answers to modernity's irreducible dilemmas. Yet they all have reconstituted the problem of modernity in these new historical contexts, in new ways.

Thus all these developments and trends constitute aspects of the continual reinterpretation and reconstruction of the cultural programme of modernity; of the construction of multiple modernities and of multiple interpretations of modernity, of attempts by various groups and movements to reappropriate modernity and redefine the discourse of modernity in their own new terms.

The new interpretations of modernity that have developed on the contemporary scene, however, especially but not only in conjunction with the new religious movements, contain some very important new components of crucial importance for the interpretation of the relation between modernity and the West. These movements – significantly including many of the postmodern ones that developed in the West – attempt to completely dissociate Westernization from modernity. They deny the monopoly or hegemony of Western modernity, and the acceptance of the Western modern cultural programme as the epitome of modernity. This highly confrontational attitude to the West, or rather to what is conceived as "Western", is in these movements closely related to their attempts to appropriate modernity and the global system on their own non-Western, often anti-Western, modern assumptions.

SPECIFICITIES OF THE NEW FUNDAMENTALIST AND COMMUNAL-RELIGIOUS MOVEMENTS

While the contemporary fundamentalist and communal-religious-national movements are indeed modern, comparable in many ways to communist or fascist movements, this does not of course mean that they do not reveal some distinct characteristics distinguishing them from those earlier movements and indeed constituting a new development on the international scene. The crucial difference between the contemporary movements and the communist and fascist ones lies in their perceptions of the confrontation between the basic premises of the cultural and political programme of modernity as it crystallized in the West and the non-Western European civilization – with very far-reaching implications for the domestic and international political arenas.

As against the apparent acceptance of the premises of this programme, or at least a highly ambivalent attitude to them combined with the continuing reinterpretation thereof that was characteristic of the earlier movements – such as the various socialist, communist and national movements and regimes which developed throughout the world – the contemporary fundamentalist and most communal-religious movements seem to promulgate a negation of at least some premises, as well as a markedly confrontational attitude to the West.

In contrast to communist and socialist movements, including the Muslim or African socialist movements in the 1950s and 1960s, the contemporary fundamentalist and religious-communal movements promulgate a radically negative attitude to some of the central Enlightenment – and even Romantic – components of the cultural and political programme of modernity, especially the emphasis on the autonomy and sovereignty of reason and of the individual. Thus the fundamentalist movements promulgate a totalistic ideological denial of Enlightenment premises, and have a basically confrontational attitude not only to Western hegemony but to the West as such, to what has been defined by them as Western civilization usually conceived in totalistic and essentialist ways. While minimizing in principle, if not in practice, the particularistic components characteristic of the communal-national movements, they ground their denial of, and opposition to, the premises of the Enlightenment in the universalistic premises of their respective religions or civilizations, as newly interpreted by them (see Khosrokhavar 1996; Jalal 1995).

The communal-national movements build on the earlier nativistic, Slavophile-like ones but reinterpret them in politically radical, modernist ways. Significantly enough, in all these movements socialist or communist themes or symbols are no longer strongly emphasized; themes of social justice are usually promulgated in terms of their own traditions, which are often portrayed as inherently superior to the materialistic, socialist Western ones. In this context, it is very interesting to note that the activists, especially in various Muslim Arab countries, who were drawn to different socialist themes and movements became very involved in the fundamentalist and also in some of the communal movements of the 1980s and 1990s (see Eisenstadt and Azmon 1975; Kuran 1993, 1997*a*, 1997*b*).

Within these movements, the confrontation with the West does not take the form of searching to become incorporated into the new hegemonic civilization, but rather of attempting to appropriate the new international global scene and modernity, as it were, for themselves, for their traditions or civilizations as they have been continually promulgated and reconstructed under the impact of their continuing encounter with the West.

IMPACT OF CIVILIZATIONAL TRADITIONS ON THE FORMATION OF MODERNITIES

The preceding analysis does not imply that the historical and cultural traditions of these societies are of no importance in the unfolding of their modern dynamics. Such importance is manifest, for example, in the fact that among modern and contemporary societies, fundamentalist movements develop and abound above all within those societies that crystallized in the framework of monotheistic – Muslim, Jewish and some Christian – civilizations, in which even in their modern post-revolutionary permutations, the political arena has been perceived as the major arena of the implementation of the transcendental utopian vision – even if such vision was couched in modern secular terms.

On the other hand, the ideological reconstruction of the political centre in a Jacobin mode has been much weaker in civilizations with other-worldly orientations – especially in India and to a somewhat smaller extent in Buddhist countries – in which the political order was not perceived as an arena of the implementation of the transcendental vision, even though given the basic premises of modernity very strong modern political orientations or dimensions have also tended to develop within them (see Eisenstadt 1999). Concomitantly, some of the distinct ways in which modern democracies developed in India or Japan – as distinct from the European or American patterns, which also vary greatly among themselves – have indeed been greatly influenced by the respective cultural traditions and historical experiences of these societies. The same is also true of the ways in which communist regimes in Russia, China, North Korea or South Asia have been influenced by the historical experiences and traditions of their respective societies (see Eisenstadt and Azmon 1975).

This, however, was of course also the case with the first, European modernity – which was deeply rooted in specific European civilizational premises and historical experience (see Eisenstadt 1987). But, as was indeed the case in Europe, all these historical or civilizational influences did not simply perpetuate the old traditional pattern of political institutions or dynamics. In all of them, both the broad, inclusivist universalisms of the great civilizational traditions and their primordial, exclusivist tendencies are reconstructed in typically modern ways, and continually articulate, in different ways specific to different historical settings, the antinomies and contradictions of modernity.

CONCLUSION: MULTIPLE MODERNITIES BEYOND THE END OF HISTORY AND THE CLASH OF CIVILIZATIONS – NEW POTENTIALS FOR CONFLICT

All these developments do indeed attest to the continuing development of multiple modernities, or of multiple interpretations of modernity – and above all to the de-Westernization of modernity, depriving, as it were, the West of its monopoly of modernity. In this broad context the European or Western modernity or modernities are seen not as *the* only real modernity but at best as one of multiple modernities – even if the West has of course played a special role not only in the origins of modernity but also in the continual expansion and reinterpretation of modernities.

While the common starting point of many of these developments was indeed the cultural programme of modernity as it developed in the West, more recent developments have given rise to a multiplicity of cultural and social formations which go far beyond the very homogenizing and hegemonizing aspects of this original version. All these developments attest to the growing diversification of the visions and understandings of modernity, of the basic cultural agendas of different sectors of modern societies – far beyond the homogenic and hegemonic vision of modernity that was prevalent in the 1950s, especially in social-science discourse. The fundamentalist and the new communal-national movements constitute one such new development, in the unfolding of the potentialities and antinomies of modernity. All these movements may develop in contradictory directions – in a more open pluralistic way as well as in the opposite, confrontational, direction, manifest in growing inter-religious or inter-ethnic conflicts.

At the same time these movements entail a shift of the major arenas of confrontation and of crystallization of multiple modernities, from that of the nation-state in particular, to new arenas in which these different movements and different societies continually interact with and cut across each other. They all aim for a worldwide reach and diffusion, through numerous returns, through the various media of communication (Eickelman and Anderson 1999). They are very politicized, formulating their programmes in highly political and ideological terms, continually reconstructing their collective identities with reference to the new global context. The debate in which they engage and confront each other may indeed be formulated in civilizational terms, but these very terms – indeed the very term "civilization" as constructed in such a discourse – are already couched in modernity's new language, in totalistic, essentialistic and absolutizing terms, and they may entail a continual transformation of these identities and of the cultural programmes of modernity. Indeed the very pluralization of life-spaces in the global framework endows them with highly ideological absolutizing orientations, and at the same time brings them into the central political arena.

Such developments may also give rise to highly confrontational stances – especially towards the West – but these stances are promulgated in continually changing modern idioms. When such clashes or confrontations become combined with political, military or economic struggles and conflicts they may become very violent. Indeed the combination of religious and modern components and orientations is characteristic of many of the fundamentalist and communal-religious movements, that bring out, on the contemporary scene, the dark side or potential of both modernity and religion. They attest to the fact that the continuing expansion of modernity throughout the world has not been very benign or peaceful – by no means has it constituted the continual progress of reason. Rather these processes have been continually interwoven with wars, violence, genocides, repression and dislocation of large sections of the population – indeed sometimes of entire societies.

Although from the optimistic point of view such wars, genocides and repressions have often been portrayed as being against the basic grain of the programme of modernity, often as survivals of premodern attitudes, it has been increasingly recognized that in fact they were very closely interwoven with modernity – both with its ideological premises and its expansion and with the specific patterns of the institutionalization of modern societies and regimes. Wars and genocide, which were not, of course, new in the history of mankind, became radically transformed and intensified, unceasingly generating tendencies to specifically modern barbarism. The most important manifestation of such a transformation was the ideologization of violence, terror and war – which would first become most vivid in the French Revolution. Such ideologization became a central component in the constitution of nation-states, which became the most important agents – and arenas – of the constitution of citizenship and symbols of collective identity, with the crystallization of the modern European state-system, with European expansion, colonialism and imperialism, and with the intensification of technologies of communication and of war. The Holocaust, which took place in the very centre of modernity, became a symbol of its negative, destructive potential, of the barbarism lurking within its very core.

But while such destructive potential is indeed inherent in modernity, and its most extreme manifestations developed within the centre of modernity, and in close relation to some components of the cultural programme of modernity, yet it also has very strong roots in the major religions. The cultural programme of some of the great religions, especially the monotheistic ones – with their claims to be the bearers of absolute truth and their strong universalistic-missionary tendencies – contained very strong aggressive and destructive potential. This was particularly notable in some of the proto-fundamentalist sects, some of which were the harbingers of the cultural programme of modernity, and above all of its Jacobin components, which can come to the fore and fuse with the religious elements in many contemporary movements.

All of the processes analysed above that have been taking place in the contemporary scene, among them the resurgence of the religious component in the construction of national and international collective identities, thus entail neither the end of history in the sense of the end of ideological confrontational clashes between different cultural programmes of modernity (Fukuyama) nor a clash of civilizations which seems to deny the basic premises of modernity (Huntington). The importance of various civilizational traditions and historical experiences in shaping the specific contours of different modern societies does not mean that these processes give rise to a number of closed civilizations, continuations of their respective historical pasts and patterns. Rather, these different experiences constitute reference points in the continuous flows and interactions between multiple modernities cutting across any single society or civilization.

While such diversity has certainly undermined the old hegemonies, at the same time it has been closely connected – perhaps paradoxically – with the development of new, multiple, common reference points and networks – with a globalization of cultural networks and channels of communication far beyond those that existed before. Moreover, the political dynamics in all these societies are closely interwoven with geopolitical realities, which are also influenced by the historical experiences of these societies yet are largely shaped by modern developments and confrontations which make it impossible to construct such closed entities. Needless to say, these processes do not even constitute a – basically impossible – return to the *problématique* of premodern Axial civilizations.

NOTES

1   It may be worthwhile noting a certain irony in the fact that the view that promulgates an overall homogenizing of the contemporary world, seemingly very close to earlier theories of modernization and convergence of industrial societies, also proclaims the end of modernity, that is, of the classical programme thereof.
2   On "new" social movements see Aronowitz 1992; Banks 1981; Jelin 1990; Karst 1993; Pizzorno 1994; West and Blumberg 1990.
3   On Axial Age civilizations see Eisenstadt 1978, 1980, 1982, 1986, 1992.
4   See also the discussion entitled "The Road to 2050. A Survey of the New Geopolitics", *The Economist*, 31 July 1999.

REFERENCES

Aronowitz, S. (1992), *The Politics of Identity. Class, Culture, Social Movements* (New York: Routledge)
Banks, O. (1981), *Faces of Feminism. A Study of Feminism as a Social Movement* (Oxford: Martin Robertson and Company)
Eickelman, D. and Anderson, J. (eds) (1999), *New Media in the Muslim World. The Emerging Public Sphere* (Bloomington: Indiana University Press)
Eisenstadt, S. N. (1978), *Revolution and the Transformation of Societies* (New York: Free Press)
_____ (1980), "Transcendental Vision, Center Formation and the Role of Intellectuals", in L. Greenfeld and M. Martin (eds), *Center and Ideas and Institutions* (Chicago: University of Chicago Press), 96–109
_____ (1982), "The Axial Age: The Emergence of Transcendental Visions and the Rise of Clerics", *European Journal of Sociology* 23:2, 294–314
_____ (ed.) (1986), *The Origins and Diversity of Axial Age Civilizations* (Albany, NY: State University of New York Press)
_____ (1987), *European Civilization in a Comparative Perspective* (Oslo: Norwegian University Press)
_____ (1992), "Frameworks of the Great Revolutions: Culture, Social Structure, History and Human Agency", *International Social Science Journal* 133, 385–401
_____ (1999), *Fundamentalism, Sectarianism and Revolutions. The Jacobin Dimension of Modernity* (Cambridge: Cambridge University Press)
Eisenstadt, S. N. and Azmon, Y. (eds) (1975), *Socialism and Tradition* (Atlantic Highlands, NJ: Humanities Press)
Friedman, J. (1994), *Cultural Identity and Global Process* (London: Sage Publications)
Fukuyama, F. (1992), *The End of History and the Last Man* (New York: Free Press)
Gauchet, M. (1998), *La Religion dans la démocratie. Parcours de la laïcité* (Paris: Gallimard)
Göle, N. (1996), *The Forbidden Modern, Civilization and Veiling* (Ann Arbor: University of Michigan Press)
Hannerz, U. (1992), *Cultural Complexity* (New York: Columbia University Press)
Huntington, S. P. (1993), "The Clash of Civilizations?", *Foreign Affairs* 72:3, 22–49
_____ (1996), *The Clash of Civilizations and the Remaking of World Order* (New York: Simon & Schuster)
Jalal, A. (1995), *Democracy and Authoritarianism in South Asia. A Comparative and Historical Perspective* (Cambridge: Cambridge University Press)
Jelin, E. (ed.) (1990), *Women and Social Change in Latin America* (Geneva, United Nations Research Institute for Social Development)

Juergensmeyer, M. (1994), *The New Cold War? Religious Nationalism Confronts the Secular State* (Berkeley: University of California Press)

Karst, K. (1993), *Law's Promise, Law's Expression. Visions of Power in the Politics of Race, Gender and Religion* (New Haven: Yale University Press)

Khosrokhavar, F. (1996), "L'universel abstrait, le politique et la construction de l'islamisme comme forme d'altérité", in M. Wieviorka (ed.), *Une société fragmentée?* (Paris, Éditions La Decouverte), 113–151

Kuran, T. (1993), "The Economic Impact of Islamic Fundamentalism", in M. Marty and R. S. Appleby (eds), *Fundamentalisms and the State: Remaking Polities, Economies and Militance* (Chicago: University of Chicago Press), 302–341

Kuran, T. (1997a), "Islam and Underdevelopment: An Old Puzzle Revisited", *Journal of Institutional and Theoretical Economies* 153 (1): 41–71.

———— (1997b), "The Genesis of Islamic Economics: A Chapter in the Politics of Muslim Identity", *Social Research* 64:2, 301–338

Marcus, G. (ed.) (1993), *Perilous States. Conversations on Culture, Politics, and Nation* (Chicago: University of Chicago Press)

Pizzorno, A. (1994), *Le radici della politica assoluta* (Milan: Giangiacomo Feltrinelli Editore)

Smolicz, J. (1998), "Nation-States and Globalization from a Multicultural Perspective. Signposts from Australia", *Nationalism and Ethnic Politics* 4:4, 1–18

West, G. and Blumberg, R. (eds) (1990), *Women and Social Protest* (New York: Oxford University Press)

12 Modes of Religious Pluralism under Conditions of Globalization

OLE RIIS

The process of globalization accelerates the general awareness of the plurality of religions. As a side effect of international communication, trade, politics and mobility, people become increasingly aware of the existence of a multitude of world views, and they are led to critically reflect on their own assumptions. Traditions legitimating the religious identity of a homogeneous region are thus challenged by globalization, in so far as supposedly universal normative standards change into insular peculiarities. Such a change of perspective may also challenge the status of religious organizations. For instance, a unit which has been a regional church for centuries becomes sect-like when seen in a global framework. These phenomena have been analysed extensively in recent studies of globalization (see for example Beyer 1994 and Robertson 1992).

The principal aim of this essay is to show that religious pluralism can develop in several modes. Religious diversity is intensified by globalization. However, it is far from evident that it results in only one general type of religious pluralism. Instead, it is more probable that globalization is leading to a plurality of pluralisms. In the following discussion, this problem will be approached from the perspective of the sociology of religion. After a brief review of various definitions of pluralism, I will elaborate upon the concept of religious pluralism by introducing a distinction of different levels of analysis and by situating the concepts of recent theoretical debates within the realm of sociology of religion. Furthermore, I will analyse different modes of religious pluralism at a national and a European level. The final section presents confrontations between different strategies of pluralism.

CONCEPT OF PLURALISM

The very term "pluralism" has several meanings depending on the respective discourse to which it refers. The concept was initially coined by Enlightenment philosophers such as Christian Wolff and Immanual Kant. Originally, it signified a doctrine about the plenitude of possible world-views combined with the invitation to adopt the universal viewpoint of a world-citizen. In present philosophy, the concept of pluralism refers to the standpoint that the world may be interpreted in several ways, or to the evaluation that science is enhanced by competition between several interpretations. In ethics and in normative sociology, it refers to the problem that modern society is no longer based on an authoritative set of norms, and thus all ethical questions are, following the terminology of Jürgen Habermas, subject to open-ended and rational discourse.

The term pluralism has spread from philosophy to other academic discourses. At the turn of the twentieth century, pragmatists such as William James reused the concept stressing the empirical implications of a pluralistic ontology. Traces of this usage of the term can still be found in cognitive sociology. Additionally, the concept of pluralism became popular in political considerations about the conditions of democracy as opposed to a monistic state apparatus, especially in the work of Harold J. Laski. Hence, in political discussions pluralism began to symbolize the ideals of multiple political parties, the decentralization of the state apparatus and the distribution of power resources in society. In economic theory and other disciplines inspired by models of rational choice, the term pluralism is associated with the idea of a free market system, which aims ensure open competition for suppliers and free choice for customers.

Pluralism may refer to all these meanings in sociology; however, social science has added further varieties of pluralism. In cultural sociology and ethnology, pluralism may refer to a fragmentation of culture into a set of sub-cultures demarcated by ethnic, linguistic, religious or other boundaries. In cognitive sociology, which studies the human interpretation of everyday life and the world at large, the concept of pluralism describes a social situation where several meaning systems are simultaneously presented as plausible interpretations of the world. In functional sociology, pluralism refers to the differentiation of society, which can be observed at the individual level as a differentiation of roles, at the organizational level as increased competition of formal organizations and at the societal level as limitations of the functions of institutions.

Within the context of social science discourse, pluralism in the sense of a recognition of multiplicity in society and as a precondition for individual choice and freedom is contrasted by two extreme opposites. Firstly, it is opposed to any form of monism, that is, a theocracy, an absolutist state, a monopoly, a total society, an alienated consciousness, a petrified cultural monolith and so on. Secondly, since the idea of pluralism implies an identifiable structure, it is simultaneously contrasted by amorphousness. Such a state may be described as anarchy, anomie – in a cognitive or normative sense – epistemological relativism, incoherent postmodernism, and so forth. Since social fields are often homologous, pluralism in one field is often correlated with pluralism in other fields of society. However, this homology is not an outcome of a mechanical law, as is demonstrated by many examples of economic, political, cultural and social fields, which diverge in their respective degree of pluralization within a society.

This brief sketch suggests that the concept of pluralism is used both in a descriptive and in an evaluative sense. In the descriptive sense, it may, on the one hand, refer to an awareness of a multitude of sub-entities, as an awareness of diversity and plurality. In the normative sense, it may express the recognition and positive acknowledgement of plurality. However, it would be a primary example for a naturalistic fallacy to conclude from the empirical fact of diversity that it should be embraced normatively. Furthermore, one may argue that there is a fundamental difference between tolerating a concrete range of differing attitudes, beliefs, values and lifestyles, and holding an abstract, universal ideal of toleration. The latter may express indifference rather than toleration, by accepting anything in principle and therefore nothing in practice. Since pluralism is a term with several meanings and associations; it is necessary to clarify its meaning in the present discussion.

A PHENOMENOLOGY OF RELIGIOUS PLURALISM

In a modern context where rationalized styles of discussion dominate in society, religious discourse is a very special type. Religions are founded on divinely revealed truths.[1] Religious discourse refers to a suprahuman agency and a transempirical sphere. The source is beyond human comprehension. Acceptance of the revealed truth is fundamentally based on belief, not by references to logic or empirical demonstration.[2] Religious groups vary according to their degree of internal pluralism, and their willingness to cooperate with other groups. There is a limit to how far a religious group can accept religious pluralism internally and externally without feeling that it compromises its identity. This does not exclude discourses within or between religious groups. Some religious groups have vivid internal discussions, some religious groups cooperate, some reach a concord and some even merge.

While all religions are characterized by referring to a transempirical source of truth and purity, it is useful, at the outset, to distinguish between different religions by assessing the scope of their symbolical claims. Whereas *universalistic* religions, for example Christianity and Islam, claim to contain the whole spiritual truth, *particularistic* religions have more specific aims and only claim partial access to that truth. While the former confront the individual with a fundamental choice and demand total commitment from their members, the latter are less demanding. They may even be combined in functional mixtures, which, for the universal religions, would be perceived as eclecticism, syncretism and heresy.[3]

As a consequence, religious pluralism seems to be less problematic when particularistic religions are involved. In this case, it is the functional limits of each religion and their appropriate combinations, and not the general principle of religious pluralism that may cause controversy and conflict. Examples of religious pluralism involving particularistic religions stretch from ancient Rome to present-day Japan. In such settings, the claims of universalistic religions are seen as undermining the whole system of religious pluralism, as shown by the critique of Emperor Marc Aurel against early Christianity. In turn, religious pluralism involving several universalistic religions, each of which claims to be the exclusive vessel of truth and purity, is precarious. It may, in fact, evolve from a state of peaceful coexistence to open conflict or a majority-minority domination.

Religious pluralism can be analysed at three consecutive social levels: at the macro-level, religious pluralism implies that the societal authorities recognize and accept a plurality within the religious field; at the meso-level, pluralism implies the acceptance of a multitude of religious organizations which function as competitive units; and finally at the micro-level, pluralism implies an individual's freedom to choose and develop her or his own private beliefs. These modes of pluralism correspond with *religious toleration, denominalization* and *religious freedom*. However, these are not interrelated in a mechanical manner. In principle, religious toleration could be organized within the framework of one latitudinarian church; denominalization could be organized by ascribing each individual to the religion of their parents; and religious freedom could imply an extreme individualization dissolving all denominations.

Issues of religious freedom are mostly discussed as prohibition of state interference in the individual's religious beliefs. However, religious freedom also implies the freedom to practice one's religion. This is not problematic as long as religious practices are regarded as rituals confined to the limited space of a church or a temple and to a limited timespan of holydays. However, problems arise when religious practices include ethics. Most religions regard themselves as something more than abstract philosophies of life. They aspire to provide a practical ethical guidance for living. This leads to a confrontation with the forces of other social fields. If the authorities of the political, economic or cultural fields feel challenged by the authorities of the religious field, they may react by narrowing its domain. In other words, they may limit religious freedom to the right to believe in something by restricting the right to act in accordance with this belief in society. Although such a reaction may be considered rational with regard to the efficiency of the economy and the state, it results in a delimitation of religious freedom in its most basic sense.

All modern constitutions, including those of totalitarian states, grant religious freedom.[4] For instance, the 1949 Constitution of the German Democratic Republic Chapter V, Articles 41–44 grants full freedom of religion and belief to each citizen as well as the right to organize denominations. It even offered state protection of religious practices. However, religious freedom was limited by one important proviso: religions were not to be misused politically, in opposition to the (socialist) constitution. Such conditional limits to religious freedom are, in fact, not a special feature of totalitarian states. They are also provided in democratic states, in so far as it is recognized that an unfettered freedom of religion may dissolve society. It is therefore imperative to pay attention to the conditions as well as to the limitations of the principle of religious freedom and its practical protection.

Religious pluralism at the individual level has several forms. It is articulated in the individual's right to choose attachment to a denomination. It should be noted that this implicitly acknowledges the expectation that individuals associate themselves with one specific denomination which claims to represent universal truth. Yet, it may also refer to individuals formulating their own view of life, by picking or mixing elements of religious belief systems according to their own preferences. In the sociology of religion, this process has been labelled "religion à la carte" (Bibby 1987) or a religious "bricolage" (Luckmann 1967). A third variety is a functional mixing of particularistic religions. This type is widespread in history, and the term bricolage does by no means adequately describe a typical Japanese mixture of Shinto baptism, Christian marriage and Buddhist burial. Despite the universalistic claims of the denominations, individuals may regard specific denominations as appropriate for specific aspects of life and engage in a reflective compartmentalization of the religious field.

To some commentators (see Hick 1985), religious pluralism implies the recognition of the common foundation of all varieties of the religious quest and the possible convergence of world religions. To others, pluralism implies mutual respect among well-specified world views, in full recognition of their differences. Both varieties support toleration. However, the first one would stress religious freedom of individuals, while the second would stress recognition of denominations as carriers of specified answers.

RELIGIOUS PLURALISM FROM THE PERSPECTIVE OF THE SOCIOLOGY OF RELIGION

The views on pluralism among sociologists of religion depend on the theoretical background assumptions of their analysis. For the sake of the following argument, one may broadly distinguish between three major strands of theoretical schools in the sociology of religion, which are associated with three main founders of sociology (see Riis 1996a): *functionalism* (Emile Durkheim), *cognitivism* (Max Weber) and *critical theory* (Karl Marx). Functionalism regards religion as an institution constitutive for social integration; cognitivism sees it as a world view providing meaning for both individuals and collectives; and critical theory interprets it as an ideology legitimating the power structure of society.

Talcott Parsons, a major representative of the *functional* approach, analyses pluralism as a "systematic differentiatedness at all levels" (see Parsons 1967 and 1995). These levels include a differentiation of roles, as well as a social and cultural differentiation. Religious pluralism means, according to Parsons, a differentiation which provides religion with a more narrowly and clearly defined place in the social and cultural system. Membership in religious organizations is based on a voluntary decision, and the content and practice of religion is privatized. This does not necessarily lead to the secularization of society but rather to a development of a "civil religion" (see also Bellah 1967). Together, the various denominations form a "moral community" in Durkheim's sense by referring to generally shared norms and values of society. In the American case, these values include freedom, toleration, justice, equality, achievement-orientation and responsibility. The value system simultaneously stresses individual values, such as freedom and achievement, and collective values which safeguard freedom. According to Parsons, the strength of the American system lies in its ability to absorb particularistic moral movements in the greater, pluralistic system through value generalization. In Europe, a similar tendency is fettered by the nation states.

From the perspective of the *cognitivist* school of sociological theory, represented for instance by Peter Berger, "... the phenomenon called 'pluralism' is the socio-structural parallel to the secularization of consciousness" (1967, 127). In his view, secularization leads to a de-monopolization of religious traditions and to an upgrading of the role of lay people. On the religious market, denominations are increasingly forced to compete among themselves and with non-religious world views. As a consequence, in order to survive and grow, religious organizations must be rationalized and bureaucratized. The religious market, which is influenced by the dynamics of consumer-preferences, needs and fashions, most notably by the preference to products harmonized with a secularized consciousness, influences the content of religious belief systems. The products become standardized as the denominations adapt their products to the majority of the consumers. Nevertheless, the denominations maintain a marginal distinction by referring to their "confessional heritage". Pluralism therefore implies that world views are relativized and that plausibility structures become precarious. Religions can no more legitimate the "world" at large; instead several religious groups seek to legitimate their particular sub-worlds through their respective belief systems. For Berger, there are only two possible strategies for religious denominations to respond to an increased pluralism. Either they must adapt to the dynamics of the religious market, or they must withdraw from it. While the first option leads to a crisis of religion, the second undermines the social basis of the church.

Critical theory, finally, regards society as subject to struggles for power and accordingly interprets religion as an instrument for legitimating group-specific interests. Although, this tradition of sociological theory is bifurcated in many branches which also differ in their views on religion (see for example Houtart, Habermas or Bourdieu), the general view can be summarized as follows. Whereas religious monopolies are generally based on an alliance with the political power, religious pluralism is characterized by contrasting channels of legitimization and, hence, by struggles for domination in the religious field. Religious organizations may have more or less influence and resources depending upon their association with either majority or minority groups. Among critical theoreticians, however, religious pluralism is not a theme which attracts much attention, especially within the Marxist tradition because religion is not ascribed an important potential for structural change and human emancipation. Yet, some sociologists of religion influenced by the critical school are trying to rectify this view (for example, Beckford 1989).

The three theoretical approaches outlined above stress different aspects of religious pluralism; however, they converge on certain points. For instance, both Parsons and Berger draw attention to the privatization of religion, to the democratization of society with its influences on denominations, to the marketization of religion, and, as possible reactions to this development, to the re-emergence of orthodoxy and fundamentalism. Additionally, their theories are based on similar empirical foundations, namely on the American experience. Nevertheless, their conclusions differ considerably. Because it expects popularization, relativization, bureaucratization and cartellization in the religious field, the Bergerian view is rather dark, pointing to anomic threats lurking behind pluralism. The Parsonian view, on the contrary, is optimistic, in so far as its scenario contains the development of general, humanitarian values which support a moral community that transcends the particular interests in society. This divergence can be explained by their underlying theoretical approach. Berger maintains that through religion a sacred cosmos is constructed and maintained. Consequently, he interprets religious pluralism as a relativization and profanization of this cosmos. Parsons, on the other hand, regards religion as a provider of norms and values for society and therefore claims that pluralism encourages the formulation of basic values for heterogeneous societies. Berger's view may be criticized for postulating a basic human need for a comprehensive world view. It can be argued, furthermore, that it neglects the possibility that a confrontation of different world views may lead to a clarification of their differences rather than to relativism. The Parsonian view, on the contrary, may be criticized for balancing social development by counter-posing two vaguely described forces: the centrifugal process of societal differentiation versus the centripetal counter force of value generalization. Behind such a theoretical move lies the hidden assumption that religion has a high potential for formulating a set of shared and, hence, integrating values. Critical theory points out that this very assumption is related to the problem of legitimation, although it tends to underestimate the role of religion in modern society.

In addition to these three classic approaches, rational choice theory has increasingly informed recent studies in the sociology of religion. Its theoretical line of argumentation is not yet well-established, and it is far too early to speak of a new "paradigm" in the Kuhnian sense (cf. Warner 1993). However, this approach takes a new and instructive angle on the issue of religious pluralism. Based on the assumption that social behaviour is an outcome of decisions of actors optimizing their chances in market-like social situations, rational choice theory elucidates some of Parsons' considerations on the functioning of religious markets and corrects some of the assumptions of Bergerian theory. According to rational choice theory, religious pluralism implies a vitalizing competition in the religious market. The dynamics of the religious market in a pluralistic society are highly influenced by the demands of consumers. The suppliers are forced to provide those services which are in demand by the consumers. This argument is supported by a series of empirical studies which presumably demonstrate that religious commitment is stronger in societies where many denominations compete unimpeded by state intervention, as is the case in the United States (Stark and Bainbridge 1985). Although some empirical evidence for this view can also be found in Western Europe, the rational choice approach to religious pluralism may be criticized for being based on vague assumptions about rationality and the compensatory functions of religion (see for example Bruce 1996, 129–168). To be sure, the metaphor of the market might illustrate some aspects of religion in modern society; but a market of eternal, spiritual goods differs substantially from a market of short-term material goods.

These theories present different aspects of pluralism. Each of them is able to elucidate certain social aspects of pluralism, which may be relevant under specific social conditions. For instance, rational choice theory may be quite illustrative for major aspects of the religious field in the USA, whereas it is less adequate for analysing the role of religion in major social conflicts. In other cases, critical theory seems more promising, such as for an analysis of the role of religion in the former Yugoslavia, where religion has re-emerged as a label for ethnic identity after two generations of socialist rule.

PUBLIC RECOGNITION OF DENOMINATIONS AS A MODE OF RELIGIOUS PLURALISM

In the sociology of religion, the American mode of religious pluralism – granting religious freedom and minimizing state intervention – is sometimes depicted as a universal ideal. However, the American model also has drawbacks, such as continuing legal struggles about the borderline of the religious field. In Western Europe, religious pluralism has evolved within a completely different socio-historical context. Appeasement after the religious wars of the sixteenth and seventeenth centuries was based on territorial religious homogeneity. The principle of *cujus regio, ejus religio* implied a continental pluralism combined with national homogeneity. Within this social context, the struggle for religious freedom was aimed at the liberation from ideologies which were supporting the hegemonic state system. In turn, religious freedom was perceived by spokesmen of religious conformity as a temptation of the people, since they feared that such freedom could lead to the dissolution of the social order.

Religious freedom has eventually been embraced by all Western European states in their respective constitutions. Nevertheless, a close connection between the state and an established church remains in some countries (see for example Davie and Hervieu-Léger 1996, Dierkens 1994). This may be seen as an anachronism, especially if contrasted with the model of the USA. It may be argued that competition is skewed on the religious market if one denomination is supported and privileged by the state. A nearby example for the contradiction between the principles of religious pluralism and the continuation of established churches can be found in Denmark (see Riis 1996b). Before the democratic constitution of 1849, all citizens were subjugated to the King's confession, that is, to the Evangelical-Lutheran church. The King mercifully gave some confessions a right to practice within his realm, such as the Huguenots, Remonstrants, Bohemian Brethren and Mosaic Jews. These rights were, however, restricted to pre-existing members within selected cities. The democratic constitution of 1849 granted full rights to the freedom of religious beliefs and practices and to the freedom of organizing congregations. At the same time, it granted the Evangelical-Lutheran Church a special status as the "Church of the Danish People'. This compromise was due to ideological and practical considerations. The church was (and still remains) an institution of public services which is expressed, for instance, in demographic registration procedures and in the administration of grave-yards. The state church has neither a synod nor an archbishop; rather, it is formally headed by the Queen as represented by her Minister of Ecclesiastical Affairs. Although the privileged denomination does receive some advantages because of its elevated status as a state church, it can be a heavy burden to carry a national religious tradition and its memories of indoctrination and suppression.

Official recognition of a denomination implies granting it the status as a public institution. In Denmark, for instance, recognition is formally achieved by being awarded the right to sign marriage certificates by the Ministry of Ecclesiastical Affairs.[5] Other privileges follow from the status as a publicly recognized denomination, including the right of denominational members to have their taxes deducted for their membership fees (a privilege which members of the state church are not granted). Furthermore, recognized denominations have an improved access to state funds for cultural activities. The Danish policy of public recognition has been quite liberal in the past decades; about one-hundred religious organizations have been recognized as public denominations. The list, going far beyond traditional Christian denominations, includes Jehovah's Witnesses as well as Buddhist, Hindu and Muslim congregations and even Old Nordic paganism. The demands of the Minister of Ecclesiatical Affairs for awarding recognition are mainly directed at securing that the applicant can be held legally responsible, that the applicant will not misuse the status and that the applying organization can be expected to continue. Until 1998, applicants were screened by the Bishop of Copenhagen, but this task has since been given to a committee of independent councillors.

The practice of public recognition just described may be criticized for being bureaucratic. A seemingly simple solution would be to take all privileges away from all religious organizations, including the Lutheran church. This, however, would imply a secularization of all public services which currently remain under church administration. It would also necessitate a revision of the constitution, a re-evaluation of church properties, a re-organization of the entire state apparatus and a complete re-organization of the Lutheran church. Hence, such a solution is far less simple than it sounds. It can be concluded that the present model expresses a specific mode of religious pluralism by elevating all major religious groups to the status of a publicly recognized denomination.

Besides individual religious freedom and denominational pluralism, the Danish system grants an internal pluralism within the state church. It is possible to establish free churches and free congregations that are affiliated with the state church, and it is possible for a group of dissenting members to employ their own pastor. The local pastor and the congregation have a broad latitude of freedom of practice as long as they agree. This policy of internal pluralism has been challenged recently by some borderline cases. Church council members who have publicly expressed beliefs contradictory to the confession have been evicted, and a pastor has been censured for publicly objecting to child baptism and formulating his own version of the ritual. Yet, being defrocked can hardly be described as a "severe punishment" for deviating from one of the central dogmas of the church, rather, it demonstrates that latitudinarianism has its limits. The state church remains a broad canopy for the large majority of Danes. The majority of its members only use the church for rites of passage. Generally, members are not especially committed to its creed, but instead they believe that most of the great religions hold basic truths. Their basic outlook is one of privatized religiosity, and their membership of the state church is based on its internal pluralism.

PILLARIZATION AS A MODE OF RELIGIOUS PLURALISM

Another way of establishing religious pluralism is to fragment society into subcultures according to religious, ethnic or other criteria. There are many varieties of this general model. A first variant is based on the isolation of religious minorities, either through enforced insulation in ghettos, or through voluntary retraction in order to avoid corrupting influences from the majority. A second variant is based on social separation of sizeable subcultures. In an ideal-type subcultural "pillar", each religious community is enabled to live a whole life from the cradle to the grave according to its own ethical standards (see Monsma and Soper 1997). According to this ideal, all social services are covered by internal institutions. This includes, among others, services such as kindergarten, schools, universities, hospitals and graveyards. It is possible to point out several historical cases which come close to this ideal type. Such processes of segmented differentiation on the basis of religious formations are generally labelled pillarization. Strategies of pillarization have in several cases formed a defensive reaction as major societal institutions are under a threat of laicization.

The Dutch experience during the first half of this century can be regarded as an example of the peaceful co-existence of different pillars. The development of the Dutch system of pillarization was a reaction against liberal politics, which aimed to privatize religion and to dissolve confessional schools. The Calvinist prime minister (1901–05), A. Kuyper, outlined "parallelism" as a social ideal ensuring the right and freedom of the major religious and ideological groups to develop independently of government influence. This corresponded with the Catholic wish for equal rights, and consequently, the divided religious factions agreed on pillarization as the great socio-political compromise. The basic idea is that since religion touches all aspects of life, social life should be organized and guided according to the religious (or secular) beliefs of people. Socialization and caring are basic functions which especially call for a religious foundation. Therefore, institutions for education and welfare must be related to and guided spiritually by specific denominations. The pillars should furthermore provide newspapers and broadcasting networks, trade unions, political parties, recreation clubs and so on. Through these efforts of restructuring, liberals and socialists became distinct pillars instead of representatives of general social interests. The Dutch constitution assures religious freedom for individuals, as well as rights for religious groups on the basis of standards of non-discrimination and equality. This constitution therefore represents a very high level of religious pluralism. The Dutch courts, for instance, recognize non-Christian holidays and burial rites.

More recently, however, tensions have evolved between the established Dutch pillars and immigrant minorities. Tensions are especially great between naturalized Dutch citizens and immigrants who come from Muslim countries. Furthermore, the system of pillarization seems to have eroded during the last decades because church-membership rates are declining and more and more people are crossing different pillars. This does not indicate that the system of pillarization contradicts religious pluralism. On the contrary, it precisely indicates its success, in so far as that system seems to have given Dutch people a better understanding of and a respect for religious diversity. In fact, the state has not taken over the whole complex of non-governmental organizations affiliated with the pillars, be they religious, ethnic or other; instead these organizations now operate on the basis of an internally pluralized clientele.

The Dutch experience represents but one example of pillarization. The relationship between the pillars in different social contexts ranges from co-existence to conflict. A prime example of social conflict that is sustained and symbolized by a pillarized structure can be found in Northern Ireland. The Netherlands and Northern Ireland both display a similar structure. In both cases, Catholics and Protestants (and Non-Confessionals) form separate subcultures with attached social services, including schools. Yet, the split between Protestants and Catholics in Northern Ireland represents a case of pillars in conflict. These contrasting cases demonstrate that the system of pillarization does not in itself lead to peaceful co-existence or social conflict. Rather, the *modus vivendi* between the pillars depends on other social factors, not least the distribution of power and resources in society at large.

This point is important because Western Europe is presently experiencing the development of a novel pillar. For a millennium, Western Europe has been dominated by Christianity; therefore the emergence of different pillars has pertained either to Christian denominations or to non-confessional positions derived from the Judaeo-Christian world-view. As a consequence of international migrations flows, however, a large number of Muslims have been incorporated into Western European societies at the end of the twentieth century (see Dassetto and Bastenier 1988, Leveau 1994). Not only do these Muslim residents share beliefs in the Quran and in the Prophet's words, but they also share the experience of belonging to a religious minority in a diaspora. Muslims are confronted by symbols which relate to the Christian background of the majority culture. These are generally taken for granted, and their religious signification is hardly realized by the majority. One obvious example is the calendar system which in Western Europe is fixed by reference to the birth of Christ rather than by reference to the Prophet's *higra* from Mecca. Muslim immigrants also share a common experience because their ethical norms and values are majorized in the Christian-secular society. Through politico-legal systems and cultural expectations, the Muslim minority is thus brought under pressure to form a proto-pillar. However, European Muslims do not belong to a unified denomination (*umma*), nor do they share a unified culture. Instead European Muslims form a group which is fragmented linguistically, ethnically and socially. Many of these particular groupings even disagree over several ethical views. Moreover, efforts by the majority to confine religion to a narrowly prescribed field, that is, as an abstract belief system held by private individuals, go against the self-understanding of Islam as a practical religion, which provides templates for good life and for a good society. Attempts by faithful Muslims to live in full accordance with Islam within Western Europe, may conflict with interests of the Christian or secularized majority.

A possible compromise for this situation which is intimately related to globalization processes and their impact on mobility and migration would be to form a publicly recognized Muslim pillar. Such a solution, however, goes against the majority interest of integrating Muslim immigrants into Western society. Furthermore, such a solution goes against the minority interest of maintaining particular Muslim traditions as symbol of an ethno-cultural heritage. If Islam in Western Europe is transformed into a sub-cultural pillar, it will be confronted with the intellectual challenge of a reinterpretation in order to be adaptable to the new societal background. It will hence be confronted with the challenge of "internal secularization" (Willaime 1996).

DILEMMAS OF PLURALISM

Religious pluralism at a societal level has hitherto been challenged by policies of monism or secularism. Monism occurs as one religious community seeks for domination over the religious field, while secularism represents a political strategy to restrict or eradicate the religious field. In societies which follow the Western, democratic paradigm, these confrontations have ended with a proclaimed victory for religious pluralism. However, the meaning of pluralism is not clarified. Therefore, new discourses concerning contradictory understandings of pluralism arise.

Religious pluralism is a term with several meanings, and accordingly there are many forms of pluralism. These forms may stress religious toleration, denominalization or individual freedom to different degrees. While a certain mode of pluralism stresses the individual's right to religious freedom, another emphasizes collective rights awarded to denominations. Religious pluralism as expressed in the right to religious freedom is based on an individualistic concept of universal rights and the principle of formal equality. Religious pluralism as articulated in collective rights of denominations builds on the idea of partial and group-specific rights and, hence, presupposes formal inequality.

Several strategies of religious pluralism may be confronted in a certain society. The elite of the religious majority may either adopt a strategy of collective or individual rights. Simultaneously, the elites of the religious minorities may follow either strategy. The situation is uncomplicated if both sides follow the same strategy. For instance, all religious elites may stress individual rights, and accordingly regard the religious field as an "open market" determined by individual choice. One example of such a constellation can be found in the United States. It is also possible that the religious elites regard the field as characterized by collective rights. One example of such a constellation can be found in systems of pillarization.

However, it is possible that the religious elites diverge concerning their understanding of pluralism. One constellation confronts a majority elite arguing for collective rights with minority representatives arguing for individual rights. Such a contradiction is typical in situations where the majority defends its traditional privileges while minority groups seek toleration for their membership. European history provides many examples of such contradictions – and they can even be traced today.

Added to this, a novel constellation of pluralistic strategies has arisen. It consists of elites of minority groups arguing for collective rights confronting the elite representing the majority arguing for abstract individual rights. Such a constellation may occur in cases when a minority elite refers to collective rights as a strategy for defending its traditional identity within a modernized society, while the majority elite uses individual rights as an offensive strategy for the functional integration of society. In such a case, the defenders of collective rights may criticize the principle of individual rights as leading to assimilation and homogenization, whereas the defenders of individual rights may criticize the principle of collective rights due to possible internal conformization by subordinating individual identities to the prescribed group standards as well as to an exclusivist distance between groups.

Such contradictions display a basic dilemma of pluralism. Toleration of a range of permissible religions in society does not necessarily lead to an enhancement of the options available to individuals. Religious pluralism at the societal level does not imply more religious freedom at the individual level, unless all religious organizations allow an internal pluralism. A policy of toleration may institutionalize totalitarian organizations which restrict the options available to their individual members. To use Kymlicka's terminology, it will be hard to find a practicable balance between prohibiting "international restriction" and guaranteeing "external protection" (see Kymlicka 1995).

The latent danger of pillarization is that it may lead to a postmodern caste system, where the life-world is entirely based on ascribed identity and status, while the pillars are unified at a systemic level through a common functioning of the state apparatus and the globalized economy. There are serious doubts as to whether ascribing certain collective privileges to a minority group will solve the material and political discriminations to which its members are subjected. This is Habermas's basic argument for accepting cultural rights only as rights of individuals (Habermas 1994). One may even argue that ascribing a minority group with certain special privileges may solidify the basic discrimination of the social system. The issue of the structural distribution of power and resources is thereby redirected to questions about corrective redistributions.

A policy of pluralism stressing religious freedom as individual rights may also contain problems. By stressing that religion is a private matter, religious interests may become fragmented. Individuals who share values and interests on the basis of their religious commitment are blocked from representing these as religious. By excluding religious organizations from major decisions in society, their potential for mobilizing their membership is simultaneously reduced. One may even regard a policy that overstresses religious freedom as an instrument for secularism which aims at diminishing the influence of religion in society. A policy which accentuates religious freedom does not inevitably lead to a homogenization. One comprehensible reaction to the "embarrassment of choice" is a commitment to an absolutist position such as religious fundamentalism.

Religious toleration presupposes a foundation of shared values. However, not all values are compatible. Even within a religion, the celebration of conflicting values may limit internal pluralism. More importantly, the values forwarded by different religions may be antagonistic. Because these religions may refer to an undisputable authority and a single truth, such value differences express tensions which may erupt in an open conflict. The optimistic vision of Parsonian theory tends to disregard such tensions. The policy of toleration is based on an expectation that various religions may co-exist peacefully and that eventual tensions may be solved through democratic legislation, that is, by majority rule. A general policy of toleration would include religious groups which are fundamentally intolerant due to their theocratic aspirations. However, such minorities may feel that their values are suppressed despite the democratic procedures of majorization. As this dilemma is unavoidable, even democratic societies are sometimes forced to set limits to religious toleration.

NOTES

1   This is a general characteristic, which needs an added modification. In some religions, such as Unitarians, Quakers and branches of Buddhism, the dogmatic core is not very explicit and firm.
2   Magic and miracles have an element of empirical demonstration; but such demonstrations are beyond human control.
3   The membership of a religion can be divided according to their acceptance of and commitment to universal claims of their respective religion.

4   The individual's right to the freedom of religious beliefs and practices is guaranteed in many instruments of international human rights law, most notably in Art. 18 of the Universal Declaration of Human Rights (1948) and Art. 18 of the International Covenant on Civil and Political Rights (1966).
5   Although the legal nomenclature changed in 1969, the general principle continues.

REFERENCES

Beckford, J. A. (1989), *Religion and Advanced Industrial Society* (London: Unwin Hyman)
——— (1999), "The Management of Religious Diversity in England and Wales with Special Reference to Prison Chaplaincy", *International Journal on Multicultural Societies* 1:1, 55–66.
Bellah, R. N. (1967), "Religion in America", in *Daedalus. Journal of the American Academy of Arts and Science*, 1–21
Berger, P. (1967), *The Sacred Canopy: Elements of a Sociological Theory of Religion* (Garden City, NY: Doubleday)
Beyer, P. (1994), *Religion and Globalization* (London: Sage Publications)
Bibby, R. W. (1987), *Fragmented Gods: The Poverty and Potential of Religion in Canada* (Toronto: Irwin Publications)
Bruce, S. (1996), *Religion in the Modern World. From Cathedrals to Cults* (Oxford: Oxford University Press)
Davie, G. and Hervieu-Léger, D. (eds) (1996), *Identités religieuses en Europe* (Paris: La Découverte)
Dassetto, F and Bastenier, A. (1988) (revised 1991), *Europa nuova frontiera dell'islam* (Rome: EL)
Dierkens, A. (ed.) (1994), *Pluralisme religieux et laïcités dans l'Union européenne (Problèmes d'histoire des religions*, vol. 5) (Bruxelles: Éditions de l'Université de Bruxelles)
Habermas, J. (1994), "Struggles for Recognition in the Democratic Constitutional State", in Amy Gutmann (ed.), *Multiculturalism: Examining the Politics of Recognition* (Princeton: Princeton University Press)
Hamnett, I. (ed.) (1990), *Religious Pluralism and Unbelief* (London: Routledge)
Hick, J. (1985), *Problems of Religious Pluralism* (London: Macmillan)
Kymlicka, W. (1995), *Multicultural Citizenship. A Liberal Theory of Minority Rights* (Oxford: Clarendon Press)
Leveau, R. (1994), "Éléments de réflexion sur l'Islam en Europe", *Revue Européenne des Migrations Internationales* 10:1, 158–166
Luckmann, T. (1967), *The Invisible Religion* (New York: Macmillan)
Monsma, S. and Soper, C. (eds) (1997), *The Challenge of Pluralism. Church and State in Five Democracies* (Lanham: Rowman & Littlefield)
Parsons, T. (1967), "Christianity and Modern Industrial Society", in T. Parsons, *Sociological Theory and Modern Society* (New York et al.: The Free Press), 385–421
——— (1995), "Religion in a Modern Pluralistic Society (1965)", in S. Bruce (ed.), *The Sociology of Religion*, vol. I (Aldershot: Edward Elgar Publishing), 481–502
Riis, O. (1996*a*), *Metoder og Teorier i Religionssociologien* (Aarhus: Aarhus Universitetsforlag)
——— (1996*b*), "Religion et identité nationale en Danemarque", in G. Davie and D. Hervieu-Léger (eds), *Identités religieuses en Europe* (Paris: La Découverte), 113–130
——— (1998*a*), "Religion Re-Emerging", *International Sociology* 13:2, 249–272
——— (1998*b*), "Modes of Religious Pluralism under Conditions of Globalisation". *International Journal on Multicultural Societies* 1:1, 20–34

Robertson, R. (1992), *Globalization: Social Theory and Global Culture* (London: Sage Publications)

Stark, R. and W. Bainbridge (1985), *The Future of Religion. Secularisation, Revival and Cult Formation* (Berkeley: University of California Press)

Warner, R. S. (1993), "Work in Progress toward a New Paradigm for the Sociological Study of Religion in the United States", *American Journal of Sociology* 98:5, 1044–1093

Willaime, J.-P. (1996), "La secularization contemporaine du croire", in L. Babès (ed.), *Les Nouvelles Manières de Croire: Judaisme, christianisme, islam, nouvelles religiosités* (Paris: Les Editions Ouvrieres), 47–62

13 Prison Chaplaincy in England and Wales – from Anglican Brokerage to a Multi-faith Approach

JAMES A. BECKFORD

This chapter analyses the changing response of the Prison Service of England and Wales towards the increase of religious diversity among prisoners.* I shall begin with some critical remarks about the concept of pluralism. My aim is to show that it is a problematic concept from a sociological point of view and that the notion of "diversity" is more appropriate in the context of my research on prison chaplaincy. Next, the extent of religious diversity in the population of England and Wales as well as among prisoners will be documented. The chapter's central argument will be that prison chaplaincy in England and Wales used to be a site of controversy, not just because of the growth of religious diversity but also because of the continuing reliance of the British state on the Church of England to act as a universal mission to all prisoners. Anglican prison chaplains were in a strange situation: as representatives of a universalist religion they were legally required by the Prison Act 1952 to facilitate the practice of other religions such as Buddhism, Hinduism, Islam, Judaism and Sikhism. They were the main agents of the British state's policy for managing religious diversity in its prisons. The profound changes that have affected their work since 1999 have gone some way towards reducing the significance of their role as brokers for other faiths. But my conclusion is that discrimination against prisoners from ethnic and religious minorities has still not completely disappeared.

PLURALISM OR DIVERSITY?

The term "pluralism" occurs extensively in sociological analyses of religion, but it presents two main problems (Beckford 2003: 73-102):

- First, pluralism refers to an ideological or normative belief that there *should be* mutual respect between different cultural systems and freedom for them all. It holds that peaceful coexistence between different cultural systems is preferable to enmity between them. And it sometimes suggests that a state of balance in the importance attached to different cultural systems is better than an ideological monopoly or a very one-sided relationship between a dominant system and subordinate systems. But much research is not about the ideology of pluralism or about the state's management of this ideology. Most research in the sociology of religion is actually concerned with religious *diversity* and with the public response to diversity. It is confusing, in my opinion, to use the concept of pluralism in both a descriptive and an evaluative sense. For the sake of clarity, then, I think that fact and value should be kept analytically separate. Pluralism is an ideological or evaluative response to empirical diversity. To be more precise, pluralism can assume many different forms. Riis (1999 and in this volume) has helpfully identified a wide range of uses to which the term "pluralism" can be put and, within them, three different ways of instituting religious pluralism: toleration, denominationalization and individual religious freedom. Each of them is an ideological model of how to manage religious diversity. State authorities have therefore adapted them selectively to the perceived and changing need for social order and the maintenance of politico-economic power structures. I argue that strong pluralism needs to be based on the right of individuals to religious freedom.
- Second, some political scientists have used pluralism for their own purposes to imply that the well-being of any society depends simply on having a plurality of competing interest groups, social classes or religions. But this perspective totally ignores the fact that *inequalities* of power or prestige can sometimes render the idea of pluralistic competition unrealistic. Relations of superordination and subordination can give rise to marginalization, exploitation and oppression. The notion of a market for religions is also vulnerable to the same objection: it distracts attention from gross inequalities and imbalances of power, opportunity and resources. We therefore need a notion of diversity that is open to the possibility that some religious groups are so much more influential and powerful than others that it is simply unrealistic to think of them as competing with each other in harmony. We need to focus on the opportunities that religious diversity creates for the perpetuation or the reduction of the power held by dominant religious groups.

There is a risk that research on religious minorities somehow implies that they necessarily represent social or sociological problems. But I want to argue that *dominant* religious groups can also be problematic, especially when they confront weaker minorities. Even when pluralism forms part of the public discourse about majority–minority relations, there is no guarantee of commitment to equal respect or equal opportunities.

But it is also necessary to analyse carefully what we mean by "religious diversity" in a country such as England and Wales. It refers primarily to a number of factors that may, or may not, be interrelated. In the first place, it refers to an increase that has taken place in the variety of religious groups operating in England and Wales since, say, 1950. Second, it refers to an increase in the number of faith communities that are separate from Christian faith traditions. Third, it refers to the growing popularity of religious and spiritual beliefs or practices which fall outside the categories of the world's major faith traditions. Fourth, it refers to the differentiation of formerly unitary faith groups into separate groupings. In a country where one religious organization used to dominate religious life, the term "diversity" registers the change from a virtual monopoly to a situation in which competition takes place between various religious organizations.

The precise configuration of all these dimensions of diversity differs from country to country in accordance with the religious history and religious composition of each. The political salience of religious diversity therefore varies with the local circumstances. The social implications of growing religious diversity are also shaped by them. This is why I think it is important to ground the study of growing religious diversity in particular cases, that is, in the framework of historical, cultural and social factors influencing the perception of diversification in any given country. And, as Riis (in this volume) has clearly demonstrated, the meaning of the term "pluralism" also varies with local circumstances and from country to country.

My reasons for insisting on a conceptual distinction between pluralism and diversity will become clearer when I explain the extent to which the treatment of prisoners from different faith traditions has historically been unequal in England and Wales. The situation has changed significantly since 1999 in the sense that facilities for the practice of religions other than Christianity have improved. Nevertheless, my conclusion is that the British state remains far from neutral in matters of religion and that it merely *tolerates* a degree of religious diversity. I do not regard toleration as a strong form of pluralism. It is a *concession* made by the powerful to the weak and, as such, it always runs the risk of being manipulated or cancelled by the former (Wilson 1995). Furthermore, "tolerance presumes a position of normative superiority – we tolerate things we do not like but believe have the right to exist" (Cooper 2004, 18).

GROWTH OF RELIGIOUS AND ETHNIC DIVERSITY

Although discussions of religious diversity frequently concern new religious movements, the New Age or the continuing fragmentation of Christian denominations, the focus of this paper is on the increase in numbers of Buddhists, Hindus, Jews, Muslims and Sikhs in England and Wales since the 1950s.[1] Table 13.1 gives a general impression of the relative size and rate of growth or decline in these faith communities (bearing in mind that they are far from being homogeneous, self-conscious communities).

Table 13.1 **United Kingdom, religious communities, in millions, 1975–2005**

	1975	1980	1985	1990	1995	2000	2005*
Christian Churches	42.6	42.5	42.4	42.3	42.2	42.1	41.9
Main religions other than Christianity							
Hindu	0.4	0.5	0.5	0.5	0.5	0.6	0.6
Jewish	0.4	0.3	0.3	0.3	0.3	0.3	0.3
Muslim	0.4	0.7	1.0	1.3	1.4	1.6	1.7
Sikh	0.1	0.2	0.2	0.2	0.3	0.3	0.4
Other religions	0.1	0.2	0.2	0.2	0.3	0.4	0.4
Percentage of population:							
Christian	76	76	74	74	73	72	70
Other religions	2	3	4	4	4	5	6
Total all religions	78	79	78	78	77	77	76

*estimated
Source: Adapted from Brierley (2003/04, 2.2).

It is not at all surprising that the growing religious diversity of the UK's population should have become reflected in British prisons.[2] In fact, the number of prisoners in England and Wales who came from religious backgrounds other than Christianity began increasing in the 1970s. Most of them were Muslims whose families had migrated to the United Kingdom from South Asia. But the first cohorts of young prisoners who had been born in the United Kingdom and whose ethnicity was Asian or Asian British began to enter prisons in significant numbers in the 1990s. The label "immigrant" was not appropriate for these British-born members of extensive, well-established communities and networks of Muslims, Hindus, Jains and Sikhs. The Prison Service of England and Wales was slow to adjust to the growing numbers of prisoners from the Caribbean, South Asia and East Africa in the 1960s and 1970s (Genders and Player 1989) and equally slow to recognize officially that Buddhists, Hindus, Muslims and Sikhs had specific religious requirements. Even in 1979 it was not clear whether religious minorities in prisons were merely tolerated or really accepted (Russell 1979).

Table 13.2 shows the evolution of religious diversity in the prisons of England and Wales between 1991 and 2003, as recorded by the annual census of prisoners' religious registrations from 1991 to 1995 and by the Local Inmate

Table 13.2 Religious registrations, all prisoners in England and Wales, 1991–2003

	1991	1993	1995	1997	1999	2001	2003	% of total in 2003	Change in % of total 1991–2003
Main Christian	32 991	30 334	30 300	36 498	39 354	36 641	39 536	54.83	-20.83
Other Christian	644	668	651	527	522	1 248	1 693	2.34	+0.86
Other main religions									
Buddhist	183	177	182	226	346	546	737		
Hindu	151	161	162	198	243	295	291		
Jewish	194	209	178	288	198	167	195		
Muslim	1 959	2 106	2 745	3 693	4 355	4 933	5 808		
Sikh	307	323	353	394	456	433	480		
Sub-total	2 794	2 976	3 620	4 799	5 598	6 374	7 511	10.41	+3.93
Other faiths	238	325	179	203	200	1 676	600		
Agnostic, atheist, none	6 866	7 415	11 420	15 840	18 555	21 329	22 756	31.56	+15.82
Non-permitted religions	68	140	129	138	153	196	2		
Total	43 601	41 848	46 299	58 005	64 382	67 464	72 098		

Data System (LIDS) after 1999. These data are the best available, but they are still problematic in some respects. For example, as many as 2000 or 3000 prisoners were missing from the census in some years; the categorization of religious identities has changed over time; and there is no way of checking the validity of claims that prisoners make about their religious affiliations or sympathies. Nevertheless, I have no reason to question the *relative* size of the registration categories. Incidentally, the category of "non-permitted religions" contains the Nation of Islam, the Church of Scientology and, until 2003, Rastafarianism.

Statistics of religious registrations for earlier years are less reliable than those for the recent past (see Table 13.3), but I estimate that between 1975 and 2003 there was a 39 per cent decrease in the proportion of prisoners identified with the main Christian Churches. By contrast, the proportion of prisoners identified with the major "other faiths" increased by 7 per cent over the same period. Meanwhile, a 30 per cent growth occurred in the proportion of prisoners who declined to identify themselves with any religion. In other words, the significance of the relatively small growth in the numbers of Buddhist, Hindu, Jewish, Muslim and Sikh prisoners becomes much greater when it is compared with the dramatic decline in the percentage of prisoners associating with mainstream Christian Churches, or indeed with any form of religious activity. The significance of these shifts in religious registrations for control over prison chaplaincy was of particular concern to me.

Table 13.3   **Religious registrations, 1975–2003, HM prisons, England and Wales**

	1975	%	2003	%	Change in percentage 1975–2003
Main Christian	30 974	94.0	39 536	54.8	– 39.2
Other Christian	240	0.7	1 693	2.3	+ 1.6
Main other faiths	1 112	3.3	7 511	10.4	+ 7.1
Agnostic, atheist, none	649	2.0	22 756	31.6	+29.6
Non-permitted religions	-	-	602	0.8	
Total	32 975	100.0	72 098	100.0	

The point for emphasis here is that, although the pattern of prisoners' religious registrations had changed radically, the arrangements for prison chaplaincy were slow to keep pace with this change until the Prison Service Chaplaincy made a commitment to introduce multi-faith principles and practices after 1999. The fact that prison chaplaincy had previously been controlled mainly by the Church of England helps to explain why so little adaptation to religious diversity had occurred.

In order to discover how the Church of England used its established position to shape the provision of prison chaplaincy for the growing numbers of prisoners from other faith communities, Sophie Gilliat and I adopted a mixed strategy of research including documentary analysis, 60 interviews, questionnaires administered to all known Church of England chaplains and Buddhist, Hindu, Jewish, Muslim and Sikh Visiting Ministers, and participant observation in 14 prisons of various types in England and Wales (Beckford and Gilliat 1998).

BROKERAGE BY THE CHURCH OF ENGLAND

Every one of the 140 prisons of England and Wales is still legally required to have a chaplain who is a clergyman of the Church of England; and about 80 per cent of all full-time Christian chaplains are Anglicans. More importantly, not a single Buddhist, Hindu, Jew, Muslim or Sikh was employed as a full-time or part-time chaplain until 2001. And most significantly, from my point of view, decisions about whether to appoint Visiting Ministers[3] to supply religious and pastoral care to prisoners belonging to "other faiths" were taken by Christian chaplains and prison administrators.

Until 1999 most full-time Anglican chaplains in the Prison Service of England and Wales were still civil servants who also happened to serve, in effect, as the mediators between religious minorities and the prison system. They were managers of religious diversity on behalf of the British state. But they were *not neutral* in matters of religion. They were also representatives of the Church of England and of Anglican forms of spirituality. As such, they tended to favour certain attitudes and practices while deprecating others. In particular, a majority of those whom Sophie Gilliat and I interviewed in the mid-1990s supported the notion that chaplaincy should be coordinated by a single agency which was the most representative religious organization in the country and which was, in their opinion, best placed, by virtue of its dominant position, to protect minorities. Some Anglican chaplains argued that the necessity for a single, clearly dominant agency to run prison chaplaincy had actually become *more* pressing because of growing religious diversity. They saw themselves as the only stable point of reference against a backdrop of change and confusion. From the point of view of many Anglican chaplains, religious diversity was merely a challenge, not a positive benefit. The responsibility for managing diversity did not generate fresh theological reflections, in the view of most of them, but it did reinforce the Anglican idea that the Church of England had a mission to all people in England and an obligation to respond to requests for help.

Another argument that Anglican chaplains deployed in defence of their position of power and responsibility was that the provision of resources and opportunities for prison chaplaincy would be greatly reduced if the British state chose to deal with all religious groups individually instead of using the Church of England as an intermediary and coordinator. This argument rested partly on the claim that the historical continuity of Church/state relations and the numerical preponderance of Anglicans in the population of England and Wales made it difficult for agencies of the state to ignore or counteract the Church's claims for chaplaincy resources. There was some support for this argument among the leaders of minority faith communities. They regarded the Church of England as a powerful source of protection against a potentially unsympathetic state. Some of them were content to seek shelter behind the Church's comforting size and established power, believing that they would be much weaker and more vulnerable if they had to pursue their own interests in direct negotiation with state agencies. They accepted the argument that all religions could benefit indirectly from the privileges that the Church of England had enjoyed for centuries.

Until the end of the twentieth century it was common for Church of England prison chaplains to justify their dominant position by stressing that their role was that of "broker" between prison administration and "other faiths" (Beckford and Gilliat 1998). They saw themselves as the go-betweens who negotiated access and resources on behalf of the "outsiders". Yet, this brokerage was regarded with considerable ambivalence on both sides. On the one hand, it was relatively difficult for the Visiting Ministers of some other faiths to feel that they could obtain equal treatment for prisoners who belonged to their faith communities. They complained that Anglican chaplains: failed to notify them about prisoners who wanted Visiting Ministers to visit them; failed to provide Visiting Ministers with enough opportunities to visit their prisoners; failed to supply adequate numbers of religious artefacts or books; and failed to obtain suitable rooms in which other faith prisoners could worship or meditate. In fact, there were numerous complaints about the lack of responsiveness among Church of England chaplains to the demands for better religious resources from other faith prisoners and their Visiting Ministers.

On the other hand, the fact that Church of England chaplains were employed in all prisons and were under an obligation to facilitate the religious and pastoral care of prisoners from *all* faith communities meant that prison authorities could not completely ignore the rights of non-Christian prisoners. The chaplains were usually well respected by prison staff and were therefore in a strong position to act effectively on behalf of *all* prisoners, regardless of their religious affiliation. There was a strong expectation that they would act as brokers – not only on behalf of prisoners from other faith groups but also on behalf of their Visiting Ministers.

The main reason for the Anglican brokerage was not that Visiting Ministers lacked appropriate skills or knowledge. In fact, most of them were ministers of religion or other religiously qualified people who visited prisoners regularly in order to offer religious, spiritual or pastoral care. Some were representatives of minority Christian groups or movements, such as Jehovah's Witnesses or the Assemblies of God. Others represented the major world religions and ancient religious traditions such as paganism, although it was not permissible for prisoners to receive Visiting Ministers from the "non-permitted religions" of Scientology, the Nation of Islam or Rastafarianism.

No Visiting Ministers were employed by the Prison Service; most of them visited prisons in their spare time, receiving only modest fees and travel expenses in return. Only ten of the Visiting Ministers on the Prison Service Chaplaincy's list in 1995 were women, nine of whom were Buddhists. According to the Prison Service Chaplaincy's own records, Visiting Ministers numbered approximately 500 in 1995, but I have good reason to doubt the accuracy of this figure. Christian chaplains found it difficult to know precisely how many Visiting Ministers were actually carrying out their duties on a regular basis. In fact, Christian chaplains were often frustrated by the lack of formality and the lack of clearly representative organizations among other faith communities. The Prison Service Chaplaincy was no different from other agencies of the state in putting pressure on Muslims or Hindus, for example, to create fully representative formal organizations that could speak unequivocally for their communities. In effect, other faiths gained the impression that they would be tolerated in prison chaplaincy on condition that they behaved and organized themselves like Christian Churches. It is not surprising, then, that tensions existed between the state-supported Christian majority and other religious minorities in prison chaplaincy. At the same time, the pressure to adopt more formal and more representative structures created tension inside some of the minority communities.

There was an implicit understanding between the Church of England and those leaders of minority faith communities who gratefully accepted its patronage in their prison chaplaincy system that the representation of religion on prison committees would be left to the Anglican chaplains. In return for abandoning claims to equality of treatment or equality of opportunity to influence chaplaincy policies, minority faith communities could rely on Anglican chaplains to defend their interests and facilitate their access to prisoners. Pragmatism tended to take precedence over principles of equality. Not surprisingly, these pragmatic arrangements depended heavily on the goodwill of individual chaplains to act as brokers for minority faiths. Some chaplains performed the role of broker with reluctance, whereas others willingly accepted the professional obligation to facilitate religious support for all prisoners without regard for their religious identity or lack of it.

RESISTANCE TO BROKERAGE

Not all members of minority faith communities were content, however, to remain dependent on the patronage, protection and goodwill of the Church of England. Some radical leaders of Buddhists, Muslims and Sikhs, for example, challenged the universalist claims of Anglican chaplains to have a legitimate mission to all prisoners who sought their support. These dissenters rejected Anglican universalism and asserted claims to equality of rights. Despite official moves to encourage dialogue between Prison Service Chaplaincy officials and the leaders of other faith communities, some of the latter still pressed for the complete reorganization of the legal and administrative framework for prison chaplaincy. In March 1996, Buddhist, Muslim and Sikh leaders presented a paper to the Secretary of State at the Home Office contending that "the central role of one particular religious denomination in the prison system is unacceptable in a multi-faith society, and ... that in the future when legislation is brought forward, it must ensure that all religions are treated equally".[4] Their aim was nothing less than the abolition of the special privileges enjoyed by Church of England chaplains in prison chaplaincy. The Commission on

British Muslims and Islamophobia (2001: 16) subsequently agreed that the reason for Muslims' scepticism about progress towards addressing the issue of religious diversity in prisons was "dependence on the discretion of individual chaplains, governors and Prison Officers". The main problem remained "structural inequality" of faith groups.

It may seem paradoxical that minorities could frame their case for equal rights in terms of their particularistic beliefs and practices, but the paradox dissolves when it is recognized that they were claiming the right of all minorities to practise their religion in their chosen manner. In this sense, particularism underlay universalism. After all, this was how sectarian movements such as Jehovah's Witnesses and Mormons had managed to contribute to the refinement of laws governing the freedom of religion in many countries since the late nineteenth century. Their position may have been strengthened by the Human Rights Act, which came into effect in 2000, and by a European Employment Directive (Council Directive 2000/78/EC) against discrimination in employment and vocational training on grounds of religion – among other things. The Employment Equality (Religion or Belief) Regulations 2003 came into effect in Great Britain in December 2003. This is an example of the impact that transnational human rights norms can have on domestic policies relating to the "management" of religious diversity (Soysal 1994).

Moreover, a Muslim member of the British House of Lords introduced a parliamentary debate on 28 October 1999 on proposed new legislation that, if enacted, would have made it a criminal offence to discriminate against a person on the grounds of religion. Lord Ahmed's view was that tolerance is an inadequate basis for the defence of religious freedom and for mutual respect among faith communities because it presumes that certain religions are inherently valuable whereas others are merely permitted by concession to operate. For this reason, I consider that tolerance and denominationalization (Riis in this volume) are weak forms of pluralism. In my view, they merely assert that only one religion, Church or state agency truly represents normality and that they alone have the power and authority to decide which other religions merit the concession of being allowed to function. Tolerance and denominationalization are not about mutual respect or equal opportunities: they are about the capacity of relatively powerful organizations to control their relatively weak competitors.

The struggle for control over the orientation of the Prison Service Chaplaincy of England and Wales was a further stage in the process whereby minorities challenged the taken-for-granted power and privilege of dominant Churches. The world of prisons is one of the relatively few areas of social life where historical links between the British state and dominant Churches remain strong. Ferrari's (1999) sceptical view about the widespread assumption that modern European states have no competence in matters of religion certainly applies to the case of Britain, despite the fact that it is not a *laïque* state:

> Depuis longtemps, l'Etat laïque a choisi de coopérer avec les communautés religieuses dans beaucoup de domaines, mais cette coopération est sélective; elle privilégie normalement les confessions religieuses plus nombreuses ou plus

anciennes et désavantage celles qui sont plus petites, plus récentes, plus éloignées des valeurs traditionellement acceptées dans la société. (Ferrari 1999, 370)

[For a long time, the secular State chose to cooperate with religious communities in many areas, but this cooperation is selective; it normally privileges the more numerous or older confessions and disadvantages those which are smaller, more recent, further away from the traditional values accepted by society.]

The situation in the Prison Service Chaplaincy of England and Wales began to change, however, in the late 1990s.

TOWARDS MULTI-FAITH CHAPLAINCY

The research on which this section is based took place between 2000 and 2004 as part of a project on the treatment of Muslim prisoners in France and England and Wales.[5] Extensive fieldwork was conducted in three English prisons for men, with less intensive observation in two women's prisons. Interviews were conducted with 68 prisoners and with 67 members of prison staff at local level and at the Prison Service Chaplaincy headquarters. In addition, six full-time Muslim chaplains were interviewed by telephone. The results of the comparison between France and Britain will appear in Beckford, Joly and Khosrokhavar (2005).

The first substantial move in the direction of re-orienting prison chaplaincy in England and Wales towards objectives that were not narrowly associated with mainstream Christianity came in 1999 with the appointment of the first Muslim Adviser to the Prison Service. The proposal was originally to ask a Muslim organization to second a staff member to the Prison Service at no cost to the public purse. After protest about the inequity of expecting Muslims to finance this post while Christian organizations were not expected to pay the costs of Christian chaplains, the Prison Service agreed to establish the post at the same grade as that of Assistant Chaplains General. As a member of the headquarters team, accountable to the Chaplain General, the Muslim Adviser came to fulfil several important functions. He provided authoritative advice to the Prison Service about the religious and pastoral needs of Muslim prisoners. It was also his responsibility to monitor the extent to which Muslim prisoners were able to fulfil their religious obligations. Furthermore, the Muslim Adviser was instrumental in liaising with Muslim organizations and in arranging training for Muslim Visiting Ministers. In short, the creation of this post was a practical, as well as a symbolic, demonstration that it was no longer acceptable that Muslims had to remain dependent on the brokerage provided by Christian chaplains. They were to have their own, direct input into chaplaincy policies and practices.

The second step towards multi-faith chaplaincy concerned the documentation provided about faith communities in prisons. The Prison Service Chaplaincy's *Directory and Guide on Religious Practices in HM Prisons*, which first appeared in 1988, had been compiled mainly by a Church of England Assistant Chaplain General. It was a compilation of the religious practices and requirements associated with the major faith communities. Subsequent editions of this well-received publication drew more on the advice of representatives from minority faith groups, but the publication in 2000 of the *Prison Service Order on Religion*[6] reflected a higher level of consultation concerning the contents. Leading representatives of faith groups had the opportunity to contribute towards the wording of sections about their particular requirements. Moreover, it was clearly envisaged that the process of revising PSO 4550 would be ongoing.

Third, it was also in the early 2000s that the Standing Consultation on Religion in Prison, which had been convened and chaired by the Chaplain General of the Prison Service, gave way to an Advisory Group on Religion in Prisons chaired by the Prison Service's Director of Regimes. It brought together not only representatives of various faith groups but also a prison Governor and members of the Prisoner Administration Group. In short, relations between the Prison Service Chaplaincy and faith groups other than the main Christian churches in England and Wales were being formalized in an administrative framework that was much wider than chaplaincy. A Working Group, chaired by the Head of the Prisoner Administration Group, also set about designing a more inclusive and even-handed vehicle for facilitating communication between the Prison Service Chaplaincy and all faith groups. The Advisory Group and the Working Group were, in turn, replaced in May 2003 by an entirely new body – the Chaplaincy Council. Some of the representatives of faith communities on the Council also serve as "faith advisers to the prison service" supplying "Religious Consultative Services", further strengthening the involvement of minority faith groups in such things as the selection and training of sessional chaplains. The Council holds up to six meetings a year. The Chaplain General chairs four of the meetings, and the others are chaired by the Director of Resettlement. Again, this arrangement signifies a more prominent role for minority faith communities and a re-positioning of chaplaincy issues in the context of wider concerns in the Prison Service with diversity, race equality and resettlement. One of the early fruits of the Council's work was the first ever national conference for 450 chaplains of all faith traditions in the autumn of 2003.

The fourth step towards multi-faith chaplaincy was the decision in 2001 to begin appointing full-time Muslim chaplains in certain prisons. At this writing, 17 of them are in post, and four further appointments are planned before the end of 2004. Full-time Muslim chaplains now enjoy the same terms and conditions of employment as their Christian counterparts; and they are required to perform the same statutory duties. In some establishments they also play a full part in the administration of chaplaincy business, with some of them representing chaplaincy on prison committees. However, the degree of their integration in the day-to-day affairs of prisons varies from prison to prison, thereby reflecting the reluctance of a relatively small proportion of Christian chaplains to accept them as professional peers. None of them has been appointed to the status of Area Co-Coordinating Chaplain yet, but in theory their career prospects are no different from those of Christian chaplains.

The final and crucial step in the process of re-orienting prison chaplaincy towards a multi-faith model was the appointment in July 2001 of a new Chaplain General. The terms and conditions of the appointment specified for the first time that the post holder would be expected to implement multi-faith policies. In the event, the new appointee was personally committed to multi-faith ideals; and he had already acquired considerable experience of putting such ideals into practice in one particular prison.

The shift towards multi-faith chaplaincy has not been without its problems, some of which were aggravated by the rapidity of the many changes that began at the end of the 1990s. For example, the appointment of a full-time Muslim Adviser to the Prison Service was widely welcomed but also gave rise to the accusation that the interests of other minority faith communities had been neglected – or sacrificed. There have also been tensions between the Muslim Adviser and a few Muslim organizations that did not always share his particular interpretation of his role. For his part, the Adviser sometimes regretted that Muslim communities did not give him the support that he needed. Moreover, the level of administrative support for the Muslim Adviser was considered by some parties to be too low to enable him to meet all his obligations fully. Finally, the lack of plans for the appointment of full-time chaplains representing faiths other than Christianity and Islam was regretted in some quarters. Overall, however, it seems as if the Prison Service Chaplaincy in England and Wales has made the transition towards multi-faith policies and practices without major difficulty, thereby reducing the salience of brokerage by Church of England chaplains.

CONCLUSION

Prisons are places where the interaction between persons from minority and majority populations can be observed with special clarity because prisons usually force prisoners to live in exceptionally close proximity to each other. The processes of residential, educational, economic, social and recreational segregation that tend to ghettoize minorities in the major cities of Britain are strong but relatively less powerful in prisons. Nevertheless, my evidence suggests that segregation along lines of religion and ethnicity is possibly even more categorical in prisons than outside. Boundaries between faith groups in prisons have great importance as markers of personal and collective identity. This applies both to pre-existing identities that can come into sharper focus in prison conditions and to new identities that can be learned, practised and intensified relatively easily in the particular circumstances of prison. In both cases, prison conditions create opportunities for experimentation with new expressions of old identities and with completely new forms of identity. Many prisoners also welcome the opportunity to symbolize their identity by means of rituals and other markers in order to signal their similarities to, and differences from, fellow inmates. For all these reasons, then, it is essential for prison authorities to treat religious and ethnic minorities even-handedly. The prisons of England

and Wales increasingly try to manage religious and ethnic diversity by involving all faith communities in institutionalized chaplaincy activities.

The adoption of multi-faith principles and practices as well as the integration of Muslim chaplains into the organizational framework of prison chaplaincy have helped to ensure that the level of satisfaction with the religious and pastoral provision made for Muslim prisoners has increased significantly since the end of the 1990s. The dissatisfactions that persist – about, for example, the quality or authenticity of halal food, the time to be spent with Muslim chaplains and the facilities available to religious minorities other than Christian and Muslim – are relative to prisoners' perception of what is provided for prisoners from other faith communities. In other words, the policy of catering specially for the needs of particular faith communities does not necessarily result in perceptions of complete equality and justice but it helps to forestall the development of the high levels of alienation observed among Muslim prisoners in other countries such as France (Khosrokhavar 2004).

Multi-faith chaplaincy, within a broader framework of commitments to the value of diversity, has gone some way towards managing the problems associated with religious and ethnic differences between prisoners in England and Wales. This approach to integration on the basis of communal identities is subject to various criticisms. Gerd Baumann (1999), for example, is critical of the tendency for multicultural and multi-faith policies to hypostatize difference and to fail to tackle racism directly. Other critics of the multi-faith approach would prefer to base equality on strictly individual rights that took no account of collective differences. The Prison Service Chaplaincy of England and Wales takes a more pragmatic view, however, of the need to acknowledge that collective differences are, de facto, integral to prisoners' identities and are therefore to be formally recognized and respected. The search for an even-handed way of achieving equal respect among faith communities in the prisons of England and Wales will continue. According to Furseth (2000), a similar policy of recognizing and implementing the rights of religious minorities to practise their faith in prisons and military establishments is also required in Norway. She acknowledges that such a policy may temporarily increase the risk that religious minorities may thereby become more controversial and more segmented from the rest of Norwegian society. Nevertheless, her conclusion, like mine, is that public policies that secure the rights of religious minorities are, on balance, likely to lead to respect for them.

The question of whether the Church of England's continuing dominance of prison chaplaincy is a suitable basis on which to seek equal respect remains open. It could be argued, for example, that a more democratic structure for prison chaplaincy would be better if it gave members of all faith groups an equal opportunity to compete for the positions of leadership at chaplaincy headquarters. This would also represent a step towards the further decoupling of statehood and national identity, thereby opening a productive space between political unity and cultural diversity.

NOTES

* This is an extensively modified version of an article published in 1999 (Beckford 1999). The reason for extensive modification is that major changes began to take place in the Prison Service of England and Wales soon after the article appeared. I have therefore chosen to write this chapter in such a way that it places the current response of prison chaplaincy towards religious diversity in its recent historical context.

1 The countries of England and Wales contain about 88 per cent of the UK's population. Since only a tiny percentage of the main religious minorities identified in Table 13.1 live in Scotland or Northern Ireland, it is safe to assume that their overall strength in England and Wales is likely to be even greater than in the UK as a whole.

2 The study of religious diversity in British prisons was conducted with Dr Sophie Gilliat between 1994 and 1997. Thanks are due to the Church of England and the Leverhulme Trust for their generous financial support. See Beckford and Gilliat, 1998.

3 Visiting Ministers were volunteers who conducted religious and pastoral activities with prisoners identified with religious groups other than mainstream Christian Churches. They were re-named "sessional chaplains" in 2003.

4 "Religion in the Prisons of England and Wales", discussion paper presented by Lord Avebury, the Venerable Khemadhammo Mahathera, Bashir Ebrahim-Khan and Indarjit Singh, House of Commons, 27 March 1996, text located at: <http://www.angulimala.org.uk/Religion%20in%20Prisons%20(Disc%20Paper).pdf>

5 The project on "Muslims in prison: a European challenge" was funded by the Economic and Social Research Council (award R000238528) and co-directed with Professor Danièle Joly.

6 HM Prison Service, PSO 4550.

REFERENCES

Baumann, G. (1999), *The Multicultural Riddle. Rethinking National, Ethnic, and Religious Identities* (London: Routledge)

Beckford, J. A. (1999), "The Management of Religious Diversity in England and Wales with Special Reference to Prison Chaplaincy", *International Journal on Multicultural Societies* 1:1, 55–66

———— (2003), *Social Theory and Religion* (Cambridge: Cambridge University Press)

Beckford, J. A. and Gilliat, S. (1998), *Religion in Prison. Equal Rites in a Multi-Faith Society* (Cambridge: Cambridge University Press)

Beckford, J. A., Joly, D. S. and Khosrokhavar, F. (2005), *Muslims in Prison: Challenge and Change in Britain and France* (Basingstoke: Palgrave)

Brierley, P. (2003/04), *UK Christian Handbook. Religious Trends* (London: Christian Research)

Commission on British Muslims and Islamophobia (1997), *Islamophobia: A Challenge for Us All* (London: Runnymede Trust)

Commission on British Muslims and Islamophobia (2001), *Addressing the Challenge of Islamophobia. Progress Report, 1999–2001* (London: Commission on British Muslims and Islamophobia)

Cooper, D. (2004), *Challenging Diversity. Rethinking Equality and the Value of Difference* (Cambridge: Cambridge University Press)

Ferrari, S. (1999), "Le droit européen en matière religieuse et ses conséquences pour les sectes", in F. Champion and M. Cohen (eds), *Sectes et Démocratie* (Paris: Seuil), 359–72

Furseth, I. (2000), "Religious Diversity in Prisons and in the Military: The Rights of Muslim Immigrants in Norwegian State Institutions", in *International Journal on Multicultural Societies* 2:1, 40–52

Genders, E. and Player, E. (1989), *Race Relations in Prison* (Oxford: Oxford University Press)

HM Prison Service (2000), *Prison Service Order on Religion*. PSO 4550 (London: HM Prison Service)

Khosrokhavar, F. (2004), *L'islam dans les prisons* (Paris: Balland)

Riis, O. (1999), "Modes of Religious Pluralism under Conditions of Globalisation", *International Journal on Multicultural Societies* 1:1, 20–34

Russell, D. (1979), "Religious Minorities in Prison", *Prison Service Journal* 35, 7–9

Soysal, Y. (1994), *Limits of Citizenship. Migrants and Postnational Membership in Europe* (Chicago: University of Chicago Press)

Wilson, B. R. (1995), "Religious Toleration, Pluralism and Privatization", *Kirchliche Zeitgeschichte* 8, 99–116

14 The Challenges of Religious Pluralism in Post-Soviet Russia

KATHY ROUSSELET

The rejection of forced secularization in Soviet Russia – the symbol no less of the liberalization and democratization process – gave rise, during the turning point of the 1980s, to the emergence of a certain ideology of pluralism, understood as the recognition of widespread religious diversity, the assertion of equality of status for the different religions, equal treatment for believers and atheists and, finally, unlimited freedom granted by the State to all religious organizations. This ideology was reflected in a tolerant attitude on the part of the Russian Orthodox Church – by far the largest in the country – towards other religions. This attitude has, however, proved short-lived. Inasmuch as the Orthodox Church has acquired increasing public prominence in recent years and the new law on freedom of conscience adopted in 1997 has considerably restricted the freedom to practise the so-called "non-traditional" religions, the question may well be asked how far it is still possible today to talk in terms of "religious pluralism". Fresh reports of persecutions of religious groups regularly reach the West. In addition to the refusals to register some communities there are cases of tax inspections and searches. Must we have recourse again to the "metaphor of the elastic" used by P. Chaunu to characterize the wide divergence between the Edict of Nantes and its revocation, namely the idea that a period of excessive liberalization is followed by an extremely restrictive religious policy?[1]

The State is confronted by a variety of problems bound up with the question of the management of religious diversity in Russia – how to redefine the separation of the Orthodox Church and the State, the position to be adopted vis-à-vis globalization and, finally, the political search for a national cement to bind together a highly atomized society. The Orthodox Church, whose voice is quite influential within the State apparatus, has also taken up a position on these questions, to which the new social doctrine of the Church published in August 2000 has provided some partial answers.

Aside from some arguable similarities with the development of religion in the West, the situation in Russia is quite distinct: the revival of the Russian Orthodox Church is taking place concomitantly with and against

283

the background of a search for a national idea on the part of the regime in power, a movement of desecularization understood as a process of religious change, and the lawful assertion of the freedom of the individual. The management of religious plurality, which should be viewed as underlined by Ole Riis (1999 and this volume) at three different levels, is bound up with the question of the definition of the individual and their place in the community – a community today conceived in terms of both the Soviet and the Orthodox heritage. The Russian Orthodox Church for its part preaches a religion of the community rather than of the individual and places the emphasis on tradition as opposed to freedom of conscience. The Orthodox Church recognizes only a dialogue of cultures based on the community. As for the Russian State, it fluctuates between several kinds of legitimation, reflecting the diverse facets of its heritage.

RELIGIOUS DIVERSITY AND SOCIAL CONFLICTS

Multinational diversity has led in Russia to the development of numerous religions: Christianity, Islam, Buddhism, Judaism, Shamanism, and so on. According to figures from the State Committee for Statistics, following an ethnic definition of religion, the percentage of those belonging to the Orthodox tradition within the Russian Federation has decreased over the last years; in 1999 they amounted to 88.95 per cent of the total population, while the figure for Muslims was 9 per cent, for Buddhists 0.6 per cent and for Jews 0.23 per cent.[2] Despite the recent migratory movements of certain Muslim peoples such as the Kazakhs, Kyrgyz and Turkmens towards their countries of origin, the percentage of Muslims significantly increased between 1959 (6.05 per cent) and 1999 (9 per cent) and demographers expect this trend to continue in the years to come.

Among the Christians in particular there is a long tradition of religious diversity resulting from the schisms within the Russian Orthodox Church (not only Raskol in the seventeenth century and the proliferation of Old Believer groups in the centuries that followed, but also the post-revolutionary schisms that gave rise, among other denominations, to the True Orthodox Church) and from the immigration of national groups, particularly in the eighteenth century. Some of these groups, notably the Germans of the Catholic or Lutheran confession and Polish Catholics, are today tending to disappear as a result of the opening up to the West and the associated emigration processes. In addition, communities stemming from foreign missions appeared in the second half of the nineteenth century – Baptists, Adventists, evangelical movements and so on – and flourished on Russian soil. Such movements were particularly active at the beginning of the 1920s. Finally, at the end of the 1980s, with the opening up of the frontiers and the development within a section of the Russian population – particularly in the large cities – of a Utopian vision of "Western normality", movements of Western origin, mainly American, evangelical groups (Rousselet 2004a) and also new religious movements (NRMs) established roots in the country. Catholicism also gained new followers, associating this faith with the development of the democracy to which they aspired and linking Orthodoxy with the Soviet past, but their numbers remain small. In general, as in the West, religious globalization, the quest for meaning in an age of uncertainty and the individualization of belief have accelerated the phenomenon of religious diversification. Since the 1970s, and particularly since the opening up of frontiers at the end of the 1980s, religious diversity is no longer related so much to ethnic diversity, but rather to the delegitimization of the majority Church.

However, this recent trend towards religious diversification should not be exaggerated. Official sources continuously speak of an increasing number of sects but the hazy definition of an NRM and of its members – should it include those who take part in the activities of the movement or only those who have requested information? – as well as the difficulty of gathering statistics, makes estimates from whatever source extremely questionable. Fear of the NRMs, propagated by some political institutions and by the hierarchy of the Orthodox Church, has led to an overstatement of the danger they represent. According to the Russian researcher Marat Shterin, at the end of the 1990s there would seem to be scarcely more than 40 000 active members and, if we add those belonging to the NRMs and charismatic churches long established in Russia, we would arrive at a figure of 300 000 persons, that is, 0.2 per cent of the population of the country. Most of the NRMs probably have no more than a few hundred members, perhaps even a few dozen members. M. Shterin cites as examples the Centre of the Mother of God, which had about 3500 members in 1997, the Movement of Vissarion with about 2000, while the Church for the Unification of World Christianity had about 1000 members in 1996. However, since 1995–1996 these various movements appear to have reached a certain ceiling, or have even declined (Shterin 2000).

As in the West, this expansion of religious belief has been accompanied by a strong sense of cultural allegiance to the Orthodox tradition, even if the attachment to the institution itself is weak (Rousselet 2000*a*). According to the results of a survey carried out in 2004 by the Levada Centre, while the percentage of those who state that they belong to the Orthodox Church is 56 per cent, church attendance itself is quite low: 6 per cent of those questioned attend church at least once per month, 18 per cent one or more times each year, 15 per cent even less often and 60 per cent not at all. Various ideas are intertwined, the assertion of individual freedom being associated with a strong sense of community and with efforts to anchor a sense of identity within a partly reinvented national tradition.

Public opinion appears to have evolved considerably in recent years. The ongoing socio-economic crisis has been accompanied by a narrowing of the sense of identity, by a recurrence of interest in Russian history and culture, the reappearance of anti-Semitism and stronger feelings of antagonism towards the West,[3] exacerbated by, among other reasons, the crisis in Kosovo. There has been an increasing hostility on the part of public opinion towards foreign religious groups. This trend is apparent in numerous surveys and is reflected, in particular, in the attitude adopted towards members of religious sects, even if macro-sociological research is unable to reflect the complexity of local circumstances, as analysed by various researchers. In response to the question "What attitude should be adopted towards the members of

Table 14.1   **What attitude should be adopted towards the members of religious sects? (%)**

Replies	1989	1994	1999
Ban such groups	4	6	14
Isolate them from society	6	12	23
Provide them with assistance	5	8	9
Leave them to their own devices	57	51	29

religious sects?", a survey carried out by the Russian Centre for the Study of Public Opinion[4] produced the replies shown in Table 14.1 above (Levada 1999, 13).

Micro-sociological research gives a slightly different picture. According to local surveys carried out by H. Heyno, K. Kääriäinen and M. Shterin in the Volga region, even where people sometimes react quite violently to the question concerning sects, they do not regard their presence as a real problem, in part no doubt because they are not interested in public affairs.

Multinational diversity could also lead to the outbreak of new, religious-based social conflicts. Post-Soviet Russia has inherited the consequences of the Stalinist nationalities policy, in particular the policy of artificially grouping together peoples from very diverse cultures and traditions. In the northern Caucasus the return to their former lands of some population groups "displaced" by Stalin during the Second World War has given rise to a high degree of tension with the new occupants, particularly since the rehabilitation of the "punished peoples" prescribed in the law of 26 April 1991 (Longuet-Marx 2000).

Several authors have noted an increase in "Islamophobia" in Russia (Malashenko, 1999),[5] encouraged by the increasing number of articles on Islamic fundamentalism in the Russian press. This Islamophobia has to be seen within the context of a long history of conflicts, in particular in Daghestan and Chechnya in the nineteenth century, although it also has more recent roots in the Soviet period when Islam was regarded as the most reactionary religion and in specific events such as the Iranian revolution, the war in Afghanistan, the conflict between Serbia and Bosnia and, above all, the two wars recently waged by the Russian Government in Chechnya. The growing number of Muslim refugees from the Caucasus in some regions of Russia, the terrorist attacks in the last years, and also the economic and social crisis have helped to create fearful attitudes towards people from the Caucasus. Recent years have also seen a growth of forms of racism against the Muslim population, as attested by public opinion surveys. Likewise, there has been an increase in acts of vandalism in Russian cemeteries in Chechnya.

With regard to the place of Islam in public life and the growth of fundamentalism in the Islamic republics of Russia, an American study carried out in 1993 in five of those republics drew attention to the variations arising from the presence, or otherwise, of the Sufi tradition: in Tatarstan, where it was absent, society was still very secularized, unlike the situation in Chechnya and Daghestan (Lehman 1997). That analysis is confirmed by more recent developments. Thus, in Daghestan, there has been a grassroots movement of re-Islamization and a radicalization of religious feelings stimulated by the economic and political crisis (Yemelianova 1999; Ware and Kisriev 2000). In the north Caucasus, alongside Sufism, the traditional form of the religion, there has been a growth of Wahhabism, a more radical form of Islam from the Middle East, which "seeks to transcend clan, tribal, ethnic and even national allegiances in an attempt to unify all the peoples of the Caucasus under the banner of religion" (Longuet-Marx 2000, 40). These groups are recruiting both from among the poor and also from among the young intellectuals who studied in the Middle East; as for the former intelligentsia, long influenced by the heritage of Soviet atheism (Siverceva 1999), it is able to acquire knowledge without passing through the traditional religious structures. But some analysts suggest that the development of Wahhabism in Chechnya cannot be explained by religious factors alone. In fact, these groups emerged during the war. Young people's motive to engage in fighting were not predominantly religious or ideological, and a lot of them would move from Islamic units to secular ones, and vice versa. They rather became Islamic to be permitted to join specific units. The expressions "wahhabi" or "integrist" therefore did not fit Chechen reality. These were labels which did not correspond to people's identities: thus, a Sufi leader could no less be an Islamic combatant (Comité Tchétchénie 2003, 36–37). To postulate links between Chechen fighting groups and al-Qaeda would also be much exaggerated, as funding mostly came from Russia rather than from the Middle-East or the Gulf region. In sum, religious conflicts, and Islamism in particular, could not be considered as immediate causes of a war which was decided elsewhere. However, the influence of Islamism would have grown with the conflict itself (Comité Tchétchénie 2003, 42). Nevertheless the Dubrovka theatre hostage-taking in October 2002, the crash of two flights in August 2004 and the Beslan catastrophe (North Ossetia) one month later have shown that the conflict is spreading far beyond Chechnya to the whole North Caucasus and other parts of Russia.

In Tatarstan, a survey carried out by Kääriäinen and Furman (2000)[6] shows that religious practice among the Tatars, as among the Orthodox Russians, is at a low level: 10 per cent go to the mosque more than once a month, 57 per cent have never read the Koran and 50 per cent do not follow the dietary rules. As regards the attitude of the Tatars towards other peoples, it is the Russians, Ukrainians and Belarusians who receive the highest percentage of positive responses, while the Chechens are at the bottom of the list with only 62 per cent of positive responses.[7] Moreover, among the Russians of Tatarstan 92 per cent have a positive attitude towards Islam, while the corresponding figure in relation to the Russians of Russia itself is 57 per cent. It would therefore seem that this region is not affected by religious conflict at the present time. However, Kääriäinen and Furman (2000, 233 et seq.) have found strong support among Tatars of the younger generation for the independence of Tatarstan, despite the fact that the attitude of young people towards the Russian population of Tatarstan is generally more positive than that of the older generations, and that the young people are, for example, more favourable to mixed marriages. While the Tatars of the older generation combine religious traditionalism with a certain degree of loyalty to the Russian State, the desire for independence on the part of the young is more closely linked to democratic values and the pursuit of freedom and legal equality. However, this desire for independence may give rise to the growth of Islamic fundamentalism, which is already apparent among a minority of Tatar youth.

In the regions where Muslims are in a minority, the situation is far from uniform. In those areas where there has been a high level of immigration of people fleeing the war in Chechnya, there is considerable tension and, in southern Russia, in the regions of Krasnodar, Stavropol and Rostov, there has been an increase in feelings of xenophobia towards peoples from the Caucasus (Vitkovskaâ and Malashenko, 1999), with the Cossack revival there also contributing to religious radicalization. On the other hand, in the *oblast* of Omsk, according to the study of V.B. Yashin (2001), there are no interreligious conflicts. The same is true for the region of Nizhni-Novgorod, which borders Tatarstan and has a very mixed population: Russians, Mordvins and Chuvash of Orthodox or pagan backgrounds, and also Muslim Tatars. A study carried out in 1995 by the Institute of Manuscripts and Old Books of the Volga region shows that most of the villages are ethnically constituted and that while the Chuvash have settled independently of any ethnic consideration it is rare to find Russo-Mordvinian villages or, even less so, Russo-Tatar villages. As for Russo-Tatar marriages, they would appear to be very much the exception. Nevertheless, ethnic conflicts appear to be virtually non-existent. While the religious practices on the confines of Orthodoxy and paganism among the Mordvins and Chuvash are apparently regarded with some suspicion, the Russians appear to show respect for the Tatars and their practices.[8]

STATE MANAGEMENT OF RELIGIOUS DIVERSITY – TOWARDS WHICH MODEL OF SECULARISM?

The State management of religious plurality is characterized by strong ambiguities. They are the result of the many different traditions existing in post-Soviet Russia, the development of the political system, conflicts between the political authorities, the place occupied by the Russian Orthodox Church in public life, and also the changes in political and religious attitudes. Behind the formal statements on the need to restore the Orthodox identity of Russia, the reality is more complex. According to some observers the war in the Balkans has destroyed any hope of turning Orthodoxy into a political ideology; it would appear that some believers have been shocked by the use of the Orthodox religion in propaganda against the West, though the desire to make use of it for political ends would seem to be mainly the work of new converts (Aleksandrov 1999).

It is no less the case that the trends in legislation are towards a "limited pluralism" as defined by A. Agadjanian (2001).

In the context of political globalization at the beginning of the decade, involving the total rejection of the Soviet regime and a search for universal values, "freedom of thought" emerged as a form of "emancipation from any all-embracing doctrine" – this definition, provided by J. Baubérot (1999) with regard to the freedom of thought characterizing French secularism, would seem appropriate to the situation at the time, even if what was essentially involved was a process of demarcation from Soviet thought. A new law on freedom of conscience, adopted in 1990, in line with international conventions, asserts freedom of conscience and religion as an inalienable right of the citizen, proclaims the equality of forms of religious belief and of the rejection of religion,[9] and clearly affirms the separation of Church and State; religious movements are granted the right to practise all religious activities and the procedure for registration which enables religious communities to acquire the status of a legal entity is very simple. This law has led to the growth of all kinds of religious activities, which have acquired a high social profile.[10]

However, since 1993 the Russian Orthodox Church has undertaken an effective lobbying campaign to have this law favourable to religious pluralism amended. It was initially in the regions that the movement towards the restriction of the rights of religious minorities emerged. Between 1993 and 1997 new laws on freedom of conscience were adopted in a third of the 89 regions of Russia, notably the regions of Kaliningrad, Tver, Tula, Kalmykiya, Riazan, Vologda, Kostroma, Tatarstan, Udmurtiya, Perm, Sverdlovsk, Khanty-Mansiysk, Tuva, Amur, Khabarovsk, Sakhalin, Yaroslavl, Ulyanovsk, Bashkiriya, Yamalo-Nenets, Buryatiya, Sakha-Yakutiya and Primoriye (Uzzell, 1997, 350 [note 1]). Moreover, laws may have existed even though they had not been made public. The definition of the so-called "traditional" religions, that is, those regarded as belonging to the Russian tradition, varied from place to place, so that, for example, in the region of Sverdlovsk Catholicism was included among them. The regions are not easily subject to international pressures on behalf of human rights and it is there, rather than at the centre, that political and economic compromises between political and religious authorities take place. It is very often the local hierarchy of the Orthodox Church that provides its expertise – not to say its permission – for the registration of any particular religious organization. As for the officials responsible for examining such cases, they are for the most part the same as those who previously worked in the Council for Religious Affairs during the Soviet period.

The situation is also evolving at the federal level. The 1997 law, drafted under pressure from the Russian Orthodox Church and against a background of geopolitical introversion, affirms in its preamble the "special role of Orthodoxy in the history of Russia". Several articles are contrary to international law and to the Russian Constitution,[11] in particular Article 8.5:

> The terms "Russia", "Russian" and their derivatives may be used in its official title by a centralized religious organization whose bodies have operated, on a legal basis, for at least 50 years from the time when the organization in question submitted a request for official registration to the registration authority.

This article reflects the equation of "Russian" with "Orthodox" which, as A. Agadjanian (2001) shows it, goes back a long way and forms part of an ancient debate on the identity of Russia. These are remnants of Soviet legislation, such as the specific treatment of "foreign religious organizations" and the obligation to register placed upon "religious organizations unable to produce a certificate attesting to their presence for at least 15 years on the territory in question"; they "may acquire legal personality provided that they are re-registered each year until they complete the stated period of 15 years" (Article 27.3). However, no body is obliged to issue certificates of 15 years' presence.

Since then, without any real change in the spirit of the law, legislation has tended towards greater conformity with the Constitution and there has been increasing flexibility and simplification in the application of such legislation. Vladimir Putin's accession to power has led to a strengthening of central authority. Several regional laws which were found to be anti-constitutional had to be brought into conformity with federal law.

But the legislation remains unstable. Drafts of a doctrine on Church–State relations were written in 2001–2002 by the General Department of the Ministry of Justice, the Department of Religions at the Academy of Public Service or the Russian parliament's Committee for Religious and Social Organizations. Some politicians such as Alexander Chuyev and Serguey Glazyev (Rodina Faction) proposed law drafts that would lead to a tighter collaboration between the State and the so-called traditional religious organizations. The Russian Orthodox Church also gave its own conception. Some regions adopted once again anti-missionary laws which limit the entry of preachers on their territory. That was the case of the Belgorod region in 2001, the Kursk one in June 2004; but these laws would not be systematically applied. On the contrary, there are regions where Catholic priests and nuns were denied entry in the region beyond any law (19). Some of them, such as the Irkutsk, Perm, Tambov, Udmurtia, Ekaterinburg and Samara ones, would renew the Soviet practice which consists in asking for the names, the age and the address of the members of religious organizations.

The federal law wasn't modified yet. But while the State recognizes religious pluralism, it gives some preference to the Orthodox Church which stands de facto as *primus inter pares*. As in other fields, the unclear implementation of law can satisfy both parties: it gives place to negotiation and informal relations.

The affirmation in law of the existence of a dominant religion has been accompanied by a concern with classifying the various religious groups and, in particular, with distinguishing the sects from other religious movements. Such a classification, which serves to articulate the policy of religious administration, has a long history which it may be worthwhile recalling. In the nineteenth century the whole question received passionate and one-sided treatment, whether by the Orthodox missionaries, who regarded the sects as heretical movements opposed to both Church and State or by the populists and Marxists, who saw such movements merely as forms of socio-economic protest. Even for a liberal such as A. S Prugavin, sects were a sign of the sickness of Russia (Prugavin, 1904). During the Soviet period the authors of both popular works and scientific studies very often divided religious groups, in a simplistic and dishonest fashion, into sects and churches, considering the sects to be more dangerous and harmful than the churches. In an arbitrary and contradictory manner they included within this term very different kinds of groups: Baptist and evangelical movements, the True Orthodox Church, religious monarchist groups and sometimes even movements of Old Believers. While such an approach was a source of embarrassment to some, since it was in contradiction with both the Soviet Constitution, which prescribed equal rights for religious groups, and with the Leninist principle of struggle against all kinds of religion without distinction, it was in line with the existing policy of the authorities towards the religious groups that refused to be registered; the principle of registration by the Council for Religious Affairs represented, in fact, a system of classification of the movements on the basis of their "harmful" character. There is no doubt that these former classifications still contribute today to the ways that the new religious movements, and indeed all religions, are seen. To the pre-revolutionary and Soviet criteria has now been added the criterion of tradition, which does no more than make explicit once again the former distinctions. On top of the distinction made between traditional and non-traditional religions has been superimposed the Soviet distinction between Russian and foreign religions as well as the distinction between religious groups having links with the State and those lying outside its control. The sect/church distinction strengthens this opposition. This trend has been accompanied by a conceptual approach similar to that observed in France. Thus if, as D. Hervieu-Léger has pointed out, the "Catholic model has proved to be extremely fruitful by providing the sole framework of reference on the basis of which the State itself has been able to construe the organization and the legal position of other religions" (Hervieu-Léger 1999, 94), the same can be said of Russia, where the relationship between the Orthodox Church and the State has provided a model for all relations between religious institutions and the State. This was particularly obvious during the Soviet period in the case of the Baptist-Evangelical Church, which was reorganized after the Second World War on a more centralized basis. All the so-called traditional religions need to be analysed from this point of view. On the other hand, the movements that do not submit to this kind of relationship are subject to discrimination, and it is not by chance that the schisms within the movements have mostly revolved around their own organization.

It would seem that the kind of tone and measures adopted with respect to the so-called "sectarian" groups during the Soviet period have resurfaced since the mid-1990s. Thus, in a document of the Ministry of the Interior dated 23 October 1996, more specifically, in a paragraph setting out measures to combat "organized crime", a number of "foreign sects" are considered to be undesirable as they could contribute to social disorder. This document, drawn up on the basis of contributions from the Ministry of the Interior, the Federal Security Service (FSB), the Ministry of Health, the Ministry of Social Welfare and the services of the Procurator General of the Russian Federation, contains references to the True Orthodox Church, Jehovah's Witnesses, the

Unification Church, the Church of Jesus Christ of Latter Day Saints, and the New Apostolic Church. These sects "are accused of being 'asocial', of rejecting constitutional obligations, of endangering the moral, psychological and physical health of citizens and of having attracted children into their ranks and broken up families". According to the document "the religious groups use humanitarian aid to attract into their ranks Russian citizens, particularly young people, and infiltrate educational, military and scientific institutions" (Dennen 1997). There are also accusations of espionage, which was the classic charge during the Soviet period.[12] In addition to the argument based on national identity – the True Orthodox Church being that much more vulnerable since it rejects, within Orthodoxy itself, the identification of the Russian Orthodox Church with Russia itself – there are two other political lines of argument used in the past: the need for the State to control religious movements and, a specifically Soviet argument, the "besieged citadel" argument based on a fear of the incursion of movements from abroad. Missionaries are still often seen as agents of imperialism and as the destroyers of national unity, particularly in the Caucasus, in the Far East and in the European frontier regions, such as Kaliningrad. More recently, a directive from the Ministry of National Education dating from summer 2000 repeated the same kind of accusation against 700 foreign religious groups, including the True Orthodox Church, the Jehovah's Witnesses and the Salvation Army and requested the principals of educational establishments to show the greatest vigilance against the risks of infiltration. This traditional perception of the so-called sectarian religious groups reflects a particular view of the relationship between the religious and political spheres and the continuing force of the model of the relationship between the dominant national church and the State.

Vladimir Putin has pursued a political project of both control and centralization. He has assimilated the administration of religious plurality to the task of strengthening the State, as is shown by the changes made in the concept of national security. While the 1997 text stressed the role of the Russian Orthodox Church in the defence of Russian spiritual values, in the new version of the concept of national security the "moral and spiritual education of the people" is seen as a matter of State policy. There is an increased control by the State over the activities of religious organizations and by the federal authorities over the subjects of the Federation. But it should be added that, in spite of an apparent strong power, the State does not seem to be capable of implementing its policy.

The activities of religious organizations are regulated by many public institutions in which the Russian Orthodox Church actually promotes its own interests: the Russian government's Commission for Religious Associations, Russian parliament's Committee for Religious and Social Organizations, coordination organizations inside some ministries such as those of Education, of Justice, of Interior or of Defense. At the regional level, the institutions, which also became numerous, are influenced by local Orthodox hierarchs. In order to control the relations between the political authorities and the religious organizations, some advocate the creation of a unique organ. Whereas the Russian Orthodox Church fears the reappearance of the Council for Religious Affairs which would limit its influence, some religious minorities support the idea, as this organ could prevent the arbitrary decisions of local authorities.

The attitude towards Muslim communities is no doubt one of the most difficult problems which the Russian State has to cope with. As F. Daucé (2001) has pointed out, there is real Islamophobia among the ruling classes. Yet there has grown up alongside this a whole ideological discourse – itself rooted in a Eurasian consciousness and propagated mainly by theoreticians of the conservative revolution or of national communism – on the alliance within Russian borders of the Orthodox and Turco-Muslim worlds. One of the current government objectives is to ban the radical movements originating in Kuwait and Saudi Arabia and regarded by some as agents of the United States, to limit the development of competing Islamic organizations and to favour those deemed to be loyal to the present government. Religious extremism is now identified with Islamic terrorism; the hostage-takings and the Beslan catastrophe provoked new waves of Islamophobia. But the actions against religious extremism — which is quite difficult to define— are often inadequate. Some mosques were closed and it becomes more and more difficult for a Muslim community to become registered. In 2004 in the Stavropol region only 8 out of 47 demands were accepted as the other ones were rejected under the pretext that some of their members would have taken part in the war. In spite of discourses on multiethnicity and multiconfessionalism, the battle against extremism easily becomes an alibi against Islam in general.

Religious pluralism is essentially used as a political resource. The Russian President continues Soviet policies, unifying different traditional movements in order to defend the State against a foreign enemy. In his declared battle against Islamic terrorism he chaired the presidential Council for Co-operation with Religious Organizations on 29 October 2004 for the first time, a council gathering 16 representatives of recognized religious organizations, political authorities and specialists of religion. The enemy could soon have another face. Russia could oppose universalism of values and political liberalism, and religion could once again be requested. Generally speaking, it seems that Vladimir Putin appeals to religion as a political resource in his foreign policy (Rousselet 2004b). The discourse held by the Russian Orthodox Church on the cohabitation of civilizations is closely akin with the one of the State about multipolarity. By stressing categories such as civilization and tradition, it conveys a vision of the international order based on inter-State relations, just on the contrary to the transnational evangelical religion, which is more diffuse and which comes from the United States (Decherf 2002). Thus religious pluralism which in Russia means the harmonious coexistence of traditions could be opposed to globalization and universalism.

The "laïcité à la russe" evolves in a post-atheistic context. Secularization of the Russian society and atheism in public institutions are important phenomena; they explain why the management of religious pluralism is so ambiguous, especially in the army and in education institutions. With respect to the army (Daucé 2001), both traditional and legal-rational forms of legitimacy are sought; at the same time, the desire to gain new support for the army from the Orthodox Church contrasts with the sociological reality of an institution with a low percentage of believers and with a long-standing tradition of atheism. As in the rest of the population, the percentage of believers tended to diminish within the armed forces in 1998–99 and the feeling of institutional allegiance is still quite weak. According to a study carried out by the army there are tensions between Orthodox Christians, Christians of other denominations and Muslims, and also between believers and non-believers, while the participation of Orthodox priests in public ceremonies and events and the blessing of military equipment helps to exacerbate such tensions.[13] The two wars in Chechnya have complicated the situation still further. The policy of the State and of the military high command fluctuates between the use of religious allusions to mobilize the Russian people, the resort to legalistic language, and an alliance with the moderate Islamic authorities against Islamic fundamentalism. However, the official positions taken by the political authorities and the Orthodox hierarchy do not give a full picture of the situation. Agreements signed at the higher level are not always applied and depend on micro-sociological factors, such as the particular religious beliefs – if any – of the head of the local military administration or the presence of trained religious personnel. While the Russian Orthodox Church conceives its action within society through its relationship with the State, as do all the so-called traditional religions that have adopted the model of the dominant church, the other religions have a less institutionalized relationship with political authority. As opposed to the official strategies of the one, the others rely on grass-roots strategies. Although public life is dominated by the agreements between the Russian Orthodox Church and the State, and although there are obviously cases of flagrant discrimination against some religious movements, that does not mean that the non-traditional religions cannot occupy a place in the public arena. However, the agreements are principally made on the basis of personal relations.[14]

With respect to religious education, the situation depends much on regional contexts. The attitude of the Federation towards the course on the bases of Orthodox Culture has changed a few times in the last years; in the secondary schools it was hindered by parents and teachers still influenced by Soviet values. Another book which deals with all world religions has been written. Some regions such as the Moscow and the Leningrad ones replaced the course on Orthodox culture by another one focused on history of religions (N. Mitrokhin 2005).

RELIGION, COMMUNITY AND TERRITORY

In view of the importance of the Orthodox Church and its role in public life, its position regarding the administration of religious plurality should not be ignored. In the new social doctrine adopted in August 2000 by the Synod of Bishops, it expressed its views on both the question of the nation and the question of secularism and freedom of conscience. It should, however, be noted that this doctrine is an officially sponsored text drawn up within the department for external relations of the Patriarchate of Moscow, being more of a compromise between different tendencies within the hierarchy than a real social doctrine fully responding to the challenges to the Russian Orthodox Church posed by the modern world. In many respects the document is extremely ambiguous, in particular as regards the relationship between the Church and the State. It is true that the new doctrine takes account of the secularization of the country, but, while affirming the separation of Church and State and accepting the resort to civil disobedience (which breaks definitively with the principle of harmony and which appears to be a response to the Declaration of Sergius), it calls for collaboration between Church and State (see Calvez 2001).

Close historical links, dating back to the very origins of Christianity in Russia, unite the Orthodox Church and the nation (Agadjanian 2001). The document of August 2000 reaffirms to some extent the idea of the Church of the majority as the "soul of the nation". While the question of the multiculturalism of the Russian State is passed over in silence – the Church ignoring the problem of its position within a plurinational and pluridenominational context – and while the concept of "universal values" so often proclaimed at the end of the 1980s and the beginning of the 1990s has disappeared, the concept of "Christian patriotism" has appeared. This is linked to the theological approach to the community within Orthodoxy, which has precedence over the rights of the individual; and this priority given to the community explains the difficult relationship that the Russian Orthodox Church has with the Western churches, including the Catholic Church.[15] The reaffirmation of the Orthodox nation is also linked with the difficulty that Russia has had in "reinventing" itself after the collapse of the Soviet Union. The affirmation, in the preamble to the 1997 Law, of the "special role of Orthodoxy in the history of Russia" is explained by the problematic distinction between Russian citizenship and Russian nationality.

The religion of the community is conceived as being very closely linked with the national territory, the symbol of both its universality and its national roots. Confronted by globalization the Orthodox Church seeks to defend what it calls its "canonical territory", referring in particular to the Epistle of Paul the Apostle to the Romans 15, 20–21:

> It is my ambition to bring the gospel to places where the very name of Christ has not been heard, for I do not want to build on another man's foundation; but as Scripture says, *They who had no news of him shall see, And they who never heard of him shall understand.*

On more than one occasion, Cyril of Smolensk, the head of the department for external relations of the Patriarchate of Moscow, has defended the principle of a "local church" with full responsibility for Christians in a particular place. A number of different concepts are involved in the opposition to the foreign missionaries on Russian territory, theological factors undoubtedly coming after other grievances of both an economic and political nature and drawing on older attitudes from the Soviet and even the pre-revolutionary periods (Rousselet 2001, 2004b).

The Russian Orthodox Church's deep roots in the community, territory and nation must be seen in relation to its attitude towards tradition, a tradition envisaged as inviolable. Religious traditionalism is linked to a conception of multiculturalism as a "symphony of cultures", as the conservation and juxtaposition of religious and community traditions, as opposed to Western neoliberalism, to a process of globalization leading to cultural uniformity, and to international standards centred on human rights. In the document on social doctrine the Russian Orthodox Church emphasizes that it is ready to cooperate with the traditional denominations and is strongly opposed to proselytism. It adds:

> 6.3. The Orthodox Church makes a distinction between the Christian denominations that proclaim their belief in the Trinity and in the divinity and humanity of Christ and the sects that reject the basic Christian dogmas. It recognizes the right of Christians of other denominations to bear witness and to provide religious education for those population groups that are traditionally attached to them, and it is opposed to all missionary activity by the sects.

The question of the rule of law and of human rights is not broached in the social doctrine proclaimed in August 2000 and there is some confusion – which is long-standing – between law and morality (Novik 2000, 260). As for freedom of conscience it is only seen in negative terms, as a principle enabling the State to survive in a "de-Christianized" environment:

> The promulgation of the principle of freedom of conscience is proof of the decline of the system of spiritual values and the loss of commitment to the salvation of the major part of society ... The affirmation of freedom of conscience as a legal principle proves that society has lost its religious aims and values. Such an affirmation is the result of massive apostasy and of an obvious misunderstanding of the mission of the Church, which is to combat sin.

As an Orthodox observer from Saint Petersburg, Dimitri Kratov, has pointed out, "in the Russian Orthodox Church, freedom of conscience has always been affirmed as coming from Christ himself". Thus, what the Synod of Bishops opposes would appear to be not so much freedom of conscience itself but freedom of conscience as a constitutional principle. It is also clear from an examination of the history of pre-revolutionary Russia that it was the minority religious groups, the Baptists and evangelical Christians, and not the Russian Orthodox Church, who called for freedom of conscience in the nineteenth century.[16]

CONCLUSION

The federal law of 1997, together with the agreements between the Russian Orthodox Church and the Federal Government regarding the army, education, culture, health and prison welfare, the establishment of close relations between the Church and the State concerning the return of property and of places of worship, and the construction of churches from public funds, reveal the existence of a new state of affairs whereby the Orthodox Church has acquired a major political role. Paradoxically, with the rejection of the Soviet system, the affirmation of freedom of thought is less and less marked, and it would seem that there has been a transition from militant atheism to a world where there is less and less place for the non-believer.

However, apart from the need to take into account the precarious balance of forces of a country whose legislation is in the process of being drafted and subject to frequent amendments, other factors complicate the overall picture. More than before even, the question of pluralism must be approached from a regional perspective. We have seen how some regional laws on religious matters were inconsistent with the federal law, how the management of religious plurality depended to a large extent on the relations between the political and religious authorities, and how, in some regions, the local Orthodox hierarchy acted as advisers to the local authorities and had a say in decisions regarding the registration of religious organizations. The management of religious plurality also sometimes operates, as the example of Omsk shows (Yashin 2001), against a background of conflicts between different administrative authorities within the same region, and the diversity of the structures responsible for the administration of religious groups has contributed to conflicts over jurisdiction and to an often ambiguous policy.

Secularism in Russia is adversely affected by two problems: the problem of the management of the Muslim communities, in particular against the background of the war with Chechnya, and the problem of the attitude to be adopted towards the new religious movements and, in general terms, towards the religious organizations of non-Russian origin that have developed in the wake of globalization. The evolution of this model of secularism, the relations between the Russian State and the Russian Orthodox Church, and the place that the latter should occupy in a religious context that is becoming increasingly diverse on account of globalization have been made difficult by the coexistence of several different traditions, which are clearly emphasized in the document on the social doctrine of the Orthodox Church: the heritage of the Byzantine "symphony", the historical relationship between the Russian Orthodox Church and the State in the nineteenth century and, finally, the atheism of the Soviet period. The different strands in the history of the relationship between the Orthodox Church and the State should help to throw light on the ambiguity of their current relationship. An additional factor is the very diversity of the models that Russia could follow. Finally, the positions taken by the various political and religious authorities and the political leaders are extremely diverse and a consensus is difficult to achieve.

Post-Soviet Russia has experienced several different forms of religious pluralism, resulting in the current rather confused state of affairs. "Pluralism-emancipation", as defined by F. Champion (1999), paradoxically has its origin in the Soviet heritage, with the religious revival being transplanted into an atheist soil. It would seem to be a response to the largely secularized state of Russian society, as well as to the need to affirm freedom of thought. Pluralism-emancipation also corresponds to the political affirmation of universal values and to the desire to enter the global civilization. But against the background of a growing ethnicization of Orthodox religion over the last decade (even if this trend has been fairly apparent since the Second World War, the survival of the Russian Orthodox Church at the time having been largely due to its patriotism and to its close links with Russian national history), this trend towards pluralism-emancipation is on the decline, and this decline is epitomized by the condemnation of all forms of atheism and the attacks on the new religious movements. Consequently, it is quite possible to talk of the re-emergence of a "limited pluralism" (Agadjanian 2001), which has its origin in a long historical tradition. There is also a pluralism of identities and communities, recognized by the Russian State and the Russian Orthodox Church, even though the superiority of the Russian nation is affirmed and the interests of the State prevail over the recognition of particular interests. This tension between the standardizing tendencies of the State and the need to take into account an acknowledged religious diversity, particularly apparent in the army and in education, is not at all peculiar to Russia and, in fact, all modern States appear to be confronted by this difficulty.

In Russia, the existence of pluralism, as guaranteed under the law, is accompanied by the affirmation of the power of the Orthodox religion to confer legitimacy upon the State; in this way, modern and traditional ways of thought appear to confront one another. Religious pluralism of the Western kind, which tried to establish itself in Russia at the beginning of the 1990s, has its roots in a particular definition of religion that presupposes the separation of the temporal and spiritual realms (see contribution of F. Champion 1999). However, as is clear from the basic principles of the social doctrine of the Russian Orthodox Church as expounded in August 2000, the Russian Orthodox religion sees the relationship between the spiritual and the temporal spheres in a different way. As against the legal definition inspired by the West, the Russian Orthodox Church puts forward another definition, which makes no distinction between the religious community and the ethnic community.

These different contradictions all relate to a central issue. Just as in the West, the administration of religious plurality depends on the identity that the different institutions involved accord to their country: is Russian society a principally Orthodox society, a secularized society or a pluri-religious society? The answer to the question, while it may be scientifically resolved, depends more generally on the political evolution of the country. It varies, more perhaps than elsewhere, in response to local factors. The ideological line of the central government, which is already multiform, and the ideas propagated by the media have to coexist at the local level with practices that often deviate significantly from the central policies. Under the impact, among other factors, of globalization – even if its formal legal effect is one of standardization – it is the local level, in Russia at least, which is the most relevant for the analysis of religious pluralism.

Finally, the Russian management of religious plurality provides an opportunity to extend the debate initiated by S. N. Eisenstadt (2000 and this volume) on the question of a "clash of civilizations", which could sound the death knell of modernity. The Russian Orthodox Church, by opposing certain religious groups, also opposes the process of globalization, which is seen as a process of hegemonic universalism controlled by the West and, in particular, the United States; it defends largely traditional values and indeed has difficulties in seeing itself within a context of Western modernity. However, the position of the Russian Orthodox Church cannot be reduced to this logic of confrontation. Thus, it is not so much in terms of a clash of civilizations that Metropolitan Cyril of Smolensk sees the relationship with the West as in terms of a juxtaposition of cultures, Europe being above all else the meeting place of traditions and cultures. The idea of a clash of civilizations seems even more inappropriate since the religious diversity that exists is recognized by the various religious groups, including the Russian Orthodox Church; plurality thus lies at the very heart of Russian civilization. However, this recognized plurality is seen within the context of tradition; the plurality resulting from globalization and modernity is criticized by the religious movements that have existed within the Russian religious environment for several centuries. And in fact, the opposition of these different movements, whether it be the Russian Orthodox Church or Muslim spiritual leaders, is focused not so much on religious plurality as on the loss of territory and the disappearance of frontiers.

NOTES

1   Chaunu, P. (1986), "La décision royale", in *La Révocation de l'édit de Nantes et le protestantisme français en 1685* (Paris: SHPF), 13–30; quoted by Baubérot 1999, 318.

2   Tul'skij, M. "Prognoz demografov", *Nezavisimaja Gazeta-Religii*, 27 September 2000.

3   The attitude towards the West nevertheless remains extremely ambiguous. While the language of confrontation seems to be increasingly marked and patriotism is accompanied by a nostalgia for Russia as a great power, the popularity of this idea does not, however, mean that citizens are ready to support their country and sacrifice themselves for its defence. Furthermore, the anti-Western views are very abstract and are distinct from the feelings expressed towards the Western peoples themselves. The attitude towards the United States of America is ambivalent. In 1998 the United States was the first on the list of countries regarded as enemies of Russia, and in second position on the list of friends. Whatever their sympathies and antipathies, many young people wish to leave Russia for – in order of preference – the United States, Germany, Great Britain or France. See Gudkov (1999, 45–46) and Zdravomyslov (1998, 46).

4   The surveys were carried out by the Russian Centre for the Study of Public Opinion in November 1989 among 1325 people, in November 1994 among 2957 people, and in March 1999 among 2000 people. The 1989 survey was carried out on the basis of a representative sample of the population of the whole of the Soviet Union, but only the results for Russia have been taken into account here. The percentage of "don't knows" is not mentioned.

5   This includes a growing number of incidents concerning the construction of mosques (*Islam v SNG* 1998, 161).

6   This survey was carried out in 1999 among 618 people, 274 of whom were Tatars.

7   The Chechens are only regarded in a positive light by 49 per cent of the Russian population of Tatarstan. This figure is, however, a cause for some surprise and gives rise to some doubts as to the reliability of the replies given by the interviewees.
8   See the archives of the Institute. The researchers, carrying out qualitative research, emphasize certain incidents, such as the construction of an Orthodox chapel by a Tatar, who was the former head of a collective farm, or the hostile attitude of villagers towards an Orthodox priest who was emphasizing the danger of Islamic expansionism.
9   There has been an increase in the number of round tables where believers and convinced atheists seek together to find the way towards "universal values".
10 For the other laws that govern the relationship between religious movements and the State in more specific fields, see Shterin, 2000*a*.
11 See the conclusions of the experts at the meeting of the Assembly for Human Rights on 23 September 1997 (*Messager ecclésial et social* n°24, supplement to *Russkaja Mysl'*, 21 October 1997; translated in *Istina*, 4, 1997, pp. 412–414).
12 This document also states: "Using religion as a cover, the foreign representatives of the above-mentioned organizations establish networks that enable them to gather sociopolitical, economic, military and other information on the processes that determine Russia's strategic position."
13 Survey carried out by L. V. Peven and V. M. Gruzdev, cited by F. Daucé; see also "Vo čto verjat soldaty?" [What do the soldiers believe in?], *Nezavisimaja Gazeta-Religii*, 23 February 2000.
14 Thus, albeit in another field, a Catholic parish particularly active in Vladivostock has established a close relationship with local women's prisons and one of the parishioners has been appointed to the Board of Patronage of one of them. It is a fact that the financial resources that some religious movements possess help to give them a place in public life.
15 The document signed in 1993 at Balamand between Catholics and Orthodox clearly showed how some Western positions, permeated by the so-called universal values of freedom of conscience, could offend the Orthodox who are less concerned by the rights of the individual than the rights of the community and tradition. Thus, in the final text of Rule No. 27 the phrase concerning "the right of each person to join the religion of his choice" was deleted and the following phrase was added: "it is for the leaders of the communities to assist their members to deepen their loyalty towards their own church and towards its tradition ..." ("Déclaration de Balamand", *Istina* 4, 1993, p. 391. See also "Une appréciation orthodoxe-catholique commune sur la Déclaration de Balamand. Consultation orthodoxe-catholique des Etats-Unis", *Istina* 1, 1996, pp. 35–40).
16 *Russkaja Mysl'*, 7 September 2000, translated in *Istina* 45:3, 2000, pp. 302–303. Nowadays the main defendants of freedom of thought and freedom of conscience are Protestants and those persons who had worked in a militant atheist context in the Soviet period.

BIBLIOGRAPHY

Agadjanian, A. (2001), "Pluralism and National Identity in Russia", *International Journal on Multicultural Societies* 2:2, 79–106
Aleksandrov, V. (1999), "Prepjatstvija služeniû i nesbyvšiesja nadeždy. O social'noj roli pravoslavija v sovremennoj Rossii" [The obstacles to service and disappointed hopes. The social role of Orthodoxy in contemporary Russia]. *Nezavisimaja Gazeta* 21:44, 10 November

Baubérot, J. (1999), "Laïcités, sectes, société", in F. Champion and M. Cohen (eds), *Sectes et démocratie* (Paris: Seuil), 314–330

Calvez, J. Y. (2001), "Une doctrine sociale de l'orthodoxie russe", *Etudes*, avril, 511–520

Champion, F. (1999), "The diversity of religious pluralism", *International Journal on Multicultural Societies* 1:2, 43–57

Comite Tchétchénie (2003), *Tchétchénie. Dix clés pour comprendre* (Paris : La Découverte)

Daucé, F. (2001), "The Military and Religious Pluralism in Russia", *International Journal on Multicultural Societies* 2:2, 107–129

Decherf, D. (2002), "Les Etats-Unis au secours des 'droits de l'homme religieux'", *Critique Internationale* 15:avril, 14–24

Dennen, X. (1997), "Les mesures prises en Russie à l'encontre de la 'Vraie Eglise orthodoxe'", *Istina* 42:4, 352–356

Dubin, B. (1997), "Religija, cerkov', obščestvennoe mnenie" [Religion, church, public opinion], *Svobodnaja Mysl'* November, 94–103

Eisenstadt, S. N. (2000), "The Resurgence of Religious Movements in Processes of Globalisation – Beyond End of History or Clash of Civilisations", *International Journal on Multicultural Societies* 2:1, 5–16

Gudkov, L. (1999), "Rossija v rjadu drugih stran: k probleme nacional'noj identičnosti" [Russia among other countries: the problem of national identity], *Monitoring obščestvennogo mnenija: èkonomičeskie i social'nye peremeny* 1:41, 39–47

Hervieu-Léger, D. (1999), "Prolifération américaine, sécheresse française", in F. Champion and M. Cohen (eds), *Sectes et démocratie* (Paris: Seuil), 86–102

Islam v SNG [Islam in the CIS] (1998) (Moscow: Institut Vostokovedenija RAN)

Kääriäinen, K. and Furman, D. (2000), "Tatary i russkie – verujuščie i neverujuščie, starye i molodye" [Tatars and Russians – believers and non-believers, old and young], in K. Kääriäinen and D. Furman (eds), *Starye cerkvi, novye verujuščie. Religija v massovom soznanii postsovetskoj Rossii* [Old churches, new believers. Religion in the mass consciousness of post-Soviet Russia] (Moscow-Saint Petersburg: Letnij sad), 209–236

Lehmann, S. G. (1997), "Islam and ethnicity in the Republics of Russia", *Post-Soviet Affairs* 13:1, 78–103

Le Huérou, A., Merlin, A., Regamey, A., Serrano, S. (2005), *Tchétchénie, une affaire intérieure? Russes et Tchétchènes dans l'étau de la guerre* (Paris, Autrement-CERI)

Levada, Ju. (1999), "'Čelovek sovetskij' desjat' let spustja: 1989–1999 (predvaritel'nye itogi sravnitel'nogo issledovenija)" [Soviet man ten years later: 1989–1999 (preliminary conclusions of a comparative study)], *Monitoring obščestvennogo mnenija: èkonomičeskie i social'nye peremeny* 3 :41, 7–15

Longuet-Marx, F. (2000), "Les sociétés du Nord-Caucase. Ethnies, conflits et traditions", *Le courrier des pays de l'Est* 1009 (October), 36–41

Lotkin, I. (1998), *Ethnological Monitoring: Omsk Region, Russian Federation* (Moscow) <http://www.unesco.org/most/monitor.htm> (in Russian)

Malašenko, A. V. (1999), "Islam v Rossii" [Islam in Russia], *Svobodnaja mysl'* 10 (1488), 44–50

Mitrohin, N. (2005), "Religija i obrazovanie v Rossii", *International Journal on Multicultural Societies* 2:3, 44–71

Novik, V. (2000), "Examen critique de quelques aspects du 'Document social' publié par le Synode de Moscou", *Istina* 45:3, 255–263

Prugavin, A. S. (1904), *Religioznye otščepency (Očerki sovremennogo sektantstva)* [Religious renegades (Aspects of contemporary sectarianism)] (Saint Petersburg: Obščestvennaja Pol'za)

"Recenser la Russie en 2002" (2003), Numéro spécial de la *Revue d'Etudes comparatives Est-Ouest* 34:4

Riis, O. (1999), "Modes of Religious Pluralism under Conditions of Globalisation", *International Journal on Multicultural Societies* 1:1, 20–34

Rousselet, K. (2000*a*), "L'orthodoxie russe entre patriotisme et individualisme", *Vingtième siècle-Revue d'histoire* 66 (April–June): 13–24

_____ (2000*b*), "La société russe et les conséquences de l'insécurité", *Revue internationale et stratégique* Summer, 101–111

_____ (2001), "Globalisation et territoire religieux en Russie", in J. P. Bastian, F. Champion and K. Rousselet (eds), *La globalisation du religieux*, Paris: L'Harmattan, 183–196

_____ (2004*a*), "La diversité évangélique en Russie: de la mission étrangère à la surenchère nationale". *Critique internationale* 22 (January): 125–138

_____ (2004*b*), "L'Eglise orthodoxe russe et le territoire". *Revue d'Etudes comparatives Est-Ouest* 35(4): 149–171

Siverceva, T. (1999), "Daghestan: the quest for national identity". *Central Asian Survey* 18(3): 359–372

Šterin, M. (2000*a*), "Novye religioznye dviženija v Rossii 1990-h godov" [New religious movements in Russia in the 1990s], in K. Kääriäinen and D. Furman, eds, *Starye cerkvi, novye verujuščie. Religija v massovom soznanii postsovetskoj Rossii* [Old churches, new believers. Religion in the mass consciousness of post-Soviet Russia], Moscow-Saint Petersburg: Letnij sad, 150–181

_____ (2000*b*), "Vzaimootnošenija meždu cerkov'ju i gosudarstvom i religioznoe zakonodatel'stvo v Rossii v 1990-e gody" [Relations between Church and State and religious legislation in Russia in the 1990s], in K. Kääriäinen and D. Furman, eds, *Starye cerkvi, novye verujuščie. Religija v massovom soznanii postsovetskoj Rossii* [Old churches, new believers. Religion in the mass consciousness of post-Soviet Russia], Moscow-Saint Petersburg: Letnij sad, 182–208

Uzzell, L. (1997), "Les restrictions aux droits des Minorities religieuses au sein de la Fédération de Russie". *Istina*, 42(4): 349–351

Vitkovskaja, G. and Malašenko, A. (eds) (1999), *Neterpimost'v Rossii: starye i novye fobii* [Intolerance in Russia: old and new phobias]. Moscow: Moskovskij Centr Carnegie

Voroncova, L. M. and Filatov, S. B. (1998), "Tatarstanskoe evrazijstvo: evroislam pljus evropravoslavie" [Tatar eurasianism: euro-islam and euro-orthodoxy], *Družba narodov* 8, 130–139

Ware, R. B. and Kisriev, E. (2000), "The Islamic factor in Daghestan". *Central Asian Survey* 19 (2): 235–252

Yashin, V. B. (2001), "The Military and Religious Diversity in Present-Day Russia: the Omsk Model". *International Journal on Multicultural Societies* 2(2): 107–127

Yemelianova, G. M. (1999), "Islam and nation building in Tatarstan and Daghestan of the Russian Federation". *Nationalities Papers* 27(4): 605–630

Zdravomyslov, A. (1998), "Kto my: 'nacionaly' ili 'graždane'?" [Who are we: 'nationals' or 'citizens'?]. *Monitoring obščestvennogo mnenija: èkonomičeskie i social'nye peremeny* 2(34): 44–47

Index

African languages, orthographies, lack 227
Albanian 142, 149, 153
Alevi Muslims 103, 104, 107
Anglo-Boer War (1899–1902) 189
assimilation 38, 102, 129, 182, 217, 223, 225, 241, 263
Australia
  multiculturalism 5
  National Language Policy 225

Baltic States
  diglossia 167
  ethnic Russians 167
    language proficiency 168
  independence 167
  language legislation 11, 131, 168–82
    purpose 168–9
  minority languages 169–74
    in education 177–9
    in the media 176–7
  nation-building 167
  statehood 180, 181
  see also Estonia; Latvia; Lithuania
Bangladesh, language conflict 123
Basque conflict 26
  arrests, social efficiency of 53, 54, 55
  background 27
  state policies (Spanish) 9, 35, 42–4
    amnesties 46
    'dirty war' 47, 55, 56
    identity 41,51–4
    language 218, 220, 232
    repression 35, 42, 44, 48, 56
    responsiveness 35, 42–4, 48, 56
  see also ETA
Belgian Linguistic Case 116, 120
Belgium 5
  language in education 120, 213 n. 44
Berger, Peter 257
  on religious pluralism 256

boundaries 23, 94, 101, 147, 222, 252, 279

Cameroon, language policy 232–3
Canada 5, 26
  French language 220–1, 222, 230
Catalan 219, 220
Chechnya
  Wahhabism 287
  wars 288, 294
Chiapas conflict 26, 30, 31
  background 28–9
Church of England, prison chaplaincy 273–6
citizenship 4, 128, 144–5, 168, 183, 248, 295
'clash of civilizations' (Huntington) 239, 240, 241, 248, 298, 299
communal-religious movements 240
  anti-West bias 244–5
  see also fundamentalist movements
conflict prevention, OSCE 127–9
Copenhagen Document (1990) 138, 139, 140
  and identity 129–30
corpus planning 10, 11
Council of Europe 7, 115, 157 n. 16, 168, 182, 192, 208
Croatia, minority languages 139
cultural diversity
  and globalization 3, 6
  political governance of 3, 4, 5, 8, 14, 129
  see also linguistic diversity; religious diversity; religious pluralism

democracy 4–5, 27, 29, 43, 109, 115, 122, 185, 252
  and language 123
  liberal democracy 233
  transition to 44, 50
Durkheim, Emile 255, 256

education 11, 73, 167, 177–9, 189,
    199–201, 247–52, 292
  bilingual 223
  and language 222–3
  minority languages in 147–52
'end of history' (Fukuyama) 240, 241,
    242, 248
endangered languages 11–12, 217, 218,
    219, 233, 234
English language, dominance 217
Estonia 139, 141, 142, 143, 144
  citizenship 183 n. 5
  Ethnic Estonians 167
  language
    in education 151, 177–8
    in elections 141, 142, 172
    in employment 143, 175
    in media 176
  Language Act 169, 170, 171, 173, 176
  language proficiency certificates 134–5
  minority language 139, 170, 171, 182
  Russians in 168
  State Language Law 134
ETA
  Basque perceptions of 40–1, 51–2
  ceasefire 48, 49, 50, 56
  homicides 39, 45
    and voting patterns 51
  support structure 39–40, 55
ethnic minorities
  identities 7
  language rights 115
ethnic violence
  case studies 26–7
  diminution, state policies 26
  and state policies 29–32
European Charter for Regional and
    Minority Languages 7, 118, 192,
    204 n. 5, 223–4
European Convention on Human Rights
    122, 141, 173, 185, 224
European Court of Human Rights
    (ECHR)
  Belgian Linguistic Case 116, 120
  judgements, language issues 207–8
extremism
  repressive vs responsive policies 37
  see also terrorism

federalism 8, 38
Framework Convention for the
    Protection of National Minorities 7,
    116, 138, 181, 204–5

French language, in Canada 220–1, 222,
    230
French Revolution 4, 248
Fukuyama, Francis 12, 240
fundamentalist movements 239–40
  anti-West bias 244–5
  revolutionary character 242
  see also communal-religious
    movements; Islamic
    fundamentalism

Georgia 140
  language training 135–6
  State Language Law 135
globalization 3, 6, 217, 283
  and cultural diversity 3, 6
  cultural globalization 243, 296–7
  political globalization 289
  religious globalization 285
  and religious pluralism 12, 251–64
governance *see* political governance

Habermas, Jürgen 5, 252, 264
Hague Recommendations (1996) 132,
    149, 206
Hawaiian 222–3, 226, 229
HCNM (High Commissioner on
    National Minorities) 128–9, 130, 131
  minority languages
    role 133–43, 148–55
    survey 132
human rights 35, 42, 52, 56, 66, 109, 123,
    185–7, 276, 289, 296
  and citizenship 4
  and international law 7, 8
  see also rights
Hume, John 72, 77
Hume/Adams Initiative 72
Huntington, Samuel P. 12, 240

identity 117
  collective identity 102, 241, 279
  complexity 128
  and Copenhagen Document 129–30
  ethnic identity 22–3, 189, 258
  and language 128
  minorities 7
  and violence 101
  see also religious identity
individuals, and human rights 5
International Covenant of Civil and
    Political Rights (ICCPR) 6, 186
  in South Africa 201–4

Irish language 230–2, 233
Islamic fundamentalism 286, 294
  Tatarstan 288
Islamophobia, Russia 286, 293
Istanbul Summit Declaration (1999) 131

Kemal, Mustafa (Atatürk) 103
Kosovo, Turkish language 142
'Kurdish'
  language criteria 101
  meaning 101
Kurdish conflict 9, 26, 96
  background 29
  civil war (1984–99) 96–100
  identity 101–4
  multilingualism 103
  nationalism 94, 104–9
  religious factor 103–4
  as rural insurgency 95, 97
  self-determination 95
  state policies (Turkish) 94
    evacuation 97
Kymlicka, Will 5, 223, 233, 263
Kyrgyzstan 140

language
  and citizenship 128
  and education 222–3
  and identity 128
  Northern Ireland conflict 62
  and social organization 128
language legislation 130
  Baltic States 11, 131, 167–82
language policies
  evaluation 219–23, 233–4
  and home use 218
  outcomes 11–12
language rights 10
  and democracy 123
  as human rights 10, 116, 118, 121–2,
    124
  and language maintenance 218
  minorities 115
  official pronouncements 117, 120, 123,
    124
  personal name choice 117
  private sphere 116–17, 118, 136–7
  public sphere 117, 136–7
  treaties, Council of Europe 121–2, 124
  unenforceability 122
languages
  dominant 217
  statistics 217

Latvia
  citizenship 183 n. 5
  Election Laws 141
  ethnic Latvians 167
  Language Law 169, 170, 174
  language proficiency certificates 135,
    144
  languages
    in education 177–9
    in media 176–7
  minority language 139, 151, 169
  Russians in 168
  State Language Law 134, 137, 143, 175
  State Language Training Programme
    130, 151, 181
  state language use 171–2
Lijphart, Arend 38
linguistic diversity
  and OSCE 10–11, 129
  South Africa 11
Lithuania
  ethnic Lithuanians 167, 179
  languages, in education 177
  minority language 169, 170, 172, 177
  Russians in 168
  State Language Law 168, 169, 170,
    173–4, 175

Macedonia 123, 130
  Albanian 142, 149, 153
Maori language 224, 225–6, 229–30
Marx, Karl 255
media, minority languages in 152–4
migration, international 3, 8, 13
minority languages
  Baltic States 169–74
  and citizenship 144–5
  Croatia 139
  in economic life 145–6
  in education 147–52
  in electoral processes 140–2
  Estonia 170
  European Charter 223–4
  HCNM
    role 133–43, 148–55
    survey 132
  Latvia 169
  Lithuania 169, 170, 172, 177
  in the media 152–4
  in non-elected public bodies 143
  OSCE area 130–1
  in private sector 143–4
  in public administration 138–40

public authorities, use 118–21
in public services 146
resource issues 137–8
rights 131
South Africa 203–9
see also endangered languages
modernity 12, 239
civilizational traditions 245–6
de-Westernization of 246
early European 246
reinterpretations 243–4, 246–7
Moldova 130, 134, 144, 146
multiculturalism 5, 7, 148, 295, 296

nationalism 21
Afrikaner nationalism 189
Basque nationalism 35
civic nationalism 123
ethnonationalism 26
Kurdish nationalism 103–4, 109
"methodological nationalism" 4
nation-building 4, 8, 10, 11, 12, 13, 14
Baltic States 167
South Africa 186
Turkey 102
nation-state 3, 4, 10, 242
Native American Languages Act (1990)
218–19
Navajo language 227
Ndebele language 188
Netherlands 5
Netherlands Antilles 232
New Caledonia, indigenous languages
220
Northern Ireland conflict 9, 26
agreements 1973–98 75–7
Anglo-Irish Agreement (1985) 62
for and against 69–70
limited success 70–1
anti-terrorist measures 66, 70
'Bloody Sunday' 65
causes 62–3
Council of Ireland 65–6, 67
EU involvement 77
Good Friday Agreement (1998) 62, 69,
74, 76–7
aftermath 85–7
referendum 76
success conditions 78
IRA 64, 69, 72
Irish Republic, involvement 64, 69
Joint Declaration (1993) 72–3, 74
language issues 62

Mitchell Principles 74
New Ireland Forum 69
political parties 63–4, 72
balance of power 83–4, 85, 86–7, 90
religious factors 63
self-determination 72–3, 74, 75
socio-economic reforms 68, 73
Sunningdale Agreement 65–6
failure, reasons for 67–8
terrorism 62, 66, 70
US involvement 77
violence 79–83
and community relations 81–3, 86
Loyalist 80–1
Republican 80

Öcalan, Abdullah 93, 94, 96, 104
O'Neill, Terence 64
OSCE (Organization for Security and
Co-operation in Europe)
area, minority languages 7, 118, 130–1
conflict prevention 127–9
and linguistic diversity 10–11, 129
Oslo Recommendations (1998) 117, 123,
132, 154, 206

Parsons, Talcott 257
on religious pluralism 255–6
PKK (Parti Karkaren Kurdistan)
defeat 9, 93, 104, 110
'revolutionary' war 96
Syrian support 96
as war machine 94
pluralism 38
vs diversity, comparison 267–9
see also religious pluralism
political governance
of cultural diversity 3, 4, 5, 8, 14
of religious pluralism 13, 14
primordialism 8, 22
prison chaplaincy, multi-faith, UK
prisons 13, 277–80
privatization, religion 257

Québécois conflict 26
background 28
Quechua 220

rational choice theory 8, 24–5, 257–8
religion, privatization 257
see also sociology of religion
religions
particularistic 253

universalistic 253
religious diversity
    Russia 13–14, 283–99
    and sociology of religion 255–8
    UK, growth 269–70
    UK prisons 271–2
    see also religious pluralism
religious freedom 258
    and ethics 254
    limitations 254–5
    Russia 289
religious identity, as public
        phenomenon 241–2
religious market 256
religious movements, resurgence
        239–41
religious pluralism 13
    Berger on 256
    and established church 258–60
    and globalization 12, 251–64
    Parsons on 255–6
    pillarization 260–2
        danger 262–3
        Dutch example 260–1
        Islam, possibility 262
        Northern Ireland example 261
    political governance of 13, 14
    in prisons 13
    see also religious diversity
rights
    collective rights 21, 262–3
    cultural rights 264
    fundamental rights 37, 42, 74, 228
    group rights 32
    individual rights 21, 263–4, 280
    minority rights 21, 38, 115, 130, 182,
        208, 221, 233, 276, 280, 289
    see also language rights; religious
        freedom
Romania 139
    Hungarian minority 131, 148
    minority languages 134, 139
Russia
    Beslan disaster 293
    Chechnya wars 288, 294
    Islamophobia 286, 293
    new religious movements 284–5
    religious diversity 13–14, 283–99
        army 293–4
        social conflict 284–8
        state management of 288–94, 298–9
    religious education 294
    religious freedom, law 289, 296–7

religious sects, public opinion 285–6
sectarian groups 291–2
secularization 293, 296
Soviet, secularization 283
Sufism 287
Wahhabism 287
Russian Orthodox Church 14, 288, 289,
        297–8
    diversity within 284
    and freedom of conscience 296
    and globalization 295
    membership 284
    revival 283–4
    special status 289–91, 294–5, 296–7
    tradition 296, 299

Saami language 220
Sardinian 225
secessionism 8, 9, 21, 26
    case studies 26–9
    explanations 22–5
secularization 259, 262, 287
secularism 103, 201, 262, 277, 288, 294
self-determination 8, 50
    Kurdish conflict 95
    Northern Ireland 72–3, 74, 75
    South Africa 192
Sinn Féin 66, 69, 72, 73, 83, 84
    broadcast ban 70
    elections, success 74
Slovakia 134, 139
social constructivism 8, 22–4
sociology of religion
    American model 258
    cognitivism 255, 256
    critical theory 255, 256–7
    functionalism 255–6
    rational choice theory 257–8
    theories 255–8
South Africa
    Afrikaans, status 194, 228
    Anglo-Boer War (1899–1902) 189
    Bill of Rights 192–3
    Constitution (1996) 189–90, 192, 193–5
        Section 6: 195–9
    education, and language choice 193,
        199–201
    English, status 228
    Great Trek 189
    ICCPR in 201–4
    language policy 189–92, 197–9
    languages 188, 189, 190
        indigenous 191, 227–8

official 191, 195, 211 n. 14, 227
linguistic diversity 11
minority concept 187–8
  application 188
  definition 188
minority languages, rights 203–9
nation-building 186
self-determination 192
'unity in diversity' 186
Spanish Civil War (1936–39) 42–3
Spanish Constitution (1978) 43
Sri Lanka 123
state-formation 4, 11, 12, 13, 14
  post-Soviet 129
statehood
  Baltic States 180, 181
  and national identity 4, 5, 280
Sufism, Russia 287
Sweden 5
Switzerland 5

Tajikistan 138
Tatarstan 287–8
  Islamic fundamentalism 288
terrorism
  Basque extremism 9, 39, 40
  extremism, distinction 39
  Islamic 293

meaning 39
Northern Ireland 62, 66, 70
state 42, 50, 55, 56
victims of 51
Turkey, nation-building 102

Ukraine 134
UN Declaration on the Rights of Persons
  Belonging to National or Ethnic,
  Linguistic and Religious Minorities
  7, 123, 156 n. 4, 201, 204
UN, Human Rights Committee 7
UNESCO 7, 204, 213 n. 45, 222
Universal Declaration on Human Rights
  156 n. 4, 265 n. 4
urbanization, Kurdish conflict 95,
  117–8, 173, 181, 188, 201, 203, 207

values, common 115

Wahhabism
  Chechnya 287
  Russia 287
Weber, Max 110, 255

Zapatista conflict *see* Chiapas conflict
Zulu language 188

137×109

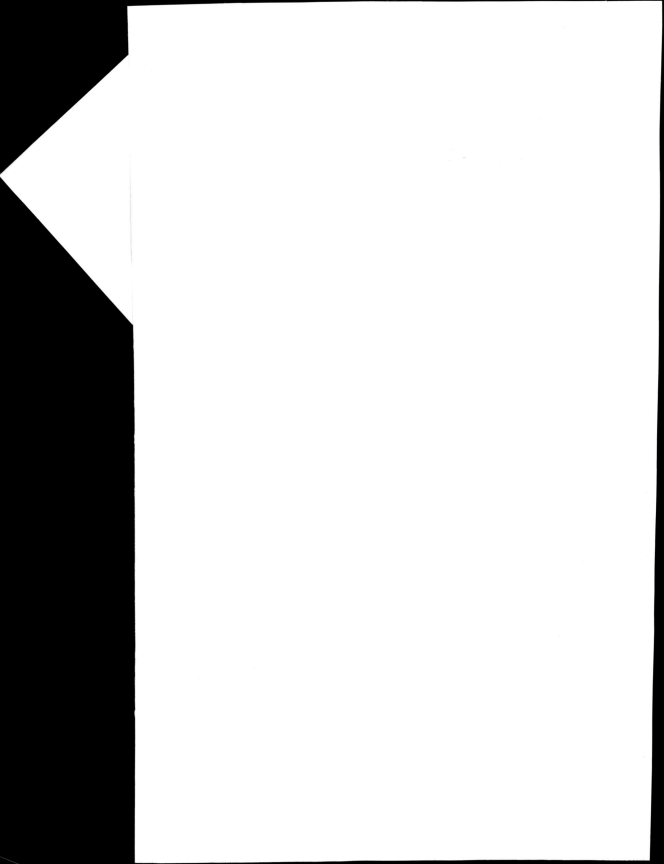